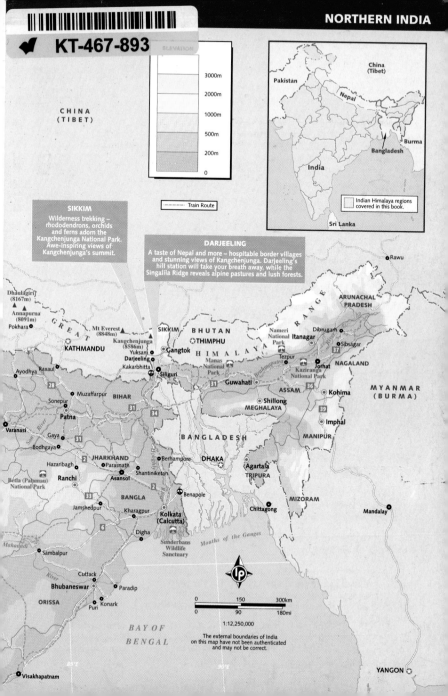

KT-467-893

ELEVATION

	3000m
	2000m
	1000m
	500m
	200m
	0

----- Train Route

CHINA
(TIBET)

China
(Tibet)

Pakistan

Nepal

Burma

Bangladesh

India

Indian Himalaya regions
covered in this book.

Sri Lanka

SIKKIM
Wilderness trekking –
rhododendrons, orchids
and ferns adorn the
Kangchenjunga National Park.
Awe-inspiring views of
Kangchenjunga's summit.

DARJEELING
A taste of Nepal and more – hospitable border villages
and stunning views of Kangchenjunga. Darjeeling's
hill station will take your breath away, while the
Singalila Ridge reveals alpine pastures and lush forests.

Rawu

Dhaulagiri
(8167m)
Annapurna
(8091m)
Pokhara

GREAT

Mt Everest
(8848m)
Kangchenjunga
(8586m)
KATHMANDU
Yuksam
SIKKIM
Gangtok
Darjeeling
Kakarbhitta

ARUNACHAL
PRADESH

BHUTAN
THIMPHU

RANGE

Nameri
National
Park
Itanagar
Dibrugarh
Sibsagar

Manas
National
Park
Siliguri

H I M A L A Y A

Tepur
Jorhat
Kaziranga
National Park
NAGALAND

Ayodhya
Raxaul

Muzaffarpur
BIHAR

31
Guwahati

Brahmaputra

36
Kohima

MYANMAR
(BURMA)

Sonepur
Patna

31

34

ASSAM
Shillong
MEGHALAYA

39

Varanasi
Gaya
31
Bodhgaya

B A N G L A D E S H

MANIPUR
Imphal

Hazaribagh
JHARKHAND
Parasnath
Berhampore
DHAKA

Shantiniketan
Agartala
TRIPURA

Betla (Palamau)
National Park
Ranchi
Asansol

BANGLA

MIZORAM

Jamshedpur
33
Kharagpur
Benapole

Chittagong
Mandalay

Mahanadi
Sambalpur

6
Digha
Kolkata
(Calcutta)

Sunderbans
Wildlife
Sanctuary

Mouths of the Ganges

River
Cuttack
Bhubaneswar
Paradip

ORISSA
Puri
Konark

BAY OF
BENGAL

0   150   300km
0   90   180mi
1:12,250,000

The external boundaries of India
on this map have not been authenticated
and may not be correct.

85°E

90°E

YANGON

Visakhapatnam

Trekking in the Indian Himalaya
4th edition – September 2002
First published – April 1986

Published by
Lonely Planet Publications Pty Ltd ABN 36 005 607 983
90 Maribyrnong St, Footscray, Victoria 3011, Australia

Lonely Planet Offices
Australia Locked Bag 1, Footscray, Victoria 3011
USA 150 Linden St, Oakland, CA 94607
UK 10a Spring Place, London NW5 3BH
France 1 rue du Dahomey, 75011 Paris

Photographs
Many of the images in this guide are available for licensing from
Lonely Planet Images.
e lpi@lonelyplanet.com.au
w www.lonelyplanetimages.com

Main front cover photograph
Sunset over the peaks of Kangchenjunga, Darjeeling, Bangla.
(Lindsay Brown)

Small front cover photograph
Trekker on the trail to Khambachen. (Richard I'Anson)

ISBN 1 74059 085 6

text & maps © Lonely Planet Publications Pty Ltd 2002
photos © photographers as indicated 2002

Printed through SNP SPrint Singapore Pte Ltd at
KHL Printing Co Sdn Bhd Malaysia

Contents

2 Contents

The Maps

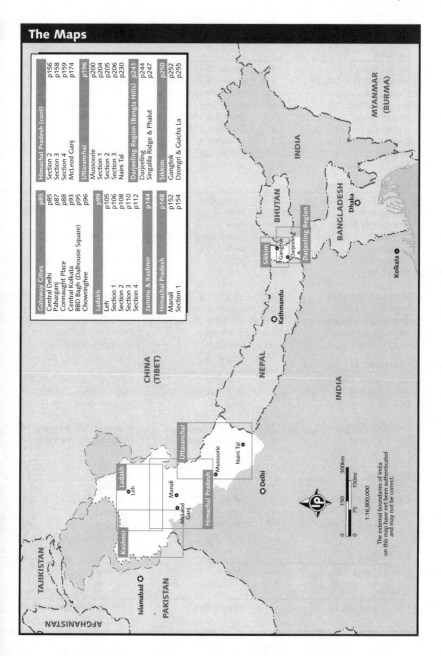

1:16,800,000

0   150   300km
0   75   150mi

The external boundaries of India
on this map have not been authenticated
and may not be correct.

The Treks	Days	Standard	Season
Ladakh			
Markha Valley	8	moderate–demanding	June–mid-Oct
Hidden Valleys of Ladakh	5	moderate–demanding	June–mid-Oct
Singge La & Lamayuru	10	moderate–demanding	June–late Oct
Remote Zanskar	10	demanding	mid-Aug–mid-Oct
Phugtal Gompa & Shingo La	7	moderate–demanding	June–early Oct
Phitse La & Baralacha La	8	demanding	June–early Oct
Kang La & Miyar Glacier	7	demanding	July–early Oct
Umasi La	6	demanding	June–early Oct
Kanji La & Shilakong Gorge	6	demanding	June–mid-Oct
Himachal Pradesh			
Hampta Pass & Lahaul	5	moderate	June–Oct
Deo Tibba Base	5	easy	June–mid-Oct
Chandrakani Pass & Malana	5	easy	May–Oct
Pin Parbati & Spiti	8	moderate–demanding	mid-June–mid-Oct
Bara Bhangal	11	demanding	mid-June–mid-Oct
Indrahar Pass	5	moderate	May–Oct
Kareri Lake	4	easy	May–June; Sept–Oct
Mani Mahesh Kailash	3	easy	June–mid-Oct
Kugti Pass & Lahaul	5	moderate–demanding	mid-June–mid-Oct
Chandra Tal & Baralacha La	4	moderate	July–mid-Oct
Tarik La & Kinnaur	5	moderate	mid-June–mid-Oct
Kinnaur Kailash	4	demanding	mid-July–mid-Oct
Uttaranchal			
Rupin Pass & Kinnaur	6	moderate	late May–June; mid-Sept–Oct
Har ki Dun & Ruinsara Lake	6	easy–moderate	May–June; mid-Sept–mid-Oct
Dodi Tal & Yamunotri	4	easy	mid-May–June; Sept–Oct
Source of the Ganges	5	easy–moderate	May–June; mid-Sept–mid-Oct
Khatling Glacier	7	easy–moderate	May–June; mid-Sept–mid-Oct
Hem Kund & Valley of the Flowers	4	easy	May–mid-Oct
Kuari Pass	5	moderate	mid-May–Oct
Rup Kund	7	moderate	mid-Sept–mid-Oct
Pindari Glacier	7	easy	May–Oct
Milam Glacier & Nanda Devi	10	moderate	May–Oct
Darjeeling			
Singalila Ridge & Phalut	5	easy	Oct–May
Sikkim			
Dzongri & Guicha La	7	easy–moderate	April–mid-May; Oct–mid-Nov

The Author

Garry Weare

Best described as a veteran trekker, Garry has trekked well over 20,000km in the Indian Himalaya since 1970. He is a director of the Australian Himalayan Foundation, a fellow of the Royal Geographical Society, a life member of the Himalayan Club, and is a consultant to the adventure travel company, World Expeditions. In between treks, he spends his time avoiding most of life's problems in the Southern Highlands of NSW, Australia.

From the Author

Thanks to my good friends, Harsh Vardhan and Wangchuk Shamshu, directors of Great Himalayan Outdoor. Sincere thanks to the guides who accompanied me, including Almas Khan, one of the most dedicated leaders this side of Kathmandu. I would also like to thank the other guides, including Prabhu Singh, Chandra Shekhar, Bhowani Singh and the Ladakhi team of Nawang Tsering, Tsering Norboo and Angchuk Nye.

Thanks to my friends from Kashmir: Meraj Din, Rauf Tramboo and Manzor Ahmed (now gainfully employed elsewhere in the Himalaya). I would also like to mention the support and advice from Rinzin Jowa in Leh, 'Sandi' Badyari in Srinagar, Manjeev Bhalla in Shimla, and Iqbal and Himanshu Sharma in Manali.

Closer to home, thanks go to Dr Jim 'Jigme' Duff and Rejane Belanger for their contribution to the Health & Safety chapter. Thanks to Erich Draganits and his associates at the Institute of Geology, University of Vienna, for their contribution to the Geology section and the boxed text in the Ladakh chapter. Thanks also to Paul Deegan in the UK for his Zanskar aside and to Bill Aitkin for allowing me to quote from one of his many works on the Indian Himalaya.

Closer to the workplace, thanks to Lindsay Brown and Sally Dillon for their support; to Angie Phelan, Marg Toohey and Janet Brunckhorst for their painstaking efforts in editing the book; and to Glenn van der Knijff and Karen Fry for all their work producing the trekking maps. Thanks also to Richard l'Anson for his critical restraint when my photos have not been quite in focus.

Dedication

To India Weare: may she eventually discover the delights of trekking in India.

Trek Descriptions

This book contains 33 trek descriptions ranging from day trips to 11-day treks, plus suggestions for side trips and alternative routes. Each trek description has a brief introduction outlining the natural and cultural features you may encounter, plus information to help you plan your trek – transport options, level of difficulty, time frame and any permits required.

Day treks are often circular and are located in areas of uncommon beauty. Multi-day treks include information on campsites, huts, hostels or other accommodation and where you can obtain water and supplies.

Times & Distances

These are provided only as a guide. Times are based on actual trekking time and do not include stops for snacks, taking photographs, rests or side trips. Be sure to factor these in when planning your trek. Distances are provided but should be read in conjunction with altitudes. Significant elevation changes can make a greater difference to your trekking time than lateral distance.

In most cases, the daily stages are flexible and can be varied. It is important to recognise that short stages are sometimes recommended in order to acclimatise in mountain areas or because there are interesting features to explore en route.

Level of Difficulty

Grading systems are always arbitrary. However, having an indication of the grade may help you choose between treks. Our authors use the following grading guidelines:

Easy – a trek on flat terrain or with minor elevation changes, usually over short distances on well-travelled routes with no navigational difficulties.
Moderate – a trek with challenging terrain, often involving longer distances and steep climbs.
Demanding – a trek with long daily distances and difficult terrain with significant elevation changes; may involve challenging route-finding and high-altitude or glacier travel.

True Left & True Right

The terms 'true left' and 'true right', used to describe the bank of a stream or river, sometimes throw readers. The 'true left bank' simply means the left bank as you look downstream.

Maps

Our maps are based on the best available references, often combined with GPS data collected in the field. They are intended to show the general route of the trek and should be used in conjunction with maps suggested in the trek description.

Maps may contain contours or ridge lines, in addition to major watercourses, depending on the available information. These features build a three-dimensional picture of the terrain, allowing you to determine when the trail climbs and descends. Altitudes of major peaks, passes and localities complete the picture by providing the actual extent of the elevation changes.

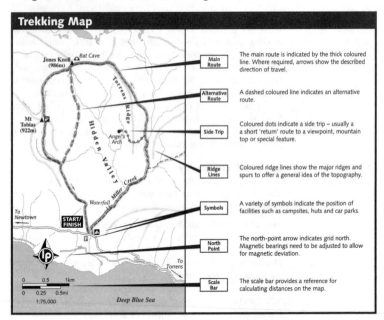

Route Finding

While accurate, our maps are not perfect. Inaccuracies in altitudes are commonly caused by air-temperature anomalies. Natural features such as river confluences and mountain peaks are in their true position, but sometimes the location of villages and trails is not always so. This may be because a village is spread over a hillside, or the size of the map does not allow for detail of the trail's twists and turns. However, by using several basic route-finding techniques, you will have few problems following our descriptions:

1. Always be aware of whether the trail should be climbing or descending.
2. Check the north-point arrow on the map and determine the general direction of the trail.
3. Time your progress over a known distance and calculate the speed at which you travel in the given terrain. From then on, you can determine with reasonable accuracy how far you have travelled.
4. Watch the path – look for boot prints and other signs of previous passage.

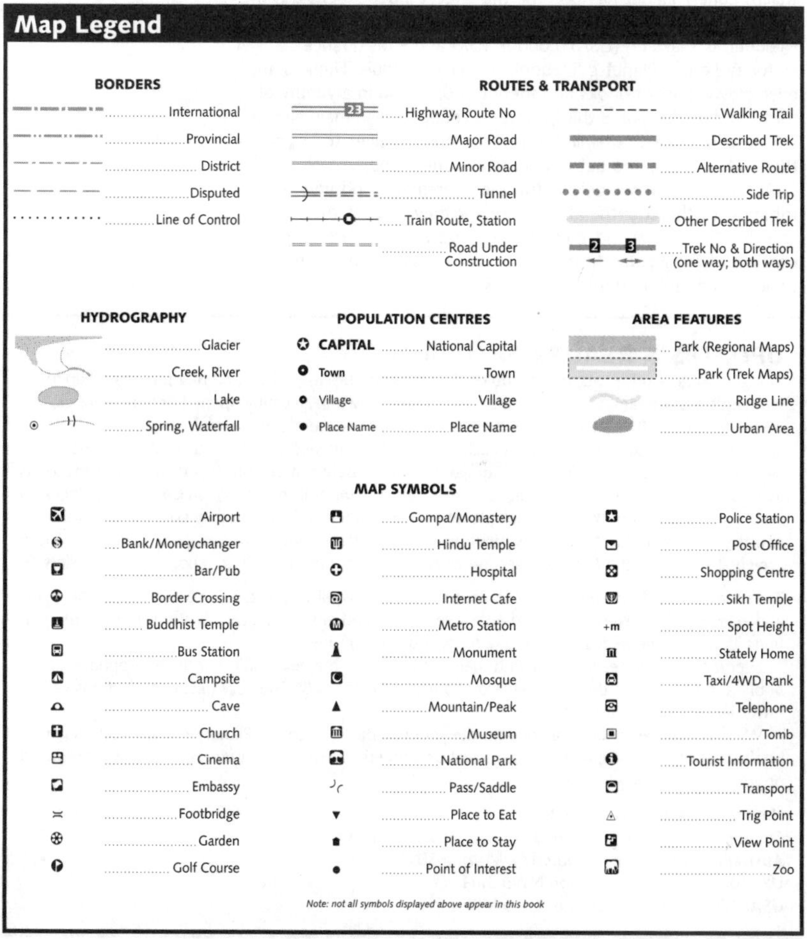

Map Legend

BORDERS

.... International
.... Provincial
.... District
.... Disputed
.... Line of Control

ROUTES & TRANSPORT

23 ...... Highway, Route No
.... Major Road
.... Minor Road
.... Tunnel
.... Train Route, Station
.... Road Under Construction

.... Walking Trail
.... Described Trek
.... Alternative Route
.... Side Trip
.... Other Described Trek
2 **3** ..... Trek No & Direction (one way; both ways)

HYDROGRAPHY

.... Glacier
.... Creek, River
.... Lake
.... Spring, Waterfall

POPULATION CENTRES

⊙ **CAPITAL** .... National Capital
⊙ **Town** .... Town
⊙ Village .... Village
● Place Name .... Place Name

AREA FEATURES

.... Park (Regional Maps)
.... Park (Trek Maps)
.... Ridge Line
.... Urban Area

MAP SYMBOLS

⊠ .... Airport
⊛ ... Bank/Moneychanger
⊡ .... Bar/Pub
⊕ .... Border Crossing
▣ .... Buddhist Temple
▤ .... Bus Station
⊞ .... Campsite
⊿ .... Cave
⊕ .... Church
⊟ .... Cinema
⊡ .... Embassy
⋈ .... Footbridge
❀ .... Garden
⊙ .... Golf Course

▣ ...... Gompa/Monastery
⊞ .... Hindu Temple
⊕ .... Hospital
⊡ .... Internet Cafe
Ⓜ .... Metro Station
⚑ .... Monument
⊡ .... Mosque
▲ .... Mountain/Peak
▥ .... Museum
⊡ .... National Park
⌒ᵣ .... Pass/Saddle
▼ .... Place to Eat
■ .... Place to Stay
● .... Point of Interest

⊞ .... Police Station
⊡ .... Post Office
⊗ .... Shopping Centre
Ⓤ .... Sikh Temple
+m .... Spot Height
▥ .... Stately Home
⊡ .... Taxi/4WD Rank
⊡ .... Telephone
■ .... Tomb
ⓘ ...... Tourist Information
⊡ .... Transport
△ .... Trig Point
⊡ .... View Point
⊡ .... Zoo

Note: not all symbols displayed above appear in this book

Foreword

ABOUT LONELY PLANET GUIDEBOOKS

The story begins with a classic travel adventure: Tony and Maureen Wheeler's 1972 journey across Europe and Asia to Australia. Useful information about the overland trail did not exist at that time, so Tony and Maureen published the first Lonely Planet guidebook to meet a growing need.

From a kitchen table, then from a tiny office in Melbourne (Australia), Lonely Planet has become the largest independent travel publisher in the world, an international company with offices in Melbourne, Oakland (USA), London (UK) and Paris (France).

Today Lonely Planet guidebooks cover the globe. There is an ever-growing list of books and there's information in a variety of forms and media. Some things haven't changed. The main aim is still to help make it possible for adventurous travellers to get out there – to explore and better understand the world.

At Lonely Planet we believe travellers can make a positive contribution to the countries they visit – if they respect their host communities and spend their money wisely. Since 1986 a percentage of the income from each book has been donated to aid projects and human rights campaigns.

UPDATES & READER FEEDBACK

Things change – prices go up, schedules change, good places go bad and bad places go bankrupt. Nothing stays the same. So, if you find things better or worse, recently opened or long-since closed, please tell us and help make the next edition even more accurate and useful.

Lonely Planet thoroughly updates each guidebook as often as possible – usually every two years, although for some destinations the gap can be longer. Between editions, up-to-date information is available in our free, quarterly *Planet Talk* newsletter and monthly email bulletin *Comet*. The *Upgrades* section of our website (W www.lonelyplanet.com) is also regularly updated by Lonely Planet authors, and the site's *Scoop* section covers news and current affairs relevant to travellers. Lastly, the *Thorn Tree* bulletin board and *Postcards* section carry unverified, but fascinating, reports from travellers.

Tell us about it! We genuinely value your feedback. A well-travelled team at Lonely Planet reads and acknowledges every email and letter we receive and ensures that every morsel of information finds its way to the relevant authors, editors and cartographers.

Everyone who writes to us will find their name listed in the next edition of the appropriate guidebook, and will receive the latest issue of *Comet* or *Planet Talk*. The very best contributions will be rewarded with a free guidebook.

We may edit, reproduce and incorporate your comments in Lonely Planet products such as guidebooks, websites and digital products, so let us know if you don't want your comments reproduced or your name acknowledged.

How to contact Lonely Planet:
Online: e talk2us@lonelyplanet.com.au, W www.lonelyplanet.com
Australia: Locked Bag 1, Footscray, Victoria 3011
UK: 10a Spring Place, London NW5 3BH
USA: 150 Linden St, Oakland, CA 94607

Introduction

The Indian Himalaya offers superb trekking possibilities. It is undoubtedly one of the most spectacular and impressive mountain ranges in the world. Compared to Nepal, the region hosts a small number of trekkers each year, but there is a steady and growing interest. Trekkers are discovering that the Himalaya Range does not end at the border of Nepal. In fact, they're finding a choice of treks that are as demanding and rewarding as those offered by the Everest and Annapurna regions.

To fully appreciate the Indian Himalaya's beauty, there is no substitute for trekking. This unforgettable experience brings you into direct contact with the country and its people, and helps to foster an appreciation of the mountain environments.

In the space of a week or two, you may trek through Hindu settlements, visit isolated

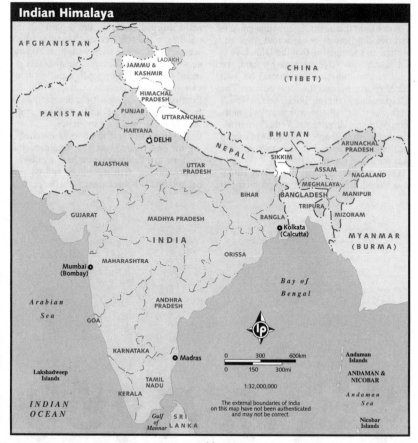

Indian Himalaya

AFGHANISTAN

JAMMU & KASHMIR — LADAKH

CHINA (TIBET)

HIMACHAL PRADESH

PAKISTAN

PUNJAB

UTTARANCHAL

HARYANA

DELHI

NEPAL

BHUTAN

ARUNACHAL PRADESH

RAJASTHAN

UTTAR PRADESH

SIKKIM

ASSAM

NAGALAND

MEGHALAYA

MANIPUR

BIHAR

BANGLADESH

TRIPURA

MIZORAM

GUJARAT

MADHYA PRADESH

BANGLA

Kolkata (Calcutta)

MYANMAR (BURMA)

INDIA

ORISSA

Mumbai (Bombay)

MAHARASHTRA

Bay of Bengal

Arabian Sea

ANDHRA PRADESH

GOA

KARNATAKA

Madras

0   300   600km

0 150 300mi

Andaman Islands

Lakshadweep Islands

TAMIL NADU

1:32,000,000

ANDAMAN & NICOBAR

KERALA

Andaman Sea

INDIAN OCEAN

Gulf of Mannar

SRI LANKA

The external boundaries of India on this map have not been authenticated and may not be correct.

Nicobar Islands

Buddhist monasteries, pitch a tent beside shepherd encampments or stay in traditional Islamic villages. On a typical trek, you will traverse the Great Himalaya Range and appreciate the sheer geographic diversity: from the verdant, forested valleys and wildflower meadows to the rugged Trans-Himalaya region. While crossing the passes, remember the many generations of pilgrims, traders and armies who have followed these trails – their journeys reflect the rich cultural history of the region. Combine this with the wildlife and forests – and the many snowcapped peaks towering above 7000m – and you have all the ingredients of a highly rewarding trek.

A constant theme throughout this guide is that trekking has its rewards and responsibilities. In recognising that the Himalaya is not just a vast adventure playground, we must aim to minimise our impact on both the environment and the local culture. The 'Responsible Trekking' boxed text (pp46–7) addresses this challenge with practical guidelines. The 'Environmental Watch' information in each trek chapter details the efforts of local and international conservation groups, plus what you can do to help.

Over the past decade, the Indian Himalaya has been beset by political problems. It is hoped that future editions may again include a comprehensive guide to trekking in Kashmir. However, for now we must be content with the many attractive alternatives in the regions of Ladakh, Himachal Pradesh, Uttaranchal, Darjeeling and Sikkim.

We offer a wealth of suggestions to help make your adventure a reality: general knowledge about the Indian Himalaya; transport advice for getting to the region and the trailhead; tips for staying healthy on the trail; a language guide; plus a special Clothing & Equipment section so you're well prepared before you leave home.

In each trek chapter, we introduce the region with a description of its geographical and historical features, and a guide to the wildlife. For each trek, we detail the best season to go, where to buy supplies and the accommodation en route. We also recommend local trekking agencies and give advice on hiring porters and packhorses. Finally, a day-by-day trek description is complemented by accurate trekking maps based on the author's experience.

The hard part is then up to you – choosing the best trek to suit your interests, and the time and funds that you have available. In a region so rich in culture and natural beauty, this is bound to be a challenge.

Facts about the Indian Himalaya

HISTORY

In many respects the history of the Indian Himalaya reflects the passage of history in northern India. After establishing power in the plains many an empire set their sights on the hills where they assumed power for a brief period or forged an alliance with the local rulers. The result is a complex cultural and political history. Some of the most important periods and significant events are linked in the chronology of north Indian history that follows:

2500–1500 BC – Indus Valley civilization of proto-Dravidians established; evidence of movement to the hills.

1500–1000 BC – Aryans (from Afghanistan and Central Asia) migrate to northern India and the Dravidians are pushed south.

1500–1200 BC – The *Vedas*, a series of hymns devoted to the Aryan Gods, composed.

800 BC – The *Upanishads*, scriptures including doctrines on philosophy, composed and later adopted by the great Hindu teachers.

563 BC – Gautama Buddha born.

500 BC – Teaching of the Buddha spreads across India.

327 BC – Alexander the Great invades India.

262 BC – Emperor Ashoka declares Buddhism the state religion.

1st century AD – Epic poems – the *Mahabharata* and the *Ramayana* – composed to commemorate the history and heroes of India. Trade links established between India and the Roman Empire as an offshoot of the Silk Road.

AD 319 – Founding of the Gupta Empire unites most of northern India.

510 – Gupta Empire defeated by the Huns, northern India divides into separate Hindu kingdoms until the arrival of the Muslim rulers in the 11th century.

8th century – Noted Hindu philosopher, Shankara, revives Hindu philosophy and teachings.

750–800 – Tantric Buddhism is popularised in the Indian Himalaya by Indian Buddhist teacher Padmasambhava.

1001–25 – Mahmud of Ghanzi attacks northern India and Kashmir.

1192 – Mohammed of Ghur gains power over northern India – emergence of the sultanate of Delhi.

14th century – Kashmir peacefully converted to Islam.

1398 – Tamerlane (Timur) raids northern India and Delhi.

1527 – Moghul rule established over northern India by Babur (a descendant of both Genghis Khan and Tamerlane). Moghul rule later established over most of the Himalayan kingdoms. The great Moghul rulers, including Humayun, Akbar, Jehangir, Shah Jahan and Aurangzeb, hold power until 1707.

1612 – East India Company establishes trading post at Surat, Gujarat.

1690–1756 – East India Company embarks on a period of expansion (established government in Bengal in 1771). In 1803 it establishes control over all of North India except the Punjab.

1784 – British government takes more direct control of East India Company affairs.

1814 – Gurkha wars with East India Company.

1857 – Indian Mutiny; East India Company brought under British government control.

1885 – Formation of the Indian National Congress.

1920 – Mohandas (Mahatma) Gandhi assumes leadership of the Congress party and pushes for independence.

14 August 1947 – Indian independence after WWII and Labour party victory in UK. Jawaharlal Nehru becomes India's first prime minister.

1947–49 – Hari Singh, the last Maharajah of Kashmir, is forced to choose between India and Pakistan. His indecision leads to full-scale war until 1 January 1949. Line of control established but further conflicts between India and Pakistan occur in 1965 and 1971.

1962 – India at war with China following dispute along India/Tibet border.

1964 – Nehru dies.

1966 – Himachal Pradesh formed, including the hill states of Chamba, Kangra, Kullu and Lahaul (granted statehood in 1971); Indira Gandhi (Nehru's daughter and no relation to Mahatma Gandhi) elected Prime Minister.

1975 – Sikkim becomes part of India following political unrest and opposition to the influence of the large number of settlers from Nepal.

1975 – Indira Gandhi declares state of emergency, loses election in 1977, re-elected in 1980, assassinated in 1984.

1984 – Rajiv Gandhi, Indira Gandhi's son, becomes prime minister until 1989.
1987 – State of Arunachal Pradesh formed.
1989 – Separatist movement gains momentum in Kashmir and, although state elections are reintroduced in 1996, political unrest continues.
1991 – Rajiv Gandhi assassinated.
1996 – Congress party defeated by BJP/United Front.
1998 – BJP secures majority government.
1999 – Kargil war between India and Pakistan.
2000 – State of Uttaranchal formed, comprising the Garhwal and Kumaon regions of Uttar Pradesh.

History of Trekking & Exploration

While pilgrims, armies and traders had for many centuries explored the Himalaya, organised trekking was closely associated with the pursuit of hunting and game that gained popularity in India in the later part of the 19th century. By the turn of the 20th century it was well under way. It was not uncommon for the British to undertake a trek from Srinagar to Gilgit or to cover the 14 stages from Srinagar to Leh as part of their annual leave. Agencies were established in Srinagar and Shimla to specialise in sport-related activities – hunting, fishing and trekking. A large retinue of porters would carry huge canvas tents and collapsible string beds. Arthur Neve's *The Tourist's Guide to Kashmir, Ladakh & Skardo*, first published in 1911, records this romantic era. It was a time when men such as Francis Younghusband, the newly installed Resident in Kashmir, ascended the forested slopes of the Lidder Valley in search of game; when Auriel Stein, living on an alpine meadow above the Sindh Valley, planned his next expedition to Central Asia; and Sven Hedin set off from Srinagar in 1906 on his second expedition to Tibet.

Mountaineering also dates from this time. Expeditions were mounted to climb the Punjab Himalaya and the Karakoram. Nanga Parbat had been attempted in 1895 by a team of British alpinists, while a recce of Nun and Kun, the highest peaks in the Punjab Himalaya, was conducted by CG Bruce in 1898. In 1902 and 1904 Arthur Neve was able to correct the mapping of some of the complex topography of the massif. Two years later American couple William and Fanny Bullock Workman took their turn, while Arthur Neve returned again in 1910. Italian Count Calciati climbed Kun in 1914, but Nun remained unclimbed until 1953. Closer to the Kashmir Valley, Kolahoi was attempted by Ernest Neve a number of times before the first successful summit attempt by Kenneth Mason in 1911.

The Karakoram also attracted much attention at the turn of the century. The first major expedition was mounted by the Duke of Abruzzi in 1909, setting out from Srinagar with several hundred porters. Although the expedition team was not able to make a serious summit attempt on K2, climbers today still refer to the standard route to its summit as the Abruzzi Ridge.

Many peaks of the Garhwal and Kumaon were also being explored. In particular, the approach to Nanda Devi was examined by WW Graham in 1883 on his attempt to ascend the Rishi Ganga. Longstaff, in 1905, explored the gorge leading to the inner sanctuary. In 1907 Longstaff returned: after climbing the high col between Dunagiri and Changabang, he again attempted, without success, to enter the inner sanctuary. He did, however, divert his energies to climbing Trisul (7120m), which at the time set the record for the highest climbed peak in the world. Longstaff also made a recce of Kamet (7756m), the second-highest peak in the Indian Himalaya, which was not climbed until 1931.

In Sikkim, Claude White, the first British Resident, spent a number of seasons from 1890 exploring the glacial systems below Kangchenjunga and later the remote Lhonak Valley in northern Sikkim. The first attempt to climb Kangchenjunga was made in 1905, while the Scottish doctor AM Kellas spent six seasons exploring the possibilities on Kangchenjunga, climbing a number of peaks along the nearby Singalila Ridge.

To assist the exploration and appreciation of the Himalaya Range, the Himalayan Club was founded in 1927. It established branches in Kashmir, Chamba, Shimla, Almora and Darjeeling. Its initial purpose was to assist

Early Pilgrim Trails into the Himalaya

From the earliest times the Himalaya has been revered as the 'abode of the gods' and a source of religious inspiration. Pilgrims wandered across the foothills in search of the river systems that flowed from the Himalaya. Beyond the Punjab, pilgrims followed the passage of the Chenab as it twists and turns between the Pir Panjal and the outer ranges of the Dhaula Dhar, while trails along the Indus Valley to Kashmir and Ladakh would have been followed since the time the Aryans first migrated to India.

Religious sites such as the one at Haridwar where the Ganges flows from the mountains to the Indian plains were established. Some pilgrims went further, searching for trails above the deep gorges, crossing landslides and forging their way through thick jungle to discover the confluences of many of the tributaries of the Ganges. Trails deeper into the mountains were established over the centuries as generations of shepherds searched for new pastures, and pilgrims continued in their quest for religious enlightenment.

Knowledge of the Himalayan trails was incorporated in the *Mahabharata*, the Vedic epic written in the 1st century AD. The Vedic gods were gradually superseded by others, including Shiva the destroyer, Vishnu the preserver and Brahma the creator. Shiva in particular was linked with the popular fertility cults of the bull and the worship of the lingam (phallic symbol). This move was to gain wider appeal with the spread of the Tantric cults and the worship of the mother goddess. This cult of sexual union was raised to divine status, with each god assigned a formal partner. For example, Shiva was associated with Parvati and Vishnu with Lakshmi. These symbols were gradually integrated into the Himalayan tradition and would later find expression in pilgrimages. For instance, the ice statue inside the sacred Amarnath Cave in Kashmir represents the divine lingam. This sign of cosmic creation would have also supported pilgrimages to many other regions of the Himalaya, including the modern-day pilgrimage to the cave of Vaishno Devi in the Jammu foothills.

It is thought that the four destinations of the *char dham* (pilgrimage to the sources of the Ganges River) – Yamunotri, Gangotri, Kedarnath and Badrinath – were founded by the time of the Mauryan Empire in the late 4th century BC. It was also a time when the Royal Highway (a predecessor of the Grand Trunk Road) was constructed across northern India.

Roads were extended across the forested ridges of the Pir Panjal Range for monks attending the third Buddhist Council in Kashmir around 250 BC. Huge camping areas were established along the trail to facilitate their safe passage. After the conference many pilgrims made their way across the Zoji La to the Indus Valley and on to Tibet. Following the course of the Indus, it would have then taken them only a few stages to reach Lake Manasarovar and Mt Kailash, the sacred 6714m peak situated close to the source of the Sutlej and the Brahmaputra (Tsangpo). While it is unclear when the first pilgrimages were made to Mt Kailash, there would have been a steady flow of pilgrims by the 3rd century BC – some 2000 years before the first European explorers were to 'discover' the mountain.

HIRA LAL DANGOL

Vishnu: a sacred figure for pilgrims.

The Great Game

The need for intelligence in 'the Great Game' (as the covert struggle between Britain and Russia came to be known) was to be the underlying motive of Himalayan exploration throughout the 19th century.

In 1820 William Moorcroft, an eminent veterinary surgeon, set off with geologist George Trebeck to cross the Himalaya to Leh before attempting to travel north over the Karakoram Pass to Kashgar. Permission was not granted so they continued to Kashmir and eventually on to Afghanistan and Bukhara where they both died in 1825. Moorcroft's journals were later recovered and published, and have made an invaluable contribution to the understanding of the geography and politics of the time.

In the 1830s a number of travellers and explorers crossed the high passes linking Kashmir, Jammu, Ladakh and Baltistan, compiling detailed information on these less-travelled routes.

Following the first of the Sikh wars in 1845 and the Treaty of Amritsar in 1846, the East India Company gained unimpeded access to the passes that defined the frontiers of northwest India. A Boundary Commission was established in 1847 and over the next two years men such as Cunningham, Strachey and Thomson travelled extensively throughout the West Himalaya.

The Great Trigonometrical Survey of India was to fill many of the gaps in knowledge regarding these complex mountain ranges. In 1856 the survey moved to Kashmir and was able to appreciate the full extent of the Karakoram Range, including K2, the second-highest peak in the world.

In 1864, Johnson, one of the survey's most able people, was authorised to cross the Karakoram Pass to the Kun Lun Range and Khotan. This notable journey indicated for the first time that the Karakoram Range was not the only significant barrier to trade and communication to Central Asia.

By this time the British considered it necessary that eastern Turkestan be a buffer zone between British India and Tsarist Russia. With this in mind, two trade missions (in 1870, and again in 1873) were mounted to Kashgar. However, by 1877 the Chinese had reasserted their power over the region; shortly after, a Russian envoy was installed in Kashgar.

These developments were of great concern, particularly in light of the geographic intelligence gathered by the surveyors who had stayed on after the second mission returned to India. They were able to ascertain that the Pamirs were nowhere as high or as formidable as the Kun Lun or the Karakoram, with the passes leading south from the Pamirs over the Hindukush easily accessible to Chitral, Hunza, Gilgit and Kashmir. Routes for a Russian advance abounded, and the area between the Karakoram, the Hindukush and the Pamirs became the focus for exploration until the end of the century.

Notable in this era were the exploits of Sir Francis Younghusband, with his epic crossing of the Mustagh Pass in 1887 and his return to Central Asia in 1889. By the time he returned to the Pamirs in 1890, a Russian territorial advance over the Hindukush was a distinct possibility. It was during this period that he obtained reliable information that the Russians intended to annex the Pamirs up to the Hindukush and the passes into Hunza and Gilgit.

Protracted negotiations ensued and, following the British offensive in Hunza, a proposal for a neutral corridor between the Hindukush and the Russian territory was accepted. In 1895 a joint Anglo-Russian Boundary Commission was appointed, resulting in the demarcation of the Wakhan Corridor – a tract of land linking Afghanistan and Sinkiang – to separate the British and Russian empires.

Sir Francis Younghusband

TAMSIN WILSON

with transport and supplies for both trekking and mountaineering teams.

During the 1930s a new style of exploration and climbing evolved in the Himalaya, typified by Eric Shipton, HW Tilman and Frank Smythe. Their expeditions in the Indian Himalaya were initially concentrated in the Garhwal, where Shipton and Smythe were members of the first expedition to climb Kamet in 1931. After the climb they explored many other peaks and passes in the vicinity. The hallmark of the team was travelling light, without complicated logistics, and often in the company of just a climbing Sherpa or two.

In 1934, Shipton and Tilman, with three Sherpas, returned to the Garhwal. The small team managed to forge a route up the Rishi Ganga to the base of Nanda Devi. (This was to lead to Tilman successfully climbing Nanda Devi on a joint Anglo-American expedition two years later). After completing their foray into the Nanda Devi Sanctuary, Tilman and Shipton and the team of Sherpas completed two challenging traverses: the first between Badrinath and Gaumukh and the second from Badrinath to Kedarnath. The second foray was an epic, with the members having little or nothing to eat for most of the expedition. Frank Smythe shared Tilman and Shipton's trekking philosophy when he spent the 1937 season climbing and exploring many of the peaks in the vicinity of the Bhyundar Valley, including Mana (7272m). The success of these mountaineers demonstrated that a small, lightweight expedition had a greater chance of achieving its goals than the huge British expeditions mounted to climb Everest in the 1920s and 1930s.

By now trekking had become an established pastime. In 1933 Ernest Neve revised the 15th edition of *The Tourist's Guide to Kashmir, Ladakh & Skardo* to reflect the increasing interest in travelling to higher and more remote valleys. Arrangements out of Kashmir could be left to Cockburns Agency or to a houseboat family and, judging by the reports retained by some houseboat families, a trusted guide and a reliable cook were the most valuable assets to any trekking party.

Crossing huge distances was no longer considered extraordinary. Consider the case of Robert Fleming, who trekked for seven months from Peking to Kashmir and received not so much as a nod of acknowledgment from the reservations clerk when he finally checked into Nedou's Hotel in September 1935.

Following Indian independence in 1947, the nature of climbing and trekking the high and remote Himalayan valleys was restructured to accommodate the political changes. For instance, the India/Pakistan partition meant it was no longer possible to trek from Kashmir to Baltistan. To the north, much of India's border with China was restricted. The war in 1962 led to the enforcement of inner line restrictions (pertaining to the restricted areas close to India's sensitive border regions with Pakistan and China) in Ladakh, Himachal Pradesh (at that time part of the Punjab hill states), Uttar Pradesh and Sikkim.

Regions such as Kashmir and the Kullu Valley attracted trekkers and climbers in the 1950s and 1960s. At the time Ladakh was off limits while the Pir Panjal Range dividing the Kullu Valley and Lahaul was as far as one could trek in Himachal. In Uttaranchal (Uttar Pradesh) similar restrictions applied and only a few of the classic treks could be undertaken without inner line permits.

The gradual lifting of restrictions in 1974 allowed trekkers to visit Ladakh, Zanskar and Lahaul while permits were no longer necessary to trek in many of the northern regions of Uttaranchal. In 1992 the regions of Kinnaur, Spiti and the Johar Valley in Uttaranchal were opened up for trekking. More remote trekking areas close to India's border regions may be possible in the future.

GEOGRAPHY

For the ancient geographer, the complexities of the Himalaya were a constant source of speculation. From the earliest accounts, Mt Kailash was believed to be the centre of the universe with the river systems of the Indus, the Brahmaputra and the Sutlej all flowing from its snowy ridges and maintaining the courses that they had followed prior to the forming of the Himalaya.

The Sutlej flows directly from Tibet through the main Himalaya Range to the Indian subcontinent, the Indus flows west until it rounds the Himalaya by the Nanga Parbat massif, and the Brahmaputra flows eastwards for nearly 1000km around the Assam Himalaya and descends to the Bay of Bengal.

It was not surprising, therefore, t.1at 19th-century geographers experienced formidable difficulties in tracing the river systems, and defining the various mountain ranges that constitute the Himalaya. Even today, with the advent of satellite pictures and state-of-the-art ordnance maps, it is still difficult to appreciate the form and extent of some of the ranges that constitute the Himalaya.

Great (Main) Himalaya Range

This is the principal mountain range dividing the Indian subcontinent from the Tibetan plateau. From Nanga Parbat (8125m) in the west, the range stretches for over 2000km to the mountains bordering Sikkim and Bhutan in the east. The West Himalaya is the part of this range that divides Kashmir and Himachal Pradesh from Ladakh. The highest mountains here are Nun (7135m) and Kun (7077m). East of Kashmir, the Himalaya extends across

to the Baralacha Range in Himachal Pradesh before merging with the Parbati Range to the east of the Kullu Valley. It then extends across Kinnaur Kailash to the Swargarohini and Bandarpunch ranges in Uttaranchal. Further east it is defined by the snowcapped range north of the Gangotri Glacier and by the huge peaks in the vicinity of Nanda Devi (7816m), the highest mountain in the Indian Himalaya. In western Nepal the range is equally prominent across the Annapurna and Dhaulagiri massifs, while in eastern Nepal the main ridgeline frequently coincides with the political boundary between Nepal and Tibet.

East of Nepal the main Himalaya Range extends across central Sikkim from the huge Kangchenjunga massif, which includes Kangchenjunga (8586m), the world's third-highest peak. The East Himalaya is breached by the headwaters of the Tista River, which forms the geographical divide between the verdant alpine valleys to the south and the more arid regions that extend north to Tibet. Trekking possibilities are at present confined to the vicinity of the Singalila Ridge, an impressive range that extends south from the main Himalaya and forms the border between India and Nepal.

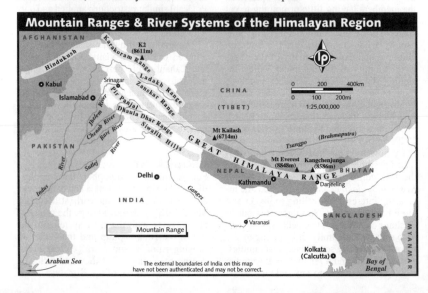

Mountain Ranges & River Systems of the Himalayan Region

Pir Panjal Range

This range is south of the main Himalaya at an average elevation of 5000m. From Gulmarg in the northwest it follows the southern rim of the Kashmir Valley to the Banihal Pass. Here the Pir Panjal meets the ridgeline separating the Kashmir Valley from the Warvan Valley. From Banihal the Pir Panjal sweeps southeast to Kishtwar and then to the east, where it forms the divide between the Chandra and Ravi valleys. Further east of the Kullu Valley it merges with the main Himalaya Range. The Pir Panjal is breached only once – at Kishtwar, where the combined waters of the Warvan and Chandra rivers meet to form the Chenab River, one of the main tributaries of the Indus.

Dhaula Dhar Range

Lying to the south of the Pir Panjal this is easily recognised as the snowcapped ridge behind Dharamsala where it forms the divide between the Ravi and the Beas valleys. To the west it provides the divide between the Chenab Valley below Kishtwar and the Tawi Valley, which twists south to Jammu. To the east it extends across Himachal Pradesh forming the high ridges of the Largi Gorge and extending south of the Pin Parbati Valley before forming the impressive ridgeline east of the Sutlej River. There it forms the snowcapped divide between the Sangla Valley and upper Tons catchment area in Uttaranchal, including the Har ki Dun Valley. Beyond the Bhagirathi River it forms the range between Gangotri and Kedarnath before merging with the main Himalaya at the head of the Gangotri Glacier.

Whether the Swargarohini and Bandarpunch ranges form part of the main Himalaya or whether they form part of the Dhaula Dhar Range is a matter of dispute. Kenneth Mason argues in *Abode of Snow* that these ranges are part of the lesser Himalaya and continue east to include the peaks to the south of Gangotri Glacier, including Kedarnath (6490m) and Kedar Dome (6831m), before merging with the Great Himalaya Range at the head of the Gangotri Glacier.

GARRY WEARE

In Uttaranchal, the Chaukhamba Range is visible at the head of the Gangotri Glacier.

Siwalik Hills

This range lies to the south of the Dhaula Dhar, with an average elevation of 1500m to 2000m. They are the first range of hills encountered en route from the plains and are geologically separate from the Himalaya. They include the Jammu Hills and Vaishno Devi, and extend to Kangra and further east to the range south of Mandi. In Uttaranchal they extend from Dehra Dun to Almora before heading across the southern border of Nepal.

Trans-Himalaya

This complex range of mountains is to the north of the main Himalaya range. It includes the Zanskar, Ladakh and East Karakoram ranges.

The Zanskar Range forms the backbone of Ladakh south of the Indus River, stretching from the ridges beyond Lamayuru in the west across the Zanskar region, where it is divided from the main Himalaya by the Stod and Tsarap valleys, the populated districts of the Zanskar Valley. The Zanskar Range is breached where the Zanskar River flows north, creating awesome gorges until it reaches the Indus River just below Leh. To the east of the Zanskar region the range continues through Lahaul and Spiti, providing a complex buffer zone between the main Himalaya and the Tibetan plateau. It continues across the north of Kinnaur before extending west across Uttaranchal, where it again forms the intermediary range between the Himalaya and the Tibetan plateau, which includes Kamet (7756m). The range finally peters out northeast of the Kali River – close to the border between India and Nepal.

The Ladakh Range lies to the north of Leh and merges with the Kailash Range in Tibet.

The East Karakoram Range is the huge range that forms the geographical divide between India and Central Asia. It includes many high peaks, including Teram Kangri (7464m), Saltoro Kangri (7742m) and Rimo (7385m), and the Karakoram Pass (5672m), historically the main trading link between the markets of Leh, Yarkand and Kashgar.

GEOLOGY

The Himalaya is one of the youngest mountain ranges in the world, resulting from the collision of India with Asia. Its deep gorges expose usually hidden geologic processes and more than 1800 million years of earth history. The evolution of the Himalaya can be traced to the Early Cretaceous epoch (130 million years ago) when the landmass which is now India broke away from Africa and Antarctica. Palaeomagnetic data indicates that after separation from Gondwanaland the Indian sub-continent moved northeast at a rate of around 18cm per year before colliding with the Asian continental crust 60 million years ago. The Indian crust started to submerge below the Asian crust and the northward movement slowed down to its present rate of around 5cm per year. The ongoing collision is still resulting in deformation, crust thickening and surface uplift. The upper continental crust of India is still shearing southwards along the major thrust zones – the oldest to the north and the youngest to the south (rather similar to the small thrusts a snow plough makes when clearing snow). These thrust zones divide the Himalaya into its major tectonic units: from north to south they are the Trans-Himalaya, Indus-Yarlung Suture Zone, Higher Himalaya, Lesser Himalaya and Sub-Himalaya.

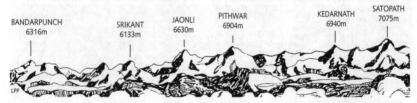

BANDARPUNCH 6316m   SRIKANT 6133m   JAONLI 6630m   PITHWAR 6904m   KEDARNATH 6940m   SATOPATH 7075m

The most prominent peaks of the western Himalaya,

Trans-Himalaya

This region is characterised by bright, coarse-grained granitic rocks, which outcrop directly to the north of the Indus-Yarlung Suture Zone. These igneous rocks originated from before the collision of India and Asia; they formed from melted oceanic crust that was originally between the two continents. The region includes the Ladakh Range, the East Karakoram and the adjoining ranges that extend to the Tibetan Plateau.

Indus-Yarlung Suture Zone

This defines the zone of collision between Indian and Asian crust. It consists of a complex series of rock bands, including deep-sea sediments and oceanic basalts; rocks from volcanic arcs; and even mantle rocks. All combine to form the so-called 'ophio-lithic melange'. This complex is reflected in the colourful appearance of grey turbitites, greenish basalts and red radiolarite that form the landscape of Ladakh. Of particular interest are the incredible geological formations in the vicinity of Lamayuru.

Higher Himalaya

This is the northernmost unit of the Indian continental crust. It extends from the Main Central Thrust of the Himalaya to the Indus-Yarlung Suture Zone. It includes the highest mountains of the Himalaya, including many of the world's 8000m peaks. The Higher Himalaya is composed of two major tectonic parts. The lower part comprises high-grade metamorphosed sedimentary rocks such as schists, gneisses and marbles; together with abundant granitic intrusions, including the spectacular mountains of Kinnaur Kailash in the Sutlej Valley, Hannuman Tibba and Deo Tibba near Manali, and the impressive Gumburanjan monolith that captures every trekker's imagination when crossing the Himalaya Range to the Zanskar. The tectonically upper part consists of low-grade metamorphosed sandstones, shales, dolomites and limestone representing mainly marine deposits of the northern Indian continental margin. This unit is frequently sighted in the high alpine valleys immediately to the south of the Himalaya Range or in Spiti – the famous 'seashells on Himalayan mountaintops' that provided early geologists with one of their most vexing puzzles.

Lesser Himalaya

This is to the south of the Higher Himalaya. The oldest rocks of the Himalaya – such as the augengneisses near Wangtu in the Sutlej Valley – belong to this unit forming the 1800-million-year-old basement for the thick deposits above. The sediments range in age from Precambrian to early Tertiary, with a major break in deposition between middle Cambrian and Eocene. The region extends across the southern mountain regions of Himachal and Uttaranchal.

Sub-Himalaya

This zone includes much of the Siwalik Hills and represents the southernmost unit. It consists mainly of sandstones and conglomerates derived from the erosion of the rising Himalaya in the north. Tectonically, it is over-thrust by the Lesser Himalaya at the Main Boundary Thrust and subsequently it over-thrusts recent sediments from the Indus-Ganges plains along the Main Frontal Thrust. This major thrust is the youngest and the most active thrust of the Himalaya, and is a major factor in the present shortening

CHAUKHAMBA
7138m   NILKANTH
6596m   KAMET
7756m   TRISUL
7120m   DUNAGIRI
7066m   NANDA DEVI
7816m   NANDA DEVI
EAST 7434m   BAMBA DHURA
6334m   PANCH CHULI
6904m

most of which can be viewed on treks in Uttaranchal.

between India and Asia. Its ongoing activity is responsible for the high seismicity of this zone, which is one reason why there has been such widespread concern regarding the large-scale construction of dams across the region.

CLIMATE

Climatically, the Indian Himalaya is varied, and can be divided into the following regions. The national newspapers have daily weather reports.

Beyond the Monsoon

Ladakh and Zanskar, Spiti, northern Kinnaur and some areas of northern Uttaranchal are isolated from the main brunt of the Indian monsoon. These regions lie to the north of the main Himalaya Range and escape the full impact of the monsoon. Humidity is always low, while rainfall is no more than a few centimetres a year.

However, it's not all good news. These regions experience some of the coldest temperatures anywhere in the world, and it doesn't warm up till the spring in late April or early May. In June, temperatures frequently reach the mid-20°Cs, snow on the passes melts and most treks can be undertaken from then until mid-October. Heavy rainstorms can occasionally be experienced in July and August, and river crossing should be undertaken with great care at this time. By September the conditions are ideal, and they normally remain so until late October, although night-time temperatures may fall below freezing. By November, the early winter snows fall on the passes closest to the Himalaya. In winter the villagers still travel, enduring the intense cold, to follow the valley floors where river crossings are no longer a problem.

Modified Monsoon

The Kashmir Valley and the lower Warvan and Chenab valleys in Jammu and Lahaul experience a modified monsoon climate. These regions lie between the Pir Panjal and the main Himalaya Ranges. Although occasional clouds break over the Pir Panjal, this does not normally cause a major disruption

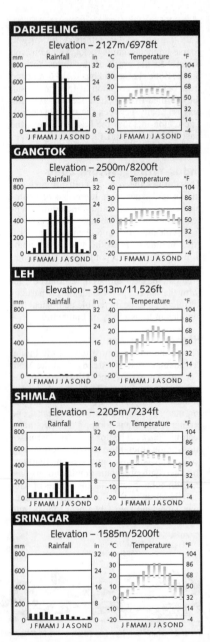

Himalayan Vegetation Zones

The Indian Himalaya can be broadly divided into three geographic zones that have a marked effect on the vegetation.

West Himalaya – North of the Himalayan Divide

This includes Ladakh, Zanskar, upper Lahaul and Spiti. It includes an alpine zone found generally from 4000m to 5000m and even higher as you move north towards the Karakoram Range. The zone is often virtually devoid of vegetation bar sage bush and the grassy meadow found alongside a watercourse. The sub-alpine zone extends from 3500m to 4000m and includes stunted junipers. A lower zone, from 3000m to 3500m, includes willows and cultivated poplars. Irrigated barley fields, sprinkled with leguminous plants, geraniums, aquilegias and louseworts, thrive in the depths of the valleys.

South of the Himalaya Range

This vast region includes the Kashmir Valley and the regions of Himachal and Uttaranchal. It supports an alpine zone from 3500m to 4500m, which includes the open grazing meadows at the higher levels, while birch groves mark the lower level of this zone. The temperate zone extends from 1500m to 3500m. Conifers, including firs, hemlocks, pines and cedars, are found between 2500m and 3500m, while oaks and blue pine are found at the lower elevations. In regions where the forests have been cleared, cornfields are found between 1800m and 3000m and rice paddies somewhat lower, between 1500m and 2000m, as in the Kashmir and Kullu Valleys.

The tropical and subtropical zone in Himachal and Uttaranchal includes long-needled pine, sal and oak forests, while thorn scrub is found closer to the Indian plains where much of the original forest belt has been cleared. In the more remote mountain districts the forest floor is covered with more luxuriant cover, including bamboo, ferns and shrubs. The upper limit of this zone is 1400m.

East Himalaya

This includes Sikkim and Darjeeling and is, in many respects, an ecological extension of eastern Nepal. The region includes an alpine zone, which extends between 3500m and 4500m, while the sub-alpine zone with junipers and dwarf rhododendrons extends from 3300m to 4000m. Note that there is an absence of birch trees in this zone. The temperate forest range extends from 1800m to 3500m and includes a band of conifers, magnolias, daphnes and rhododendrons at the upper levels, and an oak, bamboo and rhododendron band between 2000m and 3000m, while at the lower elevations there are oak, alder and chestnut trees. This merges with the subtropical forests, which are better preserved than those in the West Himalaya. Among the deciduous and evergreen forests the sal tree is the most easily identified in southern Sikkim. In the tropical zone a variety of shrubs, bamboos, palms and ferns is also found.

to the trekking season, which extends from May to mid-October. After October the day temperatures drop, but the weather is generally settled until mid-November, when the first heavy winter snows fall on the high passes. Winter (Dec–Mar) is often bleak, with heavy snow falling at lower altitudes. April and May are characterised by heavy precipitation, which falls as snow in the mountains, precluding trekking over the passes until June.

Monsoon – West Himalaya

Most of the hill states, including Kangra and Chamba, the Kullu Valley, Shimla in Himachal and most regions of the Garhwal and Kumaon in Uttaranchal, come under the influence of the Indian monsoon.

The first heavy monsoon rains fall by the end of June and continue until September. The rains tend to become progressively heavier as the monsoon continues, with the heaviest falls lasting through August till early September. Temperatures at this time of the year rise during the day to the mid-20°Cs, while at night they fall to between 5°C and 10°C. The post-monsoon period from mid-September to late October is generally settled with clear, fine days, although the daytime temperatures fall considerably towards the end of October. This weather trend continues through to December, although the daytime temperatures are often little above freezing. Winter brings heavy snow that continues till the end of March and/or early April. Snow melts on the lower ridges by May and on some of the higher passes by June during the short pre-monsoon season.

Temperatures begin to rise in May and by mid-June they can reach 20°C.

Monsoon – East Himalaya

Both Darjeeling and Sikkim are subject to the Indian monsoon that sweeps up from the Bay of Bengal, bringing heavy rainfall from early June until the end of September. The post-monsoon months (Oct & Nov) provide settled conditions, with clear views of the mountains, although night-time temperatures frequently fall below freezing above 3500m. During the pre-monsoon period (mid-March–late May), temperatures often rise to 25°C, while mid-morning storm clouds may preclude good views of the mountains.

CONSERVATION & ENVIRONMENT

Developments relating to mining, forestry, tourism and the defence of the region's sensitive political borders compound the Himalaya's environmental problems. Population growth increases the need for energy and roads and changes in land cultivation lead to overgrazing and increasingly monocultural agriculture.

The construction of large-scale dams – including the Bakra Dam harnessing the waters of the Sutlej in Himachal Pradesh; the recently constructed Tehri Dam harnessing the waters of the Bhagirathi River in Uttaranchal; and the dam construction on the Chenab below Kishtwar in the Jammu & Kashmir state – have drawn significant protests from environmentalists. Other developments, particularly in the Kullu and Parbati valleys in Himachal Pradesh, have also been a cause for concern.

Deforestation for fuel or to increase the amount of land for cultivation is a further issue. Wildlife and forest officers working in remote locations rarely command the financial resources to curtail illegal logging, stop plant hunters stripping the hill sides of medicinal herbs or to prevent poaching or hunting of protected species.

Overgrazing is common throughout the alpine regions of the Himalaya. There are few alpine meadows that have not attracted huge flocks of sheep and goats as Gaddi and Bakraval shepherds search continually for new pastures. In the lower regions the Gujar shepherds create similar problems while grazing their buffalo to supply milk and cheese to the local markets. Failure to follow a viable crop rotation has led to monoculture, particularly in Uttaranchal where chir plantations have replaced the mixed oak forest.

Road developments have also taken their toll on the environment. While it is probable that 90% of remote villages in the Indian Himalaya will be connected by road in the next few generations, it is relevant to consider that much recent construction has paid little regard to the environment or to the fact that many roads can only be used for a few months each year.

Conservation

To appreciate the environmental impact in the Himalayan regions many government reports have been commissioned. Some have incorporated developments and reforms adopted in other mountain regions of the world for example in the European Alps, North America or the New Zealand Alps. The more successful ones have taken into consideration the fact that the Himalaya is characterised by developing economies where the nature of the problems and the level of priorities are different.

In the interim a number of local organisations have formed pressure groups to try to address some of the developments. The

Himalayan Tourism – Some Further Perspectives

To ascertain the impact of tourism in the Himalaya, modern studies have tried to strike a balance between local interests and the interests of visitors, including a) tourists to hill stations b) pilgrims and c) trekkers and mountaineers.

Mountain Tourism

It is evident that most Indian hill towns have been subjected to inappropriate developments that place undue strain on the local resources.

This is particularly apparent in the more popular hill stations, including Shimla, Naini Tal, Mussoorie and Darjeeling.

Manali, in a fertile alpine valley in northern Himachal Pradesh, was an exception to the rule. However, the huge increase in the number of hotels, lodges and guesthouses in the last decade has lead to many ad-hoc developments. Orchards and natural surrounding have been destroyed with many discerning tourists now staying elsewhere in the Kullu Valley.

Development in Leh, the capital of Ladakh, has been of a different nature. Since 1974 the influx of tourism has placed considerable strain on the local resources, with many tourists demanding facilities that are almost impossible to provide. The large number of foreign tourists has also placed undue pressure on the local culture, with the Ladakhi people often discarding traditional practices for the sake of the tourist dollar.

However, Himalayan tourism has not been without some benefits. It has been a major source of employment, checking migration to the big cities. It has also stimulated local arts and crafts while increasing awareness of a region's history and culture. The influx of tourists has also provided *gompas* (Tibetan Buddhist monasteries) and *mandirs* (Hindu temples) with a vital source of income that has been channelled into preserving important buildings and wall paintings. New ideas from other regions of India – and abroad – have also helped develop fresh perspectives, and facilitated innovations such as solar heating, waste disposal and micro-hydroelectric schemes.

Pilgrimage Tourism

In the past, pilgrims made few demands on their travels through the Himalaya. Nowadays the development of roads has resulted in greater accessibility and greater numbers of pilgrims. In Uttaranchal the pilgrimage season in May and June to the Char Dham attracts something in the vicinity of 250,000 pilgrims. This has had a devastating effect on the local mountain environment. Over the last decade a number of associated interest groups, including the Gangotri Conservation Project, have been able to redress some of the worst of the developments. However, further funding is imperative in order to ensure that projects can be completed here and at the other pilgrim centres.

Trekking & Mountaineering

While a far smaller number of mountain tourists venture beyond the trailhead, the environmental and cultural problems caused by a steadily increasing number of trekkers is a cause for concern. (See the 'Responsible Trekking' boxed text for more information, pp46–7.) 'Tread lightly' philosophies have yet to be reconciled with increasing pressure on the local environment. Tin cans, plastic and other non-biodegradable rubbish are not properly disposed of, wood is used for fuel, and the demand on camping areas has resulted in streams and rivers being polluted.

There has also been a gradual undermining of cultural values. However, as with mountain tourism, trekking can help to stimulate interest in traditional handicrafts and may also provide employment and halt the trend of migration from the mountain villages to the cities. More discriminating trekkers may also act as a pressure group to help preserve threatened wildlife species and delicate areas.

magazine *Sanctuary Asia* provides updates and information regarding conservation programs in India. Some of the conservation societies involved in projects in India, either based in India or overseas, are listed under Useful Organisations (pp55–6).

NATIONAL PARKS & WILDLIFE SANCTUARIES

The creation of national parks and wildlife sanctuaries has gone some way towards protecting the endangered flora and fauna in various regions of the Himalaya. However, the Himalaya is not a wilderness region and many national parks are created in areas where people have lived for centuries. The challenges of creating a controlled environment are therefore of a different nature to those in other countries.

Ladakh

The Hemis High Altitude National Park was created in 1981 and includes an area from the south of the Indus River across the Stok Range to the Markha Valley. The preservation of wildlife has largely been successful, although there are still reports of snow leopards being stoned to death by villagers whose domestic sheep and goats are being attacked.

Kashmir

The vast Kishtwar National Park was created in the early 1980s to include the area northeast of the Warvan Valley and northwest of Chenab Valley up to the main Himalayan watershed. This ambitious plan did not, however, take into account the large-scale summer migration of the shepherds grazing huge flocks of sheep and goats on the already fragile hillsides. Closer to the Kashmir valley the Dachigam National Park legislation was more strictly enforced until the outbreak of political unrest over the last decade.

Himachal Pradesh

In Himachal Pradesh, the creation of the Greater Himalaya National Park in 1984 has helped to preserve a wide variety of fauna and flora in the Sainj, Tirthan and Jiwa to the

east of the Kullu Valley. However, there is concern that the lower reaches of these beautiful valleys may be affected by the nearby dam project in the Larji Gorge. A similar project is currently underway in the Kanawer Sanctuary in the upper Parbati Valley, designed to provide towns in the lower Kullu Valley with hydroelectricity. Close by, the Pin National Park in Spiti extends from the eastern watershed of the Parbati valley, providing a sanctuary for protected species such as the snow leopard.

The Manali Sanctuary, immediately to the west of Manali, is the most accessible sanctuary for most visitors to the Kullu Valley. (Trek through it on the Bara Bhangal trek in Himachal Pradesh.) It extends through mixed forest with many orchids and ferns to the alpine pastures where a wide variety of wildflowers thrive in summer.

Uttaranchal

In 1983 the former Uttar Pradesh (UP) government introduced restrictions on the movement of people into the Bhyundar Valley (Valley of the Flowers) and the Nanda Devi Sanctuary. It was maintained that the local shepherds, trekkers and mountaineers had damaged the flora and fauna and that a suitable period of time was necessary for these regions to regenerate. At present the Nanda Devi Sanctuary is closed to trekkers, while no overnight camping is permitted in the Bhyundar Valley.

On the border of Himachal and UP, the Govind National Park was originally established as a wildlife sanctuary in 1955. It provides many opportunities for trekkers to explore the Har ki Dun Valley and the adjacent valleys leading to Kinnaur.

Sikkim

Legislation to curb logging and deforestation of the luxuriant forests in southern Sikkim has been enforced over the last decade. The creation of the Kangchenjunga National Park, together with forest check posts and trekking permits at Yuksam has contributed to the preservation of some of the finest rhododendron and magnolia forests in the Himalaya.

WATCHING WILDLIFE

The Indian Himalaya is an exceptional region of biodiversity. Observing and identifying the plants and animals en route is sure to be a highlight. The following guide is a survey of species that trekkers are likely to see. In addition, each trek chapter features a specific 'Watching Wildlife' boxed text. For a list of books on the Indian Himalaya's natural history, see p57.

FLORA
WILDFLOWERS

The alpine regions of Himachal Pradesh and Uttaranchal provide excellent scope for appreciating the wide range of flowering plants, many of which are similar to the mountain flora of Europe and the USA.

Primula Family Mainly concentrated in the northern temperate zone, primula is herbaceous, dying down at the end of the year. The leaves commonly form an entire rosette around the stem – the actual stem being leafless – and the flowers form clusters. Some of the larger primula species are unpalatable to animals, so often grow around shepherd encampments in the Himalayan high meadows. *Primula denticulata* is very common on open grazing slopes and in shrubberies at elevations from 1500m to 4500m. It is often called the drumstick primula, named for its compact globular head of massed individual flowers. The flowers are purple to mauvish-blue, although there is a white form. Each petal is split at the top. The tooth-edged leaves crowd tightly round the plant. Both the leaves and the stem, initially around 10cm, extend up to 30cm by the end of the season.

Iris Family This herbaceous family includes the crocus genus (cultivated in the Kashmir Valley), and is worldwide in distribution. It is distinguished by its six petals and alternate leaves, usually long and narrow. Irises are characterised by three erect petals fused below into a tube and three limp petals, known as 'falls'. The rhizomes (swollen underground stems) creep along the ground, and vast numbers from the Himalayan species have been dug out by plant hunters for cultivation in Europe. *Iris kemaonensis* is common across the Himalayan alpine meadows in early spring, appearing not long after the snows melt. Often in large clumps, this bright lilac-to-purple flower with dark spots and blotches on its petals can be found in elevations up to 4000m. The flowers are solitary and virtually stalkless. Each of the three falls has a bright yellow beard. The flowers appear with the young leaves, but in due course the leaves grow longer.

Saxifrage Family Also herbaceous, the genus *Bergenia* has large leaves – their blades (the flattened part of the leaf) being 5cm or more. These leaves have leaf stalks at the base, and stout, flowering but leafless stems rising from the strong rootstock. Both *B. ciliata* and *B. stracheyi*, which are common across the Indian Himalaya, have leaf margins with bristly

Close-up of a primrose, *Primula denticulata*

hairs. *B. ciliata*, found in forests and on rock ledges, flowers from March to July; *B. stracheyi*, the common alpine species of the western part of the Himalaya, grows on open slopes and flowers from June to August. Both are found in elevations around 4000m, but *B. ciliata* also grows at much lower altitudes, appearing from 1800m. The leaves of *B. ciliata* are quite large compared to the individual flower stems, which grow white, pink or purple flowers. The leaves grow larger and turn bright red in the autumn before dying. *B. stracheyi* has shorter leaf stems and longer, pink flowers that hang in a drooping cluster.

Daisy Family Members of this large family are characterised by distinctive flower heads, composed of numerous small florets on a flower stem. There are many differences among the actual types of the florets. *Leontopodium*, the edelweiss genus, has 35 different species, many of which are fairly difficult to distinguish. Edelweiss need to be protected from the winter wet when cultivated, so these perennials persist well below the ground between growing seasons. Both *L. himalayanum* and *L. jacotianum* (smaller and more tufted) are quite common in the West Himalaya, above 3000m or more. Both are found on open slopes and flower from July to September/October. The plants have grey, woolly and tufted stems, with clusters of many small, globular white flower heads. As the dense, woolly leaves dry, they are used for tinder by shepherds.

Spurge Family This is a family of herbaceous perennials, with rootstock persisting until the next growing season. All *Euphorbia* have a milky sap, which emerges freely when the plant is damaged. The *E. wallichii* occurs in the western Himalaya and is particularly common on Kashmiri open slopes and grazing grounds, flowering from April to May. This erect plant has very leafy stems, of 30cm to 60cm in height, which terminate in several yellow flower heads in virtually flat-topped clusters. The yellow heads are actually bracts, which surround the flower and attract pollinating agents. The insignificant flowers are within. When dry, the smooth, blue-grey seeds burst open.

Rose Family The *Rosa* genus of the rose family can be distinguished by the fact that its many hard, one-seeded carpels (the female part of the flower) are enclosed within a hip – the fruit, a fleshy receptacle. *Rosa webbiana* is very common in the western Himalaya, naturally occurring at altitudes from 1500m to 4000m. From June to August, on the dry rocky slopes of Lahaul, Ladakh and across to Pakistan, this cheerful, pink-flowered rose brightens the barren hillsides. It has also been cultivated around many villages. Up to 2.5m high, it has slender branches and straight prickles. The small, rounded leaves have prickly leaf stalks. The single, five-petalled flowers, up to 7cm across, are densely clustered. The stems and leaves often turn bright pink.

Buttercup Family Many members of the buttercup family can be found in the Himalaya. The *Aquilegia* genus, for example, commonly known as the columbine or 'Granny's bonnet', has several species in the Himalaya. *Aquilegia nivalis*, of the West Himalaya, has deep-purple, solitary, nodding flowers. It flowers from June to August on high alpine slopes, scree and rocks. The unbranched stem, up to 20cm long, has only a few kidney-shaped leaves.

Caltha palustris is commonly called the marsh marigold (*palustris* means swampy). This flower is common on open slopes and grazing grounds across the Himalaya from 2400m to 4000m. A small plant, spread low to the ground, it is distinguished by relatively large, fleshy, heart-shaped leaves and terminal clusters of yellow or white buttercup-shaped flowers.

TREES

Oak Forming whole forests, this hardwood is common across the Himalaya, upward from 2100m. In a few, mostly moister areas, it is dominant right to the upper tree line. This large evergreen tree is distinguished by its globular (acorn) nuts. The leaves of the young trees have spiny marginal teeth (like a holly leaf), but on older trees the leaf has entire margins and the upper surface is dark, glossy green. It is common on steep, rocky, south-facing slopes from which the snow cover clears quickly. The trees are very important in the hill villages and cultivated areas of the temperate hill forests as they are extensively lopped for cattle fodder. The wood is used locally for building and it also gives good fuel. The bark contains much tannin.

MARGARET JUNG

Horse chestnut

Horse Chestnut A large deciduous tree of up to 30m or more in height, the horse chestnut is found in forests and shady ravines across the altitude zone from 1800m to 3000m. The trees are impressive for their large, upright pyramidal clusters of white flowers, the petals often streaked with red at the base. The leaves are distinctive, long-stalked and divided in a palm-like manner. The fruit is a leathery capsule, usually with one large shining seed. Like many trees in the Himalaya, the leaves are lopped as stock fodder. Superb forests of horse chestnuts, interspersed with maples and the Himalayan walnut tree *(Juglans regia)*, can be found towards the upper reaches of the Ganges tributaries in Kumaon and Garhwal. As with the walnut trees, the wood is often used for turned articles and the bark is used medicinally.

LPP

Rhododendron arboreum

Rhododendron Part of the heath family, this tree/shrub genus comprises more than 800 species, most of which are evergreen. Although not unique to the Himalaya, many species are distributed widely across the Indian Himalaya, with some endemic only to the eastern Himalaya and Nepal. *Rhododendron arboreum* is the most widely distributed in the Himalaya, at a range of altitudes from 1500m. It has many different forms, some reaching a height of 15m. Its flowers range from red and pink to white, usually at the higher altitudes. The mass blooms are superb in early spring. Shallow rooted, rhododendrons virtually always grow in acid soils rich in humus, although the *R. arboreum* can be found on limestone soil. Towards the upper valleys of Uttaranchal, the *R. arboreum* clings tenaciously to the hillsides in thick, branching clusters of shrubs, which are almost impenetrable. Along with birch trees, it forms the highest tree line vegetation right up to 3600m. The flowers are presented as offerings in hillside temples, and the wood is frequently used for fuel.

Chir Pine Ancient in terms of geological time, the long-leaved chir pine forms extensive forests in the Indian Himalaya, from 500m to 2700m. A large, slim, triangular tree, up to 40m high, it is distinctive for its very thick and deeply fissured rough bark. The bark drops off in broad, scaly plates. The chir grows in acid or alkaline soil without any apparent discrimination. It can cling to ravines so steep that they are virtually impossible to climb. The chir discourages undergrowth and the forest floor is thick and slippery with the fallen clusters of long, needle-like leaves. The trees are particularly drought tolerant and, occasion-ally after a very dry spell, will lose their leaves for a period before regrowth. Mature trees can withstand forest fires, but the young seedlings are not fire resistant, so repeated burnings make regeneration impossible. The edible seeds from the solitary or clustered deciduous cones are winged, and spiral down to the ground after the hot weather. The sapwood has a sweet smelling resin and the bark yields tannin, which is used for dyeing. Oil of turpentine is obtained from the wood and, although the timber is not particularly durable, it is used for construction.

MARTIN HARRIS

Chir pine (cone), *Pinus roxburghii*

Himalayan Birch Growing from 2700m up to 4300m, the birch marks the upper limit of the tree line right across the Indian Himalaya. The birch tolerates long periods of snow (and therefore dry soil), and frequently can be seen clinging in isolated, spindly clusters to the slopes of high-altitude gullies, where the snow is packed and remains long into the spring.

The Himalayan birch was first botanically described in 1880. Much more recently, the *Betula jacquemontii*, also common to the area, has been considered a separate species. The bark on the *B. jacquemontii* is white, whereas on the *B. utilis* it is brownish red. On the young trees in particular, the bark peels off round the tree in thin trans-verse sheets. It makes excellent kindling for lighting fires, and traditionally has been used as paper. The bark is used locally for waterproofing and roofing huts. The inconspicuous birch flowers appear before the leaves emerge in spring. The leaves are light green and on the *B. utilis* have less pronounced teeth margins. Frequently swept down in landslides, the thin, gnarled trunks are used by shepherds as supports for tent shelters. The Himalayan birch is often mistaken for the silver birch (*B. pendula*).

MARGARET JUNG

Himalayan birch, *Betula itilis*

FAUNA

The Himalaya supports a wide variety of mammals, although many of the species are now endangered and some are bordering on extinction. To devise a trek with maximum wildlife sightings, you need time, patience, a knowledgeable guide and a great deal of luck! For more advice regarding wildlife watching in a particular trekking region, see the Watching Wildlife boxed texts in the trekking chapters.

MAMMALS

Primates The langur, the long-tailed grey monkey with a black face, is found in the temperate forests, often in the vicinity of villages. It migrates in early spring from the temperate to the lower coniferous forests. The rhesus monkey is found at lower elevations. Smaller than the langur, it is brownish-red in colour and often seen close to towns and hill stations.

Marmot These large rodents of the squirrel family are scattered widely throughout the West Himalaya. They live in large colonies in networks of deep burrows where they hibernate during winter. Their loud whistling can be heard for a considerable distance and alerts all animals in the vicinity to oncoming danger from predators, including shepherds, who trap them for their thick, golden-brown fur. While found in Ladakh, Kashmir, Lahaul, Zanskar and Himachal Pradesh, they are less common in Uttaranchal.

Long-tailed marmot,
Marmota caudata

Bears Both Himalayan black and brown bears are widespread throughout the West Himalaya. The black bear is about 4ft to 5ft high and weighs up to 180kg. It has a smooth black coat and a distinctive white 'V' on its chest. Bears are attracted to the ripening cornfields during summer. At other times, they seek refuge in the temperate and coniferous forests before hibernating for several months in winter. Brown bears are distinguished not by the colour of their fur but by the distinctive hump above their shoulder. They are larger than the black bears and tend to be found on the high alpine pastures foraging for edible roots and grasses. They are easily startled and, like all bears, should be given ample room when encountered at close range.

Himalayan black bear,
Selenarctos thibetanus

Wolf Packs of wolves are found north of the Himalaya Range in the arid regions of Ladakh, Zanskar and Spiti. During summer they wander the highest and most remote ridges in search of lone wild goats or sheep. In early winter they descend to the valleys to prey on stray domestic animals. To protect their stock, villagers in Ladakh construct stone enclosures, often on the outskirts of their village, in order to trap the wolf or occasional snow leopard. While sightings of large packs are rare, there is a distinct possibility of hearing them in the vicinity of a settlement on winter nights.

Jungle Cat These long-legged cats are sandy-coloured to grey-brown and inhabit the temperate forests of Himachal and Uttaranchal as high as 2400m. Also known as swamp cats, they have a short, banded tail and prey on small mammals, birds and reptiles.

Snow Leopard These cats inhabit the highest and most remote regions of the West Himalaya. They are solitary creatures, with a long bushy tail. Although they are protected, villagers still occasionally kill them when they attempt to prey on domestic animals. The regions of Ladakh, Spiti and Lahaul provide the

Snow leopard,
Panthera uncia

biggest concentration of snow leopards in the world, yet even here their numbers are rapidly dwindling.

Forest Leopard In India, forest leopards are often called panthers. Some are black so their spots show up only dimly. They are larger than snow leopards and inhabit the temperate forests near villages and towns such as Naini Tal, Mussoorie and Shimla, where they prey on domestic dogs. To combat this, shepherds often place huge collars with iron spikes around the necks of their dogs.

Kiang Also known as the Tibetan wild ass, the kiang is normally found in herds of 10 to 20. They graze the high grassy plateaus in the Rupshu region east of Ladakh and the adjoining regions close to the Tibetan border.

Wild Yak These huge animals, far larger than the domestic yak, are now restricted to the Changdenmo region of Ladakh close to Tibet.

Porcupine This nocturnal animal weighs up to 15kg and is covered from head to tail in quills. It favours the lower forested elevations where it forages for potatoes and other root vegetables.

Red Fox This is of similar size and appearance to the European and North American red fox. They are rarely seen except in late spring, when their footprints may be followed in the snow. In summer they are sometimes observed on a forest trail preying on small rodents.

Pine Marten Sometimes referred to as the yellow-throated marten, it is recognised by its dark slender body and long tail, and distinguished by the yellow markings on its throat. They are normally found in the lower forested areas, where they climb trees and may prey on small birds.

Wild Sheep & Goats With few exceptions, these animals have been seriously depleted during the past 30 years. A comprehensive description of the various species and their locations is covered in George Schaller's *Stones of Silence*.

Urial, *Ovis vignei*

MARTIN HARRIS

Urial These are identified by their large, curved horns. It is the smallest of the wild sheep and can be found in Ladakh and the East Karakoram valleys, although its numbers are now seriously depleted.

Bharal (Blue Sheep) Not classified in the genus *Ovis* along with other sheep, blue sheep are distinguished by their thick, horizontal horns and the dark-blue wool on the rumps of the males. In spring they graze the high pastures of Ladakh and the Zanskar, Lahaul and Spiti. They are also found in the Nanda Devi Sanctuary. In winter they are most vulnerable to attack by snow leopards and other predators when they are in rut.

Bharal, *Pseudois nayaur*

TRUDI CANAVAN

Kashmir markhor,
*Capra falconeri
cashmiriensis*

Alpine Ibex This is one of the largest Himalayan goats. It has impressive serrated, sweeping horns and, like the bharal, selects the highest crags for protection during summer. They are found west of the Sutlej River throughout Himachal, Kashmir and West Ladakh. The wool from the underbelly is renowned for its fine quality and is used in the famous Kashmir pashmina shawl.

Markhor With their distinctive spiralling horns, these goats may be found on the Pir Panjal ranges (particularly in Kashmir), where they roam the forested slopes and open meadows.

Himalayan Tahr This heavily built goat with short, curving horns tends to favour forested ravines south of the Himalaya Range.

Serow & Goral These are classified as part of the antelope-goat family and are found throughout the Himalaya. The serow favours the forest ravines, while the goral roam the forest clearing and the lower grassy slopes.

Tibetan Antelope (Chiru) These are also classified as part of the antelope-goat family. Distinguished by their long, narrow, spiralling horns, they are now confined to the western extremity of the Tibetan Plateau. Their fine wool is prized for shahtoosh shawls, and hunting is creating worldwide concern for their survival.

Deer The Kashmir Stag, barking deer and musk deer are found in the temperate forests, although during summer they are sometimes seen in the upper forest areas on the margins of the alpine pastures.

Tahr, *Hemitragus
jemlahicus*

Kashmir Stag This is a subspecies of the red deer and is nowadays found only in the Dachigam National Park in Kashmir. In summer they roam the birch groves at around 4000m, before returning to the lower elevations in early winter. Although their numbers did increase during the 1970s and 80s, the ongoing political unrest in Kashmir has made them an easy target for poachers.

Sambar This is the largest deer in Asia, weighing up to 200kg and distinguished by a grey-brown coat. Although not a true Himalayan mammal, the sambar is regularly found at altitudes around 3000m.

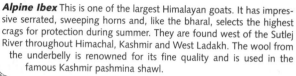

Sambars, *Cervus
unicolor*

Kakor (Barking Deer) These are short in stature with a reddish-brown body and a dog-like bark. They are found in grassy, heavily forested slopes throughout Uttaranchal, Himachal and Kashmir.

Musk Deer These deer are much sought after for their musk glands. They have curving tusks instead of horns and are mainly found in birch groves. In recent times their numbers have been seriously depleted.

BIRDS

For the novice birder, a trek is enhanced with a good field guide, a pair of lightweight binoculars and adequate time to wander the forests and meadows. To appreciate a complete variety of birdlife, trek from the foothills through the mixed oak and conifer forests to the high alpine meadows. During summer, you are likely to see at least a few of the following species. See the Books section (Natural History; p57) for guides to identification.

Lammergeier The bearded vulture, or lammergeier (literally 'lamb hawk'), nestles on inaccessible cliffs. It inhabits the entire length of the Himalaya and favours the alpine slopes during summer. With a wingspan of up to 2.8m, this magnificent bird is unique in its method of feeding on bones. Carried in the talons to a great height, the bones are dropped onto the rocks below; the bird then swoops down to feed on the exposed bone marrow. It also feeds on carcasses and in village rubbish dumps. In flight, its long, wedge-shaped tail distinguishes it from other birds of prey.

Lammergier, *Gypaetus barbatus*

Blood Pheasant Often found near water in open scrub and bamboo, rhododendron and juniper forests, this short-tailed pheasant is grey above with pale-greenish underparts contrasting with a red throat and vent. The female is a warm brown. Both sexes have coral red legs. Seen in pairs or small nyes (collective noun for pheasants), they work their way through the thickets feeding on berries and other vegetable matter. Apart from their loud, grating alarm screech, their common call is a repeated *chuk* sound.

Yellow-billed Blue Magpie Although fairly common in oak-rhododendron and coniferous forest, this shy bird hides from observers behind trees. Its beautiful long tail is flicked up when feeding. In follow-the-leader flight formation across ravines, it intersperses its heavy wing beats with glides. It has both a wheezy *peck-pecking* note as well as a high calling tone of *clear clear*.

Scarlet Minivet Often found in groups, the sight of these birds, with their scarlet and black plumage (yellow and dark grey in the case of females), flitting through the green foliage is entrancing. They are seen in gardens, and tropical and subtropical forests, and are partial to pines. They frequently emit an attractive, mellow *tweet tweet*. Constantly on the move, minivets sidle along branches, hover and drop to the ground for insects.

Yellow-billed blue magpie, *Urocissa flaviostris*

MARTIN HARRIS

Black Drongo Totally glossy black, with a characteristic 'fishtail', this bird is abundant in open areas – fields, villages and the edge of forests up to 1800m. Constantly active, it swoops after insects in the air, returns to its perch and bobs its tail. It is masterly in flight when pursuing its prey or aggressively chasing away an intruder. Bold and noisy in the mating season, it has a loud danger-warning note followed by a slow call.

Rufous Sibia This lively, cinnamon-coloured bird, with black head and wings, is common in oak-rhododendron forests and familiar around many of the Himalayan hill stations. It jerks its tail up and down when perching and is often acrobatic when searching for insects. Its song is a loud, ringing whistle. When alarmed, its crest is fully raised.

Plumbeous redstart,
Rhyacornis
fuliginosus

Plumbeous Redstart These are widely seen perched on boulders in the mountain streams of the Himalaya. The male is slate blue with a broad rufous-maroon tail that it constantly moves up and down. This bird is forever on the move, flitting from rock to rock. Feeding on fruit and insects from bushes at the water's edge, it actively hunts insects at dusk. It has a ringing song.

ENDANGERED SPECIES

There is general recognition that most wildlife species in the Indian Himalaya are endangered. Findings indicate that the numbers of Kashmir stag in the Indian Himalaya are restricted to just a handful in the Dachigam Sanctuary; that the number of snow leopards has been drastically reduced in the past few decades; and that wild sheep and goat species, including the markhor, are now almost extinct in India. The kiang is facing the same prospects in Ladakh, while the numbers of musk deer are seriously declining throughout the Indian hill states. In the East Himalaya, the red panda is similarly endangered.

While most endangered wildlife species are protected in the Indian Himalaya, the funding and resources have not been sufficient to stem other developments. The continual encroachment of mountain regions through logging and the increasing need to clear land for cultivation have contributed to the decline in wildlife numbers. Poaching has also taken its toll. Snow leopard pelts can fetch many thousands of dollars on the black market, while the skins of Tibetan wolves and lynxes are also highly prized. Musk deer are hunted for the musk gland used in the preparation of perfume, while Tibetan antelope or chiru are hunted for their fine wool for the shahtoosh shawl, although there are projects underway to determine the possibilities of breeding them in captivity.

Hunting protected sheep and goat species for their meat is a further problem. Previously inaccessible regions are now within easy reach of roads. Army personnel have exacted their toll on urial and markhor in the eastern Karakoram, while shepherds in the remote alpine valleys are responsible for the declining numbers of ibex and bharal.

Some protective measures have been enforced, including the establishment of wildlife reserves and sanctuaries. However, for creatures such as the snow leopard and red panda, the only chance of survival may be captivity breeding. Unfortunately, success rates are low, and even if successfully bred, there is no guarantee that these animals can be successfully returned to the wild.

POPULATION & PEOPLE

> From near the Nun Kun mountains and from no other spot in Asia, we go westwards through countries entirely Mohammedan, eastward among none but Buddhists, and southwards over lands where the Hindu religion prevails to the extremity of the Indian peninsula.
> **Frederick Drew, *The Northern Barrier of India*, 1877**

The Indian Himalaya marks the crossroads of Asia's three main cultures. The Kashmir Himalaya is the cultural boundary of Islam; the foothills of Jammu, Himachal Pradesh, and Uttaranchal region define the northern limits of Hinduism: while Ladakh is predominantly Buddhist. It also marks the boundaries of the Aryan and Tibetan/Mongoloid races that Frederick Drew sets out the following divisions to clarify:

race	people	religion
Aryan	Dogra	Hindu
Aryan	Pahari	Hindu
Aryan	Kashmiri	Muslim
Tibetan	Balti	Muslim
Tibetan	Ladakhi	Buddhist

This complex relationship between race, religion and people still holds today. There are many regions of the Himalaya where the people of a certain race and ancestry still subscribe to a variant religion.

The Khampa, the original inhabitants of Ladakh nowadays roam the vast Tibetan borderlands in search of pastures for their yaks and goats. The valleys are populated by Ladakhi, mostly of Tibetan origin who gradually adopted irrigation practises in order to settle in the upper reaches of the Indus Valley. There is also a sizeable Muslim community in Leh, some being descendants of trading families which settled in Leh when trade was still undertaken over the Karakoram Pass to Yarkand and Kashmir. In the outlying regions of Kargil there is a sizeable Shia Muslim community, while Zanskar has a small community of Muslims in Padum, where they settled after following the armies of Zorawar Singh in the 1830s.

The Kashmiri people trace their origins to successive Aryan migrations up the Indus Valley. While the culture was Hindu and Buddhist the majority of the people were peacefully converted to Islam in the 14th century. This is still the case today, although until 1990 nearly 10% of the Kashmir population were Hindu.

South of the Kashmir Valley are the Dogra and Pahari villagers. The Dogra are the proud hill people of Jammu, while the hill kingdoms that extend across Chamber, Kanga and into the Garwhal and Kumaon regions of Uttaranchal trace a long and mainly independent Hindu ancestry.

Among the various mountain people are shepherd groups that are often seen on the trails leading to the high Himalaya. These include the Gujar, who trace their origins from Central Asia to the northern Indian Plains and onto the Himalayan foothills. They are Muslim and yet even in Kashmir they do not intermarry or share local cultural traditions.

The Gaddi shepherds are from the region of Kangra in Himachal Pradesh. They are Hindu, and are frequently seen crossing the high passes of the Dhaula Dhar and the Pir Panjal Ranges with their large flocks of sheep and goats.

Hindu pilgrimages play an important part in the cultural fabric of the Himalaya. These include the pilgrimages to Vaishno Devi north of Jammu, and the annual trek to the Amarnath cave in Kashmir. The largest pilgrimages are in Uttaranchal to the sources of the Ganges, including Yamunotri, Gangotri, Kedarnath and Badrinath, while for Sikhs there is the pilgrimage to the sacred lake of Hem Kund.

In Sikkim and Darjeeling the people are either Hindu or Buddhist, sharing many cultural traditions with both Nepalese and Tibetan people. The original inhabitants were the Lepchas who migrated from the Assam Hills to Sikkim around the 10th century. Much later, in the 17th century, Tibetans came across the Himalaya and settled in the valleys while throughout the 19th century Nepalese migrated to Darjeeling and Sikkim. This influx of Tibetans and Nepalese forced the Lepchas to move to more remote regions in Sikkim. A more recent wave of Tibetans arrived after 1959.

RELIGION
Buddhism
The basic teachings of the historical Gautama Buddha date back to the 5th century BC. The Gautama Buddha was actually a prince who, as a young adult, renounced his standing and riches in order to follow his quest for the means of salvation. After first practising and later rejecting the ascetic lifestyle he eventually reached enlightenment after a long and intense period of meditation. Soon after, he preached his first sermon at the Deer Park at Sarnath in north India. He expounded the 'four noble truths' – that the world is full of suffering; suffering is caused by human desires; the renunciation of desire is the path to salvation; and this salvation is possible by following the 'eightfold path'. This path included the right views, resolves, speech, conduct, livelihood, effort, recollection, and meditation. Collectively they are known as the 'middle way'. The Buddha taught that by following the eightfold path we would recognise the futility of our desires and commence on the progressive stages to enlightenment, returning from one reincarnation to the next until reaching a state of nirvana, the final release from the round of rebirths. The path through this cycle of rebirths is known as *karma*, a law of cause and effect, which maintains that what you do in one life will gain (or lose) you merit in the next.

The sage Padmasambhava (750–800 AD) had a remarkable influence on the development of Buddhism in the Himalaya and was one of the foremost proponents of Tantric Buddhism. He acknowledged that the appeal of Buddhism could be widened if the tenets of Tantric Buddhism were adapted to the local animistic beliefs. This was eventually to give support to the Buddhist school known as Varjrana Buddhism – the Vehicle of the Thunderbolt.

Although Buddhism was to gain favour after the kings of Tibet invaded Ladakh in the 8th and 9th centuries, it took many generations for the Buddhist teachings to establish themselves.

One of the greatest influences came from Tibet in the 14th century when the saint Tsongkhapa propounded a new order that restored much of the traditional teachings. The Gelukpa order was to become the dominant cultural force in Tibet, while in Ladakh the monasteries of Thikse, Likir and Spitok were founded by this order in the early half of the 15th century. The order was headed by the Dalai Lama, and even today the 14th Dalai Lama undertakes regular visits to the *gompas* (Tibetan Buddhist monasteries) in Ladakh and Zanskar.

Hinduism
While the term Hinduism was coined by Arab traders in the 8th century to denote the faith of those who followed either Vishnu or Shiva, the foundations of the beliefs of the Brahmans (Brahmanism) date back to the 10th century BC.

Hinduism's beliefs evolved with the practices of the Brahman priests and incorporated many complex sacrifices and rituals. The teachings did not evolve in terms of a divine revelation or from the teaching of a particular saint or prophet, and gods and beliefs were changed to suit the circumstances. With the introduction of Buddhism and Jainism, the idea of a trinity of gods emerged, with Brahma featuring as the creator; Vishnu, the preserver; and Shiva, the destroyer and reproducer.

Essential to the beliefs of the Brahmans was the notion of reincarnation and the doctrine of karma. According to this belief, we all go through a series of rebirths or reincarnations, which will finally lead to spiritual salvation. Karma is a law of cause and effect. Bad actions will lead to a lower reincarnation, while good actions will lead to a higher rebirth and increase the chances of gaining release from the round of rebirths.

The morality of a person's action depends on whether it adheres to the *dharma* – the sacred law set out by the Brahmans and embodied in the *Gita*, a sacred text which sets out the philosophical basis for reincarnation. There are, however, many refinements, which basically depend on the emphasis placed on the believer's relationship with their god – for example, on whether it is based on love and devotion, or whether it is dependent on intellect and theology.

Most Hindus profess to be either a Vaishnava (a follower of Vishnu) or a Shaivist (a follower of Shiva). Yet it is never an exclusive arrangement. Temples devoted to Vishnu will portray a statue of Garuda, the divine eagle and Vishnu's vehicle of transport throughout the universe. Shiva, on the other hand, is less prone to rich embellishments. His presence was often associated with fertility cults and the worship of the stone lingam. The annual pilgrimage to the Amarnath Cave in Kashmir, for example, still attracts up to 20,000 pilgrims at the time of the August full moon.

Islam
The fundamental Islamic beliefs are set out in the Koran, a record of the formal utterances and discourses which Mohammed and his followers accepted as divinely inspired. It includes the famous profession of faith: "There is but one god, and Mohammed is the apostle of god". This declaration evolved in the Arabian Desert in the 7th century. For Mohammed, the essential tenet was belief in one supreme god (Allah). This god was the Being, Creator and Sustainer of the universe, the all-knowing and all-powerful arbiter of good and evil, and the final judge of all humankind.

Muslims believe that god has sent messengers or prophets to preach the unity of god and to warn them of the day of Judgement, when, it is said, those who have acted in god's faith will enter the Garden of Paradise, while the non-believers will be forever damned. These prophets, who are not workers of miracles, have included Abraham, Moses and Jesus. The last of the prophets is believed to be Mohammed – a man with no special knowledge apart from that revealed to him during his life and times in the Arabian Desert.

To gain a favourable hearing on the day of Judgement, acts of devotion must be made, including the observance of ritual prayers which are performed in set order five times a day – at daybreak, noon, midafternoon, after sunset and in the early part of the night. The acts of devotion also include ritual ablution, the giving of alms,

fasting during the month of Ramadan and a pilgrimage to Mecca. In addition, a system of social conduct is set down regarding marriage, divorce, the consumption of alcohol and the making of images. These were all later embodied in the Islamic law.

From the time that the call to Allah was first heard in the deserts of Arabia, it took nearly 700 years for it to gain a foothold in the Himalaya. It is the dominant religion in the Kashmir Valley, while much of Baltistan, including Gilgit, Hunza, Skardu, and nearby Drass and Kargil, were gradually converted. Yet this was the limit of Islam and these valleys mark the present boundaries between the Islamic and Buddhist worlds.

SOCIETY & CONDUCT
Traditional Culture
Village life in the Himalaya is shaped by the seasons and by a multitude of social and religious customs. There are few villages that do not have a *mandir* (Hindu temple), gompa or mosque and there are few passes without prayer flags or a stone cairn to ensure a safe journey. Enter any settlement and you will receive a traditional greeting, be it a *Namaste* in a Hindu village, *Jullay* in a Buddhist village or *Salaam* from the elders in a Muslim village.

Religion is an integral part of social life. In Buddhist regions the monastery provides the focus of activity, where a lama will attend the birth, marriage and death ceremonies. In traditional Hindu regions the Brahman priest will do likewise, while the mullah holds sway over a Muslim family's social and cultural needs.

Festivals and times of celebration are dictated by religious customs while even the commencement of the harvest will be determined as much by the village priest as by the weather.

The passage of the seasons is nonetheless integral to village life. As soon as the winter snow melts in the valleys, the first crop of either rice (at elevations up to 2800m) or barley (at higher elevations) is sown. Work in the fields is concentrated on maximizing the water supply – by either flooding the rice paddies or attending to the irrigation channels to ensure that the spring snow melt is channelled into the fields. Water mills are serviced and maintained, while all available labour is on hand to tend to the fields and orchards. The workload increases during the harvest period and for this reason it is often harder to secure the services of porters and horsemen at this time.

Many of the important festivals and ceremonies are held after the harvest. This is the time for weddings or to undertake journeys to distant relatives and towns.

In winter, village life centres on weaving and working in the home. This may include activities such as making copperware in remote villages in Ladakh and the Zanskar, or weaving intricate carpets in Kashmir and Himachal Pradesh. In some areas, particularly Ladakh, Zanskar, Spiti and Kinnaur, it is a time for important religious festivals, with masked dances performed over several days. It should be noted that the timings, particularly in Ladakh, have been altered in last decade or two, with some of the more accessible monasteries in the Indus valley rescheduling their festivals to attract income from tourism.

The tending of domestic animals is also determined by the seasons. For the Gujar shepherds most of the family head from the lower hills to the high mountain pastures in late spring where they tend to their buffalo throughout summer, close to where they can sell their milk and cheese. They are closely associated with the Bakraval (Gujar who own mainly goats) who are found grazing their flocks on the alpine slopes of Jammu & Kashmir. The Gaddi shepherds also follow the same migratory pattern leading their flocks of sheep and goats to the alpine regions of Himachal Pradesh.

In most other communities, the men undertake the shepherding. They establish the summer settlements in localities anywhere from a few days to a few weeks from the village location. The migration is a familiar sight on many treks from Ladakh to Uttaranchal.

On a trek you may pass the villagers taking their packhorses to the nearest roadhead or town, where they are engaged by a government department throughout the season. In other regions, including Ladakh and Spiti, it is not uncommon to come across horsemen making their way over high passes to secure timber and other building materials for house construction and repairs that are carried out in the winter.

While village life in the Himalaya is still in general harmony with the seasons it is not unusual for a member of the family to leave the village for several months each year to work in the hill stations or on the plains or even take a job with the government or army in order to provide cash income for their family.

Education in the form of schools in remote communities is also changing the fabric of traditional values and the demands for further education are sometimes incompatible with following an agrarian lifestyle. This combined with a number of other factors, including the introduction of radio and TV to remote communities, is having a significant impact on traditional rural values.

'I don't intend to look after the fields for the rest of my life' is a sentiment often expressed by the younger generation of villagers keen to make the point that the prospects of the city are more attractive than remaining in the Himalaya. This will undoubtedly have a significant impact on mountain lifestyles.

Dos & Don'ts

See also the 'Responsible Trekking' boxed text (pp46–7).

Visiting a Village Your attitude will have a significant impact on the village, particularly when you are meeting the younger generations. Bear in mind how the current pace of change impacts on their lifestyle and lend a sympathetic ear to the barrage of questions regarding your lifestyle and ambitions. Be patient when asked about their education or employment prospects and appreciate how they are trying to reconcile their ambitions with their obligations to their friends and family. This will assist you to gain a perspective as to what is happening and to the extent of cultural changes in their community.

Entering a Home Always greet villagers appropriately. Use your right hand for all social conduct and wear appropriate clothing. If invited to join a family, never throw food on the fire and do not touch cooking utensils or food while the meals are being prepared. It is also customary not to sit around or approach the hearth until you are invited to do so. As always, it is necessary to ask before taking photographs.

Entering a Place of Worship Common sense is the most important prerequisite. Wait until you are invited into the place of worship before entering, be respectful and do not take photographs without permission. With regard to dress codes, always ensure that you are modestly attired and remove your shoes. Other requirements will vary. In a mosque women should cover their head and shoulders with a shawl or scarf, while all visitors should wash hands and feet before entering. In a *gurdwara* (Sikh temple) men should cover their heads while leather items should also be removed. In a mandir do not wear leather items and in some places a headscarf must also be warn. When visiting a gompa you should also dress respectfully and approach the places of prayer in a clockwise direction.

LANGUAGE

Hindi and Urdu are the most widely understood languages in northern India. As spoken languages there is little difference between them. However, Hindi is a Sanskrit-based language written in Devanagiri script, while Urdu is a Persian language written in Arabic script.

In all of the main towns of northern India, English is widely spoken. In the mountains, however, this is not the case, and any attempt to speak a little of the local language will be to your advantage. In Darjeeling and Sikkim, and most areas of Uttaranchal and Himachal Pradesh, Hindi is widely understood. It is also the language of the Gujar and Bakraval shepherds who roam the Kashmir mountains in summer. In the outlying villages of the Kashmir Valley, the people only speak and understand Kashmiri. Similarly Ladakhi, a Tibetan-based language, is the only language understood in the more remote valleys of Ladakh and the Zanskar. In the other Himalayan regions, a number of Pahari dialects are widely used in the village areas, including Garhwali and Kumauni in Uttaranchal. For vocabulary, see pp272–7. For a full introduction to the language and pronunciation refer to Lonely Planet's *Hindi & Urdu Phrasebook*.

Facts for the Trekker

WHERE TO TREK

For experienced and first-time trekkers, the Indian Himalaya offers as many if not more opportunities than Nepal. The combination of impressive peaks, remote villages, ancient cultures and contrasting geographic regions compare with the best in the Himalaya. This guide divides the Indian Himalya into the following trekking regions:

Ladakh
The rugged Trans-Himalayan land of 'little Tibet'. Ancient *gompas* (Tibetan Buddhist monasteries) and Buddhist villages thrive beyond the confines of the Indus Valley.

Himachal Pradesh
A land of Hindu villages and temples, pristine forests and lush meadows, extending to the crest of the Himalaya Range.

Uttaranchal
Follow ancient pilgrim trails to the source of the Ganges and beyond to the summit of Nanda Devi – the highest peak in India.

Darjeeling
Trek through Nepalese settlements to alpine meadows with stunning views of Kangchenjunga – the world's third-highest peak.

Sikkim
Ascend through the finest rhododendron forests in the Himalaya to view the many peaks, including Kangchenjunga.

Suggested Itineraries

One of the most important considerations when undertaking a trek is the time and distance involved in getting to the trailhead. Essentially you need a minimum of two weeks, even for a one-week trek. You will need the extra week for travelling and spending time in Leh (or one of the many attractive hill resorts) before returning to Delhi or Kolkata.

Plan your itinerary to include rest, sightseeing, travel and acclimatisation time. See the Table of Treks (pp4–5) for details of the treks mentioned.

One Week Consider the Hampta Pass & Lahaul trek or the Chandrakani Pass & Malana trek out of Manali. The Markha Valley trek in Ladakh is extremely challenging – allow eight days! In Uttaranchal, choose between the Har ki Dun & Ruinsara Lake trek out of Mussoorie, the Pindari Glacier trek out of Naini Tal or the Kuari Pass trek. From Darjeeling, the Singalila Ridge & Phalut trek affords spectacular views of Kangchenjunga.

Two Weeks Trek from Padum in the Zanskar on the Phugtal Gompa & Shingo La trek. From Manali, undertake the Pin Parbati & Spiti or Bara Bhangal treks. In Uttaranchal, choose the Milam Glacier & Nanda Devi trek, while in Sikkim the Dzongri & Guicha La trek affords magnificent views of Kangchenjunga and a host of 7000m peaks.

Three Weeks You have time to combine treks. In the Zanskar region of Ladakh, do the Singge La & Lamayuru and Kang La & Miyar Glacier treks or visit Phugtal gompa before crossing the Shingo La. In Himachal, combine the Pin Parbati & Spiti trek with the Tarik La & Kinnaur trek; or do the Bara Bhangal trek and Kareri Lake trek out of McLeod Ganj. In Uttaranchal, choose the Kuari Pass and Rup Kund treks.

Four Weeks Exploratory trekking at its best. Savour the spirit of Tilman and Shipton in the remote valleys of Uttaranchal or the many hidden valleys in Himachal Pradesh.

Other Activities

If you're planning to combine trekking with other outdoor activities, the following may help you choose a destination.

Cycling Cycle touring on the remote mountain roads throughout Indian Himalaya has gained in popularity in the past decade. In particular, the route from Leh to Manali is high on the priority list of seasoned mountain cyclists. The ride takes 10 days to two weeks and crosses passes in excess of 5000m. Other routes include the roads leading from Manali to Spiti and onto Kinnaur; and the mountain roads linking Shimla with the Garhwal and Uttaranchal. Rides are also possible out of Darjeeling and Sikkim. For a list of operators, see Organised Treks (pp48–9) or visit the Adventure Tour Operators of India website W www.indianadventure.com.

Skiing The ski resort at Auli, close to Joshimath, is open from January through March. The Uttaranchal government offers reasonable ski packages that include ski hire, tows, lessons and accommodation. The Mountaineering Institute in Manali offers skiing courses at Narkanda near Shimla and

also out of the Kullu Valley. The two-week courses run from January to March, while advanced courses are offered in early May.

There are also opportunities for the experienced cross-country skier to follow many of the trekking routes that are under snow for up to five months of the year. For inspiration refer to Harish Kolhi's *Across the Frozen Himalaya*, an account of his winter expedition across the high passes between Ladakh and the Garhwal in 1995. There have also been a number of ambitious expeditions skiing into the Zanskar in winter while there are many opportunities to cross-country ski out of the Kullu Valley.

A heli-skiing program is run out of the Kullu Valley. The program offers weekly

Trek to a Theme

The following highlights may help you choose your trek. Whatever your interest, most itineraries include something from each of these themes, which will no doubt enhance your experience. See the Table of Treks (pp4–5) for more information.

Ancient Cultures & the Pilgrim Way

The treks in Ladakh are renowned for ancient *gompas* (Tibetan Buddhist monasteries) and villages, while Spiti and Lahaul also reflect a close affinity with the cultural history of western Tibet.

For Hindu pilgrimages, consider the annual pilgrimage to Mani Mahesh Kailash or the Source of the Ganges trek.

Mountain Panoramas

For remarkable views of the soaring peaks of the Himalaya Range, consider the Kang La & Miyar Glacier trek out of the Zanskar Valley. For views of the rugged Zanskar Range, try the Singge La & Lamayuru trek. In Himachal, the snowcapped Pir Panjal will impress above the Kullu Valley.

For spectacular views of 7000m peaks, including Nanda Devi, trek the Kuari Pass or view peaks that stretch to Tibet on the Milam Glacier & Nanda Devi trek.

Enjoy incomparable views of Kangchenjunga from the Singalila Ridge & Phalut trek or the Dzongri & Guicha La trek.

Wildflowers

While the Valley of the Flowers near Joshimath is world-renowned, there are many attractive alpine meadows in Uttaranchal.

In Himachal, the Jagatsukh Valley provides easy access to wildflowers during the monsoon months. Do the Kang La & Miyar Glacier trek to see the Miyar Valley in Lahaul.

For rhododendrons, go to Sikkim in May and appreciate the finest array of blooms in the Himalaya.

High-Altitude & Remote Challenges

Challenging traverses over the Himalaya include the Kang La & Miyar Glacier trek or the Pin Parbati & Spiti trek.

For remote trekking, it's hard to beat the Remote Zanskar trek. For well-prepared groups, Uttaranchal is the place to be, with several weeks' worth of passes and glaciers to explore.

departures from Delhi for around US$5000 per week. Contact **Greater Himalayan Outdoors** (☎ *011-6083358*, ⓔ *gho@vsnl.com*) in Delhi for details.

Mountaineering & Rock Climbing The **Himalayan Mountaineering Institute** in Darjeeling and the **Nehru Institute of Mountaineering** in Uttarkashi offer a range of mountaineering and climbing courses from January to May. Courses are also offered by the **Mountaineering Institutes** (☎ *01902-52342)*, with its head office in Manali, Himachal Pradesh. Contact the head office for their courses and the other state government courses run at Dharamsala and Brahmaur. Fees are reasonable and courses are booked on a first-come, first-served basis. Although the courses are primarily for Indian climbers, foreigners are encouraged to sign up.

For experienced climbers there are plenty of opportunities in the Indian Himalaya. However, there are only a few trekking peaks available. To climb any other peak above 6000m, apply to the **Indian Mountaineering Foundation** *(IMF;* ☎ *011-4671211;* Ⓦ *www.indmount.org; Benito Juarez Rd, New Delhi 110021)*. Allow at least three months for your application to be processed. Alternatively contact one of the recognised agents in Delhi, who will process the application on your behalf and organise porters, transport and other services.

The Mountaineering Institute in Manali offers one-week rock-climbing courses from April to December. For experienced climbers there are many opportunities to climb in Ladakh, Spiti and Kinnaur.

River Rafting River-rafting trips have been operating on many of the rivers in Ladakh, Himachal and Uttaranchal for the past 25 years. In Ladakh, a number of local operators offer one- or two-day trips down the Indus River, while longer itineraries rafting down the Zanskar River take five to seven days. In Himachal, there are day trips on the Beas River; in Uttaranchal, there are one- or two-day trips on the Ganges and its tributaries; operators in Sikkim and Darjeeling offer similar trips on the Teesta River.

Taking Photos Outdoors

Almost everywhere in the Indian Himalaya you have to allow for the exceptional light intensity. For best results shoot early in the morning and late in the afternoon – colours look washed out when the sun is high. On the coast and in the mountains where there's snow, allow for the effect of reflected light. To photograph elusive wildlife, plant yourself inconspicuously and be prepared to wait for some time. A tripod will alleviate cramped neck and finger muscles.

Always protect camera lenses with a haze or ultraviolet (UV) filter. At high altitudes the UV filter may not prevent washed-out photos. A polarizing filter can correct this problem and dramatically enhance cloud formations.

Keep film as cool as possible, especially after it has been exposed.

For a thorough grounding in the tips and techniques for photography on the road, read Lonely Planet's *Travel Photography*, by Richard I'Anson, a full-colour guide for happy-snappers and professional photographers alike.

Most of the operators offering trips also organise trekking programs; their contact details are in the trekking chapters or listed under Organised Treks (pp48–9). However, as with most adventure travel operators, some are more professional than others, and some shouldn't be allowed anywhere near the rivers! While state government regulations have attempted to close the loopholes, there are still reports of trips being offered without helmets or lifejackets – with tragic consequences. Competent operators are always happy for you to check out their experience, their guides and equipment – a necessity before parting with your money.

The Mountaineering Institute in Manali organises rafting courses on the Beas River in October and November.

WHEN TO TREK

See Climate (p22) for an explanation of the various climatic regions. Advice is also given under Planning for each trek. However, in summary, trekking seasons are determined by two factors: latitude and monsoon.

Latitude

The West Himalaya lies to the northwest of Nepal and is subject to far colder winters than many regions of Nepal, with heavy winter snows precluding trekking from mid-October to May.

Monsoon

The first monsoon rains fall in Sikkim and Darjeeling in early June. The monsoon extends across most regions of Nepal, and most of Uttaranchal and Himachal Pradesh. The rains normally fall from early July to mid-September. It is therefore advisable to trek in Darjeeling, Sikkim, Uttaranchal and Himachal Pradesh in the pre-monsoon months (May & June) or the post-monsoon months (Sept & Oct).

However, Ladakh and Zanskar, and some northern areas of Himachal Pradesh, including Spiti, lie north of the main Himalaya

Range and escape most of the monsoon rains. Here, trekking season extends from late May to late October.

WHAT KIND OF TREK?

Time, money and experience impact on most travel options, particularly trekking. You should also consider whether to backpack from lodge to lodge or to make your own arrangements – or contact a local agent to assist you – by hiring a porter or two. You may also consider having the complete arrangements made for you by a local or overseas agent (the latter will often arrange your flight as a part of the package).

Backpacking

Carrying your gear and being self-sufficient is not difficult on short treks where the load is light and the stages are easy. On a long trek, your backpack may weigh you down

Which Region, Which Month?

Use these tables to choose your trekking season:

region	season	advice
Ladakh & Zanskar	May–Oct	Likely snow on the higher passes until July.
Kashmir	May–mid-Oct	Trekking not recommended at present.
Himachal Pradesh (Kinnaur, Spiti & Lahaul)	May–Oct	Best late in the season: snow on high passes in spring; occasional monsoon rains in July and August.
Himachal Pradesh (Kullu Valley, Kangra Valley & Ravi Valley)	May–June, late Sept–early Oct	Many passes are under snow in May.
Uttaranchal	May–June, late Sept–Oct	Despite snow on higher passes in May and June, many can still be crossed. For the very well-prepared, wildflowers are best during the monsoon (July–mid-Sept).
Darjeeling/Sikkim	Apr–May, Oct–Nov	Spring is the best time for rhododendrons, while autumn usually offers the best mountain views.

pass	height	valley	open
Baralacha La	4950m	Lahaul to Ladakh	July–mid-Oct
Khardung La	5606m	Leh (Indus) to Nubra	June–Sept
Kun Zum La	4550m	Lahaul to Spiti	mid-July–mid-Oct
Pentse La	4450m	Kargil (Suru) to Zanskar	July–early Oct
Rohtang Pass	3978m	Kullu to Lahaul	mid-June–mid-Nov
Zoji La	3529m	Kashmir to Ladakh	June–mid-Oct

to the point where you see more of your feet than the mountains. It is one thing to carry your own gear for a few days, but quite another to carry it for two weeks or more. Of course this ultimately depends on your fitness and experience of trekking in mountain areas. Many trekkers compromise by hiring porters or a horse attendant to help carry the load. See also the boxed text 'Lodge-Based Trekking in India'.

Do-It-Yourself

At a hill station, you can arrange your own equipment, food and staff. If you have sufficient time and patience to organise this, either directly or through a local person, it can

be a highly rewarding experience, as well as saving you money.

However, you must be aware of the problems of dealing with a culture vastly different from your own. This is likely to affect many of your negotiations. Don't expect anything to progress too quickly, or expect a straight answer when it comes to times and stages. It is an open bargaining situation. The horsemen will naturally want to take the less demanding route, and won't lose any time in explaining to you that the passes you wish to cross are – for one reason or another – not possible for the time being. Generally, staff or horsemen are not prepared to go on an extended trek on their own. They will insist

Lodge-Based Trekking In India

Compared to the popular treks in the Annapurna and Everest regions of Nepal, there are few comparable lodge-based trekking itineraries in the Indian Himalaya. On some trails there may be a Dak Bungalow or a Forest Rest House built to accommodate forest or other government officers. There might be a parachute tent in Ladakh, while elsewhere you may expect a simple lodge run by either the state government or a local family. Then again a very basic pilgrim shelter may be just about it. Whatever is available is seldom available throughout the trek, and is basic at best. Expect simple, often dormitory-type rooms. Do not expect hot showers, thick mattresses, heating or similar creature comforts experienced in Nepal. If food is provided, expect *dhal bhat* (lentils and rice) and perhaps some vegetables, not a menu of pizza and apple pie. Indeed, it has been said that a trek in India is comparable to trekking in Nepal in the late 1960s–early 1970s.

On the majority of the treks in India, you will need to bring a tent, sleeping bag and insulated mat together with a supply of food and cooking gear. Add to this your personal gear and you will probably need to consider employing a porter or two. This will naturally impact on your budget and the choice of treks open to you.

The following is a brief summary of treks that *may* be undertaken in India without the use of a tent, and where you can expect food to be cooked for you at night.

In **Ladakh**, parachute-tent accommodation (ex–Indian Air Force parachutes) is often as good as it gets during the peak season (July & Aug). This system includes the Markha Valley trek, Phugtal Gompa & Shingo La trek and Singge La & Lamayuru trek.

In **Himachal Pradesh,** the Chandrakani Pass & Malana trek can be done without tents or elaborate organization.

In **Uttaranchal,** the GMVN and the KMVN (state-owned organisations; see Useful Organisations, p55–6) have constructed lodges on a number of trails. These include the Har ki Dun & Ruinsara Lake trek, Dodi Tal & Yamunotri trek and Source of the Ganges trek. The Pindari Glacier trek and Milam Glacier & Nanda Devi trek can be done without a tent and food supplies.

In **Darjeeling**, the Singalila Ridge & Phalut trek can be undertaken from lodge to lodge – it is, after all, very nearly in Nepal.

In **Sikkim**, there are lodges on the Dzongri & Guicha La trek. However, this is not a do-it-yourself trek, as all trekking arrangements must be made through a recognised agent in Gangtok.

Responsible Trekking

In the past 20 years the impact of trekking on the environment and cultural traditions has become increasingly apparent. Campsites are displaying all the signs of overuse, trees are lopped for campfires and fuel for porters, while litter is scattered along many of the popular trails.

Trekkers are no longer received as honoured guests in remote villages and are often regarded with suspicion; theft is increasing, as is begging. Thoughtless groups select campsites close to the villagers' source of water, and arguments arise as villagers anxious to protect grazing area confront horsemen.

Such developments have led to much discussion about the need for, and content of, more legislation. The self-regulation that has so far been the norm for trekking companies and individuals needs to be examined and, at the very least, a user-pay concept introduced to combat some of the worst effects of trekking. In the meantime, the following guidelines may help to lessen our impact on both the local culture and the environment.

Other comments on cultural and environmental matters are included in the Conservation & Environment section (pp24–6) and in the 'Environmental Watch' boxed texts in the trekking chapters.

Environment

If trekking is to become sustainable, trekkers must accept responsibility for their actions rather than placing the responsibility on the local agent or crew. It is necessary to set an example. When you arrive at a campsite begin by clearing up any garbage and filling in toilet pits and tent trenches that have been left by previous groups. This will impress the crew and illustrate a genuine concern for their environment. Also follow these guidelines:

Fires Don't encourage campfires. Bring ample supplies of kerosene, and supply a stove and kerosene for your crew.

Water Don't use detergents or toothpaste near watercourses. Wash all clothes and equipment in biodegradable soap in a bucket well away from streams or rivers.

Human Waste Disposal Contamination of water sources by human faeces can lead to the transmission of hepatitis, typhoid and intestinal parasites such as *Giardia*. Dig toilet trenches or pitch the toilet tent well away from watercourses. Burn all toilet paper and ensure all faeces are buried while trekking during the day.

Rubbish Clean up the camp on your arrival. Ensure that all nonbiodegradable items are carried out. Take reusable containers. Ensure that you bring a few additional kitbags so that bottles, tin cans and plastic items can be easily packed after use. Provide an incentive (a tip in most cases) to ensure the crew carry the kitbags back to the trailhead.

Food Bring a minimum of nonbiodegradable food. If you are employing a cook, brief him beforehand. What you don't carry in terms of tins of food you don't have to carry out as empty cans! Also ensure that you buy all major food supplies before undertaking the trek, in particular staples such as rice and flour, so as not to put pressure on the economy of local villages along the trail.

on taking a work companion with them, and this will obviously increase the cost. Consider asking other trekkers to join your party and share some of the expenses.

A cook is a valuable asset who will save you the expense of buying pots and pans, and can recommend the most suitable food. A cook can also bargain hard for you in the market, saving large amounts of time. In return, he will expect some clothing allowance, normally local walking boots, plus a decent tip at the end of the trek.

Responsible Trekking

Erosion The steepness of the Himalayan hillsides makes them particularly vulnerable to erosion. Do not destroy saplings or undergrowth. Stick to existing tracks and avoid shortcuts. Do not dig unnecessary trenches around tents.

Conservation Do not disturb or attempt to feed wildlife. Do not buy items made from endangered species, pick wildflowers or gather medicinal plants.

Cultural Considerations

The tradition of hospitality has been an integral part of the way of life of most Himalayan peoples. There were few villages where you would not be greeted on arrival, and offered tea and a place to unpack your sleeping bag for the night. Beyond the villages, the shepherds would offer similar hospitality when you reached their encampment. If at least some elements of this tradition are to be retained, it is imperative that trekkers consider their role and acknowledge their responsibilities while in the mountain regions.

To enhance your time on the trail, observe the following social and cultural considerations:

Dress Codes Wear appropriate clothing while in a village or encampment. Neither women nor men should wear high-cut shorts, although long, baggy shorts are sometimes OK for men. Women should wear trekking trousers or tracksuit pants and loose-fitting tops. When entering a home, gompa, *mandir* (Hindu temple) or *masjid* (mosque), always remove your shoes unless specifically told otherwise.

Bargaining Always be fair in bargaining situations and always keep your word. If you have promised to pay a porter for six stages that you discover later you could complete in two, so be it. The porters must be paid the agreed amount. The same applies to staff and horsemen.

Photography Never take photographs until you have secured permission. Never offer money for photographs unless there is a particular sign in a monastery requesting a donation.

Theft Don't encourage theft by leaving high-value items – including boots – around the campsite.

Washing Nudity is completely unacceptable; wear a swimsuit when bathing, even in a remote locality.

Porters & Horsemen Ensure all staff are properly clothed and equipped before commencing your trek; see the 'International Porter Protection Group' boxed text, p50.

Etiquette Never throw food into a fire whether at a campsite or in a home. It is also expedient not to touch food or cooking utensils that local people will use, particularly when trekking through Hindu regions. Also, you should use your right hand for all social interactions, whether passing money or food or any other item. Do not touch local people on the head and similarly never direct the soles of your feet at a person or religious shrine. Overt public displays of affection should also be avoided.

Gifts Avoid handing out pens, balloons and sweets to children in the villages. Do not buy local household items or religious artefacts from villagers.

Your choice of guide is vital. You are dependent on his experience and reliability, which can either make or break your trek. Before hiring a guide it is essential to check his experience and familiarity with the staff in the trek region. Once the rate has been fixed, the guide is your representative, and should be reminded of this when negotiating with the cook, the horsemen or the various other suppliers.

Remember, as the contractor of your trek, you will also be held in the position of employer should something go wrong. You should arrange insurance, clothing and equipment for all your party, have additional funds with you to deal with an emergency, and carry a comprehensive medical kit.

Local Agents

A list of agents in each region is included in the trekking chapters; contact them before or on arrival in India. Get quotes from two or three companies. You will need to ascertain their degree of expertise and competence: it is suggested that the guide has at least completed a basic mountaineering course from a recognised authority; has completed a comprehensive first-aid course; and has covered the trek you anticipate completing.

You must also, of course, carefully check what is included, particularly with regard to equipment, as there are few places to hire quality gear once you are in India.

Adventure Travel Companies

Most recognised adventure travel companies operate programs in the Indian Himalaya. The Government of India Tourist Office (GITO) in your city will have a list of recommended agents. See Organised Treks for our recommendations.

Points to bear in mind when considering these companies include their experience in handling trips to India; the leaders they employ; the food, equipment, medical kits and information they provide; insurance; and the specialist interests they cater for. Also, do they organise the air/land travel required and is the fare included in the package?

Compare the trip notes and, if possible, attend a film evening. Ultimately, any travel company is only as good as its representative in India, and this should be considered before making any commitment.

Other Considerations

Whatever option you choose, be sure to share the magic of the Himalaya with the local people. A local crew can enhance your experience in a way that is sometimes not appreciated by people wary of anything that hints of the Raj. Working with trekking parties is a valuable source of employment for local cooks, guides and horsemen, and their involvement and sense of humour can remain with you for a long time. Experiences in the Himalaya are shared experiences, and there is nothing finer than having these enhanced by a great crew.

ORGANISED TREKS
Organised Treks within India

An initial point of reference is the **Adventure Tour Operators Association of India** (**W** *www.indianadventure.com*). It focuses on the professional development of adventure sports, including trekking. The following members are based in Delhi (☎ 011); other recommended members are listed in the trekking chapters.

Greater Himalayan Outdoors *(☎ 6083358; fax 6083357;* **e** *gho@vsnl.com; Ground Floor, MG Bhavan, 7, Local Shopping Centre, Madangir, New Delhi 110062)*

Ibex Expeditions *(☎ 6912641; fax 6846403;* **e** *ibex@nde.vsnl.net.in; G-66, East of Kailash, New Delhi 110065)*

Ruck Sack Tours *(☎ 6183696; fax 6194377;* **e** *rani@nde.vsnl.net.in; B412 Som Dutt Chamber 1, 5 Bhikaji Cama Place, New Delhi 110066)*

Sea & Sky Travel *(☎ 6461027; fax 6426248; 90/60, Maiviya Nagar, New Delhi 110017)*

Shikhar Travels *(☎ 3312444; fax 3323660;* **e** *stilpl@giasdl01.vsnl.net.in; 209 Competent House, F14 Middle Circle, Connaught Place, New Delhi 110001)*

Snow Leopard Adventures *(☎ 5524389; fax 6895905;* **e** *ajeet.bajaj@gems.vsnl.net.in; 710 Kirti Shikher, District centre, Janakpuri, New Delhi 110058)*

Trek Operators Abroad

The following adventure travel companies have operated established Himalayan programmes for at least five years, while some have been in the business well over 20 years. Many of them will arrange your flight as a part of the package.

Australia & New Zealand

Peregrine Adventures *(☎ 03-9662 2700; fax 9662 2422;* **W** *www.peregrine.net.au; 258 Lonsdale St, Melbourne, Vic 3000)* also has offices in Sydney, Brisbane, Perth and Adelaide.

World Expeditions (☎ 02-9279 0188; fax 9279 0566; W www.worldexpeditions.com.au; Level 5, 71 York St, Sydney, NSW 2000) also has offices in Melbourne, Brisbane, Adelaide and Perth, and in New Zealand (below).

World Expeditions (☎ 09-522 9161; fax 522 9162; 21 Remuera Rd, Newmarket, Auckland)

Canada

Worldwide Adventures Inc (☎ 416-633 5666; fax 416-633 8667; W www.worldwidequest.com; 1170 Sheppard Ave West, Suite 45, Toronto, Ontario M3K 2A3)

France

To investigate or purchase a trek on-line, visit **Nouvelles Frontieres** at W www.nouvelles-frontieres.fr and **Allibert** at W www.allibert-voyages.com. Other companies offering treks to the Indian Himalaya include:

Club Aventure (☎ 08 25 30 60 32; W www.clubaventure.fr; 18 rue Séguier, 75006 Paris)
Terres D'Aventure (☎ 01 53 73 77 73; W www.terdav.com; 6 rue Saint Victor, 75005 Paris)

UK

Chandertal Tours & Himalayan Folkways (☎ 01323-422213; fax 417748; W www.chandertal-tours.freeserve.co.uk; 20 the Fridays, East Dean, Near Eastbourne, Sussex BN20 ODH)
Exodus (☎ 020-8675 5550; fax 8673 0779; W www.exodus.co.uk; 9 Weir Rd, London, SW12 OLT)
Explore Worldwide (☎ 01252-760000; fax 760001; W www.exploreworldwide.com; 1 Frederick St, Aldershot, Hants GU11 1LQ)
High Places (☎ 0114-275 7500; fax 275 3870; W www.highplaces.co.uk; Globe Centre, Penistone Rd, Sheffield S6 3AE)
Himalayan Kingdoms (☎ 01453-844400; fax 844422; W www.himalayankingdoms.com; Old Crown House, 18 Market St, Wotton-Under-Edge, Gloustershire GL12 7AE)
KE Adventure Travel (☎ 017687-73966; fax 74693; W www.keadventure.com; 32 Lake Rd, Keswick, Cumbria CA12 5DQ)
Martin Moran Mountaineering (☎/fax 01520-722361; W www.moran-mountain.co.uk; Park Cottage, Achintee, Strathcarron, Ross-shire IV54 8YX)
World Expeditions (☎ 020-8870 2600; fax 8870 2615; W www.worldexpeditions.co.uk; 3 Northfields Prospect, Putney Bridge Rd, London SW18 IPE)

USA

Adventure Center (☎ 800-228 8747; fax 510-654 4200; W www.adventure-centre.com; 1311 63rd St, Suite 200, Emeryville, CA 94608)
Geographic Expeditions/Inner Asia Expeditions (☎ 800-777 8183; fax 415-346 5535; W www.geoex.com; 2627 Lombard St, San Francisco, CA 94123)
Himalayan High Treks (☎ 800-455 8735; fax 415-861 2391; W www.himalayanhightreks.com; 241 Dolores St, San Francisco, CA 94103)
Journeys (☎ 800-255 8735; fax 734-665 2945; W www.journeys-intl.com; 107 April Dr, Suite 3, Ann Arbor, MI 48103-1903)
Mountain Travel Sobek (☎ 888-687 6235; fax 510-525 7710; W www.mtsobek.com; 6420 Fairmount Ave, El Cerrito, CA 94530-3606)
World Expeditions (☎ 888-464 8735; fax 415-989 2112; W www.weadventures.com; 6th Floor, 580 Market St, San Francisco, CA 94104)

GUIDES & PORTERS

A Himalayan trek is not just a question of getting from point A to point B. It provides an opportunity to appreciate the village culture; the flora and fauna; and many of the other things that bring trekkers to India. A local guide can enhance your experience. The task of showing the way is but one of many roles. Clearly, guiding is an important role, so it is necessary to ensure that your guide is fully conversant with the route before hiring him.

On shorter valley treks it may be easy to follow a well-established trail; however, a knowledgeable local guide can show you some of the hidden valleys and delights. On longer treks a guide is highly recommended; for treks with high passes a competent guide is essential.

If you decide to use a guide, it is his job to hire the porters and/or horsemen and to ensure the trek is smooth and safe. A guide can be invaluable in the case of inclement weather or an accident, when outside help may be needed, as well as helping you chat with local villagers.

Guides

The cost of hiring a local guide varies considerably. There are many self-styled guides who are worse than useless. In such cases you are better off just hiring a porter who speaks

International Porter Protection Group

The IPPG was founded in the late 1990s to provide support for the porters hired to work with trekking groups. The movement aimed to improve working conditions for porters and reduce the number of deaths and injuries due to inadequate clothing and equipment.

The group initially focused on Nepal, with the aim of increasing awareness of the plight of the porter and the responsibilities of trekking agencies and individuals.

IPPG hopes the following guidelines will be adopted by trekking agencies in India; they suggest that:

- adequate clothing be available for protection in bad weather and at altitude. This should include footwear, hat, gloves, windproof jacket and trousers, sunglasses, and access to a blanket and sleeping pad when above the snowline;

- group leaders and trekkers provide the same standard of medical care for porters, as they would expect for themselves;

- porters not be paid off because of illness without the leader or trekkers being informed;

- sick porters never be sent down alone, but with someone who speaks their language and understands the problem; and

- sufficient funds be provided to sick porters to cover land rescue and treatment.

If your trekking arrangements are being handled by an agent, insist they follow these guidelines. If you are making your own arrangements, it is imperative that you also follow the guidelines and accept responsibility for the welfare of your porters.

For further information, contact **IPPG** (*International Porter Protection Group;* e *Info@ippg.net;* PO Box 53, Repton, NSW 2454, Australia).

English. On the other hand, a professional guide recommended by a reputable organisation is worth his weight in gold. Expect to pay around Rs 400 per day for a local guide, while more professional guides will expect up to Rs 1000 plus an equipment allowance.

Porters & Horsemen

The going rate for porters will vary tremendously, depending on the trek and the season. Generally the rates will rise during harvest season (mid-Aug–mid-Sept). Horsemen and porters will bargain for better rates at the margins of the season. For example, horsemen in Manali are not keen to trek over the Shingo La to the Zanskar after mid-September, for fear they will be stranded for the winter. They may charge at least double their normal daily rate of Rs 200 per packhorse.

Where to Hire Guides & Porters

Porters or horsemen are generally hired from the roadhead or a major town before you trek. They can be organised by a local agency or you can do it yourself. A list of agencies is in the introduction to each trek.

Wages & Tipping

Expect to pay around Rs 200 per day for a porter to carry between 20kg and 30kg. However, much will depend on your negotiation skills. You may, for instance, think you have a good deal until you discover that payment is required for relocation at the end of the trek. Ensure that you spell things out or your budget will blow out. An estimate of porter or horsemen rates is in the introduction to each trek.

After a trek, it is standard procedure to tip the porters and staff. The amount will vary, but 10% to 15% of the trek wages is normal. Of course, if the trek was unduly difficult or if the porters performed extra tasks (eg, helping the cook), the tip should be more generous. In order to ensure the tips are distributed to the right people, try to tip each porter individually rather than giving the total sum to the contractor or head porter to distribute.

Items of clothing and equipment, including boots and sandshoes, are also appreciated.

Clothing & Equipment

Most porters and horsemen will expect a clothing and equipment allowance before undertaking a trek. This may include buying local rubber boots, woollen gloves and snow goggles in the market. It is your responsibility to ensure that both horsemen and porters are properly equipped. This will include the provision of a mess tent and a cooking stove plus an adequate supply of kerosene. When issuing items of equipment it is important to clarify whether they are to be returned at the end of the trek. Hiring porters through a local agency should minimise related disputes.

Porter Insurance

Most reputable trekking companies in India insure all staff, including casual staff. This is a legal requirement in India; if you hire porters directly you are technically acting as the employer and must assume the responsibility. However, you can rarely buy insurance at the same time as you are hiring, particularly in remote regions. When all is said and done, it is easier to pay a higher price through a local agency and let it deal with the problem.

WOMEN TREKKERS

On the culture of Uttar Pradesh (UP), now a part of Uttaranchal:

> The paradox of worshipping woman as a goddess and yet treating her daily as a beast of burden is central to the religious order of the UP hills. Until this neurotic dichotomy is squarely faced, the petulant spite of males will continue to breed disharmony.
>
> **Bill Aitken,** *The Nanda Devi Affair,* 1994

Attitudes to Women

While Mahatma Gandhi championed opposition to the inequalities perpetuated by the caste system, the role of women, particularly in village communities, is still subject to many medieval attitudes. In many Hindu villages in Himachal and Uttaranchal, the traditional attitudes are still prevalent. These attitudes are also found in the Islamic regions of Kashmir. By contrast, women in the Buddhist regions of Ladakh, Zanskar and Spiti enjoy a more equal status, and women trekkers are often attracted to these regions.

In simple terms, the traditional attitudes in some remote villages are that there could be something wrong with females trekking without male company. Here, your guide – who normally comes from a more educated area – can assist by explaining why you have decided to trek without male company. This can go a long way to assist women trekkers who want to spend time in the villages, visit the local school and be invited into the houses.

Trekking crews (there are rarely, if ever, women porters, horse handlers or guides) treat women with more respect, although they will always defer to any males for instructions on where to camp, etc. It is an attitude to be recognised but will change as more women trek in India – it can be overcome to some extent with good humour and patience. Women trek leaders are likely to be treated with appropriate respect.

Safety Precautions

Fortunately, gender prejudice in the mountains does not translate into acts of violence, and the mountain trails are still safe in this respect. Indeed, the attitude of males is unlikely to be anywhere near as harassing as in large cities such as Delhi or Mumbai.

It is, however, not advisable to trek on your own (a consideration for males and females). Expressions of friendliness can sometimes be misinterpreted, and misunderstandings do sometimes occur. The mention of a fictitious husband or boyfriend can deter some unwanted advances.

What to Wear

Common sense will guide you in most situations. For example, it is not advisable to wear tight jeans, high-cut shorts or tight T-shirts. When trekking, a pair of culottes or a long skirt is acceptable, although trekking pants or tracksuit bottoms should always be worn when entering some of the more remote villages. When entering a temple or mosque, it is advisable to cover both legs and arms and wear a headscarf. In short, the more you cover up, the greater the likelihood of being accepted.

When bathing, go well away from a village or encampment; washing in a river with a bathing costume is generally not acceptable. For calls of nature along the trail, an umbrella to use as a screen is an asset.

TREKKING WITH CHILDREN

Trekking with children is an ideal family holiday. Over the seasons, the author has arranged many treks for families and received much positive feedback.

A trek can be an eye-opener for children, especially when they compare the living standards of village children with their own. After initial adjustment, children quickly break down cultural barriers. Children tend not to feel the same inhibitions as adults when it comes to joining in games and being invited into local houses. It is difficult to specify a minimum age; some argue that seven is the youngest age at which the child will gain a worthwhile experience; others feel that only much older children should go on treks.

If planning a trek, try to get other families to come with you. It is also necessary that the children understand where they are going, and why they are going, well before departure. Find ways of keeping your children fully occupied; for example, devise checklists for identifying wildflowers and birds.

On the trek, don't include too many long stages. Children will tire easily and do not have the mental fortitude of adults in times of inclement weather or undue delays. Here, an obliging porter or horseman may have to carry the child for at least some of the day. This can usually be arranged. For medical advice, refer to the Health & Safety chapter and Lonely Planet's *Travel with Children*.

DANGERS & ANNOYANCES

The chances of encountering an avalanche or falling into a crevasse while trekking are minimal. Wild animals also pose minimal danger. However, the Safety on the Trek section (pp82–4) offers advice on these unlikely dangers.

A very important reminder is to avoid charcoal-fuelled fires in poorly ventilated hotel rooms; carbon monoxide poisoning has caused some deaths in the region.

Violence

While attacks on trekkers have been rare for many seasons, there have been some disturbing trends, particularly in the Kullu Valley in Himachal Pradesh, where two incidents in 2000 resulted in the deaths of foreign trekkers (see the 'Warning' boxed text, p160).

Although the state government has taken the incidents very seriously, trekking out of the Kullu Valley is by no means as safe as it was. It is recommended that trekkers employ a local agent, as there have been no recorded incidents in the area of attacks against trekking parties with local crew members.

Most governments advise tourists not to visit Kashmir (see the 'Warning' boxed text, p143). This warning includes Jammu but does not refer to Ladakh, which is generally safe for travel.

Finally, we advise staying out of Delhi and Kolkata on Independence Day (15 Aug). Nationalistic events may attract terrorist acts.

Avoid (unlikely) minor confrontations by observing traditional customs; see Society & Conduct (pp38–40).

Theft

Theft is not commonplace, although it is best not to leave a display of valuables unattended at your campsite; the temptation may prove too much for the village children. Boots, together with your washing, should always be brought inside the tent at night. It is best to lock your kitbag, although the chances of gear disappearing once it is packed up for the day are minimal.

A money belt worn around your waist beneath your clothes is one of the safest ways to carry important documents, including your passport and money. It's worthwhile placing these inside a plastic bag for rain protection.

It is advisable to keep an eye on all your gear at bus and railway stations, and to chain gear to a seat when travelling by train. Do not leave money in your hotel room; always keep your travellers cheques separate from your cheque receipts; and always keep an emergency supply of US$50 or US$100 separate from your money belt.

MAPS & NAVIGATION
Small-Scale Maps
Overall maps of the Himalaya include the Bartholomew map of the Indian subcontinent (1:400,000) and the Nelles Verlag on the Himalaya (1:1,500,000). Lonely Planet's *India & Bangladesh Road Atlas* covers many of the Himalayan regions.

Large-Scale Maps
The US Military U502 series of topographical maps covers many of the main trekking regions in India. These can be used in conjunction with the comprehensive Leomann series (1987); and the Air India trekking maps, which are upgraded versions of the state government trekking maps compiled in the early 1980s. In the introduction for each trek, the relevant map is indicated, together with other useful references.

US Military U502 Series 1:250,000
Based on the Survey of India these were revised by the US military and published in 1948. The original series were in colour and have recently been reprinted.

Leomann Map Series 1:200,000 These ridge and river maps cover most regions of the Indian Himalaya with the trekking routes depicted in three colours. It's best to use these in conjunction with the U502 Series.

Air India Map Series 1:250,000 These were produced some years ago with ridge and river sections useful to trekkers in the Indian Himalaya. The series forms the basis of other maps, including the trekking maps distributed by the Himachal Pradesh government. The sections provide a good introduction and should also be used in conjunction with the U502 series.

Buying Maps
Do not assume that you can purchase good trekking maps in India. If you are buying any of the above maps, contact a specialist map shop. Plan ahead, as they may need a month or longer to order it. Specialist map shops include:

Edward Stanford Ltd (☎ 020-7836 1321; fax 7836 0189; W www.stanfords.co.uk; 12–14 Long Acre, Covent Garden, London WC2E 9LP, UK)

Map Land (☎ 03-9670 4383; fax 9670 7779; W www.mapland.com.au; 372 Little Bourke St, Melbourne, Vic 3000, Australia)

Maplink (☎ 805-692-6777; fax 692-6787; W www.maplink.com; 30 S. La Patera Lane, Unit 5, Santa Barbara, CA 93117, USA)

Melbourne Map Centre (☎ 03 9569 5472; fax 9569 8000; W www.melbmap.com.au; 740 Waverley Rd, Chadstone, Vic 3148, Australia)

Place Names & Terminology
There are many variations between the place names in this book and names used in other maps or guides. These differences occur because there is often no universally accepted transliteration of Ladakhi or Hindi names into English. For example, we spell the world's third-highest mountain, Kangchenjunga, in accordance with the local spelling in India, even though *Trekking in the Nepal Himalaya* spells it 'Kanchenjunga' without the 'g' – the local spelling in the Nepal Himalaya!

A number of local terms are used throughout this book. For example, when trekking in Ladakh, we frequently pass Buddhist *mani* walls (walls carved with Buddhist prayers) and *chortens* (reliquaries or shrines to the memory of a Buddhist saint). In Himachal, the wandering shepherds who come from the region of Kangra are known as Gaddis. Gujar shepherds, on the other hand, frequent the less remote valleys in Kashmir, Himachal and Uttaranchal. When staying overnight on a trek, we sometimes stay in PWD huts, Forest Rest Houses or Dak bungalows where the *chowkidar* (caretaker) may be able to arrange *dhal bhat* (lentils and rice) to eat. In Ladakh, we may finish the evening off with a glass of *rakshi* (rice wine) – in the day, a bucket of *chang* (barley beer) is a less intoxicating refreshment. On some stages in Himachal, we cross a *nullah* (riverbed), while in Ladakh we cross a *la* (pass) in order to traverse a mountain range. See the glossary for a comprehensive list of terms.

Altitude Measurements

Carrying an altimeter has the disadvantage that trekkers cannot unduly exaggerate their performance after returning home. However, there is always some leeway. I have experienced Leh rise and fall nearly 100m in one day, simply by recording altimeter readings on a stormy day. Barometric pressures change considerably in mountain regions; the spot heights of mountain summits in this book are based on the Ground Survey of India and are accurate, while altitudes given in trek stages are approximate.

PERMITS & FEES
Trekking Permits

Trekking permits are generally not required in India, although some areas do require separate permission for trekking. To date, this applies to the Milam Glacier area in Uttaranchal and treks from Kinnaur to Spiti (including the Kinnaur Kailash trek), where Inner Line permits are necessary. See the following for details.

Travel Permits & Restricted Areas

There are no special travel permits required for visiting the Indian Himalaya. However, most of the Himalayan border regions close to Pakistan and China are politically sensitive, and there are Inner Line areas that place restrictions on the movements of foreigners. While restrictions have been eased in the past decade, you are still required to obtain an Inner Line permit if visiting some of the previously restricted areas, particularly in Ladakh, Himachal Pradesh and Uttaranchal. Details of current regulations are included in the trekking chapters.

The Himalayan Adventure Trust

Since 1990, the Himalayan Trust has sought to gain cooperation from Pakistan, Nepal and India to draw attention to the environmental problems affecting the Himalaya. In doing so it has drawn on worldwide support to help protect the Himalayan environment. The aims and objectives set out by the Trust include:

Support Groups
The mobilisation of support from mountaineers, trekkers, alpine clubs, adventure tour operators and the Himalayan region governments for protecting the environment, its flora, fauna and natural resources, as well as the customs and interests of the local people.

Codes of Conduct
To evolve a code of conduct and ethics to be followed by all visitors to the Himalayan region, as part of a continuing effort to maintain and sustain the well-being of the Himalayan environment.

Promoting Awareness
To hold international conferences, seminars and Himalayan tourist meets on problems relating to the Himalayan environment, and focus world attention on such matters.

Information
To exchange information, and co-operate, with other local, national and international agencies engaged in similar work.

Guidelines for Adventure Tourism
To evolve necessary guidelines – in consultation with the Himalayan countries – concerning adventure tourism, to avoid the overcrowding of trails and to achieve a fair spread of trekkers and mountaineers throughout the Himalaya.

Clean-up Programs
To encourage clean-up programs and evolve healthy environmental practices.

The area of Ladakh from 1mi (1.6km) north of the Leh-Srinagar road is generally regarded as a restricted zone for foreigners, although permission is now granted to visit the Nubra Valley, and the Pangong Lake district north of the Indus Valley. The same restrictions apply to the area 1mi east of the Leh-Manali road beyond the Baralacha La. However, the Indian government is now permitting organised groups of foreigners to visit the outlying Rupshu area closer to the disputed India-China border. These regulations are always changing so check with the local tourist office or trekking agent before setting off. It should also be noted that certain other areas, such as the Nanda Devi Sanctuary, remain closed for environmental reasons; although some exceptions have been made, the area is closed to trekkers.

In the East Himalaya, travel regulations have been eased in the past few years. A permit to enter Sikkim can be issued at the border between Bangla (West Bengal) and Sikkim at Rangpo, while trek permits can be issued in Gangtok. However, plans to ease the Inner Line restrictions in the north of the state are still on hold.

When travelling anywhere in India, it is advisable to carry your passport with you. This is your only bona fide means of identification, which you will need to show at checkpoints in Ladakh, Zanskar, Lahaul, Spiti and Kinnaur.

National Park Entry Permits

A fee is levied when entering most of the national parks in the Indian Himalaya. Fees range from Rs 20 on the Singalila Ridge National Park out of Darjeeling to Rs 100 for the first three days of a trek in the Govind National Park in Uttaranchal. Fees are considerably less for Indian trekkers. An additional fee (Rs 50 to Rs 500) is also payable for bringing still and movie cameras into the parks. Most permits are issued on entry to the national park. See the trekking chapters for details.

USEFUL ORGANISATIONS

In most of the main towns in the Indian Himalaya, state tourist offices provide informative advice. They also offer good bus and transport services, sightseeing tours and associated services for tourists. However, when it comes to trekking, they are usually not the best source of information.

Instead, you should contact the mountaineering institutes at Darjeeling or Uttarkashi. In Uttaranchal, the Garhwal Mandal Vikas Niwas (GMVN) offices in Rishikesh, Joshimath and Mussoorie; and the Kumaon Mandal Vikas Niwas (KMVN; both are state-owned organisations with trekking divisions) office at Naini Tal have staff with first-hand experience of the treks in their region. In Himachal Pradesh, enthusiastic and committed staff run the mountaineering institutes in Manali, Brahmaur and McLeod Ganj. See the relevant trekking chapter for contact details.

Conservation Organisations

The following groups promote conservation in the Indian Himalaya (many welcome donations and help from foreign visitors):

Himalayan Environment Trust (☎ 011-6215635; The Legend Inn, East of Kailash, New Delhi 110065) has been in operation since 1989. Its present focus is an ongoing environmental program in the Gangotri region in the Garhwal.

Himalayan Foundation (☎ 0542-313884; Sartoli village, PO Bgna, Nandprayag, Uttaranchal) is involved in large-scale reforestation in the Himalaya and other conservation projects in the Garhwal.

Himalayan Trust (☎ 0135-773081; 274/2 Vasant Vihar, Dehra Dun, Uttaranchal) promotes the development of isolated mountain communities while safeguarding their environmental heritage.

International Snow Leopard Trust (☎ 206-632 2421; 4649 Sunnyside Ave N, Suite 325, Seattle, WA 98103, USA) raises funds for use in developing countries, to set up parks for snow leopards, and to help finance and educate the Himalayan people regarding conservation.

Ladakh Ecological Development Group (LEDeG; ☎ 01982-3746) in Leh has been working for more than 20 years on all aspects of Ladakh's environment and cultural development.

Sikkim Development Foundation (☎ 03592-92276; Tashi Khar, Chungyeal Complex, MG Marg, Gangtok, Sikkim) formed in 1999. It aims to preserve the state's biodiversity and promote responsible tourism.

Wildlife Institute of India *(☎ 0135-620910; PO Box 18, Dehra Dun, Garhwal, Uttaranchal)* deals with conservation projects around India, including the Himalaya.

Wildlife Preservation Society of India *(7 Astley Hall, Dehra Dun, Garhwal, Uttaranchal)* formed in 1970 to promote conservation awareness.

Wildlife Protection Society of India *(☎ 011-213864; Thapur House, 124 Janpath, New Delhi)* was established to curtail illegal trafficking of wildlife, including the tiger and musk deer.

Wildlife Trust of India *(☎ 011-6326025; PO Box 3150, New Delhi 110003)* is in partnership with the International Fund for Animal Welfare. At present their Wild Aid program is promoting awareness on the plight of the chiru – the Tibetan antelope that provides the fine wool for the shahtoosh shawl. The Wildlife Trust is also involved in land regeneration and enforcing the protection of other wildlife species.

World Wide Fund for Nature *(WWF; ☎ 011-4627586; 172-B Lodi Rd Lodi Estate, New Delhi 110 003)* is the Indian headquarters of the international wildlife conservation pressure group.

DIGITAL RESOURCES

The World Wide Web provides a useful information resource for trekkers. There's no better place to start your Web research than at Lonely Planet Ⓦ www.lonelyplanet.com. Here you will find succinct summaries that will assist your travels in India, postcards from other travellers and the Thorn Tree bulletin board, where you can ask questions before you go and dispense advice when you return. You can also find updates to our guides to India and the SubWWWay section, which links you to useful travel resources elsewhere on the Web.

Check out these websites for specific advice about trekking and travel in India:

Himalayan Club *(Ⓦ www.himalayanclub.com)* features club activities and members' reports on trekking and climbing in the Himalaya.

Indian Mountaineering Foundation *(Ⓦ www.indmount.org)* details trekking and mountaineering regulations in India, plus up-to-date conservation issues.

Jammu and Kashmir Government *(Ⓦ www.jammukashmir.nic.in/)* includes sections on Ladakh and current trekking regulations.

Welcome to Himachal Pradesh *(Ⓦ www.hptdc.com)* includes general information on travelling to the Indian states and a section on Himachal Pradesh's national parks and sanctuaries.

Welcome to India *(Ⓦ www.tourindia.com)* is the official Department of Tourism website, with links to areas throughout the country.

BOOKS

There is a vast array of reading available about the Indian Himalaya but it's too much to list here. The following is our choice of 'the best of the best'. See also the Books sections in the trekking chapters.

Lonely Planet

India by Sarina Singh et al is recognised as *the* guide to travel in India.

North India by Mark Honan et al is the perfect companion to this book.

Other Guides

For trekkers to any destination, *The Mountain Traveller's Handbook* by Paul Deegan is a useful resource.

Travel & Exploration

Foreign Devils on the Silk Road; Trespassers on the Roof of the World and *Setting the East Ablaze*, a trilogy by Peter Hopkirk, offer good background reading on the areas bordering the Himalaya.

The Great Game by Peter Hopkirk is a comprehensive and highly readable account of the development of British and Russian territorial ambitions throughout the Himalaya in the 19th century.

The History of India, Volumes 1 and 2, by Romila Thapar and Percival Spear offers a general historical introduction to India.

Mountains of the Gods by Ian Cameron is a detailed account of the history of Himalayan exploration.

The Northern Barrier of India by Frederick Drew (Light & Life Publications) contains interesting geological and geographical information on the then remote regions of Jammu and Kashmir.

Travels in the Himalayan Provinces of Hindustan & the Panjab by Moorcroft & Trebeck is indispensable background reading on travels in the western Himalaya in the 1820s.

Travels in Kashmir, Ladak & Iskardo by GT Vigne (Sagar Publications) documents the author's journeys in the 1830s.

Western Himalaya & Tibet by Thomas Thomson (Cosmo Publications) and *Ladakh: Physical, Statistical & Historical* by Alexander Cunningham (Sagar Publications) are both references from the Ground Commission.

When Men & Mountains Meet and *The Gilgit Game*, both by John Keay, are two indispensable books on the history of 19th-century exploration in the West Himalaya.

Trekking & Mountaineering

Abode of Snow by Kenneth Mason is the classic on Himalayan exploration and climbing.

Across the Top by Sorrel Wilby details trekking exploits in Ladakh, Himachal Pradesh and Uttaranchal, and one of the first recorded treks by westerners through the untouched valleys of Arunachal Pradesh.

Eric Shipton – The Six Mountain-Travel Books compiled by the Mountaineers includes *Nanda Devi* and records the exploration of the Nanda Devi Sanctuary.

Exploring the Hidden Himalaya by prominent Himalayan Club members Soli Mehta and Harish Kapadia (Indus Publications) delves into the history of climbing in the Indian Himalaya.

First Across the Roof of the World by Graeme Dingle and Peter Hillary is a trekking epic.

Frank Symthe – The Six Alpine/Himalayan Climbing Books, compiled by the Mountaineers – a collection of six of Symthe's best works.

High Himalaya, Unknown Valleys, also by Harish Kapadia (Indus Publishing), outlines the treks and expeditions of one of the Himalayan Club's most active members.

Himalayan Odyssey by Trevor Braham records a climbing career that included many ascents and exploration from Sikkim to Himachal Pradesh in the post-war years.

HW Tilman – The Seven Mountain-Travel Books, compiled by the Mountaineers, includes *The Ascent of Nanda Devi*, which records the first successful ascent of Nanda Devi in 1936, and *When Men & Mountains Meet.*

A Passage to the Himalaya was edited by Harish Kapadia (Indus Publications). It is a readable assortment of climbing and trekking articles published in the Himalayan Journals over the past 70 years.

Natural History

Flowers of the Himalaya by Polunin & Stainton is essential for anyone interested in the region's flora.

Indian Hill Birds by Salim Ali (Oxford University Press) is still the best bird book available.

Flowers of the Western Himalaya by Rupin Dang (Indus Publications) includes wildflower descriptions on several treks in the Garhwal.

The Stones of Silence by GB Schaller (Vikas Publishing) provides a comprehensive, illustrated guide to the wildlife of the region.

Vanishing Tracks by Darla Hillard recounts four years of research on the snow leopard in the Dolpo region of Nepal; however, the findings are applicable to the snow leopard's survival in Ladakh and Spiti.

Buying Books

Most books are published in different editions by different publishers in different countries. As a result, a book might be a hardcover rarity in one country while it's readily available in paperback in another. Fortunately, bookshops and libraries search by title or author, so your local bookshop or library is well placed to advise you on the availability of books. For maps, see Buying Maps (p53).

The many bookshops around Janpath and Connaught Circle in New Delhi provide India's largest stock of books on the Indian Himalaya. See the trekking chapters for recommended local bookshops.

JOURNALS

The Himalayan Journal is the annual publication of the **Himalayan Club** *(PO Box 1905, Bombay 400 001)*. Copies can be purchased in selected bookshops in India and Nepal or by contacting the organisation.

Indian Mountaineer is the annual publication of the Indian Mountaineering Foundation (IMF). Copies and information can be obtained from the **IMF** *(Benito Juarez Rd, New Delhi 110 021)*.

Himal magazine is published every two months by the **Himal Association** *(PO Box 42, Patan Dhoka, Lalitpur, Nepal)*. It has informative articles about the region.

WEATHER INFORMATION

Reliable weather reports are difficult to access in the mountains. The national newspapers provide daily reports.

ACCOMMODATION

While lodge-based trekking in the Indian Himalaya is not as common as it is in Nepal, there is a variety of accommodation styles on some of the treks.

Along the trail, you may come across Public Works Department (PWD) huts, Forest Rest Houses (FRH) and Dak bungalows, many of which were constructed in the 19th century. They are run by a local *chowkidar* (caretaker) who lives nearby and faithfully maintains a register of arrivals.

On some of the treks in Ladakh, you may find parachute-tent accommodation, while in the villages you may be offered a room in a large house. In Himachal, there are basic lodges on some of the treks; in Uttaranchal, Darjeeling and Sikkim, there are both private and government-run lodges on some of the more popular routes. Basic, stone shelter huts are the norm on many of the pilgrim trails, although temporary *dhabas* (food stalls) are established during the busy pilgrimage periods.

On the more remote stages of a trek, often there will be no consistent type of accommodation or any accommodation at all. This will, in most cases, require you to carry a tent. For details of accommodation on the trek, see the Planning section for each trek. See also the boxed text 'Lodge-Based Trekking in India', p45.

For more comprehensive details of hotels *off* the trek, refer to Lonely Planet's *India* or *North India* guides.

FOOD

A healthy diet makes for a healthy trek. By adopting the best of the local food and using a little imagination or a good local cook, delicious meals can be prepared that will enhance your trekking experience.

Local Food

Besides the fruit and vegetables available in the local markets, fresh meat, eggs, pulses or dhal, cheese, ghee, flour and rice are widely available across India. Butter and dried milk can be purchased in tins. Nuts, raisins, honey, peanut butter, jams, tea, coffee, sugar, biscuits and chocolate are also available.

The cost of most locally produced food is low, including rice, flour, fruit, vegetables and pulses. The meat, tinned goods, butter, cheese, fish and dried fruit are on a par with Western prices. However, for snacks on the trek, bring a stock of dried fruit; Indian dried fruit is both expensive and of a poorer quality. This can be mixed with nuts and chocolate. Other suggested items for snacks on the trail include packets of dried soup,

herbal teas and energy bars. Australian groups often bring Vegemite and British groups often bring Marmite to give extra taste to *puris*, *parathas* and *chapattis* (all local breads).

On the Trek

If you are making your own arrangements, don't forget that many of the luxuries may also be shared with the porters, horsemen and villagers on the way. Remember that the tea-house trekking style is nowhere near as developed as it is in Nepal – if you intend to stay in houses, don't expect the gastronomic delights that you find on some routes in the Annapurna or Everest regions. Indeed, if you are trekking in Ladakh, often the only local food available is *tsampa* (roasted ground barley), butter tea, plus a few vegetables and dried apricots. In each trekking chapter there is reference to the food available locally and at the trailhead. See also Stove & Fuel (p63) for further advice.

If your arrangements are being handled for you, try to specify any dietary requirements from the outset. If you have an allergy, ensure that your leader as well as the cook and his assistant are completely clear on your requirements. A token nod of the head is not good enough. Also encourage the cook not to take too much canned or bottled food on the trek, to minimise the risk of containers being discarded along the way. See the 'Responsible Trekking' boxed text (pp46–7) for suggestions.

It is important to have a balanced diet of carbohydrates, proteins and fats on the trek; it is equally important not to miss the delicacies of Indian cooking. Try delicious *puris* or *parathas* with honey for breakfast, instead of white bread and biscuits. A succulent mutton curry, cooked with local vegetables and dhal, is much more appetising and interesting than roast mutton and boiled vegetables. Sausages, beans and chips may be OK but a simple chicken or vegetable *pulao* (savoury rice) for lunch, with chutneys and local curd, tastes so much better. It is usually quite possible to obtain fruit and vegetables that will not perish on the trek, eg, cabbages, cauliflowers, potatoes, onions and carrots. Apples are a speciality in the Kullu Valley, as are apricots in Ladakh.

Eric Shipton, the British explorer who specialised in small, lightweight expeditions in the Himalaya, reduced his requirements to just oatmeal. Food was simply calculated by multiplying the number of days by the quantity of oatmeal needed per day. Apparently, he spent considerable time debating whether salt was a luxury that could be dispensed with. For us lesser mortals, it is easy to exist quite happily for three or four weeks at a time on a substantial diet of porridge, puris and honey in the morning; with daytime snacks of nuts, raisins and tea; and an evening meal of rice, dhal and vegetables. On such treks, there is little need for freeze-dried, tinned or packaged food.

DRINKS
Alcoholic Drinks
Alcohol is freely available in all the Himalayan states except Kashmir. Bottled beer, including brands such as Golden Eagle and Rosy Pelican, is quite satisfactory and costs Rs 70 per bottle. Indian whisky, rum and gin and imported vodka cost around Rs 300 per litre depending on the quality. Imported spirits and wine are not available except in the five-star hotels in Delhi, where a premium price is charged. Alternatively, purchase a duty-free bottle before you arrive in India. Don't forget a hip flask!

Although we're not advocating over-indulgence on the trek, staff and trekkers have been known to appreciate a hot rum toddy. When trekking in Ladakh, a glass of *chang*, a barley beer, can be refreshing. It is drunk by the families when they are harvesting the fields and has a very low alcohol content. More lethal is *tongba*, available in Sikkim. Prepared in a wooden pot and drunk through a special straw, it consists of fermented millet mixed with boiling water.

Nonalcoholic Drinks
India has a wide variety of canned and bottled drinks, including the locally produced Pepsi Cola and Coca Cola. Many drinks such as bottled mango juice and apple juice are also available, while small cartons of mango, apple or peach drinks are also becoming popular. There are literally hundreds of varieties of mineral water, mostly sold in plastic bottles. It is imperative that these, together with the other bottles and cans, are disposed of with care.

On the Trek
The adage 'don't drink the water' should be remembered at all times while trekking in India. Putting iodine in the water or boiling it at night for use the following day is the most satisfactory option. See Water (p71) for more details.

Even when you are trekking way above the villages there is a need to be wary of the crystal-clear stream. Always assume that shepherds and their animals are above your water source. The only exception is if you discover a spring line – a place where the water comes straight out of the ground high on an alpine pasture. Even there you must ensure that you fill your bottle straight from the source and not at a lower point where the supply may already be contaminated. It is also necessary to ensure that you do not inadvertently contaminate the local water supply. This is especially relevant in Ladakh, where water sources are often limited. Do not camp close to the streams and, if you want to have a wash, take the water in a bowl to an area well away from its source.

While tea is the mainstay on the trek, be prepared to be flexible. Indian *chai*, a combination of tea leaves, water, milk and sugar all boiled and mixed in together, is the way Indian crews and *dhaba wallahs* (proprietors of small food stalls) believe tea should be prepared. If you want sugar and milk separately, ask at the outset and your needs may be accommodated. In the Buddhist villages in Ladakh, Lahaul and Spiti, butter tea may be offered. It is prepared by mixing tea with rancid butter and salt in a wooden churn. Provided you think of it as soup rather than tea, it's fine, particularly when mixed with tsampa.

CLOTHING & EQUIPMENT

You don't need to spend a fortune on gear to enjoy trekking, but you do need to think carefully about what you pack to make sure you're comfortable and prepared for an emergency. Taking the right clothing and equipment on a trek can make the difference between an enjoyable day out or a cold and miserable one; in extreme situations, it can even mean the difference between life and death.

This section has two parts: the first outlines the things to consider when buying the basic gear and includes an equipment check list for a trekking trip; the second part details the clothing and equipment considerations specific to the Indian Himalaya and is vital reading for all trekkers.

GEARING UP TO TREK

Considerations differ widely from trek to trek. On a short trip of a few days, you are likely to trek in shorts, a cotton shirt, warm pullover, trainers and a sun hat, plus a good jacket. However, on an extended trek involving a number of passes, it is imperative that you carry comprehensive gear.

One of the most important considerations is the type of trek you choose (see pp44–8). If you are using packhorses, weight is not such an issue as when carrying all your gear in a backpack. The check list must therefore be interpreted with a degree of flexibility. Experienced trekkers will already have an idea of what they need, but for those with less experience the following hints may prove useful.

A trek is not a fashion parade and is an ideal time to give a last wearing to cotton T-shirts or an old pair of running shoes. Remember that most of the clothing that you would take on a weekend walk is suitable for trekking the Himalayan foothills. Don't be daunted by going to the Himalaya; the weather conditions are probably on par with the conditions of most mountain regions of the world. With this in mind, purchase gear that you will be able to use when you return home. We recommend spending as much as you can afford on good walking boots, a windproof and waterproof jacket and a synthetic pile jacket. These are likely to be the most expensive items but are a sound investment, as they should last for many seasons.

The list is not exhaustive; for more advice, visit outdoor stores, talk to fellow trekkers and read product reviews in outdoor magazines.

Clothing

It's better to wear several thin layers of clothing than one or two thicker items. Layering allows you to add or remove layers as you get colder or hotter, depending on your exertion or the weather. In cool weather, begin with lightweight thermal underwear (made of wool or a 'wicking' fabric such as Capilene or polypropylene, which moves the sweat away from your body). Your lightweight shorts/trousers and T-shirts/shirt will make up the middle layer. Outer layers can consist of jumpers (sweaters), fleece jackets or down-filled jackets. Finally, there is the 'shell' layer, or wind- and waterproof jacket and pants.

Look for clothes that offer warmth, but still breathe and wick moisture away from your skin. Avoid wearing heavy cotton or denim, as these fabrics dry slowly and are cold when wet. Choose clothes that prepare you for the worst the region might throw at you.

The body loses most of its heat through its extremities, particularly the head. A wool or fleece hat and gloves can prevent this warmth being lost.

Waterproof Jacket The ideal specifications are a breathable, waterproof fabric, a hood that is roomy enough to cover headwear but still affords peripheral vision, capacious map pocket, and a good-quality heavy-gauge zip protected by a storm flap. Make sure the sleeves are long enough to cover warm clothes underneath and that the overall length of the garment allows you to sit down on it.

Equipment Check List

This list is a general guide to the things you might take on a trek. Your list will vary depending on the kind of trekking you want to do, whether you're camping or planning on staying in lodges, and on the terrain, weather conditions and time of year.

Equipment
- ☐ **backpack** or **day-pack** with **waterproof liner**
- ☐ **first-aid kit***, **toiletries** and **insect repellent**
- ☐ **food** (high-energy)
- ☐ **headtorch** (flashlight), **spare batteries** and **globe**
- ☐ **holdall** (carryall or duffel bag)
- ☐ **map**, **compass** and **guidebook**
- ☐ **map case** or **clipseal plastic bags**
- ☐ **pocket knife** (with corkscrew)
- ☐ **sewing/repair kit**
- ☐ **small towel**
- ☐ **sunglasses** and **sunscreen**
- ☐ **survival bag** or **blanket**
- ☐ **water bottle** (at least 1L per person)
- ☐ **water purification tablets**, **iodine** or **filter**
- ☐ **waterproof stuff bags**
- ☐ **trekking poles** or **stick**
- ☐ **whistle** (for emergencies)

Clothing
- ☐ **bathers** (swimsuit) for discreet bathing
- ☐ **boots** and **spare laces**
- ☐ **gaiters**
- ☐ **gloves** and **balaclava**
- ☐ **shorts** and **trousers/long dress**
- ☐ **socks** and **underwear**

- ☐ **sunhat**
- ☐ **sweater** or **fleece jacket**
- ☐ **thermal underwear**
- ☐ **trainers** (running shoes) or **sandals**
- ☐ **T-shirt** and **long-sleeved shirt** with collar
- ☐ **umbrella** (for women: use as a screen for toilet stops)
- ☐ **waterproof jacket** or **cape**
- ☐ **waterproof overpants**

Camping
- ☐ **insulating mat**
- ☐ **matches**, **lighter** and **candle**
- ☐ **sleeping bag** and **bag liner/inner sheet**
- ☐ **spare cord**
- ☐ **tent** (check pegs, poles and guy ropes)
- ☐ **toilet paper** and **toilet trowel**

Cooking Items
- ☐ **cooking, eating & drinking utensils**
- ☐ **food & fuel containers**
- ☐ **portable stove & spare parts**
- ☐ **pots & pans**
- ☐ **washing soap**

Optional Items
- ☐ **altimeter**
- ☐ **binoculars**
- ☐ **camera**, **spare film** and **batteries**
- ☐ **GPS receiver**
- ☐ **groundsheet** (lightweight)
- ☐ **waterproof, slip-on backpack cover**
- ☐ **notebook** and **pencil**

*   See the First-Aid Check List, p69

Overpants Although restrictive, these are essential if you're trekking in wet and cold conditions. As the name suggests, they are worn over your trousers. Choose a model with slits for pocket access and long leg zips so that you can pull them on and off over your boots.

Cultural Considerations Neither men nor women should wear high-cut shorts. Women should wear trousers and loose tops or a full-length skirt or dress. Nudity is unacceptable, and a swimsuit must be worn when bathing, even in remote locations.

Footwear
Your footwear will be your friend or your enemy, so choose carefully. The first decision you will make is between boots and shoes. Trainers (running shoes) or walking shoes are fine over easy terrain but, for more difficult trails and across rocks and scree, most trekkers agree that the ankle support offered by boots is invaluable. Leather boots are heavier and less water-resistant than boots lined with a fabric such as Gore-Tex, but pierce a hole in Gore-Tex–lined fabric boots – a more likely occurrence than with a leather boot – and their water resistance will go from hero to zero in an instant.

Buy boots in warm conditions or go for a walk before trying them on, so that your feet can expand slightly, as they would on a trek.

Carry a pair of camp shoes or sandals. These will relieve your feet from the heavy boots and sandals, especially, are useful when fording waterways. Spare socks are equally valuable, especially in wet conditions.

Gaiters If you will be trekking through snow, thick undergrowth or mud consider using gaiters to protect your legs and help keep your socks dry. The best are made of strong fabric, with a robust zip protected by a flap, and with an easy-to-undo method of securing around the foot.

Socks The best trekking socks are made of a hard-wearing mix of wool (70–80%) and synthetic (30–20%), free of ridged seams in the wrong places (toes and heels). Socks with a high proportion of wool are more comfortable when worn for several successive days without washing.

Sun Protection
Heat is just as much a consideration as the cold. Be sure to take a sunhat (preferably wide brimmed, with a chin strap) and sunglasses or snow goggles, especially when trekking near snow, water or sand, where reflected light can cause unexpected sunburn, even on cloudy days.

Backpack
On fully supported treks, a day-pack will usually suffice. If you are carrying your gear you will need a backpack between 45L and 90L in capacity. Most trekkers in the Indian Himalaya will also need a holdall bag; see p66.

It can be tough deciding whether to go for a smaller or bigger pack. Your pack should be large enough that you don't need to strap bits and pieces to the outside where they can become damaged or lost. However, if you buy a bigger pack than you really need there's the temptation to fill it simply because the space is there. Its weight will increase and your enjoyment decreases. Assemble the gear you intend to take and try loading it into a pack to see if it's big enough.

A good backpack should:

- be made of strong fabric such as canvas, Cordura or similar heavy-duty woven synthetic, with high-quality stitching, straps and buckles, a light-weight internal or external frame and resilient and smoothly working zips.
- have an adjustable, well-padded harness that evenly distributes weight.
- be water-resistant, with a minimum of external nooks and crannies for water to seep into; stitched seams can be treated with a sealant such as beeswax.
- be equipped with a small number of internal and external pockets to provide easy access to frequently used items such as snacks and maps.

Even if the manufacturer claims your pack is waterproof, use heavy-duty liners (garden refuse bags are ideal; custom-made sacks are available).

Tent

A three-season tent will fulfil the requirements of most trekkers. The floor and the outer shell, or fly, should have taped or sealed seams and covered zips to stop water leaking inside. Weight will be a major issue if you're carry-ing your own tent so a roomy tent may not be an option; most trekkers find tents of around 2kg to 3kg (that will sleep two or three people) a com-fortable carrying weight. Popular shapes include dome and tunnel, which are better able to handle windy conditions than flat-sided tents. Lighter-weight designs may adopt other shapes or even do without a floor.

Check you know how to pitch your tent before taking it away, and always check your poles and pegs are packed.

Sleeping Bag & Mat

Choose between down and synthetic fillings, and mummy and rectangu-lar shapes according to your needs. Down is warmer than synthetic for the same weight and bulk but, unlike synthetic fillings, does not retain warmth when wet. Mummy bags are best for weight and warmth, but can be claustrophobic. Sleeping bags are rated by temperature. The given figure (-eg, 5°C) is the coldest temperature at which a person should feel comfortable in the bag. The ratings, however, are notoriously unreliable. Work out the coldest temperature at which you anticipate sleeping, assess whether you're a warm or a cold sleeper, and choose a bag accordingly.

An inner sheet will help to keep your sleeping bag clean, as well as adding an insulating layer. They are compulsory in some youth hostels. Silk inners are the lightest, but they're also available in cotton or polypropylene.

Self-inflating sleeping mats are popular and work like a thin air cushion between you and the ground; they also insulate from the cold and are es-sential if sleeping on snow. Foam mats are a low-cost alternative.

Stove & Fuel

Fuel stoves fall into three categories: pressurised liquid fuel (Shellite/white spirits, multifuel), unpressurised fuel (methylated spirits/ethyl alcohol) or gas (butane). In India, all fuel supplies except kerosene are very hard to locate, and you can't take stove fuel on airplanes. The type of stove you take will depend on the fuel available in your destination (see p66).

Walking Poles

Consider packing a pair of lightweight telescopic poles. They help you balance and ease the jarring on your knees during steep descents.

NAVIGATION EQUIPMENT

Maps & Compass

You should always carry a good map of the area you are trekking in, and know how to read it. Before setting off on your trek, ensure that you understand the contours and the map symbols, plus the main ridge and river systems in the area. Also familiarise yourself with the true north-south directions and the general direction in which you are heading. On the trail, try to identify major landforms such as mountain ranges and gorges, and locate them on your map. This will give you a better understanding of the region's geography.

Buy a compass and learn how to use it. The attraction of magnetic north varies in different parts of the world, so compasses need to be balanced accordingly. Compass manufacturers have divided the world into five zones. Make sure your compass is balanced for your destination. There are also 'universal' compasses that can be used anywhere in the world.

How to Use a Compass

This is a very basic introduction to using a compass and will only be of assistance if you are proficient in map reading. For simplicity, it doesn't take magnetic variation into account. Before using a compass we recommend you obtain further instruction.

1. Reading a Compass

Hold the compass flat in the palm of your hand. Rotate the **bezel** so the **red end** of the needle points to the **N** on the bezel. The bearing is read from the **dash** under the bezel.

2. Orientating the Map

To orientate the map so that it aligns with the ground, place the compass flat on the map. Rotate the map until the **needle** is parallel with the map's north/south grid lines and the **red end** is pointing to north on the map. You can now identify features around you by aligning them with labelled features on the map.

3. Taking a Bearing from the Map

Draw a line on the map between your starting point and your destination. Place the edge of the compass on this line with the **direction of travel arrow** pointing towards your destination. Rotate the **bezel** until the **meridian lines** are parallel with the north/south grid lines on the map and the **N** points to north on the map. Read the bearing from the **dash**.

4. Following a Bearing

Rotate the **bezel** so that the intended bearing is in line with the **dash**. Place the compass flat in the palm of your hand and rotate the **base plate** until the **red end** points to N on the bezel. The **direction of travel arrow** will now point in the direction you need to trek.

5. Determining Your Bearing

Rotate the **bezel** so the **red end** points to the **N**. Place the compass flat in the palm of your hand and rotate the **base plate** until the **direction of travel arrow** points in the direction in which you have been trekking. Read your bearing from the **dash**.

1	Base plate
2	Direction of travel arrow
3	Dash
4	Bezel
5	Meridian lines
6	Needle
7	Red end
8	N (north point)

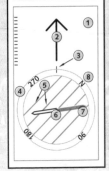

GPS

Originally developed by the US Department of Defence, the Global Positioning System (GPS) is a network of more than 20 earth-orbiting satellites that continually beam encoded signals back to earth. Small computer driven devices (GPS receivers) can decode these signals to give users an extremely accurate reading of their location – to within 30m anywhere on the planet, at any time of day, in almost any weather. The theoretical accuracy of the system increased at least tenfold in 2000, when a deliberate in-built error, intended to fudge the reading for all but US military users, was removed. The cheapest hand-held GPS receivers now cost less than US$100 (although they may have an in-built averaging system that minimises signal errors). Other important factors to consider are weight and battery life.

It should be understood that a GPS receiver is of little use to hikers unless used with an accurate topographical map – the GPS receiver simply gives your position, which you must locate on the local map. GPS receivers only work properly in the open. Directly below high cliffs, near large bodies of water or in dense tree-cover, for example, the signals from a crucial satellite may be blocked (or bounce off the rock or water) and give inaccurate readings. GPS receivers are more vulnerable to breakdowns (including dead batteries) than the humble magnetic compass – a low-tech device that has served navigators faithfully for centuries – so don't rely on them entirely.

Altimeter

Altimeters determine altitude by measuring air pressure. Because pressure is affected by temperature, altimeters are calibrated to take lower temperatures at higher altitudes into account. However, discrepancies can still occur, especially in unsettled weather, so it's wise to take a few precautions when using your altimeter.

1. Reset your altimeter regularly at known elevations such as spot heights and passes. Do not take spot heights from villages where there may be a large difference in elevation from one end of the settlement to another.

2. Use your altimeter in conjunction with other navigation techniques to fix your position. For instance, taking a back bearing to a known peak or river confluence, determining the general direction of the track and obtaining your elevation will usually give you a pretty good fix on your position.

Altimeters are also barometers and are useful for indicating changing weather conditions. If the altimeter shows increasing elevation while you are not climbing, it means the air pressure is dropping and a low-pressure weather system may be approaching.

Background photo: Trekkers establishing their campsite on a trek in Kashmir. GARRY WEARE

EQUIPMENT CONSIDERATIONS IN THE INDIAN HIMALAYA

The type of trekking you intend to do will influence the gear you require. See What Kind of Trek? (pp44–8) for advice. Note that water filters are not available in the Indian Himalaya.

Stove & Fuel

As other fuels aren't available in India, purchasing a kerosene stove once you arrive is the best option. Many of the kerosene stoves found in India's bazaars are both inexpensive (around US$10, depending on the size) and efficient. Remember to buy spare parts and an ample supply of stove pins.

Before commencing the trek, check you know how to prime the stove and dismantle it. Also test how much kerosene you will need by timing how long it takes to cook a meal and measuring the amount of fuel that is burnt.

Cooking Items

Pots and pans, enamel mugs, plates and cutlery (in fact all kitchen utensils) can be purchased in India. At most markets in the hill resorts, the price of pots and pans is determined by weight and should set you back $US5 to US$10. Cutlery and other cooking items, including metallic plates, bowls and mugs, can also be purchased in most locations.

If you have hired a cook, you can request he brings all the kitchen gear. It is also preferable to carry your own mug and cutlery during the day. This is particularly important if a trek member is sick, as it lets everyone in the group take responsibility for washing their own utensils.

Holdall

If using packhorses bring a strong duffel bag or holdall (carryall) rather than taking your expensive rucksack on the trail as it may end up in less than pristine condition after it has been tied on horses or yaks for 20 days. You should keep some items such as wet-weather clothes and a camera with you in a day-pack. The holdall should be large enough to contain all your personal gear. Strong garbage bags are ideal for lining the bag. If you have the budget, a waterproof sailing bag is highly recommended.

Compass

The majority of the treks described in this book follow well-defined trails. It is not essential to carry a compass, but it will always be an asset if you know how to use it; see the boxed text 'Navigation Equipment' (pp64–5) for advice.

Safety Equipment

Aside from the safety equipment trekkers should always carry (such as a first-aid kit and wet-weather gear), there are further items you need to bring if trekking on snow or ice. That is, if you are planning to trek across glaciers or in the early part of the season (May–early June, when there is still significant snow on the ground).

In these circumstances the basic minimum you should carry on all treks includes (these items are not readily available in India):

- **descenders**
- **harness**
- **ice axe**
- **karabiners**
- **rope** (at least 40m long) for crossing glaciers and rivers

For Independent Treks

Along with cooking items, independent trekkers will need to supply the following items for themselves and their crew:

- **fuel containers** (available in India)
- **kitbags** for food supplies, cooking gear and carrying out nonbiodegradable items (available in India)
- **mess tent** for your porters or horsemen (can be hired locally)
- **plastic jerry cans** for carrying water (available in India)
- **stoves & fuel** (bring a supply of spare parts)
- **tent** (can be hired locally)

Hiring Gear in India

In the past few seasons, a number of outlets in Indian Himalayan towns have acquired lightweight equipment for hire. A list of outlets is included in each of the trekking chapters. However, the gear may not be as good or reliable as you are used to. It may also be in short supply in trekking season. Independent trekkers are advised to bring their own tent, sleeping bag, insulated mat and backpack. For those undertaking an inclusive trek, professional agencies usually provide these items. However, it is advisable to check exactly what is provided before you leave for India.

The following hire rates were supplied by the Garhwal Mandal Vikas Nigam (GMVN; state-owned organisation) in Uttaranchal. If you anticipate hiring gear from the GMVN or any other trekking agency, contact them well in advance; supplies of gear in good condition are limited.

Equipment	security deposit	daily rate
backpack	1100 Rs	20 Rs
feather jacket	1014 Rs	25 Rs
feather mittens	248 Rs	10 Rs
four-person tent	2891 Rs	80 Rs
gaiters	182 Rs	8 Rs
kit bag	140 Rs	7 Rs
mattress	85 Rs	6 Rs
mess tent	8324 Rs	100 Rs
sleeping bag	1846 Rs	25 Rs
two-person tent	2366 Rs	65 Rs
windproof jacket	835 Rs	10 Rs

Health & Safety

Keeping healthy on your treks and travels depends on your predeparture preparations, your daily health care while travelling and how you handle any medical problem that develops. While the potential problems can seem quite frightening, in reality trekkers often complete a trek without opening their medical kit. The sections that follow aren't intended to alarm, but they are worth reading before you go.

PREDEPARTURE PLANNING

It is recommended that you have a physical and dental examination before undertaking your trek. Anyone with long-term symptoms (such as indigestion, chest pain, wheezing or coughing, back or joint problems, recurrent infections, or dental problems) should have them thoroughly investigated before leaving home. All problems are exacerbated by altitude and strenuous exercise, and seem more serious in proportion to your distance from medical help.

Health Insurance

A travel insurance policy is vital if you are going trekking. While most general travel insurances cover you against sickness while on a trek, not all cover you for emergency evacuation, which could run into many thousands of dollars if a helicopter is required. Remember that should evacuation be required some proof of insurance and of your ability to pay will save time, and perhaps even a life. Bear in mind that most embassies in Delhi or Kolkata (Calcutta) will authorise evacuation only after contacting your next of kin, which can take days.

Physical Preparation

Having made the decision to go to the Himalaya, you should then decide what standard or difficulty of trek to undertake (see p7). It's then up to you to get fit! Jogging, swimming, cycling (in fact, any regular physical exercise) is desirable. If possible, begin your programme at least three months before your

trek. Take some vigorous exercise for about one hour two or three times per week and gradually extend the duration of your outings as the departure date nears. If you plan to carry a full backpack on any walk, carry a loaded pack on some of your training jaunts. This is particularly important on the more strenuous treks, although even on shorter, easier treks the fitter you are, the more you will enjoy your trek.

Immunisations

To protect against various diseases in India, several immunisations are required. Plan ahead for your vaccinations; some require more than one injection, while some should not be given together. You should seek medical advice at least six weeks before travel.

Make sure your vaccinations are recorded and carry proof, especially for yellow fever, as this is needed to enter some countries.

Discuss your requirements with your doctor. Vaccinations you should consider for this trip include:

Diphtheria & Tetanus Vaccinations for these diseases are usually combined and are recommended for everyone. After an initial course of three injections (usually in childhood), boosters are necessary every 10 years.

Polio Everyone should keep up to date with this vaccination, which is normally given in childhood. A booster every 10 years maintains immunity.

Hepatitis A The vaccine for hepatitis A provides long-term immunity (possibly more than 10 years) after an initial injection and a booster at six to 12 months. Alternatively, an injection of gamma globulin can provide short-term protection against hepatitis A – two to six months, depending on the dose given. It is not a vaccine, but a readymade antibody collected from blood donations. It is reasonably effective and, unlike the vaccine, it is protective immediately.

First-Aid Check List

Following is a list of items you should consider including in your medical kit. Note that a wide range of medications is available for sale in India, most without need for a prescription. However, it is advisable to purchase certain items such as sunscreen and water purification tablets before arriving in India. For more details of dosage and administration of these drugs, follow the instructions of the manufacturer or the doctor who prescribed them. In cases of known drug allergy, use the appropriate alternatives.

Basic Supplies
☐ adhesive tape
☐ bandages and safety pins
☐ cotton wool
☐ elasticised support bandage – for knees, ankles, etc
☐ gauze swabs
☐ nonadhesive dressings
☐ small pair of scissors
☐ sterile alcohol wipes
☐ paper stitches
☐ sticking plasters (eg, Band-Aids, blister plasters)
☐ sutures
☐ syringes and needles – in case you need an injection in countries with medical hygiene problems (ask your doctor for a note explaining why you have them)
☐ thermometer (note that mercury thermometers are prohibited by airlines)
☐ tweezers

Medications
☐ AMS tablets – to assist in the prevention and treatment of mild mountain sickness
☐ antidiarrhoea and antinausea drugs
☐ antibiotics – consider including these if you're travelling well off the beaten track; see your doctor, as they must be prescribed, and carry the prescription with you.
☐ antifungal cream or powder – for fungal skin infections and thrush.
☐ antihistamines – for allergies, eg, hay fever; to ease the itch from insect bites or stings; and to prevent motion sickness.
☐ antiseptic (such as povidone-iodine) – for cuts and grazes.
☐ calamine lotion, sting-relief spray or aloe vera – to ease irritation from sunburn and insect bites or stings.
☐ cold and flu tablets, throat lozenges and nasal decongestant
☐ painkillers (eg, aspirin or paracetamol or acetaminophen in the USA)

Miscellaneous
☐ eye drops
☐ insect repellent
☐ multivitamins – consider for long trips, when your dietary vitamin intake may be inadequate.
☐ rehydration mixture – to prevent dehydration, eg, due to severe diarrhoea; particularly important when travelling with children
☐ sunscreen and lip balm
☐ water purification tablets or iodine

However, because it is a blood product, there are concerns about its long-term safety.

Hepatitis A vaccine is also available in a combined form with hepatitis B vaccine. Three injections over a six-month period are required, the first two providing substantial protection against hepatitis A.

Typhoid Vaccination against typhoid is recommended if it's more than three years since your last one. It is now available either as an injection or as capsules to be taken orally.

Cholera The current injectable vaccine is poorly protective with many side effects. It is not generally recommended for travellers.

Meningococcal Meningitis Vaccination is recommended. A single injection gives good protection against the major epidemic forms of the disease for three years. Protection may be less effective in children under two years.

Hepatitis B Risks in any country include receiving blood transfusions in areas where the blood may not be adequately screened; sexual contact; or needle sharing. Vaccination involves three injections and a booster.

Rabies Vaccination should be considered although it is highly unlikely that a trekker would come into contact with an infected animal. Pre-travel rabies vaccination involves having three injections over 21 to 28 days. If someone who has been vaccinated is bitten or scratched by an animal, they will require two booster injections of vaccine; those not vaccinated require more.

Japanese B Encephalitis Although the Indian Himalaya is not a high-risk area, you may consider a vaccination if making repeated visits to other regions of India. It involves three injections over 30 days.

Malaria Medication Antimalarial drugs do not prevent you from being infected but kill the malaria parasites during their development and significantly reduce the risk of becoming very ill or dying. Seek expert advice on medication, as there are many factors to consider, including the area to be visited, the risk of exposure to malaria-carrying mosquitoes, the side effects of medication, your medical history and whether you are a child or an adult or pregnant. Travellers can get advice from a doctor, travel health clinic or government health department. For more information, see Insect-Borne Diseases (p78).

First Aid

It's a good idea at any time to know the appropriate responses to a major accident or illness, and it's especially important if you are intending to trek for some time in a remote area. Consider learning basic first aid, including cardiopulmonary resuscitation (CPR), through a recognised course before you go. Ensure that you have a first-aid manual with your medical kit.

Although detailed first-aid instruction is outside the scope of this guidebook, some basic points are listed in Traumatic Injuries (pp78–9). Prevention of accidents and illness is equally important – see Safety on the Trek (pp82–4). You should also know how to summon help should a major accident or illness befall you or someone with you – see Rescue & Evacuation (p84).

Other Preparations

A suitable temperament is the most important requirement for anyone undertaking a trek in the Himalaya. If you have any doubts about whether you can cope with the demands of remote trekking for a period of weeks, do a shorter trek closer to home as a test.

If you have any known medical problems or are concerned about your health in any way, it is essential to have a full check-up before you go. It is also recommended that you have a dental check-up, while if you wear glasses take a spare pair along with your prescription.

If you need a particular medicine, take enough with you for the trip. Take part of the packaging showing the generic name, rather than the brand, as this will make getting replacements easier. It's also a good idea to have a legible prescription or letter from your doctor to prove that you legally use the medication to avoid any problems at customs.

Travel Health Guides

If you are planning to be away or trekking in remote areas for some time, you might consider taking a more detailed health guide. Lonely Planet's *Healthy Travel: Asia & India* is a handy pocket size and packed with useful information, including pre-trip planning, emergency first aid, immunisation and disease information, and what to do if you get sick on the road. Lonely Planet's *Travel with Children* also includes advice on travel health for younger children. For trekkers especially, *First Aid & Survival in Mountain & Remote Areas* by Dr Jim Duff and Dr Peter Gormley is comprehensive and easy to read.

Digital Resources

There are also a number of excellent travel health sites on the Internet. Go to the Lonely Planet website at Ⓦ www.lonelyplanet.com /weblinks/wlheal.htm for links to the World Health Organization (WHO) and the US Centers for Disease Control & Prevention, plus many other sites.

STAYING HEALTHY
Hygiene

Prevention is better than cure. Careful attention to water purification, food preparation and personal hygiene will prevent many of the diseases encountered while trekking.

The best way to prevent the diarrhoeas that can plague travellers and trekkers is to break the cycle of faecal-oral contamination by washing your hands regularly with soap and water throughout the day. This applies particularly while travelling through population centres. See also diarrhoea (p76) and malaria (p78).

Wearing clean socks, cotton underwear and a T-shirt will prevent skin infections. Chafing should be dealt with as soon as it is noticed. Toenails should be clipped short and one's feet pampered and massaged.

Water

Many diseases are carried in water in the form of bacteria, protozoa, viruses, worms and insect eggs. The number one rule is: be careful of the water, especially ice. If you don't know for certain that the water is safe, assume the worst. Reputable brands of bottled water or soft drinks are generally fine, although in some places bottles may be refilled with tap water. Only use water from containers with a serrated seal – not caps or corks. Take care with fruit juice, particularly if water may have been added. Milk should be treated with suspicion as it is often unpasteurised, though boiled milk is fine if it is kept hygienically. Tea or coffee should also be OK, since the water should have been boiled.

Water Purification The following points should be observed:

- **Boiling** Bringing water to the boil sterilises it, even at high altitudes. If the water has a lot of sediment or is heavily contaminated, boil for two minutes.
- **Iodine** Lugol's iodine solution or iodine tablets are a reliable method for sterilising water for drinking, cooking or washing. Add eight drops to 1L water and wait 30 minutes. Wait longer if the water is very cold or particularly polluted. Iodine tablets are best purchased in your own country. Do not add flavouring crystals or rehydration solution to your drinking water until sterilisation is complete.
- **Water Filters** Lightweight water filters are available. They are only effective if they combine physical and chemical filters. Water filters provide an alternative to those who do not like the taste of iodine. They are not available in India.

Food

Be particularly careful to ensure everyone washes their hands thoroughly with soap before preparing food. All water used for preparing food and washing dishes must be sterilised. Salads should be soaked for half an hour or more in water containing one teaspoon of Lugol's solution for every 4L. Vegetables and fruit should be washed with purified water or peeled where possible.

Stopping at wayside teashops is part of the trekking experience. Be selective: choose clean premises with healthy-looking owners and freshly cooked food. Consider carrying your own cup and eating utensils.

Nutrition A healthy diet makes for a healthy trek. If you do not pay attention to the food you are eating or if you simply lose your appetite, you can soon start to lose weight and place your health at risk.

Make sure your diet is well balanced. Cooked eggs, tofu, beans, lentils and nuts are all safe ways to get protein. Fruit you can peel (bananas, oranges or mandarins, for example) is usually safe, and a good source of vitamins. Note that melons can harbour bacteria in their flesh and are best avoided. Try to eat plenty of grains (including rice) and bread. Remember that although food is generally safer if it is cooked well, overcooked food loses much of its nutritional value. If your diet isn't well balanced or if your food intake is insufficient, you could consider taking vitamin and iron pills.

Common Ailments

Blisters This problem can be avoided. Make sure your walking boots or shoes are well worn in before your visit. At the very least, wear them on a few short walks before tackling longer outings. Your boots should fit comfortably with enough room to move your toes; boots that are too big or too small will cause blisters. Similarly for socks – be sure they fit properly, and wear socks specifically made for walkers; even then, check to make sure that there are no seams across the widest part of your foot. Wet and muddy socks can also cause blisters, so even on a day walk, pack a spare pair of socks. Keep your toenails clipped but not too short. If you do feel a blister coming on, treat it sooner rather then later. Apply a simple sticking plaster, or preferably one of the special blister plasters, which act as a second skin. Follow the maker's instructions for replacement.

Fatigue A simple statistic: more injuries occur towards the end of the day than earlier, when you're fresher. Although tiredness can simply be a nuisance on an easy walk, it can be life threatening on narrow exposed ridges or in bad weather. You should never set out on a walk that is beyond your capabilities on the day. If you feel below par, have a day off. To reduce the risk, don't push yourself too hard – take rests every hour or two and build in a good half-hour lunch break. Towards the end of the day, reduce the pace and increase your concentration. You should also eat properly throughout the day, to replace the energy used up. Nuts, dried fruit and chocolate are all good energy-giving snacks.

Knee Pain Many trekkers feel the judder on long steep descents. When dropping steeply, reduce the strain on the knee joint (you can't eliminate it) by taking shorter steps – leave your legs slightly bent and ensure that your heel hits the ground before the rest of your foot. Some walkers find that tubular bandages help, while others use high-tech, strap-on supports. Walking poles are very effective in taking some of the weight off the knees.

Cuts & Scratches Even small cuts and grazes should be washed well and treated with an antiseptic such as povidone-iodine. Dry wounds heal more quickly, so where possible avoid dressings, which can keep wounds wet. Infection in a wound is indicated by the skin margins becoming red, painful and swollen. More serious infection can cause swelling of the whole limb and of the lymph glands. The patient may develop a fever, and will need medical attention.

Chafing This is sometimes a problem in the groin, armpits, and on elbows or the backside. Wear well-rinsed soft cotton underwear;

wash, dry and powder the skin with talcum powder; or apply Vaseline.

MEDICAL PROBLEMS & TREATMENT

While most trekkers will not encounter any major medical problems, you will be trekking in remote areas, often with a week or more of travelling between you and medical facilities.

Even if you do not have a medical background, do record as much information as possible if a member of your party falls sick. This may later assist trained medical staff in the case of prolonged illness or evacuation. Record the duration of the complaint, its severity and location, and any symptoms such as cough and chest pains, palpitations, headaches, numbness, tingling, abdominal pain, and urinary or bowel symptoms. Note whether the victim is taking, or is allergic to, any drugs; along with factors that help or make the condition worse. Take the temperature, and pulse and respiration rate, feel the abdomen, and record the urine output and colour.

At altitude (above 3000m), always suspect acute mountain sickness (read the boxed text on pp74–5). When examining the person, a well-lit, quiet place is ideal. Remember also that a confident, reassuring approach works wonders when a patient is injured or sick.

Environmental Hazards

At high altitude, if you lie with half your body in the shade and half in the sun, it is

Warning

Self-diagnosis and treatment can be risky, so you should always seek medical help. An embassy, consulate or five-star hotel can usually recommend a local doctor or clinic. Although we do give drug dosages in this section, they are for emergency use only. Correct diagnosis is vital.

Note that we have used generic rather than brand names for drugs throughout this section – check with a pharmacist for locally available brands.

Everyday Health

Normal temperature is oral 37.0°C (98.4°F), rectal 37.6°C (99.7°F). The normal adult pulse rate is 60 to 100 per minute (children 80 to 100, babies 100 to 140). As a general rule the pulse increases about 20 beats per minute for each 1°C (2°F) rise in fever. Normal urine output is at least 500ml (one pint) of pale yellow urine per day.

Respiration (breathing) rate is also an indicator of illness. Count the number of breaths per minute: between 12 and 20 is normal for adults and older children (up to 30 for younger children, 40 for babies). People with a high fever or serious respiratory illness breathe more quickly than normal. More than 40 shallow breaths a minute may indicate pneumonia.

possible to get sunburn and frostbite at the same time! The best way to describe the trekking environment in the Himalaya is *extreme*. Sudden changes in the weather are to be expected. The air can be very dry so scarf and lip balm are essentials.

Sun Protection against the sun should always be taken seriously. Particularly in the rarefied air and deceptive coolness of the mountains, sunburn occurs rapidly. Slap on sunscreen (at least SPF 15+) and a barrier cream for your nose and lips, wear a broad-brimmed hat whenever the sun appears and protect your eyes with good quality sunglasses with UV lenses, particularly when walking near water, sand or snow. If, despite these precautions, you get yourself burnt, calamine lotion, aloe vera or other commercial sunburn relief products will soothe.

Snow Blindness This very painful condition is caused by UV light reflected from snow or ice. To prevent it use good sunglasses with protection underneath and at the sides. Symptoms include red, watery eyes and blindness. It lasts for two or three days, and is treated with cold compresses and painkillers.

Heat Few trekkers prepare for the heat in the Himalaya as much they do the cold, an oversight that can lead to illness.

Prickly Heat This is an itchy rash caused by excessive perspiration trapped under the skin. Keeping cool, bathing often and using talcum powder or prickly heat powders should relieve the symptoms.

Dehydration & Heat Exhaustion Dehydration is a potentially dangerous and generally preventable condition caused by excessive fluid loss. Sweating and inadequate fluid intake are the most common causes in trekkers, but other important causes are diarrhoea, vomiting, and high fever – see Diarrhoea (p76) for advice about treatment.

The first symptoms are weakness, thirst and passing small amounts of very concentrated urine. This may progress to drowsiness, dizziness or fainting, and finally, coma.

It's easy to forget how much fluid you are losing via perspiration while you are trekking, particularly if a strong breeze is drying your skin quickly. You should always maintain a good fluid intake – a minimum of 3L a day is recommended.

Dehydration and salt deficiency can cause heat exhaustion. Salt deficiency is characterised by fatigue, lethargy, headaches, giddiness and muscle cramps; salt tablets are overkill, just adding extra salt to your food is probably sufficient.

Heatstroke This is a serious, occasionally fatal, condition that occurs if the body's heat-regulating mechanism breaks down and the body temperature rises to dangerous levels. Long, continuous periods of exposure to high temperatures and insufficient fluids can leave you vulnerable to heatstroke.

The symptoms are feeling unwell, not sweating very much (or at all) and a high body temperature (39° to 41°C or 102° to 106°F). Where sweating has ceased, the skin becomes flushed and red. Severe, throbbing headaches and lack of coordination will also occur, and the sufferer may be confused or aggressive. Eventually the victim

Acute Mountain Sickness

If someone is seriously ill at altitude and you are not completely sure of the cause, call it acute mountain sickness (AMS) and descend.

AMS, also called altitude sickness, is a common and potentially fatal disease. It is caused by the failure to acclimatise to the low levels of oxygen at high altitude.

Acclimatisation to altitudes above 3000m takes time. The body undergoes a number of physiological changes. Some are immediate, such as increased pulse and respiratory rate, while others, such as the increase in red blood cells or changes in the acid-base balance, take days or weeks.

Mild AMS

The above changes, together with the effects of intense sunlight, hard walking and dehydration, may cause any of the following mild acclimatisation symptoms:

- loss of appetite
- fatigue
- headache
- nausea
- dizziness
- sleeplessness
- mild shortness of breathe on exercising
- interrupted breathing while asleep, followed by gasping (Cheyne-Stokes breathing)

Severe AMS

This is the accumulation of fluid (oedema) in the lungs and/or the brain. Fluid in the lungs is called high-altitude pulmonary oedema (HAPE). Fluid in the brain tissue is called high-altitude cerebral oedema (HACE). These may occur together or separately, rapidly or gradually over a period of days.

Night time is a particularly dangerous period for people suffering AMS. Sleeping naturally lowers the respiratory rate and Cheyne-Stokes periodic breathing can exacerbate the lowering of the oxygen level in the blood. Partners and attendants are tired or asleep themselves and a sudden worsening of the patient's condition may be missed. A typical pattern is for someone to go to bed with symptoms of mild AMS and to develop severe symptoms while asleep. Many people, including doctors, have woken to find their partners dead. Vigilance, especially at night, and the preparedness to take drastic action are essential to avoid death. An early warning sign of impending AMS is a resting pulse of more than 110 beats per minute (check in the morning and at night in bed).

To examine a person for AMS, take a good history and ask about the symptoms mentioned for mild AMS and, more specifically, severe AMS, as follows:

Symptoms of HAPE

Symptoms include any of those described for mild AMS, and:

- shortness of breath: which persists at rest (more than 12 to 14 breaths per minute)
- coughing: often with frothy, blood-stained sputum
- severe fatigue
- drowsiness
- pains in the chest or upper body
- wet sounds in the lungs on deep inspiration place your ear on the bare skin of the patient's

will become delirious or convulse. Hospitalisation is essential; in the interim, get victims out of the sun, remove their clothing, cover them with a wet sheet or towel and then fan continually. Give fluids if they are conscious.

Cold While most trekkers experience a rapid drop in temperature at least once or twice during their trek, you are unlikely to encounter the following conditions if you are sensible and well equipped.

Hypothermia Too much cold can be just as dangerous as too much heat. Hypothermia occurs when the body loses heat faster than it can produce it and the core temperature of the body falls.

It is surprisingly easy to progress from very cold to dangerously cold due to a combination of wind, wet clothing, fatigue and hunger, even if the air temperature is above freezing. It is best to dress in layers; silk, wool and some of the new artificial fibres

Acute Mountain Sickness

back below the shoulder blades and compare with a healthy person

Symptoms of HACE

Symptoms include any of the symptoms described for mild AMS, and:

- severe headache – does not respond to mild painkillers; is often aggravated by lying down
- nausea and vomiting: which may become pronounced and prolonged
- loss of coordination: inability to do the 'heel-to-toe' walking test
- loss of mental abilities (eg, memory, arithmetic)
- double, blurred or failing vision
- drowsiness
- severe fatigue

Prevention & Treatment

- Ascend slowly – have frequent rest days, spending two to three nights at each rise of 1000m. If you reach a high altitude by trekking, acclimatisation takes place gradually and you are less likely to be affected than if you fly directly to high altitude.
- If possible, it is always wise to sleep at a lower altitude than the greatest height reached during the day. Also, once above 3000m, care should be taken not to increase the sleeping altitude by more than 300m per day.
- Drink extra fluids. The mountain air is dry and cold and moisture is lost as you breathe. Evaporation of sweat may occur unnoticed and result in dehydration.

- Eat light, high-carbohydrate meals for more energy.
- Avoid alcohol as it may increase the risk of dehydration.
- Avoid sedatives.

Pressure Bags Portable pressure chambers have revolutionised the management of AMS. More and more trekking groups and mountaineering parties carry one.

The victim is placed in the bag, which is continuously pressurised by a foot pump. It appears that sessions in the bag reverse the symptoms of mild AMS, while severe AMS victims can be resuscitated prior to evacuation.

A major limitation in their use is claustrophobia, while damage to eardrums is a possibility. Their major application is in plateau situations.

Drug Therapy This is no substitute for descent, and should only be used to buy time while descending with the patient (eg, if the weather is extreme or if you are on a plateau and it will take some time to lose altitude). Diamox (acetazolamide) may be given morning and night for acclimatisation symptoms. It appears to prevent AMS in some people. It will not mask the onset of AMS. If the person is getting worse, descend. Side effects are numbness or tingling of digits and lips. These are not serious.

Oxygen If available, oxygen should be given at the rate of 2L to 6L per minute, depending on the patient's condition. Once again, the only guaranteed treatment is early and adequate descent.

---

are all good insulating materials. A hat is important, as a lot of heat is lost through the head. A strong, waterproof outer layer (and a 'space' blanket for emergencies) is essential. Carry basic supplies, including fluid to drink and food containing simple sugars to generate heat quickly.

Symptoms of hypothermia are exhaustion, numb skin (particularly toes and fingers), shivering, slurred speech, irrational or violent behaviour, lethargy, stumbling,

dizzy spells, muscle cramps and violent bursts of energy. Irrationality may take the form of sufferers claiming they are warm and trying to take off their clothes.

To treat mild hypothermia, first get the person out of the wind and/or rain, remove their clothing if it's wet and replace it with dry, warm clothing. Give them hot liquids – not alcohol – and some high-kilojoule, easily digestible food. Do not rub victims: instead, allow them to slowly warm themselves. This should be enough to treat the early stages of hypothermia. The early recognition and treatment of mild hypothermia is the only way to prevent severe hypothermia, which is a critical condition.

Frostbite This refers to the freezing of extremities, including fingers, toes and nose. Signs and symptoms of frostbite include a whitish or waxy cast to the skin, or even crystals on the surface, plus itching, numbness and pain. Warm the affected areas by immersion in warm (not hot) water or with blankets or clothes, only until the skin becomes flushed. Frostbitten parts should not be rubbed. Pain and swelling are inevitable. Blisters should not be broken. Get medical attention right away.

Infectious Diseases
Diarrhoea Simple things like a change of water, food or climate can all cause a mild bout of diarrhoea, but a few rushed toilet trips with no other symptoms is not indicative of a major problem. More serious diarrhoea is caused by infectious agents transmitted by faecal contamination of food or water, by using contaminated utensils, or directly from one person's hand to another. Paying particular attention to personal hygiene, drinking purified water and taking care of what you eat are all important measures to avoid getting diarrhoea on your trek. See also Water and Food (both p71).

Dehydration is the main danger with any diarrhoea, particularly in children or the elderly as dehydration can occur quite quickly. Under all circumstances fluid replacement (at least equal to the volume being lost) is the most important thing to remember. Weak black tea with a little sugar, soda water, or soft drinks allowed to go flat and diluted 50% with clean water are all good. With severe diarrhoea, a rehydrating solution is preferable to replace minerals and salts lost. Commercially available oral rehydration salts (ORS) are very useful; add them to boiled or bottled water. In an emergency you can make up a solution of six teaspoons of sugar and a half teaspoon of salt to 1L of boiled or bottled water. You need to drink at least the same volume of fluid that you are losing in bowel movements and vomiting. Urine is the best guide to the adequacy of replacement – if you have small amounts of concentrated urine, you need to drink more. Keep drinking small amounts often. Stick to a bland diet as you recover.

Gut-paralysing drugs such as diphenoxylate or loperamide can be used to bring relief from the symptoms, although they do not actually cure the problem. Only use these drugs if you have no option but to continue with your trek. These drugs are not recommended for children under 12 years, or if you have a high fever or are severely dehydrated.

Severe Diarrhoea Where diarrhoea is profuse and watery, contains blood or mucus, is accompanied by fever, or does not improve after 48 hours, antibiotics may be required. Gut-paralysing drugs should be avoided.

In these situations, a stool test may be necessary to diagnose what bug is causing your diarrhoea, so you should seek medical help urgently. Where this is not possible, the recommended drugs for bacterial diarrhoea (the most likely cause of severe diarrhoea in travellers) are norfloxacin 400mg twice daily for three days or ciprofloxacin 500mg twice daily for five days. These are not recommended for children or pregnant women. The drug for children is co-trimoxazole, with dosage dependent on weight. A five-day course is given, Ampicillin or amoxicillin may be given in pregnancy, but medical care is necessary.

Giardiasis The parasite *Giardia lamblia* causes giardiasis. Symptoms include stomach cramps, nausea, a bloated stomach, watery, foul-smelling diarrhoea and frequent gas. Giardiasis can appear several weeks after you have been exposed to the parasite. The symptoms may disappear for a few days and then return; this can go on for several weeks.

You should seek medical advice if you think you have giardiasis, but where this is not possible, tinidazole or metronidazole are the recommended drugs. Treatment is a 2g single dose of tinidazole or 250mg of metronidazole three times daily for five to 10 days.

Amoebic Dysentery This is characterised by a gradual onset of low-grade diarrhoea, often with blood and mucus. Cramping abdominal pain and vomiting are less likely than in other types of diarrhoea, and fever may not be present. It will persist until treated and can recur and cause other health problems. If you think you have amoebic dysentery, you should seek medical advice; treatment is the same as for giardiasis.

Fungal Infections Sweating liberally, probably washing less than usual and going longer without a change of clothes all expose long-distance trekkers to fungal infection, which, while an unpleasant irritant, presents no danger.

Fungal infections are encouraged by moisture, so try to wear loose, comfortable clothes, wash when you can and dry yourself thoroughly. Try to expose the infected area to air or sunlight as much as possible and apply an antifungal cream or powder such as tolnaftate.

Hepatitis This is a general term for inflammation of the liver. It is a common disease worldwide. There are several different viruses that cause hepatitis, and they differ in the way that they are transmitted. The symptoms are similar in all forms of the illness, and include fever, chills, headache, fatigue, feelings of weakness and aches and pains, followed by loss of appetite, nausea, vomiting, abdominal pain, dark urine, light-coloured faeces, jaundiced (yellow) skin and yellowing of the whites of the eyes. People who have had hepatitis should avoid alcohol for some time after the illness, as the liver needs time to recover.

Hepatitis A is transmitted by contaminated food and drinking water. You should seek medical advice, but there is not much you can do apart from resting, drinking lots of fluids, eating lightly and avoiding fatty foods. Hepatitis E is transmitted in the same way as Hepatitis A; it can be particularly serious in pregnant women.

There are almost 300 million chronic carriers of Hepatitis B in the world. It is spread through contact with infected blood, blood products or body fluids (eg, through sexual contact, unsterilised needles and blood transfusions, or contact with blood via small breaks in the skin). Other risk situations include having a shave, tattoo or body piercing with contaminated equipment. The symptoms of hepatitis B may be more severe than type A and the disease can lead to long-term problems such as chronic liver damage, liver cancer or a long-term carrier state. Hepatitis C and D are spread in the same way as Hepatitis B and can also lead to long-term complications.

There are vaccines against hepatitis A and B, but there are currently no vaccines against the other types of hepatitis. Following the basic rules about food and water (hepatitis A and E) and avoiding risk situations (Hepatitis B, C and D) are important preventative measures.

HIV & AIDS Infection with the human immunodeficiency virus (HIV) may lead to acquired immune deficiency syndrome (AIDS), which is a fatal disease. Any exposure to blood, blood products or body fluids may put the individual at risk. The disease is often transmitted through sexual contact or dirty needles. There is also a chance that the blood used for transfusions has not been properly screened and this in turn could spread HIV/AIDS. However, fear of HIV infection should never preclude treatment for serious medical conditions.

Meningitis This is an infection of the brain's lining, which can occur in epidemics and is often fatal. Vaccination gives protection against some forms of the disease (meningitis A and C). Symptoms are fever, a severe headache that is made worse if the knees are bent up to the chest, neck stiffness, nausea, vomiting and loss of consciousness. Treatment is ciprofloxacin, 500mg eight hourly plus amoxicillin 500mg six hourly.

Rabies This fatal viral infection is not common in the Indian Himalaya. However, it is always sensible to avoid contact with dogs, cats and monkeys as their saliva may be infectious. Any bite, scratch or even lick from an animal should be cleaned immediately and thoroughly. Scrub with soap and running water, and then apply alcohol or iodine solution. If bitten or scratched, seek medical help promptly to receive a course of injections, which can prevent the onset of symptoms and death.

Tetanus This disease is caused by a germ that lives in soil and in the faeces of horses and other animals. It enters the body via breaks in the skin. The first symptom may be discomfort in swallowing, or stiffening of the jaw and neck; this is followed by painful convulsions of the jaw and whole body. The disease can be fatal. It can be prevented by vaccination, so make sure you are up to date with this vaccination before you leave.

Tuberculosis This is spread by droplet infection. It usually affects the lungs, producing a cough that is often accompanied by bloodstained sputum, low fever and weight loss. It is a chronic disease – that is, it develops slowly and can last a long time. A healthy person is less likely to contract it than someone who is run-down and debilitated. It is exceedingly unlikely that a trekker will contract TB, but it is not uncommon to come across villagers suffering from it. TB requires hospital diagnosis and long-term treatment.

Insect-Borne Diseases

Malaria This serious and potentially fatal disease is spread by mosquito bites. It is extremely important to avoid mosquito bites and to take tablets to prevent this disease. Symptoms range from fever, chills and sweating, headache, diarrhoea and abdominal pains to a vague feeling of ill-health. Seek medical help immediately if malaria is suspected. Without treatment, malaria can rapidly become more serious and can be fatal.

If medical care is not available, malaria tablets can be used for treatment. You need to use a different malaria tablet from the one you were taking when you contracted malaria. The standard treatment dose of mefloquine is two 250mg tablets and a further two six hours later. For fansidar, it's a single dose of three tablets. If you were previously taking mefloquine and cannot obtain fansidar, other alternatives are malarone (atovaquone-proguanil; four tablets once daily for three days), halofantrine (three doses of two 250mg tablets every six hours) or quinine sulphate (600mg every six hours). There is a greater risk of side effects with these dosages than in normal use if used with mefloquine, so medical advice is preferable. Be aware also that halofantrine is no longer recommended by the WHO as emergency standby treatment, because of side effects, and should only be used if no other drugs are available.

Travellers are advised to prevent mosquito bites at all times. The main messages are:

- wear light-coloured clothing
- wear long trousers and long-sleeved shirts
- use mosquito repellents containing the compound DEET on exposed areas (prolonged overuse of DEET may be harmful, especially to children, but its use is considered preferable to being bitten by disease-transmitting mosquitoes)
- avoid perfumes or aftershave
- use a mosquito net impregnated with mosquito repellent permethrin – it may be worth taking your own
- impregnating clothes with permethrin effectively deters mosquitoes and other insects

Japanese Encephalitis Mosquitoes transmit this viral infection of the brain. Most cases occur in rural areas as the virus exists in pigs and wading birds. Symptoms include fever, headache and alteration in consciousness. Hospitalisation is needed for correct diagnosis and treatment. There is a high mortality rate among those who have symptoms; of those who survive many are intellectually disabled.

Traumatic Injuries

Sprains Ankle and knee sprains are common injuries in hikers, particularly when trekking over rugged terrain. To help prevent ankle sprains, you should wear an all-leather boot with adequate ankle support.

If you do suffer a sprain, immobilise the joint with a firm bandage, and relieve pain and swelling by keeping the joint elevated for the first 24 hours and, where possible, by using ice (or anything frozen) on the swollen joint. Take simple painkillers to ease the discomfort. If the sprain is only mild, trekking with a limited weight should be possible within a day or two. For more severe sprains, seek medical attention as it may be necessary to have an X-ray to rule out the possibility of a broken bone.

Major Accident Falling or having something fall on you, resulting in head injuries or fractures, is always possible when trekking, especially if you are crossing steep slopes or unstable terrain. Following is some basic advice on what to do if a major accident does occur; detailed first-aid instruction is outside the scope of this guidebook (see also First Aid, p70). If a person suffers a major fall:

1) Make sure you and other people with you are not in danger.
2) Assess the injured person's condition.
3) Stabilise any injuries, such as bleeding wounds or broken bones.
4) Seek medical attention.

If the person is unconscious, immediately check whether they are breathing – clear their airway if it is blocked – and check whether they have a pulse (feel the side of the neck rather than the wrist). If they are not breathing but have a pulse, you should start mouth-to-mouth resuscitation immediately. In these circumstances it is best to move the person as little as possible in case their spine is damaged. Keep the person warm by covering them with a blanket or dry clothing; insulate them from the ground if possible.

Check for wounds and broken bones – ask the person where they have pain if they are conscious, otherwise gently inspect them all over (including their back and the back of the head), moving them as little as possible. Control any bleeding by applying firm pressure to the wound. Bleeding from the nose or ear may indicate a fractured skull. Don't give the person anything by mouth, especially if they are unconscious.

Indications of a fracture (broken bone) are pain, swelling and discoloration, loss of function or deformity of a limb. Unless you know what you are doing, you shouldn't try to straighten an obviously displaced broken bone. To protect from further injury, immobilise a nondisplaced fracture by splinting it; for fractures of the thigh bone, try to straighten the leg gently, then tie it to the good leg to hold it in place. Fractures associated with open wounds (compound fractures) require urgent treatment as there is a risk of infection. Dislocations, where the bone has come out of the joint, are very painful, and should be set as soon as possible – seek medical attention.

Broken ribs are painful but usually heal by themselves and do not need splinting. If breathing difficulties occur, or the person coughs up blood, medical attention should be sought urgently, as it may indicate a punctured lung.

Internal injuries are more difficult to detect, and cannot usually be treated in the field. Watch for shock, which is a specific medical condition associated with a failure to maintain circulating blood volume. Signs include a rapid pulse and cold, clammy extremities. A person in shock requires urgent medical attention.

Some general points to bear in mind:

• Simple fractures take several weeks to heal, so they don't need fixing straight away, but they should be immobilised to protect them from further injury. Compound fractures need much more urgent treatment.
• If you do have to splint a broken bone, remember to check regularly that the splint is not cutting off the circulation to the hand and foot.
• Most cases of brief unconsciousness are not associated with any serious internal injury to the brain, but as a general rule in these circumstances, any person who has been knocked unconscious should be watched for deterioration. If they do deteriorate, seek medical attention straight away.

Respiratory Problems
Respiratory problems are common at altitude and are often associated with a cough.

Sore Throat Stop smoking (if a smoker), gargle warm salt water and use steam inhalations and antiseptic lozenges. If the problem is severe or persistent, use an appropriate antibiotic.

Cardiopulmonary Resuscitation

These notes on cardiopulmonary resuscitation (CPR) are a reminder for those with training. If you don't know CPR, a training course is highly recommended. If a person collapses for whatever reason, don't panic! Before approaching or handling the victim, be aware of any danger to yourself and take appropriate action. Determine if the victim is conscious or unconscious: shake the victim firmly by the shoulders, ask for their name, and command them to squeeze your hand. If they don't respond, they are unconscious and you must proceed as follows:

The ABC Method
Airway Quickly turn the victim on the side with head tilted backward and face turned slightly down. Clear the mouth of vomit, loose teeth or foreign material.

Breathing Check for breathing by listening and feeling at the victim's mouth and nose. If not breathing, quickly turn the person on their back and tilt the head back, then give five quick breaths, mouth to mouth, with their nose pinched closed. Now feel the carotid pulse in the groove alongside the windpipe. If there is a pulse, give mouth-to-mouth breathing at the rate of one breath every five seconds.

Circulation If the pulse is absent this means the heart has stopped and that heart compression must be started. This is a specialised technique, which requires training on dummies. Do not practise on living people. Compress the lower half of the breastbone one-third of the depth of the chest slightly faster than once a second. Kneel beside the patient, rock from your hips, with arms locked straight and the heel of the palm on the lower half of the breastbone – one hand on top of the other. For adults, after 15 compressions give two full breaths (making sure the head is in full backward tilt). For children, the ratio is five compressions to one breath. Stop compression and check for the carotid pulse every two to three minutes. If the heart restarts, continue with mouth-to-mouth breathing only, at the rate of one breathe every five seconds.

Assessment of the Victim
Once airway, breathing and circulation are established, do a primary survey of the whole body. This is done to assess quickly the victim's injuries, as one obvious injury may distract from other problems. If the victim is conscious, ask them where it hurts. Feel lightly around the head and look for blood. Feel and squeeze the shoulders, arms, and hands, the chest, pelvis, legs and feet. Apply gentle pressure to the belly and finally feel underneath the person for pooling blood. When all injuries have been dealt with, a thorough secondary survey should be performed. Always suspect head, neck or spinal injury.

Care of the Unconscious (But Breathing) or Semiconscious Victim
Place the victim on the side with the top leg bent at the hip and knee to stabilise the body (lateral position). Maintain the backward head tilt. Monitor the breathing and the pulse, and provide protection from the elements.

Sinusitis An infection of the sinus cavities around the nose, sinusitis has symptoms of facial pain (with either a sudden or slow onset), fever and nasal discharge of pus. The treatment is the same as for a sore throat, plus nasal washouts with warm salt water (an eighth of a teaspoon of salt in two thirds of a glass of water), and the use of an antibiotic and a nasal decongestant.

Bronchitis The early morning chorus of coughing in the Himalaya is mostly chronic bronchitis. This infection of the respiratory tubes is marked by a cough that is especially productive early in the morning, when large amounts of phlegm may be expectorated. It can become a chronic condition. Treatment is with steam inhalations and antibiotics.

Pneumonia An infection that has invaded the lung tissue, pneumonia is indicated by shortness of breath, fever, headaches and often chest pain. Treatment is as for bronchitis, plus descent and evacuation.

For many years, acute mountain sickness was mistaken for pneumonia but AMS is far more likely to be the cause of respiratory distress at altitude than pneumonia. See the 'Acute Mountain Sickness' boxed text (pp74–5).

Bites & Stings

Bedbugs These live in various places, but particularly in dirty mattresses and bedding, evidenced by spots of blood on bedclothes or on the wall. Bedbugs leave itchy bites in neat rows. Calamine lotion or a sting-relief spray may help.

Bees & Wasps These are usually painful rather than dangerous. Calamine lotion or a commercial sting-relief spray will ease discomfort and ice packs will reduce the pain and swelling. However, in people who are allergic to them, severe breathing difficulties may occur; urgent medical care is required.

Leeches These may be present in damp rainforest conditions; they attach themselves to your skin and suck your blood. Trekkers often get them on their legs or in their boots. Salt or a lit cigarette end will make them fall off. Do not pull them off, as the bite is then more likely to become infected. Clean and apply pressure if the point of attachment is bleeding. An insect repellent may keep them away.

Lice All lice cause itching and discomfort. They make themselves at home in your hair (head lice), your clothing (body lice) or in your pubic hair (crabs). You can catch lice through direct contact with infected people or by sharing combs, clothing and the like. Powder or shampoo treatment will kill the lice and infected clothing should be washed in very hot, soapy water and left in the sun to dry.

Snakes To minimise your chances of being bitten, always wear boots, socks and long trousers when walking through undergrowth where snakes may be present. However, snakes are very rare in the Indian Himalaya, and you can confidently expect them to move away well before you approach.

Snake bites do not cause instantaneous death and antivenins are usually available. Immediately wrap the bitten limb tightly, as you would for a sprained ankle, and then attach a splint to immobilise it. Keep the victim still and seek medical help. Cover the bite site with sticking plaster and do not rinse the clothing surrounding the bite – the preserved venom will help identify the snake and the correct antivenin. Under no circumstances apply a tourniquet or attempt to suck out the poison.

Ticks You should always check all over your body if you have been walking through a potentially tick-infested area as ticks can cause skin infections and other more serious diseases. If a tick is found attached, press down around the tick's head with tweezers, grab the head and gently pull upwards. Avoid pulling the rear of the body as this may squeeze the tick's gut contents through the attached mouth parts into the skin, increasing the risk of infection and disease. Smearing chemicals on the tick will not make it let go and is not recommended.

Women's Health

Walking is not particularly hazardous to your health, however, women's health issues can be a bit trickier to cope with on the trail. Maintaining personal hygiene is vital for good health but is not always easy. Make sure you regularly change your underwear (cotton is best) and try to at least sponge wash daily.

Menstruation A change in diet, routine and environment, as well as intensive exercise, can all lead to irregularities in the menstrual cycle. This in itself is not a huge issue and your cycle should return to normal when you return to a more regular lifestyle.

Pregnancy If you are pregnant, it is not advisable to trek in the Indian Himalaya. Even normal pregnancies can make a women feel nauseated and tired for the first three months, while medication will be limited if you are ill. Food cravings are also unlikely to be satisfied by the diet available on a trek.

Thrush (Vaginal Candidiasis) Antibiotic use, synthetic underwear, tight trousers, sweating, contraceptive pills and unprotected sex can all lead to fungal vaginal infections, especially when travelling in hot, humid or tropical climates. Symptoms include itching and discomfort in the genital area, often in association with a thick white discharge. The best prevention is to keep the vaginal area cool and dry, and to wear cotton rather than synthetic underwear and loose clothes. Thrush can be treated by clotrimazole pessaries or vaginal cream. If these are not available, a vinegar or lemon-juice douche, or yoghurt, can also help.

Urinary Tract Infection Dehydration and 'hanging on' can result in urinary tract infection and the symptoms of cystitis, which can be particularly distressing and an inconvenient problem when out on the trail. Symptoms include burning when urinating, and having to urinate frequently and urgently. Blood can sometimes be passed in the urine. Drink plenty of fluids and empty your bladder at regular intervals. If symptoms persist, seek medical attention because a simple infection can spread to the kidneys, causing a more severe illness.

For more information on women's health while travelling, see Lonely Planet's *Healthy Travel Guides: Asia & India*.

SAFETY ON THE TREK

A trek in the Himalaya can be a most exhilarating and fulfilling experience and for many it is a wonderful introduction to one of the world's finest mountain ranges. However, as with all outdoor activities, a trek should not be taken lightly and you should be well-prepared before leaving the trailhead.

If trekking independently in a wilderness situation, do not trek with fewer than three members. This will ensure that if there is an accident, one member can remain with the injured party while the other goes to seek help. If you become separated from the group and lose the trail – do not panic. Do not attempt to take shortcuts or continue further into a wilderness area as that is likely to lead you into further problems. If

---

Walk Safety – Basic Rules

- Allow plenty of time to accomplish a walk before dark, particularly when daylight hours are shorter.

- Don't overestimate your capabilities. If the stage gets too tough, give up and head back.

- If possible, don't walk on your own. Always leave the details of your intended itinerary and route, including your expected return time, leaving someone responsible before you set off.

- Before setting off, make sure you have a relevant map, compass and whistle.

---

you encounter inclement weather, do not continue. Wait until the weather clears before crossing high passes or swollen rivers and if at all uncertain retrace your tracks.

By taking a few simple precautions, you'll significantly reduce the odds of getting in trouble. See the 'Walk Safety – Basic Rules' boxed text.

For advice on the clothes and equipment you should take with you, consult the Clothing & Equipment chapter.

Crossing Rivers

The first rule of crossing rivers in the Himalaya is *do not remove your boots*. These can provide invaluable ankle support as the boulders on the riverbed are continually moving and can easily crush a foot or ankle.

Before crossing, look for areas where the river is braided and test the depth of the deeper water by throwing a rock in it. If you are carrying a large backpack, ease one arm out of the pack and unclip the buckle of the waist strap. In this way, should you lose your balance and be swept downstream, it's easier to slip out of your backpack instead of being dragged under. As you move off it is advisable to link arms (don't hold hands), face slightly downstream and cross the river diagonally moving gradually with the current.

Do not attempt a crossing if the water level is above thigh height. If crossing a glacially fed river wait till the morning when the water level has dropped. Neither should you rely on blind faith by jumping from boulder to boulder. While many local people adopt this, they are more sure-footed than you, and should you slip there is often no comeback.

Lightning

If a storm brews, avoid exposed areas. Lightning has a penchant for crests, lone trees, small depressions, gullies, caves and cabin entrances, as well as wet ground. If you are caught out in the open, try to curl up as tightly as possible with your feet together and keep a layer of insulation between you and the ground. Place metal objects such as metal-frame backpacks and walking poles away from you.

Glacial Crossings

Treat all glacial passes with respect. If you do not have the technical expertise you can still safely cross a glacier, but only in the company of a trained and well-equipped guide.

Each season there are instances of trekkers and local people falling into crevasses with tragic consequences. Walking across glaciers requires the use of ropes, ascenders, crampons and ice axes – essential gear for any trekking party. Ensure that the guide knows the terrain and that no group members wander at will during the crossing.

Wild Animals

While encounters between trekkers and wild animals are rare, it is worth noting that many hundreds of villagers are attacked by bears each season. When moving through a forest region, particularly in the early evening, it is worth making some noise so as not to startle any wild animal in the vicinity. If you should encounter a bear do not turn and run. Instead, stop, make no movement and back off slowly. In most cases the bear will move away from you. Generally they will only charge if they feel endangered or trapped. If an encounter is imminent, drop into a foetal position and cover your neck in order to minimise the chances of serious injury.

I have encountered both black and brown bears at close quarters (well, reasonably close) without incident. They, like most wild animals, will not attack unless they feel threatened.

Domestic Animals

When approaching a village or shepherd encampment, try to alert someone's attention to your presence so that the dogs can be chained up. If you are attacked outside of the village or encampment, ward off the dog with your stick or walking pole, or try to grab a small rock. A well-aimed rock will at least temporarily frighten off the dog and give you time to proceed safely.

Yaks are temperamental and it is wise not to move too close to a herd grazing on the high pastures in Ladakh. Buffalo, too, should be avoided. They are nervous of your scent (unless you are with a Gujar shepherd), although there is little chance that they would actually attack.

Rock Falls

While many trekkers will witness major rock avalanches from a distance, many injuries (sometimes fatal) are sustained each season from minor rock falls. Some situations in which accidents commonly occur are described below.

When trekking up a stone-laden gully, you should not attempt to ascend while anyone is directly above you. If a small rock or boulder is dislodged it can have dire results.

The second situation to avoid is one where goats and sheep are grazing above the trail. Be aware that the animals are forever dislodging rocks and stones. Once their velocity increases they can cause severe injury.

Finally, take care if trekking in an area that is prone to rock falls or landslides. Watch out for any continuous series of falling pebbles or stones. This is particularly relevant during or after heavy rainfall when crossing extensive scree slopes.

Flash Floods

It is never advisable to camp close to the confluence of two streams or close to a river course. If there is a flash flood, within a short time a stream will turn into a torrent, which will dislodge boulders and unconsolidated terrain further up the valley.

Rescue & Evacuation

Organising the evacuation of an injured person requires that you first ascertain the severity of the injury and how the patient is to be evacuated. This can vary considerably.

If someone in your group is injured or falls ill and can't move, leave at least one person with the victim while the others go for help.

If the victim is not in dire straits, it is best to organise for a riding horse or porters to carry the victim as quickly as possible to the nearest trailhead.

This may not be as daunting as it seems. On many extended treks a shortcut to the trailhead can often be completed in a day or two. Send someone reliable ahead to organise transport and medical arrangements.

Emergency Communications Unfortunately, there is nothing of the sort you can rely on in the Indian Himalaya. Where you're going, mobile (cell) phones have limited or no reception.

Search & Rescue Organisations If you should go missing in the mountains, the State tourist authorities or the police may alert the Indian Army or the Indo-Tibetan Border Police Force. However, there is a limit to what they can do and the resources they have at their disposal. The police may also mount a search and rescue operation. However, this again will take time and will not usually be undertaken without instructions from the relevant authorities.

Helicopter Rescue & Evacuation If the evacuation requires a helicopter you will need to contact the nearest police or army post, which will pass on your message by radio. Ensure that comprehensive details are conveyed, including the patient's medical condition, their full name, nationality, passport number, age and sex.

Indicate the degree of urgency (eg, most immediate, victim in danger of dying). Give a detailed description of the location of the victim, draw a map or send a marked map, and indicate the altitude. If you intend to move, clearly indicate your evacuation route.

In most cases the Indian Army will not send a helicopter unless they are sure of payment. The victim's embassy will need to be contacted. Many embassies will not authorise an immediate evacuation, irrespective of the circumstances, until they are satisfied that the victim is insured or that the next of kin is prepared to foot the bill. This process can take many hours, even days.

Helicopter evacuation is expensive, costing from US$3000.

Most companies offer insurance to cover emergency evacuation that also includes trekking within the normal range of tourist activities. This insurance must be purchased before arriving in India.

Death

If someone dies in the mountains, take their details and passport to the nearest police post. Do not attempt to cremate or dispose of the body until the police arrive. This is essential, even if the nearest police post is many days away. The police will help with arranging evacuation or burial, and advise you of the necessary procedures.

Gateway Cities

Most international travellers bound for the hills will find themselves travelling through either Delhi (for Ladakh, Himachal Pradesh and Uttaranchal) or Kolkata (Calcutta; for Darjeeling and Sikkim). Basic stopover and transport information is given here; for more detail see Lonely Planet's *Delhi* and *India* guides.

Delhi

☎ 011 • pop 11 million
Delhi is the capital of India and its major international transport hub. In summer (when most visitors pass through en route to the Himalaya) the city is uncomfortably hot, with temperatures regularly above 40°C. Most people only spend one or two days here, arranging money, flights or train tickets to the hills. That said, Delhi is an endlessly fascinating city. To spend more time in Delhi and other states of northern India, visit in autumn. This is one of the best times to trek and after you return from the hills the temperatures will be starting to fall throughout the rest of India. It is also an ideal time to head on to Nepal if you decide to trek in both countries.

ORIENTATION

Delhi consists of two parts. Old Delhi is a warren of bazaars and backstreets that contains most of the city's Muslim and Moghul monuments. New Delhi is, by contrast, a planned and spacious city, created as a colonial capital by the British. Its hub is a huge circle known as Connaught Place, where you find most airline offices, banks, travel agents, tourist offices and mid-range hotels. It's divided up like slices of a pie and these blocks are named alphabetically.

Janpath, running south of Connaught Place, is one of the most important streets and has several tourist offices and many handicraft stalls. South of here are the government buildings, museums, residential districts and Chanakyapuri, the diplomatic enclave.

In between Old and New Delhi is the area known as Paharganj. This is the main budget travellers' area with many guesthouses, restaurants and email centres. At the eastern end of Paharganj is New Delhi train station, where most foreigners buy their tickets.

INFORMATION

See p258 for a list of tourist offices in Delhi that cater to each trekking region.

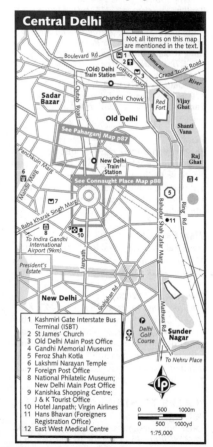

Central Delhi

Not all items on this map are mentioned in the text.

1 Kashmiri Gate Interstate Bus Terminal (ISBT)
2 St James' Church
3 Old Delhi Main Post Office
4 Gandhi Memorial Museum
5 Feroz Shah Kotla
6 Lakshmi Narayan Temple
7 Foreign Post Office
8 National Philatelic Museum; New Delhi Main Post Office
9 Kanishka Shopping Centre; J & K Tourist Office
10 Hotel Janpath; Virgin Airlines
11 Hans Bhavan (Foreigners Registration Office)
12 East West Medical Centre

0   500   1000m
0   500   1000yd
1:75,000

Money

There's a 24-hour **State Bank of India** and a **Thomas Cook** counter at the International arrivals hall, before you go through customs and immigration.

Most of the foreign banks in Delhi change money. With a Visa/Plus card you can get cash rupees from 24-hour ATMs at Citibank, Hong Kong & Shanghai Bank and Standard Chartered Bank. You can still get cash advances over the counter during normal working hours. Banks include:

American Express *(☎ 3325221; Wenger House, A-Block, Connaught Place)*
Bank of America *(☎ 3722332; DCM Bldg, Barakhamba Rd)*
Citibank *(☎ 3712484; Jeevan Bharati Bldg, Outer Circle, Connaught Place)*
Hong Kong & Shanghai Bank *(☎ 3314355; ECE House, 28 Kasturba Gandi Marg)*
Standard Chartered/Grindlays *(☎ 3732260; 17 Sansad Marg/Parliament St)* & *(☎ 3721242; 10 H-Block, Connaught Place)*
Thomas Cook *(☎ 3368359; Hotel Imperial, Janpath)*

Post

Poste restante mail can be collected from the **Foreign Post Office** *(Market Rd)*, near the New Delhi Main Post Office. Beware that poste restante not marked to New Delhi will end up at the inconveniently situated Old Delhi Post Office.

Visa Extensions

The **Foreigners Regional Registration Office** *(☎ 3319489; fax 3755185; 1st Floor, Hans Bhavan, Tilak Bridge)* organises extensions.

Medical Services

The **East West Medical Centre** *(☎ 4623738, 38 Golf Links Rd)* has been recommended by many travellers. Charges are high by Indian standards, but worth it for the good treatment.

There is a convenient 24-hour pharmacy at **Super Bazaar** in Connaught Place. Call ☎ 102 for an ambulance.

PLACES TO STAY
Paharganj

Some popular hotels include *Hotel Vivek* *(☎ 3512900, 1534–1550 Main Bazaar)*, *Hotel Payal* *(☎ 3520867, 1182 Main Bazaar)*, *Anoop Hotel* *(☎ 3529366, 1566 Main Bazaar)* and *Hare Krishna Guest House* *(☎ 3521413, 1572 Main Bazaar)*. Rooms cost from Rs 200; Rs 400 with bath.

Hotel Namaskar *(☎ 3621234, 917 Chandiwalan)* and *Major's Den* *(☎ 3629599, 2314 Laksmi Narayan St)* have been recommended. Both charge Rs 200 to Rs 400.

Mid-range places include the *Hotel Gold Regency* *(☎ 3540101, 4350 Main Bazaar)*, with rooms for Rs 800 to Rs 1000, and *Metropolis* *(☎ 3525492, 1634 Main Bazaar)*, with air-con rooms from Rs 700 to Rs 1100 (plus 10% service charge and 12.5% luxury tax on rooms priced above Rs 500).

Connaught Place

The other main accommodation area is Connaught Place. *Hotel Palace Heights* *(☎ 332 1419; C-Block, Connaught Place)* is popular, with singles/doubles for Rs 300/400, including air-cooler and common bath; air-con doubles cost Rs 700. Both the *Ringo Guesthouse* *(☎ 3310605; 17 Scindia House, Connaught Lane)* and *Sunny Guesthouse* *(☎ 331 2909; 152 Scindia House, Connaught Lane)* charge Rs 125/250, or from Rs 350 with bath.

Mid-range places include the *YMCA Tourist Hotel* *(☎ 3361915, Jai Singh Rd)*, with singles/doubles for Rs 500/570, Rs 950/1400 with air-con and bath; and the *YWCA International Guest House* *(☎ 3361517, 10 Sansad Marg)*, with rooms for Rs 550/850. *Hotel Marina* *(☎ 3324658, G-Block, Connaught Place)* has many superior facilities, including a bar and 24-hour coffee shop, charging around Rs 2600/3200.

PLACES TO EAT

Most hotels in Paharganj have good rooftop restaurants. Some of the best include the *Anoop*, *Vivek* and *Hare Rama*. Also highly recommended is the *Metropolis restaurant*.

Dining in Connaught Place tends to be more expensive. Favourites include *The Host (F-Block, Connaught Place)*, *Gaylords (Connaught Circus)* and *United Coffee House (E-Block, Connaught Place)*. Serving authentic Indian cuisine, the *Anand Restaurant (Connaught Lane)* is popular.

GETTING THERE & AWAY
Air
Delhi is the main international and domestic gateway to the Himalaya. For details of domestic flights, see the boxed text 'Flights from Delhi' (p90).

Arrival Many international flights to Delhi arrive and depart in the small hours of the morning. If this is your first time in India, it is worth getting a pre-paid taxi into town. Also reserve a room in advance or call the hotel at the airport. Make sure that you get some coins for the phone when changing money. Be particularly aware of taxi drivers who will try to steer you to a hotel of their choice. If you have a direct connection to the Himalaya, transfer to the domestic terminal (Terminal 1) 7km away. Delhi Transport Corporation buses connect the international and domestic terminals (Rs 10).

Departure If you are leaving Delhi in the early hours of the morning, get your hotel to book a taxi the evening before. They're hard to find at night, although you can always go to one of the upmarket hotels and take a taxi from the rank. When leaving

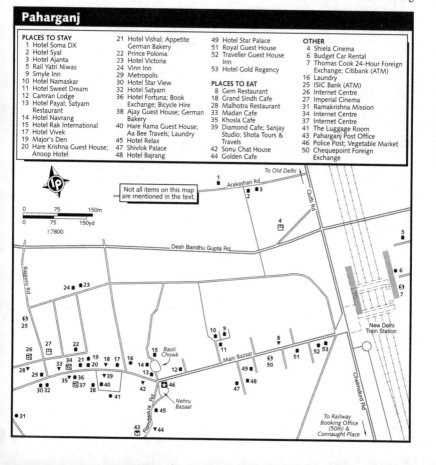

Paharganj

PLACES TO STAY
1 Hotel Soma DX
2 Hotel Syal
3 Hotel Ajanta
5 Rail Yatri Niwas
9 Smyle Inn
10 Hotel Namaskar
11 Hotel Sweet Dream
12 Camran Lodge
13 Hotel Payal; Satyam Restaurant
14 Hotel Navrang
15 Hotel Rak International
17 Hotel Vivek
19 Major's Den
20 Hare Krishna Guest House; Anoop Hotel
21 Hotel Vishal; Appetite German Bakery
22 Prince Polonia
23 Hotel Victoria
24 Vinn Inn
29 Metropolis
30 Hotel Star View
32 Hotel Satyam
36 Hotel Fortuna; Book Exchange; Bicycle Hire
38 Ajay Guest House; German Bakery
40 Hare Rama Guest House; Aa Bee Travels; Laundry
45 Shivlok Palace
48 Hotel Bajrang

49 Hotel Star Palace
51 Royal Guest House
52 Traveller Guest House Inn
53 Hotel Gold Regency

PLACES TO EAT
8 Gem Restaurant
18 Grand Sindh Cafe
28 Malhotra Restaurant
33 Madan Cafe
35 Khosla Cafe
39 Diamond Cafe; Sanjay Studio; Shota Tours & Travels
42 Sonu Chat House
44 Golden Cafe

OTHER
4 Shiela Cinema
6 Budget Car Rental
7 Thomas Cook 24-Hour Foreign Exchange; Citibank (ATM)
16 Laundry
25 ISIC Bank (ATM)
26 Internet Centre
27 Imperial Cinema
31 Ramakrishna Mission
34 Internet Centre
37 Internet Centre
41 The Luggage Room
43 Paharganj Post Office
46 Police Post; Vegetable Market
50 Chequepoint Foreign Exchange

Not all items on this map are mentioned in the text.

0   75   150m
0   75   150yd
1:7800

To Old Delhi
Arakashan Rd.
Qutb Rd.
Desh Bandhu Gupta Rd.
Rajguru Rd.
New Delhi Train Station
Baoli Chowk
Main Bazaar
Chelmsford Rd.
Ramdwara Rd.
Nehru Bazaar
To Railway Booking Office (50m) & Connaught Place

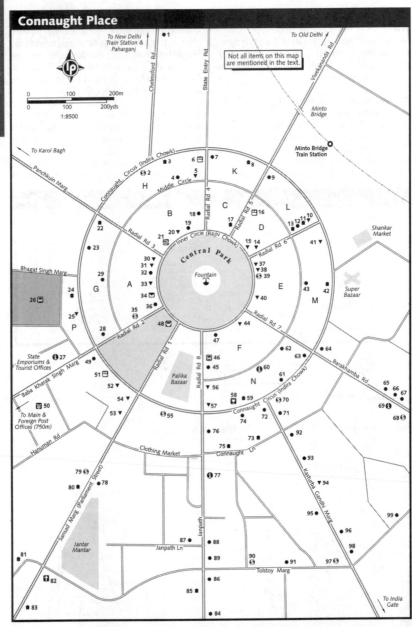

Connaught Place

To New Delhi Train Station & Paharganj

To Old Delhi

Not all items on this map are mentioned in the text.

Minto Bridge

Minto Bridge Train Station

To Karol Bagh

Panchkuin Marg

Connaught Circus (Indira Chowk)

Middle Circle

Bhagat Singh Marg

Radial Rd 3

Inner Circle (Rajiv Chowk)

Central Park

Fountain

Radial Rd 4

Radial Rd 5

Radial Rd 6

Radial Rd 7

Radial Rd 2

Radial Rd 1

Radial Rd 8

State Entry Rd

Chelmsford Rd

Vivekananda Rd

Shankar Market

Super Bazaar

State Emporiums & Tourist Offices

Baba Kharak Singh Marg

Palika Bazaar

Connaught Circus (Indira Chowk)

Barakhamba Rd

To Main & Foreign Post Offices (750m)

Hanuman Rd

Clothing Market

Connaught Ln

Samsad Marg (Parliament Street)

Jantar Mantar

Janpath Ln

Janpath

Kasturba Gandhi Marg

Tolstoy Marg

To India Gate

1:8500

Connaught Place

PLACES TO STAY

3	Hotel 55
8	York Hotel
11	Nirula's Hotel
13	Hotel Jukaso Inn Downtown
17	Hotel Palace Heights
22	Hotel Marina
24	Hotel Alka; Vega
42	Hotel Blue; Hotel Bright
59	Central Court Hotel
73	Sunny Guest House; Anand Restaurant
75	Ringo Guest House; Don't Pass Me By Cafe; Don't Pass Me By Travels
80	The Park
81	YMCA Tourist Hotel; Y Tours & Travels
83	YWCA International Guest House; VINstring Holidays
85	Hotel Imperial; Thomas Cook

PLACES TO EAT

5	Nizam Katri Kebab
10	Nirula's Complex; Pegasus
14	The Embassy
15	Pizza Pizza Express
20	Cafe 100
25	McDonald's
30	Keventers
31	Wenger's
33	Rodeo
37	Kovil; Pizza Hut
38	Berco's
40	United Coffee House; Ruby Tuesday's
41	Domino's Pizza
44	The Host
52	Gaylords
53	Kwality; People Tree
54	DV8
56	Nirula's
57	Wimpy
94	Parikrama; Tarom

OTHER

1	Railway Booking Office
2	Standard Chartered/ Grindlays Bank
4	Cox & Kings
6	Plaza Cinema
7	Alcohol Shop
9	English Book Store
12	Ashok Travels & Tours
16	Odeon Cinema
18	Bookworm
19	New Book Depot
21	Hub Internet Centre
23	Gulf Air
26	Local Bus Station
27	Delhi Tourism Corporation; Bangla Tourist Office
28	Royal Jordanian
29	Alcohol Shop
32	American Express
34	Post Office
35	American Express Bank (ATM)
36	Kinsey Bros
39	24-Hour Standard Chartered/ Grindlays Bank (ATM)
43	Singapore Airlines
45	Indian Airlines
46	EATS Airport Bus
47	Sita World Travels
48	Prepaid Autorickshaw Kiosk
49	Khadi Gramodyog Bhavan
50	Hanuman Mandir
51	Regal Cinema
55	24-Hour Citibank (ATM); Air India
58	The Blues Bar
60	Delhi Tourism Corporation; DSIDC Cyber Cafe
61	Jet Airways; Sahara
62	Aeroflot
63	Cozy Travels
64	British Airways
65	Malaysian Airlines
66	Emirates
67	Kuwait Airways
68	Bank Of America
69	Uttaranchal Tourist Office
70	Hongkong & Shanghai Bank (ATM)
71	Air Canada
72	Air France
74	Delhi Transport Corporation
76	Budget Car Hire
77	Government of India Tourist Office; Delhi Photo Company
78	Swissair
79	Standard Chartered/ Grindlays Bank (ATM)
82	Free Church
84	Chandralok Bldg (Himachal Pradesh Tourist Development Corporation); Delta Airlines; Druk Air; Japan Airlines
86	Central Industries Emporium
87	Map Sales Office
88	Lufthansa Airlines; Budget Car Rental
89	Royal Nepal Airlines Corporation (RNAC)
90	Deutsche Bank (ATM)
91	Jagson Airlines
92	Pakistan International Airlines
93	American Center
95	British Council
96	Asiana Airlines; Ethiopian Airlines; Kuwait Airways
97	Credit Lyonnaise
98	Ambadeep Bldg: Thai Airways; United Airlines; Sahara India; Scandinavian Airlines (SAS)
99	KLM-Royal Dutch Airlines; Northwest Airlines; El Al Israel Airlines; Uzbekistan Airways

Delhi, all baggage must be X-rayed and sealed before check in.

There are retiring rooms at both the domestic (☎ 3295129) and international (☎ 545 2011) terminals, which you can use if you have a confirmed departure within 24 hours. Ring in advance, as these are often full.

Airline Offices Unfortunately in India, you need to visit the airline office to make any progress with your arrangements.

Domestic Airlines The following airlines also have offices at the domestic terminal, which is a good place to make a booking (you may even get a same-day connection):

Indian Airlines (☎ 4620566, airport 5665433, 5665317; Malhotra Bldg, F-Block, Connaught Place)

Jagson Airlines (☎ 3721593, airport 5675545; 12E Vandana Bldg, 11 Tolstoy Marg)

Jet Airways (☎ 685 3700, airport 5665404; 40 N-Block, Connaught Circus)

Flights from Delhi

destination	airline	frequency	foreigners price (US$)
Bagdogra (for Shiliguri)	Jetair	daily	190
Bagdogra (via Gauhati)	Indian Airlines	3 weekly	190
Dharamsala (Gaggal)	Indian Airlines	3 weekly	150
Jammu	Indian Airlines	daily	110
Jammu	Jetair	2 daily	110
Kolkata	Indian Airlines	3 daily	205
Kolkata	Jetair	2 daily	205
Kolkata	Alliance	4 weekly	205
Kullu	Jagson	daily	135
Dharamsala	Indian Airlines	3 weekly	145
Leh	Alliance Air	daily	110
Leh	Jetair	daily	112
Srinagar	Indian Airlines	daily	120
Srinagar	Jetair	2 daily	120

International Airlines The international airlines offices are:

Air France (☎ 3738004; 7 Atma Ram Mansion, Scindia House, Connaught Circus)
Air India (☎ 3736446/7; 2nd Floor, Jeevan Bharati Bldg, Connaught Place)
British Airways (☎ 6540911; 11th Floor, Gopal Das Bhawan, Barakhamba Rd) also represents Qantas in Delhi. Qantas sales and bookings can be made here.
Gulf Air (☎ 3324293; G 12, Connaught Place)
KLM – Royal Dutch Airlines (☎ 3357747; Prakesh Deep Bldg, 7 Tolstoy Marg)
Lufthansa Airlines (☎ 3323310; 56 Janpath)
Malaysian Airlines (☎ 3313448; 10th Floor, Ashoka Estate Bldg, 24 Barakhamba Rd)
Pakistan International Airlines (PIA; ☎ 373 7791; Kailash Bldg, 26 Kasturba Gandhi Marg)
Royal Nepal Airlines Corporation (RNAC; ☎ 3321164; 44 Janpath)
Thai Airways International (THAI; ☎ 6239133; Park Royal, American Plaza, Nehru Place) also has a more convenient sales office in the Ambadeep Building, Kasturba Gandi Marg.
Virgin Airlines (☎ 3343290; Hotel Janpath, Janpath)

Bus

Delhi's Interstate Bus Terminal (ISBT) is at Kashmiri Gate, north of Old Delhi train station. Facilities include 24-hour left-luggage (Rs 10 per day), a State Bank of India branch, post office and a couple of restaurants. State transport offices operating here include:

Delhi Transport Corporation (DTC; ☎ 3354518)
Haryana Roadways (☎ 2961262)
Himachal Roadways Transport Corporation (HRTC; ☎ 2968694)
UP Roadways (☎ 2968709)

The Anand Vihar Bus Station, 15km north, handles services to Kumaon. However, for long-distance buses to the Himalaya, check directly with the state tourist offices (see Tourist Offices, p258). They operate a number of buses from convenient locations in New Delhi. There are also many private bus companies with booking offices in Paharganj and Connaught Place.

Train

The best place to make rail reservations is the **Foreign Tourist Booking Office** (open 7.30am–5pm, Mon–Sat) upstairs in the New Delhi train station. You can pay in foreign currency (cash, travellers cheques and credit cards) at the desk to the left and in rupees (with an encashment certificate) at the desk to the right. Make sure you fill in a reservation slip to avoid an longer wait.

The **main ticket office** (open 7.45am–9pm Mon–Sat, 7.45am–1.50pm Sun) is located on Chelmsford Rd, between the New Delhi train station and Connaught Place. It is well organised but incredibly busy. Take a numbered ticket from the counter as you enter the building, then wait at the allotted window.

Remember that there are two main train stations in Delhi – Delhi train station in Old Delhi, and New Delhi train station at Paharganj. If you are departing from the Old Delhi train station, allow 30 minutes to an hour to get there. An auto rickshaw will cost around Rs 50.

Many travellers opt for the bus for travelling to Himachal Pradesh, but for Chamba (for Brahmaur) or Dharamsala (for McLeod Ganj), it's possible to travel overnight by train to Pathankot in the Punjab, from where it is a three-hour bus ride to McLeod Ganj or a six-hour ride to Chamba. If you want to break up the long bus ride, *Shatabdi* trains head to Chandigarh, from where you can get a bus to McLeod Ganj or Manali.

For travel to Uttaranchal, catch a train to Dehra Dun or Haridwar before taking the bus to Mussoorie, Uttarkashi or Joshimath, which do not have train services. For the Kumaon district of Uttaranchal, the closest rail station is at Kathgodam, 35km south of Naini Tal. See the table ('Major Trains from Delhi', p92) for times and fares.

Taxis

Taxis can be hired in Delhi for trips to the Himalaya. The best bet is to check the interstate taxi stand at Delhi Gate, near the Ranjit Hotel. You will get the best deal with a taxi returning to the hills, so you don't have to pay the return fare (as you would if hiring a taxi out of Delhi). For example, expect to pay around Rs 6,500 for a car retuning to Manali. Alternatively, there are several companies along Janpath (close to the Imperial Hotel). Ambassador cars cost around Rs 2000 a day for the first 200km, including your driver. After this, add Rs 10 per km (Rs 20 if hiring the car on a one-way trip), plus Rs 500 for the overnight halting fee. Interstate road taxes are generally included in this rate.

GETTING AROUND

Auto-rickshaws are the most popular way to get around Delhi, though you will have to haggle for a reasonable fare. Fares are around Rs 30 from Paharganj to Connaught Place and Rs 50 from Paharganj to Old Delhi train station.

Bus Services to the West Himalaya

While there are many private bus companies operating out of Delhi, the following list includes some of the state bus services operating from the Interstate Bus Terminal (ISBT; Kashmiri Gate) or from the terminal at Anand Vihar (AV).

destination (departure point)	duration	semideluxe/ superdeluxe (Rs)
DTC		
Haridwar (ISBT)	8 hrs	120/160
Mussoorie (ISBT)	8 hrs	250/350
Rishikesh (ISBT)	6 hrs	150/250
Himachal Pradesh Tourist Development Corporation (HPTDC)		
Almora (AV)	12 hrs	260/na
Leh (ISBT)	3 days	1000/na
Manali (ISBT)	15 hrs	450/na
Naini Tal (AV)	9 hrs	200/na
Ranikhet (AV)	12 hrs	165/na
Shimla (ISBT)	9 hrs	290/na
HRTC		
Dharamsala (ISBT)	12 hrs	250/na
Kullu (ISBT)	14 hrs	250/450
Manali (ISBT)	16 hrs	250/450
Shimla (ISBT)	10 hrs	180/360
UP Roadways		
Dehra Dun (ISBT)	7 hrs	200/300

AV – Avand Vihar Bus Station
ISBT – Interstate Bus Terminal

To/From the Airport

The international terminal (Terminal 2) is 20km from the centre. **Ex-Servicemen's Air Link Transport Service** *(EATS;* ☎ *3316530)* has a regular bus service between both the international and domestic terminals and Connaught Place (Rs 50 plus Rs 5 per large piece of baggage). They will drop you off or pick you up at most major hotels if you ask.

Just outside the international terminal is a prepaid taxi booth. Don't give the driver your voucher until you have arrived at your

Major Trains from Delhi

train no & name	departs (departure point)	arrives	sleeper/1st class (Rs)
To Dehra Dun			
4041 Mussoorie Exp	10.15pm (OD)	8.00am	113/377
2017 Shatabdi Exp	7.00am (ND)	12.40pm	465/910
To Haridwar			
2017 Shatabdi Exp*	7.00am (ND)	11.22am	465/910
4041 Mussoorie Exp	10.15pm (OD)	5.40am	113/377
To Howrah			
2302/2306 Rajdhani**	5.00pm (ND)	9.55am	1345/2190/3825
2382/2304 Poorva Exp	4.15pm (ND)	4.15pm	302/1102
To Kathgodam			
5013 Ranikhet Exp	10.45pm (OD)	6.15am	105/361
To New Jalpaiguri			
5622 North East Exp	6.45am (ND)	9.40am	317/1615
2424 Rajdhani Exp**	5.15pm (ND)	2.10pm	1470/2365/4130
Pathankot			
4033 Jammu	9.10pm (OD)	7.55am	149/520
1077 Jhelum Exp	9.50pm (OD)	8.40am	149/520
To Shimla			
4095 *Himalayan Queen****	6.00am (ND)	17.15pm	120/410

OD – Old Delhi, ND – New Delhi
*   Fares for Shatabdi Express trains are AC Chair/AC Executive Class
**   Fares for Rajdhani trains are AC Three Tier/AC Two Tier/AC First Class
*** Change at Kalka for narrow gauge to Shimla (departing noon, 5½ hours)

destination. A prepaid taxi from the domestic terminal to Connaught Place/Paharganj costs Rs 150/170. From the international terminal, the cost is around Rs 200/220. There is a 25% surcharge between 10pm and 6am.

Kolkata (Calcutta)

☎ 033 • pop 12 million

Densely populated and frequently polluted, Kolkata can be an ugly and desperate place. Yet it's also one of the country's more fascinating centres and has long been acknowledged as the cultural capital. The best time to combine a trek to Darjeeling, Sikkim or Nepal with a visit Kolkata is from October onwards, when the monsoon rains have finished and temperatures on the plains have dropped to bearable levels.

ORIENTATION

Kolkata sprawls along the eastern bank of the Hooghly River. If you arrive from anywhere west of Kolkata by rail, you'll come into the immense Howrah Station and have to cross the Howrah Bridge into the centre of Kolkata. Getting around Kolkata is slightly confused by the renaming of city streets, but most taxi drivers still use the old names.

For visitors, the more relevant parts of Kolkata are in the areas around BBD Bagh and Chowringhee. BBD Bagh, formerly Dalhousie Square, is the hub of the central business district (CBD). South of BBD Bagh is the open expanse of the Maidan along the river. East from that is the area known as Chowringhee, where Sudder St is the most popular centre for travellers.

INFORMATION
See p258 for a list of tourist offices in Kolkata.

Money
There are offices for **American Express** (☎ 2489471, 21 Old Court House) and **Thomas Cook** (☎ 2803907; Chitrakoot Bldg, 230A AJC Bose Rd).

On Chowringhee Rd, there are branches with ATMs for **Citibank**, **State Bank of India** and **Standard Chartered/Grindlays**. **Standard Chartered/Grindlays** also have ATMs near the Main Post Office, as does the **Hong Kong Bank**.

The **State Bank of India** has a 24-hour counter in the new terminal at the airport.

Post
The **Main Post Office** (BBD Bagh) has an efficient poste restante service (to claim mail you need your passport). For posting parcels, the **Park St Post Office** in Chowringhee is more reliable.

Visa Extensions
The **Foreigners Registration Office** (☎ 247 3301, 237A AJC Bose Rd) is the place for visa extensions.

Medical Services
Medical queries can be directed to any of the large hospitals, or these clinics:

Dr Paes, Vital Medical Services (☎ 2825664; 6 Ho Chi Minh Sarani; 9.30–11am)
Wockhardt Medical Centre (☎ 4754320; 2/7 Sarat Bose (Landsdowne) Rd; 11.30am–2pm)

PLACES TO STAY
Budget travellers' accommodation is centred on Sudder St. Kolkata also has a collection of **YMCAs** and **YWCAs** (singles/doubles cost around Rs 300/500) but they are often full.

Popular hotels include **Centrepoint Guest House** (☎ 2442867, 20 Mirza Ghalib St), charging from Rs 250 or Rs 450 with air-con,

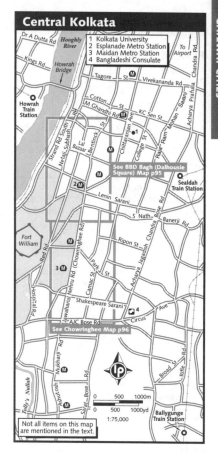

Central Kolkata

Dr A Dutta Rd | Hooghly River
Kings Rd
Howrah Bridge

1 Kolkata University
2 Esplanade Metro Station
3 Maidan Metro Station
4 Bangladeshi Consulate

To Airport

Tagore St
Vivekananda Rd

Howrah Train Station

Cotton St
M Ghandhi Rd
KC Sen St

Strand Rd South
Netaji Subhash Rd
Bentinck St
Lal Bazaar
Chittaranjan Ave
College St
Raja Ram Mohan Sarani
Acharya Pratulla

Sealdah Train Station

See BBD Bagh (Dalhousie Square) Map p95

Lenin Sarani

S Nath
Banerji Rd

Fort William
Red Rd
Jawaharlal Nehru Rd (Chowringhee Rd)
Ripon St
Acharya Jagadish Chandra Bose Rd

Camac St
Park St

Hospital Rd
Shakespeare Sarani

Jawaharlal Nehru Rd
AJC Bose Rd
Circus
Ave
Broad St
Rifle Rd

See Chowringhee Map p96

Mukharji Rd
Ashutosh Mukharji Rd
Sarat Bose Rd

Tally's Nullah

0   500   1000m
0   500   1000yd
1:75,000

Ballygunge Train Station

Not all items on this map are mentioned in the text.

and **Hotel Maria** (☎ 2450860, Sudder St), with singles/doubles from Rs 200/300.

In the mid-range and within easy walking distance of BBD Bagh, **Hotel Crystal** (☎ 2266400, 11 Dr M Ishaque Rd) charges Rs 500 for rooms with a TV and phone or Rs 800 with air-con. **CKT Inn** (☎ 2440047, 12A Lindsay St) is also recommended, charging Rs 700/1100 with air-con, a TV and bath.

Fairlawn Hotel (☎ 2451510, 13A Sudder St) has singles/doubles for US$50/60, plus taxes. This is a piece of Kolkata where the Raj still lives. The hotel is crammed with memorabilia and pre-war furnishings. The tariff includes three meals and afternoon tea.

PLACES TO EAT

Finding good food at reasonable prices is no problem in the Sudder St area. Places to try include the *Blue Sky Cafe (cnr Sudder St & Chowringhee Lane)*; *Zurich's*, further along Sudder St; and *Khalsa Restaurant*, just off Sudder St. *Jharokha (8A Lindsay St)* is a rooftop restaurant on the 10th Floor above Hotel Lindsay. It offers great views over Kolkata and inexpensive meals.

Mid-range and upmarket restaurants include the *Kwality Inn (17 Park St)*; the *Amber Hotel (11 Waterloo Rd)*; and the *Astor Hotel (15 Shakespeare Sarani)*, which has a beer garden and barbecue every evening.

GETTING THERE & AWAY
Air

From Kolkata to Bagdogra, Indian Airlines fly four times a week and Jetair twice a week for US$80. If you're flying to Delhi, choose from Indian Airlines (twice daily); Jetair (twice daily) and Alliance (four weekly); each charge US$200. Most airline offices are around Chowringhee:

Air France *(☎ 2408646; Chitrakoot Bldg, 230A AJC Bose Rd)*
Air India *(☎ 2822356; 50 Chowringhee Rd)*
Bangladesh Biman Airlines *(☎ 2292844; 30C Chowringhee Rd)*
British Airways *(☎ 2883451; 41 Chowringhee Rd)*
Cathy Pacific *(☎ 2403312; 1 Middleton St)*
Gulf Air *(☎ 2477783; Chitrakoot Bldg, 230A AJC Bose Rd)*
Indian Airlines *(domestic ☎ 2364433; 39 Chittaranjan Ave)*
Jet Airways *(domestic ☎ 2292227; 18 Park St)*
Royal Nepal Airlines Corporation *(RNAC; ☎ 2888549; 41 Chowringhee Rd)*
Thai International Airways *(☎ 2801630; 229A AJC Bose Rd)*

Bus

The only buses that travellers use with regularity are those from Kolkata to Shiliguri and New Jalpaiguri (en route to Darjeeling). The *Rocket Service* costs Rs 160, leaving at 6pm, 7pm and 8pm and arriving the next morning.

Buses generally depart from the Esplanade bus stand area at the northern end of the Maidan, but there are a number of private companies with their own stands.

Train

If you have flown in to Kolkata and don't plan to spend much time here, check in at the airport's rail reservation desk. They have an air-travellers quota reserved for same-day or next-day travel on the main expresses.

Kolkata has two main train stations. Howrah, on the west bank of the Hooghly River, handles most trains, including services to Delhi and the western Himalaya. Trains to New Jalpaiguri or Sikkim leave from Sealdah station on the east side of the Hooghly River. For the times and fares of the major trains, see the table (p97).

The **Tourist Train Booking Office** *(1st floor, 6 Fairlie Place; Mon–Sat 9am–1pm & 1.30–4pm, Sun 9am–2pm)* is near BBD Bagh. Another office at 14 Strand Rd sells advance tickets on routes into and out of Delhi, Chennai (Madras) and Mumbai (Bombay). If paying in rupees you must have your encashment certificates.

For a small fee (about Rs 50), agents in and around Sudder St can get tickets for you, often at short notice.

GETTING AROUND

Kolkata's bus system is very crowded, with fares from Rs 2. There is also a private minibus service, which is slightly faster, and has slightly higher fares. Out of peak hour, it is a relatively fast, cheap way to get to areas outside the city centre.

India's first underground train system includes a station near Sudder St – the Park St Metro Station. Tickets cost Rs 3 to Rs 7.

As with Delhi's taxis, you will have to negotiate hard to get a fair price before you get into a Kolkata cab. Few meters work or are in use. From Howrah station to Sudder St costs upwards of Rs 40.

Kolkata is the last bastion of the human-powered rickshaw, although they are now restricted to small areas in the city centre. Across the river in Howrah there are auto- and cycle-rickshaws.

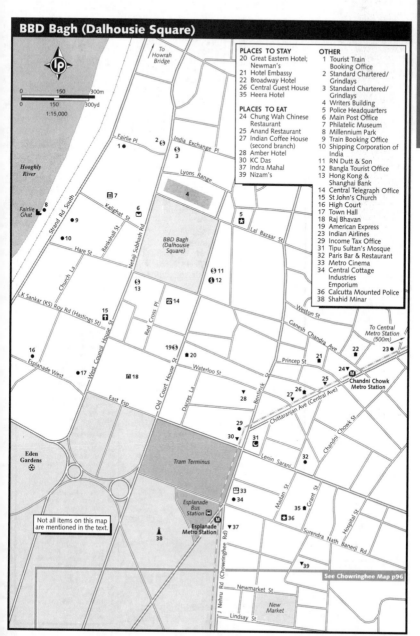

BBD Bagh (Dalhousie Square)

PLACES TO STAY
20 Great Eastern Hotel; Newman's
21 Hotel Embassy
22 Broadway Hotel
26 Central Guest House
35 Heera Hotel

PLACES TO EAT
24 Chung Wah Chinese Restaurant
25 Anand Restaurant
27 Indian Coffee House (second branch)
28 Amber Hotel
30 KC Das
37 Indra Mahal
39 Nizam's

OTHER
1 Tourist Train Booking Office
2 Standard Chartered/ Grindlays
3 Standard Chartered/ Grindlays
4 Writers Building
5 Police Headquarters
6 Main Post Office
7 Philatelic Museum
8 Millennium Park
9 Train Booking Office
10 Shipping Corporation of India
11 RN Dutt & Son
12 Bangla Tourist Office
13 Hong Kong & Shanghai Bank
14 Central Telegraph Office
15 St John's Church
16 High Court
17 Town Hall
18 Raj Bhavan
19 American Express
23 Indian Airlines
29 Income Tax Office
31 Tipu Sultan's Mosque
32 Paris Bar & Restaurant
33 Metro Cinema
34 Central Cottage Industries Emporium
36 Calcutta Mounted Police
38 Shahid Minar

To Howrah Bridge

Hooghly River

Fairlie Pl

India Exchange Pl

Lyons Range

Fairlie Ghat

Strand Rd South

Kalighat St

Bankshall St

Netaji Subhash Rd

Hare St

Church La

K Sankar (KS) Roy Rd (Hastings St)

Red Cross Pl

BBD Bagh (Dalhousie Square)

Lal Bazaar St

Weston St

Ganesh Chandra Ave

To Central Metro Station (500m)

West Council House St

Old Court House St

Dacres La

Waterloo St

Princep St

Chandni Chowk Metro Station

Esplanade West

East Esp

Bentinck

Chittaranjan Ave (Central Ave)

Chandni Chowk St

Eden Gardens

Tram Terminus

Lenin Sarani

Maidan St

Grant St

Esplanade Bus Station

Esplanade Metro Station

Hospital St

Surendra Nath Banerji Rd

Nehru Rd (Chowringhee Rd)

See Chowringhee Map p96

Newmarket St

New Market

Lindsay St

Not all items on this map are mentioned in the text.

0   150   300m
0   150   300yd
1:15,000

Chowringhee

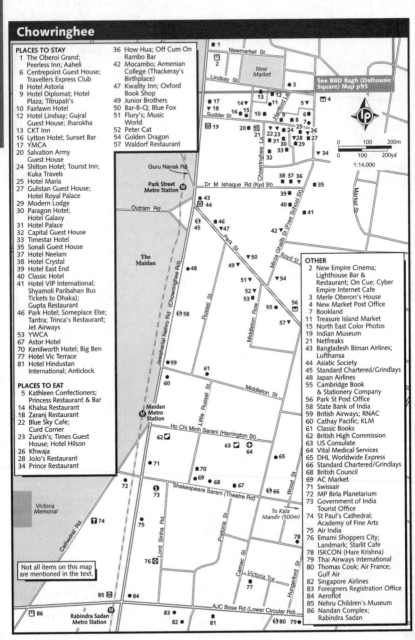

PLACES TO STAY
1 The Oberoi Grand;
  Peerless Inn; Aaheli
6 Centrepoint Guest House;
  Travellers Express Club
8 Hotel Astoria
9 Hotel Diplomat; Hotel
  Plaza; Titrupati's
10 Fairlawn Hotel
12 Hotel Lindsay; Gujral
  Guest House; Jharokha
13 CKT Inn
16 Lytton Hotel; Sunset Bar
17 YMCA
20 Salvation Army
  Guest House
24 Shilton Hotel; Tourist Inn;
  Kuka Travels
25 Hotel Maria
27 Gulistan Guest House;
  Hotel Royal Palace
29 Modern Lodge
30 Paragon Hotel;
  Hotel Galaxy
31 Hotel Palace
32 Capital Guest House
33 Timestar Hotel
35 Sonali Guest House
37 Hotel Neelam
38 Hotel Crystal
39 Hotel East End
40 Classic Hotel
41 Hotel VIP International;
  Shyamoli Paribahan Bus
  Tickets to Dhaka);
  Gupta Restaurant
46 Park Hotel; Someplace Else;
  Tantra; Trinca's Restaurant;
  Jet Airways
53 YWCA
67 Astor Hotel
70 Kenilworth Hotel; Big Ben
77 Hotel Vic Terrace
81 Hotel Hindustan
  International; Anticlock

PLACES TO EAT
5 Kathleen Confectioners;
  Princess Restaurant & Bar
14 Khalsa Restaurant
18 Zaranj Restaurant
22 Blue Sky Cafe;
  Curd Corner
23 Zurich's; Times Guest
  House; Hotel Hilson
26 Khwaja
28 JoJo's Restaurant
34 Prince Restaurant

36 How Hua; Off Cum On
  Rambo Bar
42 Mocambo; Armenian
  College (Thackeray's
  Birthplace)
47 Kwality Inn; Oxford
  Book Shop
49 Junior Brothers
50 Bar-B-Q; Blue Fox
51 Flury's; Music
  World
52 Peter Cat
54 Golden Dragon
57 Waldorf Restaurant

OTHER
2 New Empire Cinema;
  Lighthouse Bar &
  Restaurant; On Cue; Cyber
  Empire Internet Cafe
3 Merle Oberon's House
4 New Market Post Office
7 Bookland
11 Treasure Island Market
15 North East Color Photos
19 Indian Museum
21 Netfreaks
43 Bangladesh Biman Airlines;
  Lufthansa
44 Asiatic Society
45 Standard Chartered/Grindlays
48 Japan Airlines
55 Cambridge Book
  & Stationery Company
56 Park St Post Office
58 State Bank of India
59 British Airways; RNAC
60 Cathay Pacific; KLM
61 Classic Books
62 British High Commission
63 US Consulate
64 Vital Medical Services
65 DHL Worldwide Express
66 Standard Chartered/Grindlays
68 British Council
69 AC Market
71 Swissair
72 MP Birla Planetarium
73 Government of India
  Tourist Office
74 St Paul's Cathedral;
  Academy of Fine Arts
75 Air India
76 Emami Shoppers City;
  Landmark; Starlit Cafe
78 ISKCON (Hare Krishna)
79 Thai Airways International
80 Thomas Cook; Air France;
  Gulf Air
82 Singapore Airlines
83 Foreigners Registration Office
84 Aeroflot
85 Nehru Children's Museum
86 Nandan Complex;
  Rabindra Sadan

Not all items on this map
are mentioned in the text.

Colour and character abound in the Indian Himalaya. **Top Left:** In Sikkim, the Enchey Monastery is home to about 100 monks of the Nyingmapa order. **Top Right:** A young girl from Pulga in the Parbati Valley, Himachal Pradesh. **Middle Right:** A woman from McLeod Ganj, Himachal Pradesh. **Bottom:** A monk at morning puja in Thikse, Ladakh.

Spoilt for choice – bring a tent and revel in the five-star locations. **Top Left:** Miyar Glacier, on a challenging trek from Ladakh to Himachal Pradesh. **Top Right:** Lakeside at Dodi Tal, Uttaranchal. **Bottom:** Views of Chaukhamba Range from a campsite above Auli in Uttaranchal.

Major Trains from Kolkata

train no & name	departs (departure point)	arrives	sleeper/1st class (Rs)
To Dehra Dun/Haridwar			
3009 Doon Exp	8.15pm (H)	7.25am	311/1156
To Delhi			
2301 Rajdhani Exp*	5.00pm (H)	10.00am	1500/2470/4270
2203 Poova Exp	9.15am (H)	9.25pm (next day)	383/1080
To New Jalpaiguri (for Darjeeling & Sikkim)			
3143 *Darjeeling Mail*	7.15pm (S)	8.15am	210/565
5657 Kangchenjunga Exp	6.25am (S)	6.25pm	174/604
To Pathankot (for Dharamsala)			
3073 Himgiri Exp	11.00pm (H)	10.30am	43/1331

H – Howrah, S – Sealdah

*Fares on the Rajdhani are for AC Three Tier/AC Two Tier/AC First Class

To/From the Airport

The airport is 17km northeast of the city centre. It's possible to change money at the international terminal. In the adjacent domestic terminal, there's an accommodation booking service and a train reservation desk.

A public minibus (No S10) runs from BBD Bagh to the airport (Rs 10). The metro also goes out to Dum Dum, but stops 5km short of the airport. An onward bus/taxi to the airport costs Rs 5/50.

For a taxi from the airport, it's cheaper to go to the prepaid kiosk where you are assigned one. The fare is around Rs 160 to Sudder St. If travelling in the opposite direction, expect to pay 25% more.

Ladakh

Ladakh is a land of high passes on the borderland of India and Tibet. It is an integral part of the Jammu & Kashmir (J&K) state and consists of three main populated regions. The first is Leh and the upper Indus Valley. This is the cultural heartland of Ladakh where many *gompas* (Tibetan Buddhist monasteries) and forts reflect the deep Buddhist heritage of the region. The Zanskar Valley is the second region. Also with a Buddhist culture, it is a comparatively isolated valley to the south of the Indus Valley. The third main region of Ladakh includes Kargil and the Suru Valley, to the west of Leh and further down the Indus Valley. It was an integral part of Baltistan until 1947, and supports an Islamic culture that can be traced back to the 15th century, when the region was converted to Islam.

Geographically, Ladakh is one of the most rugged regions of the entire Himalaya Range. It is often referred to as the Trans-Himalaya because of its position between the Great Himalaya Range and the vast Tibetan Plateau. It is also one of India's highest regions, with altitudes, even in the depths of the valleys, rarely below 3000m.

The treks in all three regions appreciate Ladakh's cultural history and the rugged geography of the Trans-Himalaya. Most treks are demanding and at altitude, so trekkers should acclimatise in Leh and Padum before setting out.

CLIMATE

Ladakh is one of the driest regions in northern India. Leh, the capital of Ladakh, experiences an average of only 110mm of rainfall per year and heavy snowfalls are rare, making it one of the driest places in the Indian subcontinent. Ladakh's position to the north-east of the Himalaya Range isolates it from the Indian monsoon. However, areas to the south of the Indus Valley and closer to the Himalaya Range experience a higher rainfall. Padum, in the Zanskar Valley, is subject to the occasional heavy storm that breaks

Highlights

The 15th-century Spitok Gompa overlooks the Indus River.

- Witnessing herds of blue sheep high above the Markha Valley (p113)

- Visiting ancient gompas while trekking beyond the Indus Valley (p116)

- Crossing the high passes of the Zanskar Range for great views across the Trans-Himalaya (p123)

- Sharing a glass of butter tea or *chang* (barley beer) in the Buddhist villages throughout the region

over the Himalaya Range in July and August, while in winter the heavy snowfalls block the passes to the rest of Ladakh.

Ladakh is also the highest region in India, with elevations rarely below 3000m and often reaching above 3500m. This, and its northerly inland location, ensures extremely cold temperatures. In winter, the daytime temperatures are seldom above freezing.

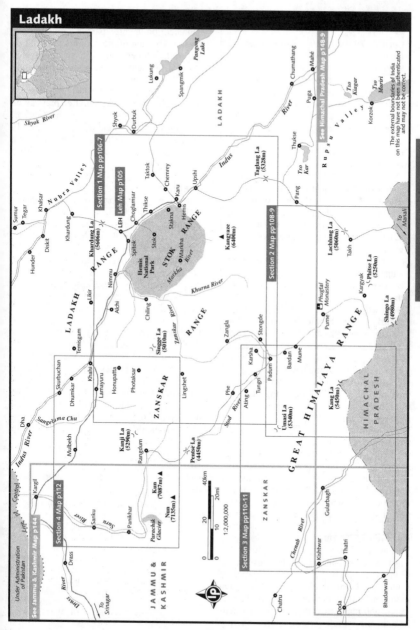

Ladakh

LADAKH

Shyok River

Panggong Lake

Lukung

Spangmik

LADAKH

River

Chumathang

Mahé

Tso Kiagar

Tso Moriri

Puga

Korzok

R u p s u   V a l l e y

Shyok

Durbuk

Section 1 Map pp106-7

Nubra Valley

Sumur
Tegar

Khalsar

Khardung La (5606m)

LEH Leh Map p105

Taktok

Chemrey

Karu

Upshi

Indus

Taglang La (5328km)

Tso Kar

Pang

Lachlung La (5060m)

To Manali

Diskit

Hunder

Khardung

Nimmu

R A N G E

Spitok

Stok

Hemis National Park

Choglamsar

Thikse

Stakna

Hemis

STOK

Markha

RANGE

Kangyaze (6400m)

Section 2 Map pp108-9

Takh

Phtse La (5250m)

Kargyak

L A D A K H

Likir

Temisgam

Alchi

Chiling

Markha River

Khurna River

Phugtal Monastery

Purne

Shingo La (4990m)

Sangelama Chu

Khalsi

Skurbuchan

Dhumkar

Lamayuru

Honupatta

Photaksar

Singge La (5010m)

Zanskar River

RANGE

Zangla

Stongde

Karsha

Bardan

Mune

ZANSKAR

Lingshet

Phe

Ating

Tungri

Padum

Kang La (5450m)

G R E A T   H I M A L A Y A   R A N G E

H I M A C H A L   P R A D E S H

Umasi La (5340m)

Zild River

Dha

Mulbekh

Indus River

Rangdum

Kanji La (5290m)

Pentse La (4450m)

Section 3 Map pp110-11

ZANSKAR

Kargil

Sanku

Panikhar

Suru River

Kun (7087m) ▲

Nun (7135m) ▲

Parachik Glacier

Section 4 Map p112

Drass

J A M M U   &   K A S H M I R

Drass River

To Srinagar

Under Administration of Pakistan

See Jammu & Kashmir Map p144

Line   of   Control

See Himachal Pradesh Map p148-9

Gularbagh

Chenab River

Kishtwar

Thatri

Chatru

Doda

Bhadarwah

0   40km
0   10   20   20mi
1:2,000,000

LADAKH

Warning

Ladakh's sensitive borders with Pakistan and China have been a source of continual problems. India's war with China in 1962 meant that Ladakh was not open to foreigners until 1974 and major regions of eastern Ladakh were off limits until the early 1990s.

India's ongoing dispute with Pakistan is the main reason for the huge military presence in Leh and other areas. This war is being fought on the Siachen Glacier in the eastern Karakoram, and is costing around $1 million a day. This area is completely off limits to foreigners.

In May 1999, fighting erupted along the India-Pakistan ceasefire line close to the town of Kargil. The Kargil-Srinagar road was closed for the rest of the year. It also severely disrupted traffic on the road from Kargil to Padum and the Zanskar Valley.

While a sense of normality has returned to Kargil, we recommend you check the latest advice from your embassy before travelling to this part of India.

Similarly, the Umasi La trek (pp137–40) should only be attempted after checking the travel advisories regarding the Kishtwar region.

The maximum daytime temperatures in Leh are around -3°C in January, while at night they can fall to -15°C. In spring, temperatures begin to rise, and by early summer they reach the mid-20°Cs.

By autumn (early-Sept–mid-Oct), day temperatures fall to between 10° and 15°C, while any instability caused by the Indian monsoon gives way to settled conditions. Towards the end of October, there is usually one significant pre-winter storm lasting two or three days, while the first of the heavy winter snows fall in December.

INFORMATION
When to Trek

The trekking season extends from early June to late October. In July, the combination of a late spring snowmelt and the occasional monsoon downpour may cause river levels to rise and make trekking difficult, particularly in the remote gorges. Storms in July and August are not uncommon and snowfalls can occur on the high passes throughout the season. The first of the winter snows fall by the mid-October, although an unseasonal storm in September can bring a premature end to the season.

Bear in mind that the Rohtang Pass on the road linking Manali and Leh may not be open until at least mid-June. In the Zanskar, the snow on the Pentse La is normally cleared for vehicles by late June, although it is possible to trek across the pass earlier in the season.

Maps

Refer to both the Leomann 1:200,000 series and US military U502 1:250,000 series for planning and trekking. See the Planning section for each trek for details of specific map requirements.

Note that Leomann's Ladakh sheets do not meet up with their Himachal Pradesh ones! Fortunately, the 'gaps' in the Himalaya Range are irrelevant to most of the treks in this chapter.

Buying Maps Neither the Leomann nor the US military series are available in Leh and must be purchased prior to arriving in India. However, copies of the Nelles Verlag 1:350,000 *Ladakh & Zanskar* and a locally published trekking map of Ladakh can be purchased in Leh for Rs 200 each. Although neither has as much detail as the larger-scale sheets, they at least cover all the main trails over the Himalaya Range.

Books

For a cultural and historical background of the region, read:

The Cultural History of Ladakh, Volumes 1 & 2 by Snellgrove and Skorupski
A History of Ladakh by AH Francke
Himalayan Art by Madanjeet Singh
Ladakh by Heinrich Harrer
Ladakh: Crossroads of High Asia by Janet Rizvi
Himalayan Caravans, also by Janet Rizvi, which has a wealth of information on the former caravans trading between Ladakh and Central Asia
A Journey into Ladakh by Andrew Harvey, which provides some relevant spiritual reflections while on the trail

Watching Wildlife

While trekking across the Trans-Himalaya region of Ladakh, you may spot **bharal** grazing the high ridges, while **ibex** or **urial** may also be seen from a distance in the more sheltered valleys. The best time to view these species is October. Schedule time in the vicinity of the high passes (for bharal) and in the remote valleys (for ibex and urial).

If you have ambitions to see a **snow leopard**, Ladakh and the Zanskar have the largest concentration in the West Himalaya. However, you will need plenty of time and luck! In the early 1990s, two eminent naturalists from Delhi spent two winters in Ladakh before recording their first photos of the snow leopard at the head of the Markha Valley. Equally as elusive is the **lynx**, with a short tail and black-tipped ears, which also preys on bharal.

In early winter, packs of **wolves** may be heard (but seldom seen) near the villages, perhaps searching for a domestic yak that has strayed from the herd. Wild **yaks** are found in the vast open plateaus of Chang-chenmo, while **kiangs** are found in the remote regions of Rupshu and Changtang.

Brown bears may be sighted in the remote valleys in the vicinity of Rangdum and areas of the Zanskar Valley. This is also the habitat of **marmots** whose shrill whistles alert other wildlife when danger approaches.

The birdlife of Ladakh includes many species that migrate from the Indian subcontinent to Central Asia in the summer. They include **black-necked cranes**, which breed in the lakes of eastern Ladakh. The **citrine wagtail** is another summer visitor, as is the **horned lark**, which is attracted to the vast high-altitude meadows. Large flocks of **grandala** also favour high-altitude meadows, as do **streaked** and **great rosefinches** and **common ravens**.

Tibetan partridges, **snowcocks** and **chukars** can be found in the scant high-altitude undergrowth. This is also the habitat of **lammergeiers**, while **golden eagles** prey on marmots, **pikas** and even small **goats**. **Himalayan griffons**, with their distinctive upturned wings, may be seen searching for prey high above the scant pastures, a habitat shared by another bird of prey – the **merlin**. **Tibetan snowfinches** and **black-billed magpies** are common in the villages of Ladakh, while **white-tailed rubythroats** are found alongside the mountain streams.

The wetter regions of Ladakh are to the immediate west of the Himalaya Range. Here there is an abundance of flowering plants, including a variety of **geraniums**, **aquilegias** and **lousewarts**. The forested regions are confined to the remote valleys where **willows**, **poplars** and **rose bushes** thrive at altitudes between 3000m and 3500m. This also provides a natural haven for wildlife, including birds, although the low rainfall prevents a wide range of wildflowers growing. Heading north, the meagre rainfall peters out and the flowering plants are mostly confined to the banks of irrigation channels.

You can find many of these books at Leh bookshops, including the **Otdon Bookshop** and **Bookworm** on Old Fort Rd, and the **Leh Ling Bookshop** on Main Bazaar Rd.

Information Sources

For information about road conditions, contact the **PWD Office** *(Fort Rd, Leh)* or go to the local bus station, where the drivers will have the latest. For trekking information, contact the **J&K Tourist Office** *(☎ 52297)* in Leh, 3km from the centre of town on the road to the airport. For general inquiries, the small counter in the same building as the Foreign

Exchange is far handier. Otherwise, you could visit one of the many trekking agencies in Leh.

Place Names

The transliteration of Ladakhi names has meant that place names in guidebooks and brochures are often spelt in a number of ways. For example, the famous gompa at Thikse is also known as *Tiksey*, *Thiksey* or *Tiksey*. Similarly, the southern region of Ladakh is referred to as the *Zanskar*, *Zangskar* and *Zaskar*. Generally, if the place sounds the same then it is the same.

Leh & the Indus Valley

Leh and the upper Indus Valley is the cultural heart of Ladakh. This is a region whose cultural horizons are closer to Tibet than to India. Ancient Buddhist heritage is reflected in the numerous gompas and forts atop sugarloaf mountains in this rugged, barren land. The region is drained by the Indus River, where outlying valleys and passes have been followed by generations of pilgrims and traders, and successive rulers have attempted to expand the borders of Ladakh way beyond the Indus Valley.

Today, the borders are still subject to political dispute. Since the Chinese occupation of Tibet in the 1950s, Ladakh's connections with Tibet have been severed, while India's war with China in 1962 further exacerbated the problem. Ladakh remained closed to foreigners until 1974.

Treks out of the Indus Valley head south, crossing the Stok Range en route to the Markha Valley. Treks from Lamayuru cross the outlying ridges of the Zanskar Range. There are fine views to the Ladakh Range and the many peaks and glaciers of the East Karakoram Range. To the south, views across the Zanskar Range extend to the snowcapped peaks of the Himalaya.

HISTORY

The history of crossing the high passes and trails across Ladakh can be traced to its original inhabitants – the Khampa – who roamed from Tibet across the windswept passes in search of new pastures. They settled, for example, on the Nimaling plains in the upper Markha Valley and discovered verdant grazing areas close to the Baralacha La and the Zanskar Valley along routes that are still followed today.

The trails along the confines of the Indus valley were followed by pilgrims from the time of the Third Buddhist Congress in Kashmir in the 3rd century BC. The trails beyond Lamayuru and Leh were also explored, although it was not until the coming of the Mons (Buddhist missionaries from India) that settlements were established. In the following centuries, migrations from lower down the Indus Valley facilitated the introduction of irrigation to Leh and the upper Indus Valley.

By the 7th century, there was a gradual migration of Tibetans from Guge (West Tibet). Forts and palaces were constructed and Ladakh's influence began to stretch beyond the Indus Valley. The Tantric sage Padmasambhava wandered the trails along the main mountain valleys of the West Himalaya. In the 11th century, the renowned teacher Ringchen Brangpo is said to have established many of the monastic sites in the remote locations across Ladakh and Tibet.

In the following centuries, a new era of pilgrims, traders and armies travelled between Leh, Guge, Spiti and Lahaul and regularly crossed the high passes and remote gorges south of the Indus Valley. While trail information was passed on through generations of pilgrims and traders, it was not until the 19th century that European travellers familiarised themselves with Ladakh's topography. Notable examples include the travels of Moorcroft and Trebeck in the early 1820s; the journeys of GT Vigne between 1835 and 1838; and the Boundary Commission of Cunningham, Stratchey and Thomson in the late 1840s.

The Great Trigonometrical Survey of India was completed in Ladakh in 1863, filling many gaps about the formidable mountainscape. By then, a regular flow of Europeans reached Leh via Kashmir and the Zoji La or via the Kullu Valley and the Baralacha La. Their horizons were set on the Karakoram Pass and the markets of Central Asia, and the routes were followed with increasing regularity until the borders closed 50 years ago.

NATURAL HISTORY

The region's main mountains are the Ladakh, Stok and Zanskar Ranges. Another major feature is the Hemis National Park, stretching from the south banks of the Indus Valley across to the Markha Valley and east to the Zanskar River.

There are many areas beyond the villages where the willow and bush provide a haven

Festivals of Ladakh & Zanskar

Festivals are an integral part of Ladakh's culture. Normally extending over a couple of days, they commemorate an important event in the religious calendar or mark the end of the harvest period. Traditionally the festivals were held in winter to coincide with the Tibetan New Year, while also providing a respite from the intense cold. A notable exception to this is the famous Hemis Festival, which celebrates the life and teaching of the sage Padmasambhava in June or July.

Nowadays, with tourism playing an important part in the local economy, some gompas have changed their festivals to fall in the summer. There is also the annual Ladakh Festival, held in Leh during the first two weeks of September.

These are the festivals scheduled for Ladakh and Zanskar until 2007:

festival	2003	2004	2005	2006	2007
Chemray	21–22 Nov	10–11Nov	29–30 Nov	18–19 Nov	7–8 Nov
Hemis	9–10 July	27–28 June	17–18 June	6–7 July	25–26 June
Karcha	26–27 July	14–15 July	3–4 July	22–23 July	11–12 July
Lamayuru	15–16 July	4–5 July	23–24 June	12–13 July	2–3 July
Leh & Likir	28 Feb–1 Mar	18–19 Feb	6–7 Feb	26–27 Feb	15–16 Feb
Losar*	24 Dec	12 Dec	1 Jan	21 Dec	10 Dec
Phyang	31 Jul–1 Aug	19–20 July	7–8 Aug	27–28 July	16–17 July
Sani	11–12 Aug	30–31 July	18–19 Aug	8–9 Aug	29–30 July
Stok	12–13 Mar	29 Feb–1 Mar	17–18 Feb	8–9 Mar	25–26 Feb
Thikse	12–13 Nov	31Oct–1 Nov	18–19 Nov	8–9 Nov	28–29 Oct

*Losar is celebrated at all gompas

LADAKH

for birdlife. The black-billed magpie is a common visitor to the villages. Birds of prey, including the lammergeier, soar above the highest pastures.

ACCESS TOWN
Leh
☎ 01982 • alt 3505m

The capital of Ladakh, Leh is in a small, fertile valley north of the Indus River. The town is also at the base of the Khardung La, the first of the high passes formerly crossed by trading caravans en route to the Karakoram Pass and the markets of Central Asia. Although these trading routes have been closed since 1947, the Leh Bazaar retains much of its character, while the Victory Fort and King's Palace provide a fitting reminder of Ladakh's rich cultural history.

For tourist information in Leh, see Information Sources (p101).

Supplies & Equipment It is advisable to purchase your food and fuel supplies in Leh. There is no shortage of fresh fruit and vegetables in the market, which also has a wide range of tinned and packed food. Supplies of flour, rice, sugar and cooking oil should also be purchased. Biscuits and basics are all you can rely on buying at the trailhead or on the trail.

Good-quality trekking gear is normally reserved for organised groups, and the leftovers are hardly recommended. It is advisable to bring your own tent, sleeping bag and insulated mat. Kerosene stoves and cooking gear can be purchased in Leh and may be sold back at a discount at the end of the trek. A rudimentary medical kit can also be compiled in Leh.

Trekking Agents Leh has many agencies operating in summer. Most are run by knowledgeable and friendly staff. Recommended agencies include:

Gypsy's World Adventure (☎ 52735;
  White House, Fort Rd)
Rimo Expeditions (☎ 53257, *Hotel Kamglachan*)
Mountain Journeys (☎ 51248, *Main Bazaar Rd*)

Explore Himalayas (☎ 52727, Main Bazaar Rd)
Ecotours (☎ 52918; Shamshu Complex, Fort Rd)

Most agencies in Leh will offer a complete package, including food, a guide and a cook, horses, tents and all cooking equipment. Charges range from US$30 to US$40 per day per person for groups between two and four. Expect prices to drop to US$25 to US$35 for larger groups.

Alternatively an agent may be able to organise pack horses or mules for you; budget for a minimum of Rs 300 per day per horse. Allow a few days for arrangements to be made as a message may have to be sent to the villager, who may need time to get the horses to the trailhead. It is also worth remembering that prices will rise during the harvest period in September, when many villagers are fully engaged in their fields and have little inclination to undertake a trek.

Places to Stay & Eat There are a number of guesthouses and hotels in Leh. Most are run by friendly Ladakhi families and are often an extension of their family home. These places are generally clean, basic and of solid construction in the traditional two-storey, whitewashed style. Leh is not a big place, and you can check out a few hotels on foot in an hour or so; see the Leh map. You should be able to bargain for considerably less than the government rates, except in busy July and August. The **Old Ladakhi Guest House** (☎ 52951), in the Old Town area, is recommended. It charges from Rs 200.

Changspa, about 2km northwest of the Old Town, is a popular area for trekkers. Guesthouses include the **Eagle Guest House** (☎ 53074), charging Rs 100 to Rs 250; **Asia Guest House** (☎ 53403), Rs 250 to Rs 500; and **Oriental Guest House** (☎ 53153), Rs 300 to Rs 500.

More upmarket hotels include the **Omisa La** (☎ 52119), which offers discounted rates of around Rs 800 when rooms are available; and the **Lotus Hotel** (☎ 53129) in Upper Karzoo, with similar rates.

Most hotels have restaurants offering a wide range of dishes. In the Main Bazaar area is the **Amdo Restaurant**. The **Summer Harvest**, near the Hotel Yak Tail; the **Tibetan Kitchen** in the Hotel Tso-Khar; and the **Hotel Ibex Bar & Restaurant** are all popular choices.

Getting There & Away Choose from air or bus travel when heading to Leh.

Air From Delhi, daily Alliance Air (US$110) and Jet Air flights (US$112) go to Leh (June–Sept). At other times, flights operate three or four times a week depending on demand. From Srinagar, the weekly service to Leh (US$55) is heavily booked. There is also a twice weekly flight from Jammu (US$65).

Remember that Leh is 3500m above sea level and the altitude will take its toll for the first couple of days. Take it easy and allow time for acclimatisation before trekking. If you're flying out of Leh, note that flights are sometimes cancelled because of bad weather. Allow for a day or two in Delhi before catching your flight home.

Road The military road from Manali to Leh is generally open from mid-June to early October. It's a two-day drive; the A-class bus (Rs 1000) halts overnight at the tented camp at Sarchu, while the B-class bus (Rs 400) stops overnight at Keylong. The alternative is to hire a 4WD for up to Rs 11,500 one way.

The Leh to Srinagar highway was an option until the outbreak of political unrest in Kashmir in 1989.

Local Transport The bus station south of Leh Bazaar services most of the outlying villages and gompas. If you are carrying a lot of gear, arrive early, as space on the roof is often as limited as space inside the bus. Timetables are altered frequently, so it is best to enquire at the bus station the day before travel. Prices and details are included in the Planning section for each trek.

Taxis or 4WDs are a convenient alternative. If you band together with others, the fare is reasonable. There are fixed rates for such outings and you will have to bargain hard to get a discount.

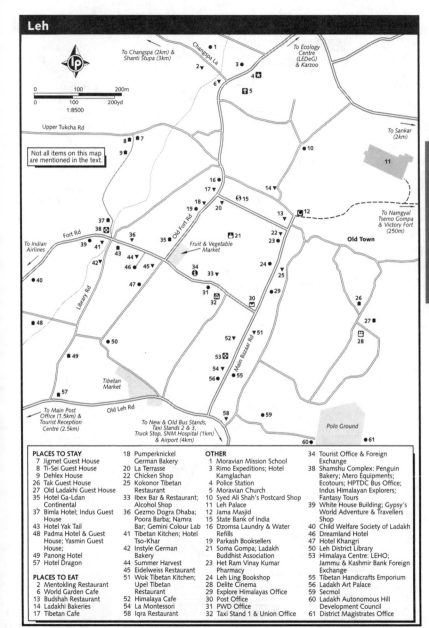

LADAKH

Leh

To Changspa (2km) &
Shanti Stupa (3km)

Changspa La

To Ecology
Centre
(LEDeG)
& Karzoo

0   100   200m
0   100   200yd
1:8500

Upper Tukcha Rd

Not all items on this map
are mentioned in the text.

To Sankar
(2km)

To Indian
Airlines

Fort Rd

Old Fort Rd

Fruit & Vegetable
Market

Old Town

To Namgyal
Tsemo Gompa
& Victory Fort
(250m)

Library Rd

Main Bazaar Rd

Tibetan
Market

To Main Post
Office (1.5km) &
Tourist Reception
Centre (2.5km)

Old Leh Rd

To New & Old Bus Stands,
Taxi Stands 2 & 3,
Truck Stop, SNM Hospital (1km)
& Airport (4km)

Polo Ground

PLACES TO STAY
7 Jigmet Guest House
8 Ti-Sei Guest House
9 Dehlex House
26 Tak Guest House
27 Old Ladakhi Guest House
35 Hotel Ga-Ldan
   Continental
37 Bimla Hotel; Indus Guest
   House
43 Hotel Yak Tail
48 Padma Hotel & Guest
   House; Yasmin Guest
   House;
49 Panong Hotel
57 Hotel Dragon

PLACES TO EAT
2 Mentokling Restaurant
6 World Garden Cafe
13 Budshah Restaurant
14 Ladakhi Bakeries
17 Tibetan Cafe

18 Pumperknickel
   German Bakery
20 La Terrasse
22 Chicken Shop
25 Kokonor Tibetan
   Restaurant
33 Ibex Bar & Restaurant;
   Alcohol Shop
36 Gezmo Dogra Dhaba;
   Poora Barba; Namra
   Bar; Gemini Colour Lab
41 Tibetan Kitchen; Hotel
   Tso-Khar
42 Instyle German
   Bakery
44 Summer Harvest
45 Eidelweiss Restaurant
51 Wok Tibetan Kitchen;
   Upel Tibetan
   Restaurant
52 Himalaya Cafe
54 La Montessori
58 Iqra Restaurant

OTHER
1 Moravian Mission School
3 Rimo Expeditions; Hotel
   Kamglachan
4 Police Station
5 Moravian Church
10 Syed Ali Shah's Postcard Shop
11 Leh Palace
12 Jama Masjid
15 State Bank of India
16 Dzomsa Laundry & Water
   Refills
19 Parkash Booksellers
21 Soma Gompa; Ladakh
   Buddhist Association
23 Het Ram Vinay Kumar
   Pharmacy
24 Leh Ling Bookshop
28 Delite Cinema
29 Explore Himalayas Office
30 Post Office
31 PWD Office
32 Taxi Stand 1 & Union Office

34 Tourist Office & Foreign
   Exchange
38 Shamshu Complex: Penguin
   Bakery; Mero Equipments;
   Ecotours; HPTDC Bus Office;
   Indus Himalayan Explorers;
   Fantasy Tours
39 White House Building; Gypsy's
   World Adventure & Travellers
   Shop
40 Child Welfare Society of Ladakh
46 Dreamland Hotel
47 Hotel Khangri
50 Leh District Library
53 Himalaya Centre: LEHO;
   Jammu & Kashmir Bank Foreign
   Exchange
55 Tibetan Handicrafts Emporium
56 Ladakh Art Palace
59 Secmol
60 Ladakh Autonomous Hill
   Development Council
61 District Magistrates Office

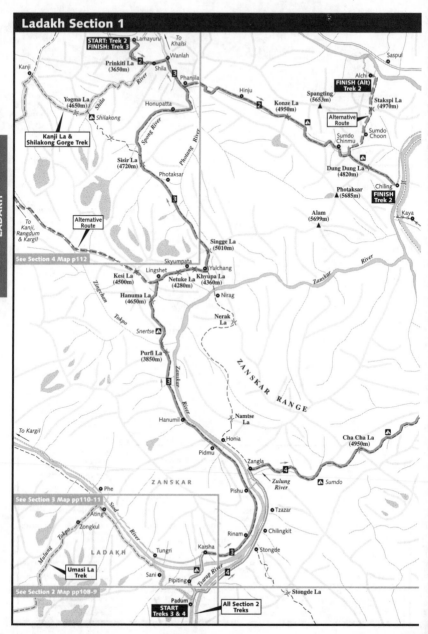

Ladakh Section 1

LADAKH

START: Trek 2
FINISH: Trek 3

Lamayuru

To Khalsi

Kanji

Prinkiti La
(3650m)

Wanlah

Shila

Phanjila

Saspul

Alchi

FINISH (Alt)
Trek 2

Yogma La
(4650m)

Shila

Hinju

Konze La
(4950m)

Spangting
(5663m)

Stakspi La
(4970m)

Shilakong

Honupatta

Alternative
Route

Sumdo
Choon

Kanji La &
Shilakong Gorge Trek

Spong River

Photang River

Sumdo
Chinmu

Sisir La
(4720m)

Photaksar

Dung Dung La
(4820m)

Chiling

See Section 4 Map p112

Alternative
Route

Photaksar
(5685m)

FINISH
Trek 2

To
Kanji,
Rangdum
& Kargil

Alam
(5699m)

Kaya

Singge La
(5010m)

Skyumpata

Yulchang

Lingshet

Zanskar
River

Kesi La
(4500m)

Netuke La
(4280m)

Khyupa La
(4360m)

Hanuma La
(4650m)

Nirag

Zanskar

Tokpo

Nerak
La

Snertse

Purfi La
(3850m)

Z A N S K A R   R A N G E

Zanskar

River

Hanumil

Namtse
La

Cha Cha La
(4950m)

Honia

Pidmu

Zangla

Sumdo

To Kargil

Phe

Z A N S K A R

Pishu

Zulung
River

See Section 3 Map pp110-11

Syad
River

Ating

Zongkul

Malung
Tokpo

Tokpo

L A D A K H

Tungri

Karsha

Tzazar

Rinam

Chilingkit

Stongde

Umasi La
Trek

Sani

Pipiting

Tsarap River

Stongde La

See Section 2 Map pp108-9

Padum

START
Treks 3 & 4

All Section 2
Treks

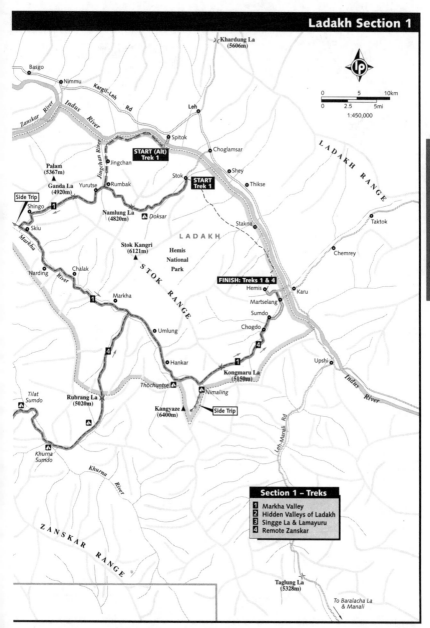

Ladakh Section 1

Khardung La
(5606m)

Basgo

Nimmu

Kargil–Leh Rd

Leh

Spitok

Choglamsar

START (Alt)
Trek 1

Jingchan

Palam
(5367m)

Shey

Ganda La
(4920m)

Rumbak

Stok

START
Trek 1

Thikse

Side Trip

Shingo

Yurutse

Namlung La
(4820m)

Doksar

LADAKH RANGE

Skiu

Stakna

Taktok

LADAKH

Chemrey

Stok Kangri
(6121m)

Hemis
National
Park

Narding

Chalak

FINISH: Treks 1 & 4

Markha

Hemis

Karu

Martselang

Sumdo

Umlung

Chogdo

Upshi

Hankar

Kongmaru La
(5150m)

Indus River

Rubrang La
(5020m)

Thochuntse

Nimaling

Tilat
Sumdo

Kangyaze
(6400m)

Side Trip

Khurna
Sumdo

Leh–Manali Rd

Khurna River

Section 1 – Treks

1 Markha Valley
2 Hidden Valleys of Ladakh
3 Singge La & Lamayuru
4 Remote Zanskar

ZANSKAR RANGE

Taglung La
(5328m)

To Baralacha La
& Manali

0   5   10km
0   2.5   5mi
1:450,000

LADAKH

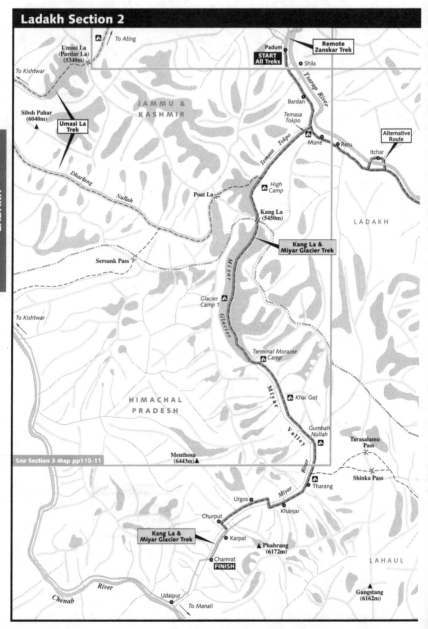

Ladakh Section 2

To Ating

Umasi La
(Pardar La)
(5340m)

To Kishtwar

Padum
**START
All Treks**

**Remote
Zanskar Trek**

Shila

Bardan

JAMMU &
KASHMIR

Tsarap River

Sibsh Pahar
(6040m)

**Umasi La
Trek**

Temasa
Tokpo

Temasa Tokpo

Mune   Reru

Itchar

**Alternative
Route**

Dharlang

Nullah

Poat La

*High
Camp*

Kang La
(5450m)

LADAKH

Sersank Pass

**Kang La &
Miyar Glacier Trek**

*Glacier
Camp 1*

Miyar Glacier

To Kishtwar

*Terminal Moraine
Camp*

HIMACHAL
PRADESH

Miyar Valley River

Khai Got

*Gumbah
Nullah*

Tarasalamu
Pass

See Section 3 Map pp110-11

Menthosa
(6443m)▲

Shinka Pass

Tharang

Urgos

Miyar River

Khanjar

Churput

**Kang La &
Miyar Glacier Trek**

Karpat   ▲Phabrang
(6172m)

Chamrat
FINISH

LAHAUL

Udaipur

To Manali

Chenab River

▲
Gangstang
(6162m)

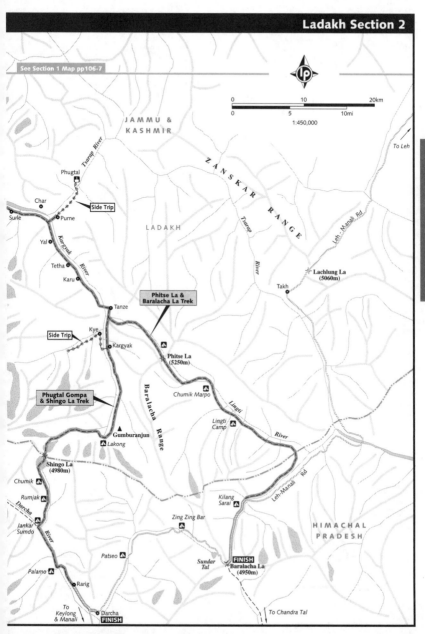

See Section 1 Map pp106-7

0   10   20km
0   5   10mi
1:450,000

To Leh

JAMMU &
KASHMIR

Tsarap River

Phugtal

Char

Side Trip

Surle

Purne

LADAKH

ZANSKAR RANGE

Tsarap River

Leh–Manali Rd

Yal

Karyuk River

Tetha

Karu

Lachlung La
(5060m)

Takh

Tanze

Phitse La &
Baralacha La Trek

Side Trip

Kye

Kargyak

Phitse La
(5250m)

Baralacha Range

Chumik Marpo

Lingti

Phugtal Gompa
& Shingo La Trek

Gumburanjun
Lakong

Lingti
Camp

Lingti River

Shingo La
(4980m)

Chumik

Leh–Manali Rd

Rumjak

Kilang
Sarai

Darcha

Jankar
Sumdo

River

Zing Zing Bar

HIMACHAL
PRADESH

Palamo

Rarig

Patseo

Sundar
Tal

FINISH
Baralacha La
(4950m)

To
Keylong
& Manali

Darcha
FINISH

To Chandra Tal

LADAKH

LADAKH

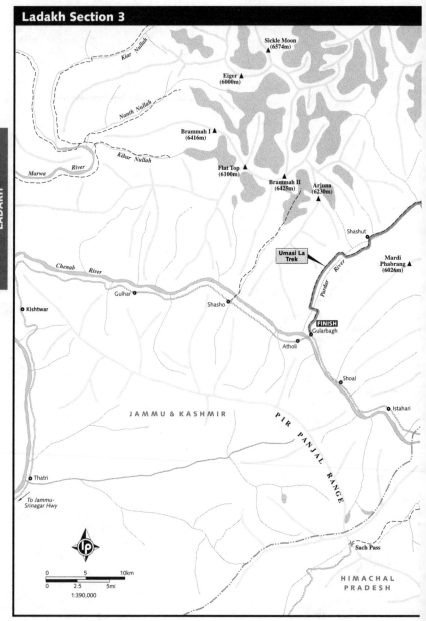

Ladakh Section 3

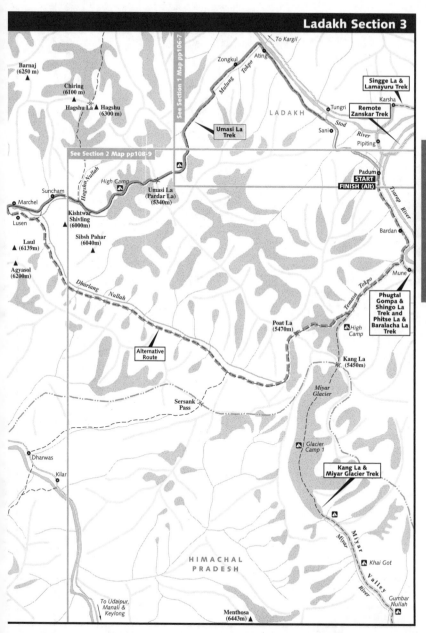

Ladakh Section 3

LADAKH

Barnaj (6250 m)

Chiring (6100 m)

Hagshu La ▲ Hagshu (6300 m)

See Section 1 Map pp106-7

To Kargil

Zongkul   Ating

Malung   Tokpo

Singge La & Lamayuru Trek

Karsha

LADAKH

Tungri

Remote Zanskar Trek

Umasi La Trek

Stod

Sani

River

Pipiting

See Section 2 Map pp108-9

Hagshu Nullah

High Camp

Umasi La (Pardar La) (5340m)

Padum
START
FINISH (Alt)

Suncham

Marchel

Lusen

Laul ▲ (6139m)

Agyasol (6200m)

Kishtwar Shivling (6000m)

Sibsh Pahar (6040m)

Dharlang   Nullah

Bardan

Tsarap River

Mune

Phugtal Gompa & Shingo La Trek and Phitse La & Baralacha La Trek

Tsarap Tokpo

Poat La (5470m)

High Camp

Alternative Route

Kang La (5450m)

Miyar Glacier

Sersank Pass

Glacier Camp 1

Dharwas

Kilar

Kang La & Miyar Glacier Trek

HIMACHAL PRADESH

Miyar

Khai Got

Valley

To Udaipur, Manali & Keylong

Miyar River

Menthosa (6443m) ▲

Gumbar Nullah

LADAKH

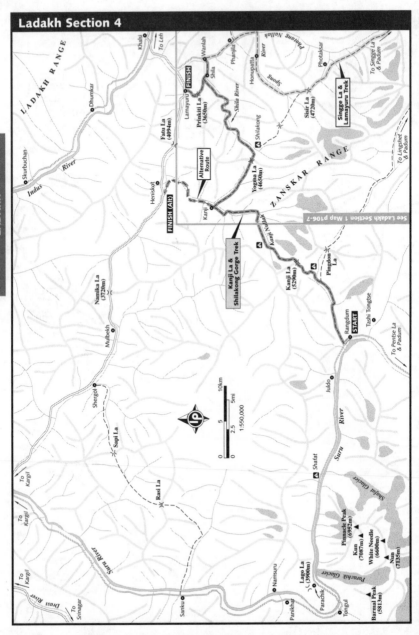

Ladakh Section 4

Markha Valley

Duration	8 days
Distance	106km
Difficulty	moderate–demanding
Start	Stok
Finish	Hemis
Nearest Town	Leh (pp103–5)
Public Transport	yes

Summary Ladakh's most popular trek, traversing the Stok Range and visiting Buddhist villages and gompas.

While this trek is easily accessible from Leh, it is by no means easy. Acclimatisation is the key to success, particularly as there are three pass crossings in the 5000m range. Spending extra time in Leh before commencing the trek is recommended. If short on time, consider the alternative route out of Spitok for the first two stages before ascending the Ganda La (4920m).

Impressive views from the passes extend north to the Ladakh Range and the East Karakoram and south across the rugged Zanskar Range to the snowcapped peaks of the Himalaya Range.

This trek in the Hemis National Park leads through many Buddhist villages where villagers supplement their traditional income by erecting parachute-tent accommodation (supplied courtesy of the Indian Air Force) or allocating small tracts of land for camping. During July and August, these campsites may be crowded. However, beyond the villages, there are plenty of campsites where you can gain a sense of isolation.

PLANNING
When to Trek
This trek can be undertaken from early June to mid-October.

What to Bring
Whether you bring a tent depends on your choice of overnight shelter. Whichever option you select, ensure you have a good sleeping bag and sleeping mat. If camping, bring a supply of food, a stove and sufficient kerosene for the entire trek.

Maps
Refer to the Leomann series 1:200,000 *Sheet 3 (Leh, Zanskar and Nubra Valley)*. Also refer to Nelles Verlag 1:350,000 *Ladakh & Zanskar* sheet and the US military U502 series 1:250,000 maps *NI 43-08 ref Leh* and *43-12 ref Martselang*.

Accommodation
If planning a night in Stok, there is the comfortable *Hotel Highland* with doubles for Rs 700. There are also a number of smaller guesthouses. There are no guesthouses at Hemis but there are several places to camp either on the outskirts of the village or in the outdoor restaurant next to the gompa.

On the trek, tea stalls or similar basic shelter is available in most of the villages, including Rumbak, Shingo, Skiu, Markha, Hankar and Sumdo. In and beyond the villages, there are also many parachute tents offering tea, soft drinks and accommodation. However, from mid-September to early June, many of the parachute tents are taken down. There are plenty of camping areas in the villages where you can expect to pay around Rs 50 per night to pitch your tent.

GETTING TO/FROM THE TREK
Bus services to Stok depart Leh at 8am and 5pm daily (Rs 15, one hour), while 4WDs cost Rs 320. From Hemis, the daily bus to the Leh Bazaar leaves at around 11am (Rs 15, 1½ to two hours). The 4WD fare is Rs 825.

THE TREK (See map pp106–7)
Day 1: Stok to Doksar
3–4 hours, 10km

On arrival at Stok, allow time to visit the **Stok Palace** (3520m) at the entrance to the village. It was built in the 1840s to house the Ladakhi royal family after they had been exiled from Leh by the Dogra army. The museum has a remarkable display of ornaments from the royal family, plus *thangkas* (Buddhist religious paintings), traditional clothing and jewellery. Entry costs Rs 30. The gompa, which has some fine masks and frescoes, is behind the museum.

Head towards the entrance of the Stok Gorge about 3km south of the village. The

LADAKH

trail gradually ascends the true left of the gorge for a further 3km before crossing the almost-dry riverbed a number of times. The crossings are well marked by stone cairns – the abundance of horse and sheep dropping will also show that you are on the right track!

From the entrance to the gorge it is around two hours to the shepherd encampment at **Doksar** (4440m). Water is at a premium here, particularly later in the season and a trickle may have to suffice for the overnight camp.

Alternative Route: Spitok to Rumbak
6–7 hours, 22km
If you have doubts about acclimatisation, consider the alternative trek for Days 1 and 2, which bypasses the Namlung La. The trek commences from Spitok gompa (just below Leh airport). It then crosses the bridge over the Indus River before following an undulating trail on the true left bank of the Indus for 6km to 7km to the confluence with the Jingchan River. Follow the trail up the Jingchan Valley to **Jingchan** village (3750m). On the following day, ascend to Rumbak and Yurutse.

Day 2: Doksar to Yurutse via Namlung La
5–6 hours, 13km
The trail to Namlung La heads up the scree slope to the west of the camp. Look out for blue sheep grazing the meagre vegetation. Just above the camp, there are fine views towards the Stok Kangri, while to the north the views extend beyond the Indus Valley to the Ladakh Range.

Namlung La (4820m) is a double pass, consisting of two rocky ridges about 500m apart. The second ridge to the west is the true pass, marked by colourful prayer flags. Panoramic views stretch down the Indus Valley. To the west, trails in the vicinity of the Ganda La can be appreciated.

The outlying fields of **Rumbak** village (3950m) are about 1km below the pass. The one-hour descent is steep in places (particularly the first 400m over loose scree) before the trail heads to the true right of the valley. If trekking from Stok to Rumbak in one day, a number of *campsites* are above the village.

From Rumbak, cross the bridge over the Jingchan River and follow the trail on the true left of the valley to the settlement of **Yurutse** (4180m). Camping and accommodation may be at a premium here, so follow the trail beyond the village for about 2km to the first of a series of established *campsites* at approximately 4300m.

Day 3: Yurutse to Skiu via Ganda La
8 hours, 18km
Depending on your campsite location, follow the main trail that heads to the true right of the valley. From the highest campsite, about 3km above Yurutse, take the right fork in the trail and ascend the yak pastures towards the pass. A number of *chortens* (reliquaries or shrines to the memory of a Buddhist saint) define the trail, while to the north magnificent views showcase the snowcapped Stok Kangri. Allow around three hours from Yurutse to the pass.

From the **Ganda La** (4920m), views extend south to the Zanskar Range and the distant summits of the Himalaya Range. After the initial descent, the trail leads to the true right of the valley to the outlying fields of **Shingo** village (4090m). There are many *campsites* above the village along with *parachute tents*.

From Shingo, the trail heads into a narrow gorge. The initial descent is on the true left of the valley before the trail regularly recrosses the stream throughout the 5km to 6km stage to Skiu. The walls of the gorge are particularly impressive, while the willow, poplar and rose bushes attract a variety of birdlife.

Skiu gompa (3380m) marks the confluence of the rivers coming from Shingo and the Markha Valley. The gompa is affiliated with Hemis and has been completely reconstructed in the past decade. There is also a lone cypress tree close to the campsites. **Skiu** village is a further 1km up the Markha Valley.

Side Trip: Zanskar Gorge
12km return, 5 hours
If you can afford a rest day, this is a worthwhile trip. From Skiu the route leads down the true right of the valley through the settlement of **Kaya** (3350m), complete with

apricot orchards and a tiny village gompa. Beyond the village, the trail continues down the Markha Valley to the confluence of the Zanskar River. The confluence is marked by a small chorten from where you can appreciate the scale of the Zanskar Gorge. A road will eventually be built along this section linking the villages of the Markha Valley to Chiling and the Indus Valley.

Day 4: Skiu to Markha
6–7 hours, 18km

There is a wooden bridge over the Markha River 1km beyond Skiu village. Do not cross it – follow the trail on the true right of the valley. The trail crosses a number of side streams for 6km to 7km before it crosses a substantial bridge over the river to the settlement of **Narding** (3530m). The trail remains on the true left of the valley for a further 3km before it crosses the river via another good bridge to the settlement of **Chalak** (3620m). Just beyond, there are a series of ancient **chortens** and an impressive mound of bharal horns.

The trail returns to the true left of the valley for 2km before reaching a solitary house and fields. Watch out for the trail here as the route descends to the valley floor and crosses the braided waters of the Markha River. There is no bridge, so wet boots may be the order of the day before continuing on the true left of the valley to a substantial campsite complete with a *lodge* and *tea stall* about 500m below Markha. To reach the village, continue beyond the *campsite* and cross the main bridge over the river.

Markha (3800m) is a substantial village, with a derelict fort on the hillside and a small gompa. Just above the village, the gompa is worth a visit if you can find the caretaker.

Day 5: Markha to Thochuntse
4–5 hours, 12km

The trail from Markha village continues through the barley fields. After 2km, it passes an impressive gorge that heads south to the Zanskar Valley (see the Remote Zanskar trek, pp128–30). Just beyond, the trail crosses the Markha River a number of times. There are no bridges – if the river is high,

consult the villagers regarding the alternative trail (of sorts) that winds high above the river on the true right of the valley.

It is 4km from Markha to the village of **Umlung** (3850m). From here, the trail remains on the true right of the valley. About 2km beyond Umlung the valley widens and the imposing peak of **Kangyaze** (6400m) can be appreciated.

Hankar (3980m) is the highest village in the Markha Valley. The village is scattered over several sheltered valleys while the village school is alongside the main trail. Beyond the highest section of the village, the trail follows the tributary of the river flowing from Nimaling. After 1km, the trail crosses a stone bridge to a series of fields owned by the villagers of Hankar and the campsite of **Thochuntse** (4250m).

Day 6: Thochuntse to Nimaling
2½–3 hours, 7km

Beyond Thochuntse, the trail steadily ascends to a series of grassy ridges before a steep gully leads to the lower elevations of the vast Nimaling plains. As the gradient eases, a series of *mani walls* (walls carved with Buddhist prayers) and chortens decorate the route, while the huge peak of Kangyaze looms to the south.

The *camping areas* at **Nimaling** (4730m) stretch across a large undulating plain immediately to the south of the Nimaling stream. Yak herders from Hankar, Umlung and Markha live in the stone settlements during summer. They also provide basic food and accommodation. Remember that inclement weather can build quickly in this area and snowfalls are not uncommon in July and August.

Side Trip: Kangyaze Base
4–5 hours, 8km return

From Nimaling, there is a fine opportunity to trek towards the base of Kangyaze and gain further views across the Zanskar Range. From camp, head south and across a series of yak-grazing pastures. While there is no established trail, it is easy to follow the lie of the land, which ascends about 300m to the snowfields at the base of the peak.

LADAKH

Day 7: Nimaling to Sumdo via Kongmaru La

6–7 hours, 18km

From Nimaling, the trail leading to the Kongmaru La is visible. From camp, cross the stream before ascending the ridge to the north, which heads to the base of the pass. The short steep ascent to the pass is rewarded with fine views to Kangyaze. Trekking from camp to the pass should require no more than two hours.

Kongmaru La (5150m) is the highest pass on the trek, with a bird's-eye view of the Indus Valley and Ladakh Range. Bharal may be seen grazing in the vicinity of the pass.

A steep 500m-descent leads to a small shepherd encampment and *accommodation* for trekkers coming from Sumdo and Hemis. The trail enters a narrow gorge, crossing the main stream on several occasions as it drops steeply for more than 600m, reaching the highest village of **Chogdo** (4000m). The track may not always be in good condition, as flash floods wash away the hillside every few seasons. The resulting trail erosion clearly illustrates the delicate nature of the mountain terrain in Ladakh. Indeed, due to a recent flood, there are no camping areas in the fields at Chogdo. It is necessary to continue to Sumdo (3730m), 3km down the valley.

The well-marked trail from Chogdo to **Sumdo** is on the true left of the valley and leads to a pleasant *campsite*. **Shang gompa** is 1km up the side valley.

Day 8: Sumdo to Hemis

3 hours, 10km

Although a 4WD track has been constructed as far as Sumdo, there is currently no scheduled bus service linking the village to Martselang and the Indus Valley. The 4WD trail follows the true right of the valley before crossing a road bridge to the true left bank and the outskirts of **Martselang** (3450m).

Remain on the true left of the valley to the substantial chorten and mani walls above Martselang. Turn west and follow the side trail that cuts across the open scree slopes to **Hemis village** (3650m). Just before the village, the trail meets the road coming from the

Indus Valley. It is easy to avoid the road: follow the trail leading directly up to the village.

The **Hemis gompa** is one of the most important in Ladakh. It is the principal gompa of the Drukpa order, and the head monk administers all the associated monasteries in Ladakh and the Zanskar. It was established in the 17th century under the patronage of the famous Ladakhi ruler Singge Namgyal, and since then has enjoyed the financial support of successive royal families. The gompa provides caretaker monks for the gompas at Leh, Basgo and Shey.

The annual Hemis festival attracts more than its share of local visitors and tourists. Held during the full moon in June/July, it is attended by many villagers who travel from throughout Ladakh and the Zanskar. The highlight is a series of masked dances commemorating the deeds of the Buddhist figurehead Padmasambhava, the sage who introduced Tantric Buddhism to the Himalaya. Every 11 years, a huge thangka, one of the largest in the Tibetan world, is displayed on the walls of the Hemis courtyard.

To fully appreciate the position of the monastery, and gain insight into the meditative practices pursued by the monks, visit the monks' hermitage. It's about a one-hour climb from behind the monastery.

Hidden Valleys of Ladakh

Duration	5 days
Distance	65km
Difficulty	moderate–demanding
Start	Lamayuru
Finish	Chiling
Nearest Town	Leh (pp103–5)
Public Transport	yes

Summary A fine alternative to the Markha Valley trek, crossing the high ridges of the Zanskar Range to Buddhist villages and gompas beyond the Indus Valley.

This trek follows the hidden valleys of Ladakh – beyond the confines of the Indus Valley. From the passes, enjoy fine views of the East Karakoram, Ladakh Range and the rugged ridges of the Zanskar Range. Extra days in Leh or Lamayuru are essential for acclimatisation.

After Wanlah (Day 1) the villages are less commercial. You will need to be more self-sufficient than on the Markha Valley trek.

Consider extending the trek to the Markha Valley. This is now logistically easier since a bridge has been constructed over the Zanskar River near Chiling. See pp113–16 for the Markha Valley trek.

PLANNING
When to Trek
The trek can be undertaken from early June until mid-October, although both the Dung Dung La and the Konze La are subject to snowfalls as early as mid-September.

What to Bring
For Days 2 to 5, a tent, sleeping bag, food and fuel supplies are necessary.

Maps
Refer to the Leomann series 1:200,000 *Sheet 3 (Leh, Zanskar and Nubra Valley)* and also to *Sheet 2 (Kargil, Zanskar & Nun Kun)* for the initial trek stages out of Lamayuru. Also refer to the Nelles Verlag 1:350,000 *Ladakh & Zanskar* sheet and to the US military U502 series 1:250,000 *NI 43-08 ref Leh*.

Accommodation
At Lamayuru, there are a number of lodges, including *Hotel Dragon* and *Hotel Shangri La.* Both have rooms from Rs 150 to Rs 200. There is a camping ground just below the road, charging Rs 100 per tent. Parachute-tent accommodation is in the vicinity of Wanlah, Hinju, Sumdo Chinmu and Chiling.

The villagers maintain the campsites and charge around Rs 50 for the night.

GETTING TO/FROM THE TREK
The six-hour bus service from Leh to Lamayuru departs around 7am. Trucks are a convenient alternative. The fare for both bus and truck is Rs 70, while 4WDs cost around Rs 2150 one way.

At present, a weekly bus service runs from Chiling to Leh (Rs 60, four hours). A prearranged 4WD is a convenient alterna-tive (Rs 1450), saving you the effort of trudging down the dusty 4WD trail in search of transport on the Kargil-Leh road.

THE TREK (See map pp106–7)
Day 1: Lamayuru to Wanlah via Prinkiti La
3–4 hours, 10km

From **Lamayuru** village (3430m), follow the trail leading down the valley for 2km before diverting up the ridge to the east, leading to the Prinkiti La. The gradual as-cent from Lamayuru to the pass should not take much more than an hour.

The **Prinkiti La** (3650m) affords views across the barren landscape of the Zanskar Range. From the pass the trail enters a narrow gorge, following a dry streambed down to the confluence with the Shilakong Valley. It is a further 2km to 3km descent past the houses at **Shila** (3200m) to the village and gompa of Wanlah. There is an established *campsite* just north of the bridge over the Wanlah River.

Wanlah gompa was established at the same time as the Lamayuru gompa and is nowadays serviced by the monks from Lamayuru. The gompa has a commanding position looking up the Shilakong Valley and the main assembly hall is open most of the day. A donation of Rs 50 is expected.

Wanlah village (3150m) has been con-nected by road with Khalsi (to the north in the Indus Valley) for the past decade. An irregu-lar bus service runs between Wanlah and Khalsi, but this is about the only transport apart from the occasional truck and the daily school bus. There are plans to extend the road to Hinju and eventually to Lingshet.

Day 2: Wanlah to Hinju
4–5 hours, 13km

Cross the main bridge and follow the 4WD road along the true right bank of the valley. The trek heads up the road for around 1½ hours to Phanjila.

The village of **Phanjila** (3410m) is at the entrance to the Hinju Valley. It boasts a school and some apricot orchards. The fields extend 2km to 3km up the valley towards Hinju. Road construction is now underway

Lamayuru Legends

Lamayuru is one of the oldest sites in Ladakh. Legend has it that a vast lake once filled the upper reaches of this valley. The sage Naropa miraculously breached this. The site of the breach was revered, and became the location of the gompa, which was built in the 10th century. One of the original gompas is just beyond the main assembly hall and has been recently renovated.

The gompa subscribes to one of the oldest Tibetan schools, the Kargyupa order, which was followed by the noted sages Marpa (1012–97) and Milarepa (1040–123). For many outlying gompas in the region, the doctrinal distinctions are merely technical – for example, those at Wanlah, Phanjila and Khalsi, although affiliated with Lamayuru, also have close cultural links with the main Drukpa gompa at Hemis.

and will eventually alter the trail route and the character of the valley. For now, follow the trail on the true right of the valley until it enters a narrow gorge. Switch for a short distance to the opposite bank before crossing back to the true right. There are small bridges to assist with the crossings.

Hinju village (3720m) has three main settlements: lower Hinju, the main village, and upper Hinju, about 3km further towards the Konze La. The main village has about 15 houses, some with solar heating. There is a choice of *campsites* about 2km above the village – an ideal base for the Konze La.

Day 3: Hinju to Camp via Konze La
6–7 hours, 15km

From the camp above Hinju, a steady climb passes the settlement of upper Hinju and some goat enclosures. The trail then gradually winds down to the valley floor and past a lone yak herder's encampment to the base of the pass.

From the encampment, continue up the valley floor for 2km before commencing the ascent. The trek to the pass from Hinju takes about 3½ hours, although the time may vary

considerably when the approach to the pass is under snow. From the **Konze La** (4950m), there are views to the Ladakh Range and the Karakoram, and of the Stok Range and the main ridges of the Zanskar Range to the east.

The descent is quite steep, over loose moraine that follows an ill-defined trail to the true left of the main valley. Once down to the valley floor, it is a short distance to the first *camp* (convenient if trekking in the opposite direction). The trail remains on the true left of the valley, crossing some small side ridges before descending to a number of *yak herders huts* (approximately 4500m), which are occupied in summer by villagers from Sumdo Chinmu.

Day 4: Camp to Dung Dung La Base
3–4 hours, 12km

From camp, cross the main river and follow the trail on the true right of the valley. The trail ascends a side ridge with potential *campsites* above the main valley. It then descends to the valley floor before crossing the river and following an irrigation channel down to the village of **Sumdo Chinmu** (4300m).

There is a small gompa close to the village and some large stone statues of the *Maitreya Buddha* (the Buddha to come) nearby. The trail remains on the true left of the valley for a further 2km before winding down to the valley floor (4250m), covered in a thick canopy of willow trees and wild rose bushes. There is a further river crossing before reaching a small side stream flowing from the nearby peaks, including Photaksar (5685m). This is also the base of the Dung Dung La and the point at which the trail splits to Alchi (see Alternative Route).

To reach the actual base of the Dung Dung La, a short, if rather steep, ascent over an intermediary ridge (4430m) is required. The ascent will take about one hour, passing a profusion of edelweiss and other wildflowers, which survive on Ladakh's minimal rainfall. From the ridge, there are views to the Konze La. A delightful meadow and *campsite* is at 4400m. It is shared with yak herders from Chiling village, who graze their animals here in summer.

Alternative Route: Alchi via the Stakspi La

2 days, 30km

This route is an alternative way to end the trek. From Sumdo Chinmu, follow the trail down the valley past the base of the Dung Dung La. This entails following a rough trail that crosses the river several times before it diverts to a side ridge north of the valley. The trail leads up and over to the village of Sumdo Choon (note: Sumdo Choon means little village, and Sumdo Chinmu, big village).

At **Sumdo Choon** (4450m), the small gompa is affiliated with Alchi. There is an impressive statue of the Maitreya Buddha in the adjoining temple and a nearby *campsite*.

Above the village, the trail leads to the base of the pass from where there is a short, steep ascent to the **Stakspi La** (4970m) and fine views of the Ladakh Range. (I recall night falling mid-trek many seasons ago after a long, tiring ascent from Alchi, but there were superb views in the early morning.)

The trail descends quite steeply to a small grazing area and shepherds shelter and a possible *campsite*. From here, it is a three-hour trek down to **Alchi** (3200m) before a further 4km along the 4WD road to the Alchi bridge and the main highway to Leh.

The temple complex at Alchi was founded in the 11th century when the noted teacher, Ringchen Brangpo, was sent by a local Tibetan king to lay the foundations for Buddhist gompas throughout Ladakh and the Zanskar. Due to its sheltered location, Alchi has remained intact to the present day.

The major point of interest at Alchi's gompa stems from the fact that the Tibetans, being newly converted to Buddhism, did not have the artistic skills necessary to decorate the temples. Artists from the Kashmir Valley (whose Buddhist temples have long been destroyed) were therefore commissioned to complete the walls and entrances.

For a complete survey of the Alchi temples, and a detailed history of the other gompas in Ladakh, refer to Volume 1 of Snellgrove and Skorupski's *The Cultural History of Ladakh*.

From the Kargil-Leh Rd there is a daily 7am bus to Leh (Rs 35, two hours).

Day 5: Dung Dung La Base to Chiling via Dung Dung La

6 hours, 15km

It is not a particularly steep ascent from camp to the pass. The trail winds past yak herders' camps before gradually crossing a series of scree slopes to the **Dung Dung La** (4820m). Here, you'll enjoy unrivalled views – north to the Ladakh Range, east across the Stok Range and south to the Zanskar Range, while the course of the Zanskar River can also be appreciated.

The route from the pass follows the contours along a high ridge for about 2km before a long and gradual descent towards Chiling village. There are views to the confluence of the Markha and Zanskar Rivers and to the upper reaches of the Markha Valley towards the Kongmaru La. About halfway down, the trail leads through a small settlement at 4270m, where a lone woman from Chiling works the fields. From the settlement, a short, steep descent leads towards a subsidiary valley just above Chiling. The trail is ill-defined after heavy rain and your crew are in for a good two hours work before reaching Chiling.

Chiling village (3550m) provides much of the copper work entering the Leh market. The main village is up a ridge above the established *campsite* and is well worth the visit. The village is now connected to Nimmu (north, on the Kargil-Leh road) by a 4WD road alongside the Zanskar River. Plans are afoot to continue the road south towards the Zanskar Valley and east to the Markha Valley.

Padum & the Zanskar Valley

The tiny Zanskar kingdom is wedged between the main Himalaya and the Zanskar Range. It comprises two narrow valleys – the Stod Valley in the northwest and the Tsarap Valley in the southeast –and extends north to where the Zanskar River enters the impressive gorges of the Zanskar Range.

Until a generation ago, it took villagers a week or more to reach the roadhead just

LADAKH

Ladakh: Physical, Statistical & Historical

Lieutenant Joseph Cunningham was one of a handful of distinguished travellers who trekked across Ladakh in the mid-19th century. Following the Treaty of Amritsar in 1846, an agreement between the British authorities and the new Maharajah of Kashmir permitted the British to assume at least partial responsibility to defend the vast territories of the Jammu and Kashmir State (J&K), including Ladakh.

In 1847, a Boundary Commission was established with three members: Lieutenant Henry Stratchey, Dr Thomas Thomson and its leader, Lieutenant Cunningham. The Commission required each member to undertake extensive travels across Ladakh to the Tibetan borderlands. Cunningham's findings were recorded in *The Physical Geography of Western Tibet*, while his book *Ladakh: Physical, Statistical & Historical* remains one of the most important works of the time and was recently reprinted in Delhi.

Ladakh: Physical, Statistical & Historical followed the standard format of the time. It was a government publication, a gazette that demanded factual information and granted little scope for reflection. Separate chapters covered geography, mountains, rivers, lakes, roads, the climate, commerce, government, people, history, religion and language that would be hard to match in present-day guide books!

Cunningham outlined all the major trails into and out of Ladakh. These included the track over the Zoji La from Kashmir to Ladakh; the route from Kishtwar over the Umasi La to the Zanskar and Leh (compiled by Dr Thomson); a route from Manali over the Baralacha La to the Indus Valley and Leh; the route to the north of the region over the Karakoram Pass to Yarkand and Khotan; and the northwest road from Baltistan and Skardu up the Indus Valley. These are routes which we can only dream of today, as most either cross or go close to sensitive international borders.

The height of every major pass to and from Ladakh is listed – they were calculated based on the time required to boil water, so most are only accurate to the nearest 200ft. All important bridges are also classified into either stone, wooden or others such as rope-suspension bridges and the famous twig bridges. Of the twig bridges, Cunningham wrote that they were both difficult and dangerous – something that trekkers up to a decade ago would experience on many treks in the Zanskar. The fording of rivers in summer also occupies Cunningham's attention. He recommends they be attempted by 10am before the levels rise with the spring snow melt – sound advice that should still be heeded today.

Cunningham comprehensively describes the wild animals. Diagrams of the wild yak and the kiang are illustrated in great detail. He also outlines the distribution of the markhor and the Marco Polo sheep long before the species were in danger of extinction. Indeed, his report – like so many of the day – provided a basis for both political intelligence and sport, and marked the beginning of an era when sportsmen undertook hunting trips across the West Himalaya and Ladakh for months at a time.

outside Kargil. In 1976 the region was opened to tourism and by 1981 a 4WD road was completed linking Kargil and Padum. This has opened up a wide range of trekking possibilities, either by heading over the Zanskar Range to Leh and the Indus Valley or traversing the Himalaya Range to Himachal Pradesh.

Crossing the passes over the Zanskar Range affords extensive views of both the Ladakh Range and the peaks of the East Karakoram. By contrast, when crossing the Himalaya Range, the views are often confined to the peaks and glaciers in the immediate vicinity.

HISTORY

Zanskar – the Hidden Kingdom is an apt assessment of a region that never figured on any of the trade routes. A quick reference to the main trails that evolved over 2500 years (see the boxed text 'Ladakh: Physical, Statistical & Historical') reveals that armies and traders over the centuries bypassed this isolated kingdom en route to Ladakh. Indeed the 'hidden' location of the Zanskar ensured that few travellers had reason to visit, even though the gompas and villages were well established by the 10th century.

Authentic records of Zanskar follow the wanderings of the scholar Ringchen Brangpo during his 11th-century search for 108 gompa sites. Legend has it that, at the same time, the sage Naropa meditated at the site of Sani gompa.

By the late 14th century, Buddhist monks and scholars ventured over the passes from the Indus Valley to establish gompas at Mune, Lingshet and Karsha for the Gelukpa order. Two centuries later, monks from the Drukpa order (affiliated to the Ladakh royal family) founded the gompas at Bardan and Zangla villages.

It was not until the early 19th century that Europeans travellers reached the Zanskar. One of the first was Hungarian scholar Coso de Koros, who spend the best part of a year in 1826–27 translating the Buddhist texts from Ladakhi to English.

In the early 1830s Dogra general Zorawar Singh led his army over the Umasi La during his conquest of Ladakh and the Zanskar. In 1834 he reduced the powers of the royal families in both Padum and Zangla to a nominal status and established the fort at the village of Pipiting, just north of Padum. He is also said to have paid a local guide a small fortune to lead his army across the Zanskar Range to the Indus Valley, to mount a surprise attack on the King of Ladakh.

While many of the high passes and secluded valleys were known to the likes of Moorcroft and Vigne, it was not until June 1948 that Thomas Thomson, a member of the East India Company's Boundary Commission, crossed the Umasi La to reach Padum. After recording the necessary data, he continued to Ladakh and the crest of the Karakoram Pass.

Many travellers were to follow in the latter half of the 19th century, discovering the snowbound passes linking the Zanskar to the Suru, Chenab and Indus Valleys.

NATURAL HISTORY

The Zanskar Range forms the backbone of southern Ladakh. It includes several peaks above 6000m and is separated from the Himalaya Range by the Zanskar Valley. It is breached only once, where the Zanskar River flows north creating a series of huge gorges before flowing into the Indus River.

There are no national parks in the Zanskar. However, as is the case throughout Ladakh, the Buddhist culture ensures that wildlife is preserved, except when wolves or snow leopards attack the villagers' domestic animals.

The wilderness regions close to the Zanskar gorges are renowned for wildlife, including brown bears and ibex. Herds of urial have been spotted roaming the high ridges way above the Zanskar River.

The alpine meadows near the Himalaya Range support a variety of wildflowers. However, the selection is in no way comparable to the verdant valleys of Himachal Pradesh.

ACCESS TOWNS
Padum
☎ 01983 • alt 1000m

On a plateau above the confluence of the Stod and Tsarap Rivers, Padum is the administrative centre of the Zanskar. It is not a very inspiring town, with concrete buildings and heaps of fuel cans and engine parts, discarded here after the road journey from Kargil. The outlying fields, settlements and gompas provide an attractive diversion.

Information If you are making trek arrangements in Padum, allow a few days to organise porters or horses. Tsering Namgyal at the **Tourist Office** (☎ 45017) will assist you and has many contacts.

Supplies & Equipment The development of the road from Kargil has made the region more accessible. Supplies can be purchased at Padum at a premium price. Kerosene, biscuits, rice, flour, and a supply of eggs, fresh fruit and vegetables are available as soon as the road from Kargil is open (late June–late Oct). The occasional bottle of rum also finds its way into the stores. However, buy luxury supplies in Leh.

There is practically no trekking equipment for sale or hire in Padum. Make arrangements before leaving Leh.

Trekking Agents Tsering Namgyal (see Information, above) is a great first stop for assistance. There is also **Zanskar Mountain**

LADAKH

LADAKH

Travel (☎ *45018, Hotel Haftal*), which can arrange horses and staff. A local guide, **Sonam 'Jimmy' Stobgais** has also been recommended and can be contacted via the Tourist Office.

Expect to pay somewhere between Rs 200 and Rs 400 per horse, depending on demand and season. During the harvest period (late Aug–Sept), it is likely that charges will rise. The going rate for crossing the Kang La or Umasi La is Rs 400 to Rs 500 per porter per stage, plus assistance with their supplies, clothing and equipment.

Places to Stay & Eat The majority of trekkers choose to camp on arrival at Padum. The rather dirty *campsites* are close to the Tourist Office in the centre of Padum. They also attract a few less than honest individuals so keep a close eye on your gear.

Alternatively, there are a number of lodges, which are open just for the season. The best is the *Hotel Ibex* next to the bus stop, with rooms for Rs 400. Close by, the *Hotel Haftal* has basic rooms for Rs 200. The *Snowland* has a more peaceful location above the main bazaar, with rooms for around Rs 200. There is also the *J&KTDC Tourist Bungalow*, in the same compound as the Tourist Office, with rooms for Rs 50.

The *hotels* and a number of *tea stalls* prepare noodles and various other Ladakhi-cum-Tibetan dishes.

Getting There & Away For most people, the timing of a trek out of Padum is determined by the opening of the road from Kargil over the Pentse La. The pass is normally cleared by late June and generally remains open until late October.

The Kargil-Padum road journey takes two days with an overnight stop, normally at Rangdum. The bus service runs every other day (Rs 240, July–mid-Oct), and is normally heavily booked.

Getting a truck from the Kargil bazaar is an alternative. Truck prices are about the same as the bus. A seat in the cabin is likely to be more comfortable than sitting in the back. Either way, look forward to two very dusty days.

You can also hire 4WDs from Kargil to Padum. Expect to pay Rs 8000, or around Rs 11,000 from Leh.

For the intrepid, there are winter trails linking the Zanskar Valley with the Indus. From late January through February, villagers follow the route over the snow bridges that form in the depths of the gorges. When the ice begins to thaw, they follow a route over the Cha Cha La to the Khurna Valley and then trek down to its confluence with the Zanskar River. Here, there are places to ford the Zanskar River to reach Nimmu and Leh. The locals favour this route in the spring, until the snows on the Pentse La begin to thaw in May. To gain a sense of winter trekking conditions, see the boxed text 'Winter in the Zanskar', p127.

Kargil
☎ 01985 • alt 2187m
At the confluence of the Suru and Drass Rivers, Kargil is a Muslim region with a sizeable Shia presence. Most tourists will encounter the main bazaar and the labyrinth of alleyways leading to the river.

In 1999, Kargil and the nearby India-Pakistan ceasefire line was the focus of a protracted war between the two countries. The town was regularly shelled by Pakistani forces and was off limits to foreigners for most of the season. Since then, an air of normality has returned and a steady flow of trekkers stay in Kargil en route to Rangdum and the Zanskar. However, seek the most up-to-date information before visiting Kargil; see also the Warning boxed text (p100).

Information The **Tourist Office** is next to the taxi stand, just off Main Bazaar Rd. However, it has no great information on local areas or the Zanskar.

Supplies & Equipment If you choose Kargil as your base for a trek, fruit, vegetables and other basics can be purchased in the bazaar. Tinned food and luxury items should be brought from Leh. Biscuits and basics can also be purchased at Rangdum.

Although a stock of trekking gear may be available for hire at the Tourist Office, most

Environmental Watch

The increasing numbers of trekkers in Ladakh over the past 20 years have taken their toll on the fragile mountain environment. Some campsites on the popular trails bear the mark of continuous use with an array of tin cans, plastic bags and other nonbiodegradable material deposited across the meadows and in the willow groves and irrigation channels. While conscientious villagers and trekkers clean some sites, others are nothing less than a disaster by the end of the season. This is particularly evident in camping areas beyond the villages where there is little or no effort to clean up after the parachute tents are packed up in September. A voluntary trekking fee to finance a clean up by the agents from Leh at the end of season would be a short-term solution. In the meantime, ensure your crew adhere to minimal impact trekking codes and always provide an example by helping to clean up on arrival at camp.

Concerns about wildlife have led to increased surveillance of endangered species. In the Hemis National Park, a program has been introduced to help villagers protect domestic animals from predators (eg, snow leopards and lynx) so that villagers don't shoot them. However, species such as the Marco Polo sheep and the Tibetan gazelle (gowa) are reduced to critical numbers. The chiru (Tibetan antelope) is also endangered. Proposals such as the establishment of sanctuaries need to be implemented without delay. Contact the **Jammu & Kashmir Wildlife Department** (☎ 01982-52171) in Leh.

Culturally, there are few villages where the children have not adopted the 'one pen' mantra. There is also increasing evidence of theft, particularly in some areas of the Zanskar. However, there have been a number of positive developments. Signs at the entrances to gompas invite trekkers to make donations, which go a long way to assist in the preservation of the buildings and wall paintings, while also supporting the local schools run by the monks. You can make a difference by making a donation or supporting one of the foundations that have contributed to the building of schools and medical facilities in the region. Alternatively, contact the **Ladakh Ecological Development Group** (LEDeG; ☎ 01982-3746) in Leh. They hold regular film evenings detailing their work and ways in which you can help.

---

treks out of Rangdum and Padum are unlikely to return to Kargil. It is advisable to make your arrangements from Leh.

Places to Stay & Eat Most hotels survive on the handful of tourists travelling to the Zanskar. There are two *J&KTDC Tourist Bungalows*. One is up the hill past the hospital; it has a variety of rooms and charges Rs 200 to Rs 400. The other is more convenient, next to the bus station, with rooms for Rs 50. *Hotel Tourist Marjuna* has a nice garden and rooms for Rs 200.

There is very little to recommend the restaurants in Kargil. A number of small restaurants and *dhabas* (tea stalls or restaurants) in the *main bazaar* offer a limited range of dishes.

Getting There & Away There is a daily bus service from Leh to Kargil (Rs 220/150 A class/B class, 10 hours). Hiring a 4WD will cost Rs 3700.

Singge La & Lamayuru

Duration	10 days
Distance	136km
Difficulty	moderate–demanding
Start	Padum
Finish	Lamayuru
Nearest Town	Padum (pp121–2)
Public Transport	yes

Summary A popular but challenging traverse of the Zanskar Range, visiting remote villages and gompas that evoke Ladakh's ancient Buddhist culture.

In July and August, a steady flow of trekkers complete this demanding traverse. As the trek altitudes do not fall below 3000m, a few days in the vicinity of Padum – visiting the outlying gompas and forts – is recommended.

After completing two easy days alongside the Zanskar River, there follows a week of crossing passes (often more than

LADAKH

one per day) that leave little doubt that you are in the rugged Trans-Himalaya. Views from many of the passes provide a further reminder of the terrain, as the Zanskar River forges its way through deep gorges to meet with the Indus River.

A road is being constructed from Wanlah that will eventually extend to Lingshet. When this is completed, Days 6 to 10 will need to be adapted; instead, trek from Lingshet to Kanji following stages in the Kanji La & Shilakong Gorge trek (pp140–2).

PLANNING
When to Trek
Monks and villagers normally cross the highest passes by early June. The passes are open until late October.

What to Bring
Unless you are prepared to sleep in a basic shelter hut on some stages of this trek, you should bring a tent. A stove, fuel and food for the stages where there are no lodges should be brought from Padum.

Maps
Refer to the Leomann series 1:200,000 *Sheet 3 (Leh, Zanskar and Nubra Valley)*. Also refer to Nelles Verlag 1:350,000 *Ladakh & Zanskar* sheet and the US military U502 series 1:250,000 map *NI 43-12 ref Martselang* and *NI 43-08 ref Leh*.

Accommodation
There are lodges and parachute tents on most but not all stages of the trek. There is a choice of accommodation at Lingshet, and lodges or parachute tents at Karsha, Pishu and Hanumil. At Snertse, there may be only basic shelter huts (possibly occupied by local shepherds). At the base of the Singge La, there may be no accommodation (if you don't have a tent, overnight at the settlement at Yulchang). From here on, there are either parachute tents or lodges at Photaksar, Honupatta and Wanlah.

Lamayuru has a number of lodges, including the *Hotel Dragon* and the *Hotel Shangri La*. Both have rooms from Rs 150 to Rs 200. Alternatively, there is a camping

group just below the road that charges Rs 100 per tent.

If you are carrying your own tent, expect to pay about Rs 50 in camping fees when you are in the vicinity of a village.

GETTING TO/FROM THE TREK
For travel to Padum, see Getting There & Away (p122). From Lamayuru, it is advisable to be at the trailhead by 7am when the first truck and bus convoys pass by. Expect to pay Rs 70 for the six- to seven-hour drive to Leh.

THE TREK (See map pp106–7)
Day 1: Padum to Karsha
2 hours, 6km
If you're coming from Kargil, it is possible to drive straight to Karsha and bypass this first day. This very short stage allows time to visit the Karsha gompa, one of the most important in the Zanskar region. The route is clearly visible from Padum and can, if you choose, lead through some villages away from the road. Follow the trail from Padum to **Pipiting** village before cutting across the fields to the bridge over the Stod River. The *campsite* is just to the south of the bridge, close to banks of the river.

After settling at camp, it is 1km to the village before a steady climb through the labyrinth of alleyways to the entrance of **Karsha gompa**. On a hillside commanding views of the entire valley and the Himalaya Range, it is the largest gompa in the Zanskar region. It attracts monks from the surrounding villages, and up to 100 may be in attendance at one time. The site was probably founded in the 10th century, while the main prayer hall and monks' quarters would have been built in the early 15th century, when the Gelukpa order was popularised in Ladakh.

The monks are particularly keen to show you around. For a donation of Rs 100, they will invite you for tea in the courtyard above the main Assembly Hall, from where you can enjoy views of the Zanskar Valley.

Day 2: Karsha to Pishu
4–5 hours, 14km
Head through **Karsha** village to the main trail, where you begin a dry, dusty and undulating

walk to Pishu. From Karsha (3600m), the trail descends gradually to the village of **Rinam** (3550m) and follows the banks of the Zanskar River to **Pishu** (3470m).

Like all villages in Zanskar, the entrance to the village is marked by a long mani wall and chortens. There is a grassy *campsite*, complete with a spring, below the village and close to the river. There is also a *parachute tent* in the vicinity.

This easy stage allows time to visit **Zangla** village and the nearby gompa.

Day 3: Pishu to Hanumil
4–5 hours, 13km
This is another relatively level stage following the Zanskar River. From Pishu, the trail follows the riverbank for 2km before ascending a dry plateau with sweeping views of the Zanskar region.

The village of **Pidmu** (3420m) is about halfway. The trail heads north through barley fields before descending to the riverbank to complete the 6km to 7km to Hanumil.

Hanumil (3380m) comprises just a few houses, and is at the mouth of an impressive side gorge. The *campsite* is a short distance past the village with fine views down the Zanskar Gorge. There is also a *tea house* where arrangements can be made for overnight accommodation. Hanumil, Pishu and Pidmu, together with Chazar and Honia on the other side of the river, constitute the tiny kingdom of Zangla.

Day 4: Hanumil to Snertse via Purfi La
5–6 hours, 14km
Before leaving Hanumil, check with the villagers as to whether you will need extra supplies – there is no guarantee of food or accommodation on this stage. The trail winds high above the Zanskar River for 5km to 6km before commencing the ascent to the Purfi La. Occasional cypress trees, wild roses and a selection of herbal plants grow on the scree slopes.

Views from the **Purfi La** (3850m) stretch south to the Himalaya Range, while to the north you can appreciate what lies ahead to the camp at Snertse. It doesn't look good!

There is a steep 500m descent to the Zingchan Tokpo followed by a steady 400m ascent to the camp. The descent takes the best part of an hour (although Ladakhi guides do it in 15 minutes). The bridge over the Zingchan Tokpo marks the boundary of Zanskar and Ladakh. There is welcome shelter of poplar and willow trees just beyond the bridge before you summon enough strength to complete the next ascent. There is a small shepherd encampment at **Snertse** (3710m), above a dusty *campsite*.

Day 5: Snertse to Lingshet via Hanuma La
6–7 hours, 17km
A steep 400m climb leads out of the narrow gorge above the Snertse campsite. In spring, this section is easier as you can simply ascend the snow bridges. Beyond the gorge the gradient eases to reach a shepherd camp about two hours beyond Snertse. Continue along the dry valley floor for a further 2km before taking the north fork in the valley that ascends to the Hanuma La. The last 2km to 3km to the pass is not demanding, while the time from Snertse to the pass is 3½ to 4 hours.

The **Hanuma La** (4650m) is marked by two large chortens and prayer flags, with spectacular views north to the Singge La and the rugged Zanskar Gorge. The snow-capped peaks of the Ladakh Range can also be appreciated. Below, Lingshet gompa is visible on the opposite side of the valley.

The descent is quite steep with many switchbacks followed by a short climb over an intermediary ridge before a long and gradual descent to Lingshet. There are a number of *campsites* a couple of kilometres before the village. Otherwise, continue to Lingshet where the *campsite* and *parachute tents* are just beyond the gompa. There is also a police checkpoint where your passport will be inspected. The time from the pass to the village is around three hours.

Lingshet gompa (4650m) was founded by the Gelukpa order with its teachings from Tibet. There is, however, an older site further down the valley that may date back to the same time as Sani and Alchi, when Buddhism was first established in Ladakh. There are normally 20 to 30 monks in attendance, and the gompa serves the outlying villages of Nirag, Yulchang and Skyumpata.

Alternative Route: Lingshet to Rangdum
3 days, 60km

From Lingshet, there is an alternative trail leading to Rangdum. The route crosses the Kesi La (4500m) to the north of the Hanuma La. Beyond the pass is the tiny settlement of Pingdon. The trail then heads over the Pingdon La, before passing the base of the Kanji La en route to Rangdum. In places the trail is hard for horses.

Day 6: Lingshet to Base of Singge La
5–6 hours, 15km

The trail from Lingshet gradually ascends the first of the intermediary passes, the **Netuke La** (4280m), before the long descent to the river at 3920m, just below the settlement of **Skyumpata** (4100m). It's a further tiring ascent for 1½ hours to the **Khyupa La** (4360m). The trail leads on for a further 3km to a *campsite* and *tea house* run by villagers from the nearby **Yulchang** settlement. A further 3km on is the **Singge La base** (4400m) where there is an adequate, albeit rocky, campsite beside the spring, which eventually cascades down to the Zanskar River 1500m below. *Parachute tents* may be available; if not, stay overnight at the *camp* above Yulchang.

Day 7: Base of Singge La to Photaksar via Singge La
6 hours, 15km

The climb up the rather steep scree slope to the pass takes about 1½ to two hours. Frozen waterfalls from the limestone cliffs form an impressive sight above the trail. The **Singge La** (5010m), literally the Lion Pass, is the highest pass on the route to Lamayuru. From the crest of the pass, views extend to the outlying ridges of the Zanskar Range and the snowcapped peaks of the Himalaya Range to the south. Note also the remarkable 6000m peak immediately to the west of the pass.

Continue with a short descent to the true left of the valley floor. The trail then heads

towards the true right of the valley and a stone shelter hut before recrossing the valley to the scant grazing pastures and a side stream that may take a little time to ford.

Beyond the side stream, the trail ascends some 5km to 6km to an intermediary ridge that leads to the Photang Valley and **Photaksar** (4100m), which supports two small gompas serviced by monks from Lamayuru. There is a choice of *campsites* opposite or just above the village. *Parachute tents* should also be available. The time from the pass to the village is around four hours.

Day 8: Photaksar to Honupatta via Sisir La
6 hours, 17km

From the campsite opposite Photaksar, continue 2km to the Photang River and cross the bridge to the true left of the valley. There follows a gradual climb for about two hours to the base of the Sisir La. Follow the well-defined trail that ascends a side ridge before completing the final steep climb to the pass.

From the **Sisir La** (4720m), the views back to the Singge La and the main Zanskar Range are particularly impressive. On stormy days, the dramatic light will make every photographer a professional! Also note that the small pass at the head of the valley to the west marks the route to the Shilakong Valley and an alternative trail to Wanlah. Immediately below, the trail heads down the scree slope to the valley floor before continuing on the true left of the valley for 5km to the first of a number of *campsites* above Honupatta village. The time from the pass is around three hours.

Three chortens mark the entrance to **Honupatta** (3900m), while the huge, ancient cypress tree in the village is adorned with Buddhist prayer flags. There are some *lodges* in the village for accommodation and food.

Day 9: Honupatta to Wanlah
5 hours, 15km

From Honupatta, the trail descends into a very impressive gorge with sheer rock walls rising nearly 1000m above the river course. Remain on the true left of the river for 6km, before a large chorten marks the confluence

Winter in the Zanskar

If you are determined – and you will need to be – to visit the ancient kingdom of Zanskar during winter, you will need a pair of insulated boots, a four-season sleeping bag and a towel. Yes, a towel.

The most direct route into the kingdom is along the floor of a gorge that has been carved out over aeons by the Zanskar River. In summer, the river is a foaming brown torrent, navigable only by raft. But in winter, as temperatures drop as low as a heart-stopping -40°C, the river solidifies. During January and February, it is usually possible to walk on the frozen surface. The ice may be just a few centimetres thick, or frozen to a depth of a metre of more. Occasionally it is possible to drop to your hands and knees in order to stare through glass-ice and study boulders the size of television sets that have been lifted off the bed of the river and suspended mid-stream.

A traverse of the frozen river (which is known locally as the Chadur) takes four to five days from the trailhead at Chiling to the village of Hanumil. The route along the Chadur changes by the hour, as the river constantly defrosts and re-freezes. It is imperative that a knowledgeable Zanskari guide is hired to find the safest route through this frozen labyrinth (even the most experienced mountaineers employ these services). Camp is made each evening on the riverbank, in caves and occasionally in dwellings. A tent can be a blessing as porters' fires always smoke out any enclosed space in a matter of minutes.

Walking on frozen water is not for the faint hearted, and dunkings in the almost-freezing river do occur. In these situations, survival time is measured in just a few minutes, so avoid leaving anyone – foreigner or local – on their own at any time.

If you do decide to brave the Chadur, you will be rewarded by the sight of ice formations unlike anything, anywhere on earth. It is a privileged opportunity to enjoy Zanskar at a time when the valley is virtually devoid of tourists. But don't forget your towel; you will need it to bring your feet back to life after one of the obligatory wading sessions through water so cold that it flows with the viscosity of oil.

Paul Deegan, April 2001

with the Photang River. Do not cross the bridge here (it leads up the valley towards Photaksar); remain on the true left for 100m and cross the next bridge. Shortly after, the trail crosses another bridge back to the true left of the gorge. Just beyond, the trail meets the road development from Wanlah, which may in the next few seasons extend to Honupatta.

Follow the 4WD track out of the gorge before crossing the substantial bridge to the true right of the valley. The dusty track then leads to the apricot orchards of **Phanjila** (3270m). It is a further 5km to 6km along the true right of the valley to the village and gompa at Wanlah.

Wanlah gompa is high above the village. It was founded at the same time as the Lamayuru gompa and is now serviced by the monks from Lamayuru. The main assembly hall and many of the other building have recently been restored and painted. A donation of Rs 50 is expected.

Wanlah (3150m) boasts some *tea houses* while the *campsite* is on the far side of the main bridge. It is also connected by road to Khalsi and the Kargil-Leh road, although the buses are at present irregular.

Day 10: Wanlah to Lamayuru via Prinkiti La
3–4 hours, 10km

Follow the true right of the Shilakong Valley for 2km to **Shila** village. Cross the bridge over the river and ascend to the chortens and prayer flags that mark the turn-off to Prinkiti La. The small gorge is devoid of vegetation and is a rather featureless route to the pass.

From the **Prinkiti La** (3650m), enjoy views across to the Sisir La and the adjoining ridges of the Zanskar. A one-hour descent leads to the village and gompa of **Lamayuru** (3430m).

For lodgings in Lamayuru, see Accommodation (p124). For information about its famous gompa, see the boxed text 'Lamayuru Legends' (p118).

Remote Zanskar

Duration	10 days
Distance	158/170km
Difficulty	demanding
Start	Padum
Finish	Hemis/Stok
Nearest Town	Padum (pp121–2)
Public Transport	yes

Summary This trek samples the Markha and Indus Valleys, passing through spectacular wilderness and impressive gorges before visiting Buddhist villages and gompas.

The remote trails and the absence of villages between Zangla and the Markha Valley deter all but the most adventurous trekkers. The high water levels in the gorges in July and August may also restrict trekkers. Staying at intermediary campsites and doing shorter stages are the only option until water levels drop in September.

The climb to the first pass – the Cha Cha La (4950m) – is steep. The trail (of sorts!) through the gorges often involves crossing landslides and boulder fields that will test even the best Ladakhi horse attendants. Even in autumn, most stages will be 'wet-boot days' until you reach the Markha Valley and the established trail to Hemis and the Indus Valley.

Allow sufficient time to acclimatise by doing day walks to the forts and gompas around Padum.

PLANNING
When to Trek
The trek is normally open by mid-June. However, there will still be heavy snow on the passes. The trails are usually open until mid-October. Beware that, in July and August, the streams in the gorges can turn into torrents, making the many river crossings difficult and sometimes dangerous.

What to Bring
Carry a tent, food and fuel for at least a week, plus a length of rope for river crossings. A pair of sandshoes will also be handy if your boots don't dry out.

Maps
Refer to the Leomann series 1:200,000 *Sheet 3 (Leh, Zanskar and Nubra Valley)*. Also refer to Nelles Verlag 1:350,000 *Ladakh & Zanskar* sheet and the US military U502 series 1:250,000 map *43-12 ref Martselang*.

Accommodation
While there are parachute tents in Zangla, that is about it until the Markha Valley. Beyond Zangla, there is no food and accommodation available.

There are no guesthouses at Hemis but there are several campsites either on the outskirts of the village or in the outdoor restaurant next to the gompa.

GETTING TO/FROM THE TREK
For travel to Padum, see Getting There & Away (p122). From Hemis, the daily bus service to Leh (Rs 15, 1½ to two hours) leaves at around 11am.

If you plan to end the trek in Leh, see Getting There & Away (p104).

THE TREK (See map pp106–7)
Day 1: Padum to Zangla
7 hours, 20km
There is a choice of routes to Zangla. The first goes via Karsha gompa, and then continues down the true left of the Zanskar Valley to Pishu village, where you cross the bridge to Zangla. (See Days 1 and 2 of the Singge La & Lamayuru trek, pp124–5) The alternative route is to cross the bridge over the Tsarap River at Padum, and follow the 4WD road down the true right of the Zanskar Valley via the village of Stongde.

From Padum, the trail to Zangla crosses the main bridge over the Tsarap River and follows the 4WD road to **Stongde** (3500m), where there is an impressive gompa, affiliated to Karsha. The trail continues past the villages of **Chilingkit** and **Tzazar** en route to **Zangla** (3370m).

The largest house in Zangla is home to the current king of Zangla. Although he now fulfils a nominal role, the royal family lineage can be traced back to the times when the Zanskar was split. One side of the family ruled from Padum, and the other

Top Left: Lamayuru is one of the oldest sites in Ladakh; its gompa dates back to the 10th century.
Top Right: Look but don't touch. For now, Kashmir's breathtaking North Sonamarg Range is out of safe reach for trekkers. **Bottom:** Rangdum Gompa in Ladakh, where early winter snows bring a new perspective to trekking.

Trekking in Himachal Pradesh. **Top:** A Buddhist village in the Miyar Valley. **Bottom:** Trekkers rest at Hampta Pass in the Pir Panjal Range.

from Zangla. During the invasion of Zorawar Singh in 1834, the king of Padum was killed. On hearing of this the king of Zangla was able to reach an accord, which allowed him to retain a nominal rule over the nearby villages of Honia and Chazar, and the villages of Hanumil, Pidmu and Pishu on the far side of the valley. The head monk at Spitok is related to this family, and also administers the Zangla gompa, which is on the cliff just beyond the village.

Day 2: Zangla to Sumdo
3 hours, 9km
Follow the trail beyond the chortens, up past the former fort high above the village. From here, the trail follows the Zulung Valley upstream with many river crossings. After about 8km there is a *campsite* at 3800m that marks the junction of the main valley and a small valley coming from the north. There is a wooded grazing area with sufficient shade in which to spend a restful afternoon before crossing the Cha Cha La on the next stage.

Day 3: Sumdo to Camp via Cha Cha La
6 hours, 16km
The trail diverts from the main valley along a rough scree path for several kilometres, before entering a large dry side valley to the south, which marks the entrance to the pass. The trail ascends a series of glacial steps to the base of the pass. The final 200m to the pass is hard going, but the fine views back to the Himalaya Range beyond Padum are well worth the effort.

From the top of the **Cha Cha La** (4950m), the trail drops steadily. The time down to the first *camp* at approximately 4000m is about two hours.

Day 4: Camp to Tilat Sumdo
6 hours, 17km
Care must be taken when making the numerous river crossings on this stage. Six hours is the average walking time in autumn. In summer, when the water levels are higher, you may be forced to do this stage in two days, walking only in the morning when the water levels are lower. There is no shortage of *campsites*, which are identified by thousands of sheep pellets. These are a legacy of the large flocks of sheep brought from the Rupshu region each autumn to trade for grain in the Zanskar Valley.

About 5km before Tilat Sumdo, there is a small cave set in a limestone cliff just above the trail. In the cave there is reported to be a rock statue or lingam representing Lord Shiva, for childless Ladakhi women to touch in order to become fertile.

Tilat Sumdo (3750m) at the junction with the Khurna Valley is a delightful sandy campsite. It is also a convenient base to explore some of the remote gorge country nearby, which is famed for its wildlife.

Some maps and guide books show a trail down the Khurna River from Tilat Sumdo to the Zanskar River and on to the confluence with the Markha Valley. This is a late winter or early spring trail, which the locals follow after some sections of the ice on the Zanskar River, begin to melt. There is no summer trail along the Zanskar River between the Khurna and Markha Rivers.

Day 5: Tilat Sumdo to Base of Rubrang La
5–6 hours, 15km
The trail climbs alongside the Khurna River for 2km to 3km, to the confluence with a side river from the north. Here the track leaves the main valley, and climbs a series of rocky cliffs. This section is subject to constant landslides making it difficult for laden horses. The trail to the Rubrang La continues up the valley for a further 7km to 8km to a grassy *campsite* at the base of the pass at 4350m.

On these sections of the trek you encounter Khampa nomads, who come from the eastern region of Ladakh. The Khampa follow a nomadic lifestyle, very similar to that of the original inhabitants of Ladakh. They live in tents made of yak hair and rely on the produce of their yaks, goats and sheep. To supplement their income, they tend horses owned by the wealthier families from the Rupshu region. It is not uncommon to see them herding many hundreds of horses across these high grazing areas throughout the summer.

LADAKH

Day 6: Base of Rubrang La to Markha via Rubrang La
6 hours, 17km

The climb to the **Rubrang La** (5020m) takes about two hours. The trail ascends through a gully, which opens out just below the pass. To the north are uninterrupted views of the Stok Range. A small spring line is 3km below the pass; this is a convenient *camping area* for parties coming from the Markha Valley. The trail descends into a large gorge that leads down to the confluence with the Markha River. **Markha** village (3850m) is 2km below the confluence on the far side of the valley.

Days 7 to 10: Markha to Hemis/Stok

From Markha village, the trek can be completed in three or four days. The options are: go up the valley to Nimaling, and cross the Kongmaru La to Hemis (47km); or continue down the Markha Valley, and cross the Ganda La to Stok (59km). See the Markha Valley trek (pp113–16) for details of these routes.

Chortens

The *chorten* (or *stupa* in Tibetan; a reliquary or shrine to the memory of a Buddhist saint) is found throughout the valleys and trails in Ladakh and the Zanskar.

Originally the chorten was a built to serve as a monument where the ashes of important Buddhist teachers and lamas were buried. However, over time it also served to commemorate the important events in the life of the Buddha and as a reminder of the five elements of the cosmos – earth, wind, fire, air and ether.

At the entrance to some towns and villages, the chorten has a passage cut through the base through which travellers pass before entering. Many of the chortens along the trails in Ladakh and the Zanskar are found in a series of three with each painted a different colour. The white chorten represents knowledge, yellow represents wisdom and black represents the protector, with each of the chortens being given a fresh coat of paint after an important festival or after the death of a wealthy villager.

Phugtal Gompa & Shingo La

Duration	7 days
Distance	113km
Difficulty	moderate–demanding
Start	Padum
Finish	Darcha
Nearest Town	Padum (pp121–2)
Public Transport	yes

Summary One of the most popular treks in the Zanskar, visiting Buddhist villages and gompas before crossing the Himalaya Range to Lahaul and the Kullu Valley.

This trek has appealed to many trekkers in the past two decades. Acclimatisation is not an acute problem as the stages to the Shingo La (4980m) provide time to adjust. In June and July, the approach to the pass will be under snow while the trails across the scree slopes and terminal moraine to the south of the pass seem to change by the season.

There is no shortage of campsites and lodges while visiting the villages and their gompas (of which Phugtal gompa is the highlight). However, trekkers without tents will face a dangerous disadvantage if crossing the Shingo La during inclement weather.

PLANNING
When to Trek
The Shingo La is normally open from early June to early October, although the winter snows remain on the pass for most of the season. An occasional storm in September may disrupt trekking plans.

What to Bring
While this trek is popular, there have been tragic accidents with groups of trekkers being caught by storms while crossing the Shingo La. A tent should be carried together with food and fuel supplies for three or four days. Snow gaiters are also useful, particularly early in the season.

Maps
Refer to the Leomann series 1:200,000 *Sheet 3 (Leh, Zanskar & Nubra Valley)* for

the northern section of the trek as far as Purne. For the southern sections, refer to *Sheet 5 (Kullu Valley, Parbati Valley & Central Lahaul)*. Also refer to Nelles Verlag 1:350,000 *Ladakh & Zanskar* sheet and the US military U502 series 1:250,000 *43-12 ref Martselang* for the stages as far as the Shingo La. For the stages south to Darcha, refer to *43-16 ref Palampur*.

Accommodation

There are basic lodges and/or parachute tents on most (but not all) stages of the trek. Lodges or tented accommodation is available at Mune, although many trekkers continue to the lodge and campsite at Reru. At Purne, there is a choice of parachute tents and a couple of lodges. There are either lodges or tents at Tetha, Karu and Tanze, while Kargyak has a choice of lodges only. Lakong, at the base of the Shingo La, has a parachute tent. Once over the Shingo La, there is no guarantee of accommodation until you reach the parachute tents at Jankar Sumdo. At Darcha there is a choice of lodges and tents.

The lodge charges are around Rs 50 per bed plus food. If camping, expect to pay around Rs 50 to pitch your tent.

GETTING TO/FROM THE TREK

For travel to Padum, see Getting There & Away (p122). From Darcha, the bus to Manali (Rs 85) leaves early in the morning. There are also a number of buses to Keylong, from where you can catch the onward connection to Manali (Rs 72, six hours).

Heading north, there are regular truck convoys that may provide transport to the Indus Valley and Leh.

THE TREK (See map pp108–9)
Day 1: Padum to Mune
6 hours, 17km
The first 10km to Bardan is along a rather dusty 4WD road and can be completed in around three hours. **Bardan gompa** (3620m) is one of the most important in the valley. It is attached to the Drukpa order and has close ties with Hemis. The main assembly hall was extensively renovated a decade

ago, while the huge prayer wheel is famed as one of the largest in Ladakh. A donation of Rs 50 to Rs 100 is expected.

From Bardan, the 4WD track continues along the true left of the Tsarap River before ascending to a plateau, and the village and gompa at **Mune** (3750m). About 1km south of the village, the pleasant *camping ground* has a good supply of water. (Note: the campsite on the map near Mune is on the Kang La & Miyar Glacier trek, and is not passed en route to Mune.)

Day 2: Mune to Purne
8–9 hours, 22km
The trail cuts across the Mune plateau to the nearby village of **Reru** (3750m), which marks the current extent of the road construction. There is a willow plantation just above the village and a school, funded by the Swiss Foundation, that provides education for intermediate students.

There is a short climb before the trail descends quite steeply to the banks of the Tsarap River. The village of **Itchar** (3650m) is on the opposite side of the valley, about 6km from Mune. If heading for Purne, there is no need to cross the bridge here. However, there is a good *campsite* below the village should you opt for an easy day and continue to Purne the following day.

The main trail heading south follows the true left bank of the Tsarap River. It passes a number of small settlements, including **Surle** (3670m), while the village of Char is visible across the valley about 3km before Purne. Continue on the true left of the valley to the confluence of the Tsarap and Kargyak Rivers.

Cross the bridge over the Kargyak River and climb to **Purne** (3700m), where a couple of *lodges* sit alongside a shady *campsite*.

Side Trip: Phugtal Gompa
4 hours, 11km return
This side trip is a highlight of the trek and is best completed the morning before taking on Day 3. From Purne, the trail to Phutgal follows the true left bank of the Tsarap River for 4km to 5km before it reaches a bridge over the river. From the bridge it is a further 1km to **Phugtal gompa** (3850m).

LADAKH

The sight of the gompa on the limestone cliff never fails to impress. The main assembly hall is carved out of a huge cave, with the monks' quarters scattered down the hillside. Also look for the ancient cypress tree on the cliff above the gompa. Inside the gompa is an inscription to Coso de Koros, one of the first Europeans to visit the Zanskar region and the first to translate the Buddhist texts from Ladakhi into English. A donation of Rs 100 is expected, to assist with facilities for the school, where students from the nearby Phugtal village receive an elementary education. Monks will also serve tea together with the ubiquitous butter tea and *tsampa* (roasted ground barley).

Day 3: Purne to Tetha
2 hours, 6km
Before beginning this stage, we strongly recommend the side trip to Phugtal gompa. There is ample time to then continue to Tetha. Recross the bridge over the Kargyak River and follow the true left of the valley through the settlement of Yal (3930m). The trail gradually ascends to a large fertile plateau that supports some prosperous whitewashed villages, including Tetha (3950m).

Day 4: Tetha to Kargyak
5 hours, 14km
From Tetha, the trail is marked by well-maintained chortens to the village of Karu (3990m). Substantial stone walls line the track, protecting the barley fields from straying pack animals. This is a problem during the trekking season and can cause disputes between villagers and trekking parties.

After Karu, the trail descends back to the riverbank to the newly constructed bridge just below the village of Tanze (3850m), on the true left of the valley. There is a willow plantation project in a large enclosure, an example of recent initiatives in the region sponsored by the J&K Forest department.

It is a further 4km to 5km to the village of Kargyak (4050m), the highest permanent settlement in the Zanskar region. There is no shortage of *campsites* alongside the river, and a couple of the *houses* in the village provide accommodation and meals.

Side Trip: Into the Himalaya Range
10km return, 4 hours
An extra day could be spent wandering the valley opposite Kargyak. The valley affords

Geological Observations in the Zanskar

A trek across the Zanskar offers a wide range of geological features associated with the metamorphic rocks of the Higher Himalaya Crystalline (the high Himalaya) and the sedimentary rocks of the Tethyan Himalaya (the Trans-Himalaya).

The contrast between the two geological units is evident when trekking between Padum and Kargyak. The Kargyak Valley partly follows the prominent fault – the Zanskar Shear Zone – that marks the limit of the Higher Himalaya Crystalline to the south and the Tethyan Himalaya to the north. The Himalayan Crystalline forms the rugged snowcapped peaks of the Himalaya Range, while the multicoloured sediments constitute the more smoothly shaped Zanskar Range.

Above the Zanskar Shear Zone, green and grey shales, grey sandstones and yellowish dolomite represent the oldest sediments of the Tethyan Zone. The green volcanic rocks that are clearly visible near Phugtal gompa or white quartzites near Tanze and Kargyak are distinctly younger.

However, the most striking feature on the trek to the Shingo La is the huge Gumburanjun peak (see Day 5), about 10km southwest of Kargyak village. The mountain is almost entirely formed by white granite, although some sedimentary beds floating in the granite are still recognisable. By Himalayan standards the granite is very young – just 22 million years old – and resulted from the melting process during the recent formation of the Himalaya. While the peak can be admired from afar, it is not recommended to get too close to the rock face. Rock falls are frequent, as they are in many other areas of the Zanskar.

spectacular views of the glaciers and snow-fields of the Himalaya Range and the smaller settlements en route create an interesting trek.

Cross the bridge over the Kargyak River to the true right. Descend for 1km to the small settlement of Kye. Head west and gradually ascend the alpine valley that leads across yak-grazing pastures to the terminal moraine and snowfields that define the Himalaya Range.

Day 5: Kargyak to Lakong
4–5 hours, 14km
Remain on the true right of the valley as you continue across the yak-grazing pastures full of edelweiss towards the impressive rock monolith known as **Gumburanjan**. After passing the rock face, it is a further 2km onto the shepherds encampments, which are known locally as **Lakong** (4470m).

Just before the main alpine meadow, cross the small rock bridge over an upper tributary of the Kargyak River. There is also a basic *dhaba* and many *campsites* with panoramic views up the valley to the Himalaya Range.

Day 6: Lakong to Jankar Sumdo via Shingo La
9–10 hours, 22km
The trail climbs steeply at first before cross-ing an extensive alpine tract that leads to-wards the base of the Shingo La. About 4km from Lakong, there is a river crossing over a torrent that flows from the glaciers north of the pass. In spring and early summer, there may be a snow bridge here, at other times wet boots are unavoidable.

The ascent to the Shingo La is not hard by Himalayan standards. It can be done in 1½ to two hours across snowfields (early in the season) and scree (from August onwards).

Distinctive rock cairns and prayer flags mark the **Shingo La** (4980m). It is set be-neath an impressive backdrop of 6000m peaks defining both the Himalaya and Bara-lacha Ranges. Horse attendants may follow a route immediately to the west about 100m lower than the actual pass.

The configuration of the glacier to the south of the pass is constantly changing, and so is the trail. The descent route has changed a number of times in the past few seasons. The current trail leads to the true right of the ice and moraine, and includes a steep 400m descent to the glacial floor.

The trail continues on the true right of the broad glacial valley, descending gradually past several *campsites* to a grassy area known as **Rumjak** (4290m). Rumjak is about 5km to 6km from the pass and it is a further 5km to 6km across sparse vegetation and scree slopes to **Jankar Sumdo** (3860m). This stretch should take about three hours.

A short steep descent leads to Jankar Sumdo. Cross the substantial bridge over the Darcha River to a large *campsite* and *parachute tents* offering shelter and food.

Day 7: Jankar Sumdo to Darcha
7 hours, 18km
The trail continues on the true right of the valley, weaving through boulder fields and across several side streams and meagre grazing pastures to **Palamo** (3600m).

Cross the stone bridge high above the Darcha River to the true left of the valley and continue down to the village of **Rarig** (3500m). This is now the trailhead, although the road can be avoided by taking the many shortcuts to **Darcha** (3350m). Many *dhabas* line the road and a *campsite* sits beside the river. There is also a police checkpoint where you will need your passport.

Phitse La & Baralacha La

Duration	8 days
Distance	109km
Difficulty	demanding
Start	Padum
Finish	Baralacha La
Nearest Town	Padum (pp121–2)
Public Transport	yes

Summary A more demanding alternative to the Shingo La trek, with two high passes en route to Lahaul and Himachal Pradesh.

Only a few trekkers cross the Phitse La each season. Apart from the first four days in the Zanskar Valley, this is essentially a wilder-ness trek – although shepherds from Kargyak occasionally graze their yaks on the north side of the pass.

Beyond the encampments, the trail is often ill-defined and includes at least one river crossing requiring respectful caution.

On reaching the Baralacha La, there is a choice of either hitching a ride to Darcha and Keylong or extending the trek across the alpine pastures to Chandra Tal, before heading south over the Rohtang Pass to Manali and the Kullu Valley.

PLANNING
When to Trek
The Phitse La is normally passable by early June, although there is snow on the pass for most of the season. The pass is open until early October. Occasional storms in September may disrupt trekking plans.

What to Bring
A tent is a must, while food and fuel supplies should be carried for at least four days, for the stages between Tanze and the Baralacha La. A length of rope is handy for the river crossing near the Lingti campsite.

Maps
Refer to the Leomann series 1:200,000 *Sheet 3 (Leh, Zanskar & Nubra Valley)* for the northern section of the trek to Purne. For the southern sections, refer to *Sheet 5 Himachal Pradesh (Kullu Valley, Parbati Valley & Central Lahaul)*. Also refer to the Nelles Verlag 1:350,000 *Ladakh & Zanskar* sheet and the US military U502 series 1:250,000 *43-12 ref Martselang* for the stages as far as the Phitse La. For the stages onto the Baralacha La, refer to *43-16 ref Palampur*.

Accommodation
There are basic lodges and/or parachute tents available as far as Tanze. Lodges or tents are available at Mune, although many trekkers continue to the lodge and campsite at Reru. At Purne, there is a choice of tent and lodge accommodation. There are either lodges or parachute tents at Tetha, Karu and Tanze. Beyond Tanze there is nothing until you reach the dhabas in the vicinity of the Baralacha La.

En route to Tanze, expect to pay Rs 50 to sleep in a parachute tent or lodge, or to pitch your tent for the night.

GETTING TO/FROM THE TREK
For travel to Padum, see Getting There & Away (p122). From the Baralacha La, you may get a seat on one of the buses coming from Leh. However, the best option is to hitch a ride on a truck to Darcha (about Rs 50) and from there catch the local bus to Keylong. From Keylong, several buses travel to Manali daily (Rs 72, six hours).

THE TREK (See map pp108–9)
Days 1 to 3: Padum to Tetha
See Days 1 to 3 (pp131–2) of the Phugtal Gompa & Shingo La trek.

Day 4: Tetha to Tanze
4 hours, 10km
Follow Day 4 (p132) of the Phugtal Gompa & Shingo La trek but stop near Tanze for the night.

Day 5: Tanze to Phitse La Base
7 hours, 15km
Shortly after Tanze, the trail to the Phitse La heads up a side gorge that ascends steeply out of the Kargyak Valley. The climb is steep for nearly 500m until the head of the gorge. A short walk back across the plateau will provide a bird's-eye view down the Kargyak Valley to Purne. There is a good *campsite* a few kilometres up the valley – in fact, the best between Tanze and the pass. However, to make an early start over the Phitse La, continue up the valley to a more restricted *campsite* at the base (approximately 4800m).

Day 6: Phitse La Base to Lingti Camp via Phitse La
7 hours, 15km
The climb to the pass is short and steep, with the final ascent up a scree slope to the well-defined **Phitse La** (5250m). There are views across to the Himalaya Range, while the climb up the small ridge to the north of the pass affords panoramic views across the Zanskar Range.

The descent crosses a series of scree slopes and is steep in places to **Chumik Marpo** (4880m). This is an ideal *campsite* if you're coming from the opposite direction. The area is grazed by yak herders from Kargyak in summer and is the only settlement on this route between Tanze and Darcha. From the camp, the trail follows a series of ridges before dropping into a narrow gorge to the main **Lingti Valley**. Continue down the valley to the first main tributary of the Lingti River and camp for the night at approximately 4400m.

Day 7: Lingti Camp to Kilang Sarai
6–7 hours, 16km

This stage enters Himachal Pradesh. Cross the main tributary early in the morning; the high water level in summer could present difficulties, but from September, this and the other side rivers are easier to negotiate. The trail winds across ridges covered with juniper and past dilapidated mani walls before reaching the confluence of the Tsarap and Lingti Valleys. The route heads up the Tsarap Valley across extensive pastures, which form the upper grazing limits of the Gaddi shepherds from Himachal Pradesh. A few kilometres on, the military road from Leh crosses the valley below the **Kilang Sarai** (4600m), where there is an adequate *campsite*.

Day 8: Kilang Sarai to Baralacha La
3 hours, 8km

From camp, the trail joins the Leh-Manali road to the **Baralacha La** (4950m). The steady climb is rewarded by impressive views of the peaks, many of which are above 6000m. Between the switchbacks on the road, you can take shortcuts until you reach the pass. The Baralacha La is one of the most historically famous passes in the Himalaya – for centuries, it marked the trading border between the Kullu Valley and Ladakh. It is a double pass, at the convergence of the Tsarap Valley in the north, the Chandra Valley to the south, and the Bhaga Valley to the west. There is no shortage of *campsites* on the pass, complete with wildflowers and an impressive mountain backdrop.

Kang La & Miyar Glacier

Duration	7 days
Distance	108km
Difficulty	demanding
Start	Padum
Finish	Chamrat
Nearest Town	Padum (pp121–2)
Public Transport	yes

Summary One of the most demanding treks over the Himalaya, with spectacular views and a 28km glacier.

You must be well prepared for this trek, which involves a high pass crossing over the Kang La (5450m) and at least one night camping on the Miyar Glacier – one of the longest glaciers in the West Himalaya.

To acclimatise, complete another trek in Ladakh or the Zanskar prior to setting off. Alternatively, reserve at least a week to see the gompas and forts in the Zanskar Valley.

There is no obvious route over the Kang La; the profile of the glaciers on both sides of the pass changes by the season. Only trekkers experienced in travelling at altitude and over this type of terrain should consider this trek.

The incredible peaks south of Kang La are ripe for exploration. Add to that the complete change of geography in the verdant Miyar Valley, Gaddi shepherd encampments and distinctive Buddhist settlements for a trek full of highlights.

The road construction up the Miyar Valley will undoubtedly change the character of the villages and the last stages of the trek. Construction will eventually extend to Tharang.

PLANNING
When to Trek
The Kang La is normally open from early July to early October. August and September are the best months as the Miyar Valley is north of the Pir Panjal Range and does not attract the heaviest of the monsoon rains.

What to Bring
A tent, sleeping bag, one or two lengths of rope, ice axes and karabiners are necessary. Carry food for five or six days, as there is

little in the way of supplies until the villages in the lower Miyar Valley.

Maps
Refer to the Leomann series 1:200,000 *Sheet 2 (Kargil, Zanskar & Nun Kun)* and *Sheet 4 (Chamba, Dhaula Dhar Passes, Pagni Valley & Lahaul)*. Sheet 2 covers the area to the north of the Kang La, while Sheet 4 covers the southern Miyar Valley. However, the sheets do not join up and neither sheet actually covers the Kang La. The Nelles Verlag 1:350,000 *Ladakh & Zanskar* sheet only includes the trek as far as the upper Miyar Valley, but at least covers the pass. Also refer to the US military U502 series 1:250,000 *43-12 ref Martselang* for the stages from Padum to just over the Kang La and *Palampur ref 43-16* for the stages in the Miyar Valley.

Accommodation
After Padum, there is no indoor accommodation until Urgos (Day 6). There is a Forest Rest House and PWD Rest House on the outskirts of Udaipur.

GETTING TO/FROM THE TREK
For travel to Padum, see Getting There & Away (p122). The road is being extended up the Miyar Valley and at present there is a twice daily bus service connecting Udaipur with Chamrat (Rs 15, two hours). From Udaipur, three or four buses a day head to Keylong (Rs 70, six hours). From Keylong, there is transport to Manali, Darcha and Leh; see Getting There & Away (p185).

THE TREK (See map pp108–9)
Day 1: Padum to Temasa Tokpo Camp
4 hours, 13km
From Padum, follow the 4WD track to the village of **Bardan** (3620m). Bardan gompa is one of the most important in the Zanskar and has close ties with Hemis.

Continue for 3km along the main trail to Mune as far as the Temasa Tokpo. Cross the bridge and divert from the main trail. The route heads south and ascends scree slope for 200m to 300m to a small grassy *campsite* (3800m) with spring water.

Day 2: Temasa Tokpo Camp to Kang La Base
7–8 hours, 17km
The trail, an ill-defined shepherd track over the boulder fields, ascends the true right of the valley. However, the trail does not divert far from the course of the river, although there are a number of side streams to negotiate. There are also many potential *campsites* en route that may serve as intermediary camps while you acclimatise. As you climb, views down to the Tsarap Valley provide an incredible profile of the Zanskar Range.

The **base camp** (High Camp) at 4800m is unremarkable. It is a small grassy area just below the confluence of two valleys. The valley to the west leads to the Poat La and the Dharlang Valley, while the valley to the southeast leads to the Kang La.

Day 3: Kang La Base to Glacier Camp 1 via Kang La
8–9 hours, 20km
This can be a tough stage. Group members should rope up before reaching the snowfields. From camp, head up the southeast valley. An ill-defined trail leads to the edge of the terminal moraine before a steep ascent over boulders and snowfields reaches a vantage point immediately below the pass. On the upper section of the snowfield, watch out for the hidden crevasses.

The **Kang La** (5450m) is 1.5km to 2km long, enclosed to the north by rock cliffs and to the south by snow walls. The route tends to lead towards the centre of the pass, avoiding the obvious crevassed sections before reaching a consolidated snowfield on the south side. There is a gradual descent for 250m to 300m to the main glacier floor.

Beyond the pass, the route tends to lead towards to the centre of the Miyar Glacier. It is spectacular country ringed by many 6000m peaks and hanging glaciers, while the summit of Menthosa (6443m) can be seen to the south of the valley. The route along the glacier's upper sections crosses extensive snow and ice fields that are mostly covered in scree. However, the walking is comparatively easy, reaching a selection of camps on the glacier at around 4800m.

Day 4: Glacier Camp 1 to Terminal Moraine Camp
5–6 hours, 13km

After the exhilaration of crossing the pass, it is hard to mentally prepare for what can be a tiring stage. The initial route is comparatively straightforward – down the centre of the glacier – until the terminal moraine. Just below, a major side glacier flows into the Miyar Glacier from the east. From here, keep a close lookout for rock cairns that define the best route through the moraine. This is especially difficult early in the season when all but the largest of the boulders are under snow. The last 5km to 6km through the terminal moraine can be particularly tiring. A grassy *campsite* at approximately 4200m provides relief beside a series of glacial lakes.

Day 5: Terminal Moraine Camp to Gumbah Nullah
5 hours, 15km

Beyond the moraine, follow a shepherd trail that leads across the alpine pastures. There are a number of **Gaddi shepherd encampments**. Do not approach the camps until you have the shepherds' attention as their dogs will need to be chained up. Several side streams require crossing before you reach a prominent rock known locally as **Khai Got** (4100m). There are silver birch trees on the opposite side of the valley marking the upper limit of the tree line.

It is a further two hours (approximately 6km) to one of the many campsites in the vicinity the **Gumbah Nullah** (4050m), which flows from the east.

Day 6: Gumbah Nullah to Urgos
6–7 hours, 17km

From the Gumbah Nullah, the trail heads across alpine pastures where the shepherds have constructed log bridges over the side streams. Gaddi shepherds from Himachal Pradesh share these pastures with yak herders from the Zanskar, who bring their animals over the Shingo La and the nearby Tarasalamu Pass in July and August. The meadows are carpeted with wildflowers that thrive as soon as the spring snows melt by mid-July. This is an idyllic *campsite* if you have time.

From the meadows south of the alpine plateau, fine views extend down to villages of the lower Miyar Valley. Look west to see the snowcapped peaks of the Pir Panjal Range, on the far side of the Chenab River.

The trail remains on the valley's true left as it descends steeply for 200m to the highest village of **Tharang** (3500m) before crossing a wide alluvial fan to **Khanjar** (3450m). Descend for a further 2km before crossing a bridge over the Miyar River to the substantial village of **Urgos** (3250m). There is a small gompa and the mani walls and chortens reflect the deep-seated Buddhist culture.

Urgos is also close to the base of Menthosa (6443m). An optional trek can be taken up the side valley to the west of Urgos to appreciate the mountain's lower flanks.

Day 7: Urgos to Chamrat
4 hours, 13km

From Urgos, head down through pea and maize fields and alongside a number of irrigation channels to the village of **Churput** (3050m). Cross the bridge over the Miyar River to the village of **Karpat** (3010m). It is then a few kilometres down the valley to the village of **Chamrat** (2950m), from where a local bus runs to Udaipur.

Umasi La

Duration	6 days
Distance	95km
Difficulty	demanding
Start	Padum
Finish	Gularbagh
Nearest Town	Padum (pp121–2)
Public Transport	yes

Summary Follow the former trading route over the Himalaya Range to the Hindu villages in the Pardar district.

Before considering this trek, check with your embassy (see the 'Warning' boxed text, p138) for advice regarding the safety of travel in the vicinity of Kishtwar.

While the route over the Umasi La is not as technically demanding as the trek over

Warning

At the time of writing, this trek is in the *for reference only* category, with advisories warning against travel in the vicinity of Kishtwar in the J&K State. However, the recent completion of the road from Lahaul now provides an alternative route to Himachal Pradesh that avoids Kishtwar region.

Check with the Tsering Namgyal in Padum for an update; see Information (p121). He is keen to point out that during 2001 a number of trekkers crossed the Umasi La either en route to Gularbagh or to undertake a challenging double traverse of the Himalaya returning via the Poat La to Padum. This is, by all reports, a spectacular trek (see the Alternative Route, Day 5).

the Kang La, trekkers should carry a rope and ice axes. Additional days should also be reserved for acclimatisation before crossing the pass. Beyond the pass, a number of Buddhist villages maintain close cultural and social contact with the Zanskar region. Hindu villages are found on the final stage towards the Chenab Valley, although the influence of Ladakhi traders is still evident in the vicinity of Gularbagh.

The vegetation levels south of the Umasi La are also clearly defined, from the high alpine pastures and silver birch trees to the upper conifer bands. Lower down the Pardar Valley, mixed conifer and oak forest lives near apple orchards and rice fields.

PLANNING
When to Trek
The Umasi La is normally passable by early June, although the winter snows do not melt until late July. The pass remains open until early October.

What to Bring
Bring a tent, sleeping bag, a rope length or two, together with ice axes and karabiners. Carry at least five days of food supplies, although some basic supplies of rice, flour and biscuits may be available in Suncham and Marchel.

Maps
Refer to the Leomann series 1:200,000 *Sheet 2 (Kargil, Zanskar & Nun Kun)* and the Nelles Verlag 1:350,000 *Ladakh & Zanskar* sheet. See the US military U502 series 1:250,000 *43-12 ref Martselang* for the stages from Padum to the Umasi La, and *43-11 ref Anantnag* for the lower stages to Gularbagh.

Accommodation
After Padum, there is no accommodation until Marchel. At Marchel's Forest Rest House, the *chowkidar* (caretaker) should be able to serve meals. Budget for about Rs 100 per room. Expect to pay around Rs 50 if you are camping in the vicinity of the villages.

GETTING TO/FROM THE TREK
For travel to Padum, see Getting There & Away (p122). The road from Kishtwar to Gularbagh was completed in 1992, while the road from Keylong in Lahaul was completed in 2001. From Gularbagh there is no current bus service to Lahaul and Manali. For now, trucks are the only alternative.

THE TREK (See map pp110–11)
Day 1: Padum to Zongkul
6–7 hours, 20km
From Padum, follow the road past the monastery at Sani to the Tungri Bridge. Do not cross the bridge, but follow the trail on the true right bank of the Stod River to the village of **Ating** (3600m) and the entrance to the Zongkul Valley. **Zongkul gompa** (3800m) is 3km to 4km up the valley, high above the valley floor. According to legend, the monastery was founded by the sage Naropa in the 11th century. Today it is serviced by half a dozen monks from Sani gompa. There is a choice of *campsites* below the gompa.

Day 2: Zongkul to Umasi La Base
6–7 hours, 14km
From Zongkul gompa, the trail leads up the true left of the Mulung Tokpo to a natural rock bridge. Cross the river here and ascend the grassy meadows (ideal for an intermediary campsite) before the route diverts up a steep ridge to enter a side valley, on the true right of the main valley. There follows

a tiring stage through an extensive boulder field to a wide glacial valley. A cluster of stone shelters and a small grassy meadow mark the overnight *camp* at 4400m.

Day 3: Umasi La Base to High Camp via Umasi La
7 hours, 13km

From camp, begin the climb up the glacial valley. The glacier is not heavily crevassed and the distance to the base can be covered in 1½ hours. The trek to the **Umasi La** (5340m) then diverts up the moraine-strewn trail to the glacier's true left. The route, marked by rock cairns, becomes progressively steeper. Just below the pass is a very steep section up an ice gully (if coming from the opposite direction, a rope belay would be handy).

The **Umasi La** is just a small gap in the cliff wall, marked by the usual array of prayer flags offered by monks from the Bardan and Sani gompas, who regularly cross the pass. Thomas Thomson was the first European to cross the pass in late June 1848. From his account, he was denied the views, reaching the pass during a heavy snowstorm. Yet he did not neglect his duties and set about boiling a pan of water. The water finally came to the boil at 180.3°F (82.2°C), from which he was able to calculate the height of the pass to be at least 18,000ft (5490m) – about 150m higher than the present-day calculation.

From the pass, a steady descent leads to a large snowfield (crevassed in places) that flows into a larger glacier from the south. Before the confluence of these glaciers, the trail turns north (along the valley's true right), offering impressive views of the Kishtwar Himalaya. There is a flat, if somewhat rocky, *campsite* at 4890m, beneath a huge rock overhang where the porters prefer to spend the night.

Day 4: High Camp to Suncham
8 hours, 18km

From the porters' camp, descend a steep 300m to 400m beside the hanging glacier to the main glacial valley floor. On reaching the glacier, the walking is easier. Follow the glacier down the valley for about 3km before heading to the lateral moraine on the true right of the valley. The route is again marked by rock cairns through the moraine.

The trail through the moraine descends to a small sandy *campsite* before a further steep descent over a grassy slope to a broad alpine valley. The trail remains on the true right of the valley to the confluence of the Hagshu Nullah and some Bakraval shepherd encampments in a birch grove at 3500m. To the south, the peak of Kishtwar Shivling (6000m) rears above the valley. It was first climbed by the British climbers Stephen Venables and Dick Renshaw in 1983.

A few kilometres down the valley, the trail crosses a large boulder field before reaching **Suncham** (3250m).

Day 5: Suncham to Marchel
3 hours, 8km

This comparatively short stage allows time to explore the Buddhist villages in the upper Pardar Valley. From Suncham, the trail descends on the true right of the valley to the confluence of the Dharlang Nullah (and the route to the Poat La – a pass to the southeast of the Umasi La leading back to the Zanskar Valley).

Descending to Marchel, the trail passes several small villages founded when Ladakhi farmers migrated to the region about seven generations ago. **Marchel** (2790m) and the nearby village of **Lusen** have simple gompas, which are periodically serviced by monks from the Bardan and Sani gompas in Zanskar. Other ties with Zanskar are also maintained and marriages are arranged on both sides of the Himalaya.

Alternative Route: To Padum via Poat La
5 days, 90km

While the author has not completed this challenging trek, the Bakraval shepherds regularly follow the route up the Dharlang Valley. Reserve two or three days for this section before crossing the Poat La.

The route over the **Poat La** (5470m) is marked by cairns that avoid the crevassed sections of the glacier south of the pass. Once over the pass it is a short descent to the high camp (at the base of the Kang La). See Days

LADAKH

1 and 2 (p136) of the Kang La & Miyar Glacier trek for details of the campsite and the following stages to Padum (in reverse).

Day 6: Marchel to Gularbagh
8 hours, 22km

From Marchel, the trail heads down the true right of the valley. Grand views extend to the Chenab Valley and across to the Pir Panjal Range beyond Atholi. The well-defined trail descends to **Shashut** (2600m), where there is a simple Hindu temple.

Below Shashut village, cross a substantial wooden bridge to the true left of the valley, then pass a series of excellent *campsites* amid deodar and conifer trees. Logging operations are also evident further down the valley. The trail recrosses the Pardar River further down the valley before reaching a series of settlements set amid chestnut, oak and deodar forest.

The small bazaar at **Gularbagh** is just above the confluence of the Pardar and Chenab Rivers. People here are of Ladakhi origin, traders who originally settled in the upper Pardar Valley. The town of **Atholi**

Pardar Valley

Until the 1830s, the Pardar district was an integral part of Chamba (now Himachal Pradesh). From 1820 to 1825, the locals supported the Chamba forces in their invasion of the Zanskar region. Allegiances changed a decade later.

After invading Ladakh and Zanskar, Zorawar Singh, the army general from Jammu, led his Dogra forces back over the Umasi La on the return route to Jammu. The Pardar people were suspicious of the Dogra, particularly when a small party of troops was left behind to 'facilitate communications' with Ladakh. The Pardar people killed the Dogra contingent. On hearing of this, Zorawar Singh returned the following year (1836) and annexed the region to Jammu. This is the main reason why the region is now part of the Jammu & Kashmir State, rather than Himachal Pradesh, and why the Himachal border (formerly Chamba) is about 15km up the Chenab Valley to the southeast of Gularbagh.

(2250m) lies on the south side of the valley. It is the district headquarters, with primary and middle schools as well as a police station.

Kanji La & Shilakong Gorge

Duration	6 days
Distance	80km
Difficulty	demanding
Start	Rangdum
Finish	Lamayuru
Nearest Towns	Padum (pp121–2), Kargil (pp122–3)
Public Transport	yes

Summary Essentially a wilderness trek, following remote trails over the outlying ridges of the Zanskar Range and through spectacular gorges to the ancient gompa at Lamayuru.

Rangdum offers many trekking possibilities, including this route over the Kanji La (5290m). For acclimatisation, we recommend a few days camping in the open meadows just beyond Rangdum gompa or at the nearby village of Tashi Tongtse.

While villages on this trek are rare, the high passes and spectacular gorges compensate. From the ridge above the Kanji La, it is possible to see the summit of K2 – the second-highest mountain in the world. Other views reach to the Stok and Ladakh Ranges. The Shilakong Gorge, with its deep canyon walls and striking rock faces, adds a further dimension to the trek. Take care on the many river crossings in July and August.

PLANNING
When to Trek

The trek is possible from early June to mid-October, although expect snow on the Kanji La until early July. Summer storms in the Shilakong Gorge, and the water levels in June and July, should also be considered.

What to Bring

Carry a tent and stove, plus food and fuel supplies for at least five days. A length of rope may be required for some river crossings.

Maps

Refer to the Leomann series 1:200,000 *Sheet 3 (Leh, Zanskar & Nubra Valley)* and *Sheet 2 (Kargil, Zanskar & Nun Kun)*. Also refer to Nelles Verlag 1:350,000 *Ladakh & Zanskar* and the US military U502 series 1:250,000 *NI 43-07 ref Kargil* and *NI 43-08 ref Leh*.

Accommodation

In Rangdum, there are roadside dhabas, and plentiful campsites in the vicinity of the gompa. Some campsites are in the meadows close to the upper reaches of the Suru River, well away from the Kargil-Padum road. Consider heading a few kilometres south to the village of Tashi Tongtse. The villagers regard themselves as being part of the Zanskar, even though the village is north of the Pentse La.

Camping is the best option en route. Because only a few trekkers undertake this trek, there are no lodges apart from those in Lamayuru and nearby Wanlah. There are no camping fees on most stages of the trek, although you can expect to pay a fee of Rs 50 in the vicinity of Kanji and Wanlah. Guesthouses at Lamayuru include the *Hotel Dragon* and *Hotel Shangri La*; both have rooms from Rs 150 to Rs 200.

GETTING TO/FROM THE TREK

To reach Rangdum from Kargil or Padum, the choice is between the bus that operates every other day or hitching a ride on a truck. From Kargil/Padum, the charge is around Rs 200/120 (10/6 hours) for either bus or truck. An expensive alternative is a 4WD; from Kargil to Rangdum, budget for around Rs 4000; from Padum you may be fortunate to get a seat for around Rs 200 if the driver is anxious to return to Kargil.

The local bus from Lamayuru to Leh departs around 7am (Rs 70, six hours). For the same fare, trucks are a convenient alternative.

THE TREK (See map p112)

Day 1: Rangdum to Kanji La Base
5–6 hours, 13km

The monks at **Rangdum gompa** (3980m) come from nearby villages **Tashi Tongtse** and **Juldo**. The gompa was founded about 200 years ago and is affiliated with the

Gelukpa order, the Dalai Lama's sect. Entrance to the gompa is Rs 50.

The trail to Kanji follows the valley to the north of Rangdum. The route depends on the water level in the river. Early in the season, it is easier to follow the trail on the true left of the valley. Later in the season, when the river crossings are less of a hazard, it doesn't matter which side of the valley you follow. After ascending the valley for a few kilometres, there is a shepherds hut on the true left bank. From the hut, a series of rather tiring ups and downs continues for several kilometres before reaching the **Kanji La base** (4250m).

The *campsite* is at the junction of the main valley and the one leading to the Kanji La. It is a small, rocky plateau 50m above the water's edge. To reach it you must cross the main river (a stream later in the season). This may require ropes if the river is flooded. Supplies will have to be offloaded from the horses as the trail is unsuitable for laden animals. There is scarcely space for tents, and the horse attendants rarely spend a good night here – they have to watch the horses in case they take off, back to the greener pastures of Rangdum.

Day 2: Kanji La Base to Camp via Kanji La
6–7 hours, 15km

An early start is imperative for this stage. There are no side streams en route to the pass, so water must be carried with you. Doing the climb in the shade should leave you sufficient reserves to reach the pass by mid-morning. From camp, the trail climbs through a narrow gorge, with a distinct possibility of wet boots. The valley opens out and you can appreciate the huge, jagged ridges of the Zanskar Range. The average time required to reach the **Kanji La** (5290m) is three to four hours.

From the pass, there are views back to the Himalaya Range, and ahead to the peaks of the Karakoram. For even better views, including **K2**, climb for 10 to 15 minutes up either of the ridges directly above the pass.

Care is needed on the initial descent from the pass. The trail down a steep gully is difficult under snow early in the season. It then winds down the true left of the valley and across boulder fields, reaching a broad scree plateau. Cross the plateau and continue for several kilometres until the trail drops steeply to the main valley floor. The time required from the pass is two to three hours.

There is a small, grassy *campsite* after this last steep descent, which is often used by trekkers from Kanji village. This is the best overnight option, although there are several *campsites* near the meadow a further 2km down the gorge.

Day 3: Camp to Kanji Village
3 hours, 9km

The trail continues down a small tree-lined gorge and recrosses the stream several times until it reaches an open grazing area. The meadow is frequented by yak herders from Kanji village. Remain on the true right of the valley, which winds and turns for several kilometres. En route you will probably meet villagers from Kanji, either with their flocks or tending the outlying barley fields. There is no need to cross the main river until you reach the gorge immediately above the village. Either *camp* here or check out the possibility of *camping* in one of the enclosures in the vicinity of **Kanji** (3875m).

Kanji village is quite a prosperous settlement by Ladakhi standards, consisting of 20 or so families who farm the immediate area.

Alternative Route: Kanji Village to Heniskot
2–3 hours

If time is at a premium, descend through the Kanji Gorge to the village at Heniskot on the Kargil–Leh road. The trail through the gorge is well maintained, although river crossings can be problematic after heavy rainfall.

The village of **Heniskot** (3550m) is on the far side of the Kargil-Leh road, and is approached through a small gorge down the valley from where the trail meets the road. Hitch a ride on at truck over the Fatu La (4094m) to Lamayuru (Rs 15); the trip should take less than an hour.

Day 4: Kanji Village to Shilakong via Yogma La
4 hours, 17km

Follow the trail that heads up the valley to the east of Kanji Village. There are many *campsites* in the surrounding alpine meadows. The gradual approach to the **Yogma La** (4650m) is on a well-defined trail. From the pass, there are views towards the Zanskar Range and the distinctive (unnamed) 6000m peak at the head of the gorge. A short, steep descent leads to the upper reaches of the gorge and the *campsite* known as **Shilakong** (3800m).

Day 5: Shilakong to Wanlah
6–7 hours 16km

The ridge immediately to the east of Shilakong leads to the Sisir La and the trail from Padum to Lamayuru; see the Singge La & Lamayuru trek (pp123–7). It is therefore likely that, as the road extends from Wanlah to Honupatta, this will become the preferred route to/from the Zanskar.

The trail down the Shilakong Gorge frequently crosses the Shila River. At times the trail forges a route through a thicket of bushes and willow trees, while occasionally it ascends the scree slopes to avoid the river. The gorge is very impressive as it penetrates one of the main folds of the Zanskar Range. The walls sometimes rise 1000m above the river.

The occasional rock cairn is often the only indication of which side of the gorge to follow, until it opens out above the settlement of **Shila** (3200m). It is a further 2km to the village and gompa at **Wanlah** (3150m).

Day 6: Wanlah to Lamayuru via Prinkiti La
3–4 hours, 10km

Retrace the route to Shila and the entrance to the small gorge leading to the Prinkiti La. The entrance is marked by a chorten and prayer flags. The route up the gorge is almost devoid of vegetation and often becomes hot and tiring by mid-morning. From the **Prinkiti La** (3650m), enjoy fine views of the Zanskar before the descent to **Lamayuru** (3430m).

Jammu & Kashmir

The regions of Jammu and Kashmir, including the summer capital of Srinagar and the winter capital Jammu, form part of the vast state of Jammu and Kashmir (J&K). Within J&K state the Jammu and Kashmir regions have been subject to political unrest since the 1990s. Lonely Planet strongly advises trekkers not to travel here (see the Warning boxed text). The following information is for background interest only, unless the security situation changes. The region of Ladakh also falls within J&K state, although it is generally safe for travel.

The Kashmir Valley was, until recent geological times, a vast lake with a water level around 200m to 300m above the present valley floor. The pressure of water eventually cleared the blockage of silt and rocks to the north of the valley. What remains is one of the most fertile regions in northern India.

The Pir Panjal Range encloses the valley to the west and south, rising on average to elevations of around 5000m. To the north, the North Sonamarg Range provides an equally impressive backdrop, including the sacred peak of Harimukh (5135m). To the east, the Amarnath and Kolahoi Ranges rise above Sonamarg and Pahalgam and extend south to the Pir Panjal. The ramparts of the Kashmir Valley are breached only once, to the north of the valley, where the Jhelum River flows through a gorge en route to the Indus River.

South of the Kashmir Valley is the region of Jammu, including the city of Jammu. The region extends north across rugged mountain terrain to the southern rim of the Kashmir Valley. It also includes the Kishtwar region, where the Chenab River forges through the Pir Panjal and Dhaula Dhar Ranges and the Siwalik Hills en route to the Indian Plains.

Until 1989 Kashmir was one of the most popular trekking destinations in India. Many groups followed the treks out of Pahalgam into the Lidder and Sindh Valleys each season from May until mid-October. However, with the onset of political unrest, there was a dramatic decline in trekking in the region. It

halted altogether when a group of foreign trekkers were taken hostage from their camp close to Lidderwat in July 1995. One was beheaded and it is assumed that the others were later killed by members of a little-known fundamentalist group operating in the valley.

INFORMATION

The following treks are out of the hill station in Pahalgam (2140m) in Kashmir. Lonely Planet strongly advises trekkers not to visit this region while the current security situation persists. The following information is provided *only* as a starting point, and *only* in the hope that the situation does improve.

Kolahoi Glacier & Tar Sar

From **Pahalgam**, the trek follows a jeep road along the West Lidder Valley to the village of **Aru** (2410m). The next short stage leads through conifer forest and meadows to the *campsite* at **Lidderwat** (3050m). From here, it is a full day's trek to view the impressive peak and glacier of **Kolahoi** (5452m), passing a number of Gujar shepherd encampments en route. After returning to Lidderwat, it is a further day to the alpine lake of **Tar Sar** (3900m).

JAMMU & KASHMIR

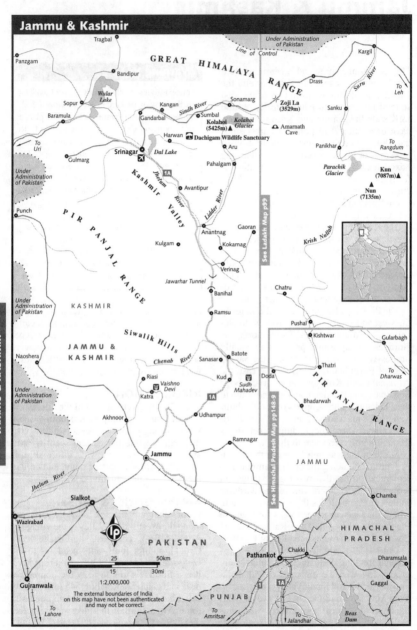

Jammu & Kashmir

Tragbal

Panzgam

GREAT HIMALAYA

Line of Control

Under Administration of Pakistan

Kargil

Bandipur

RANGE

Drass

To Leh

Saru River

Wular Lake

Kangan

Sindh River

Sonamarg

Zoji La (3529m)

Sanku

Sopur

Gandarbal

Sumbal

Kolahoi (5425m)▲

Kolahoi Glacier

Baramula

Harwan

Amarnath Cave

Panikhar

To Uri

Gulmarg

Srinagar

Dal Lake

Dachigam Wildlife Sanctuary

Aru

To Rangdum

Under Administration of Pakistan

Kashmir Valley

Jhelum River

1A

Pahalgam

Parachik Glacier

Kun (7087m)▲

Avantipur

Lidder River

Nun (7135m)

Punch

PIR PANJAL RANGE

Gaoran

Krish Nullah

See Ladakh Map p99

Anantnag

Kulgam

Kokarnag

Under Administration of Pakistan

KASHMIR

Verinag

Jawarhar Tunnel

Chatru

Banihal

Ramsu

Pushal

Siwalik Hills

JAMMU & KASHMIR

Kishtwar

Gularbagh

Naoshera

Chenab River

Sanasar

Batote

Thatri

To Dharwas

Riasi

Vaishno Devi

Kud

Sudh Mahadev

Doda

PIR PANJAL RANGE

Katra

Bhadarwah

Akhnoor

1A

Udhampur

See Himachal Pradesh Map pp148-9

Ramnagar

JAMMU

Jammu

Jhelum River

Sialkot

Chamba

Wazirabad

HIMACHAL PRADESH

PAKISTAN

0   25   50km

0   15   30mi

1:2,000,000

Dharamsala

Gujranwala

The external boundaries of India on this map have not been authenticated and may not be correct.

Pathankot

Chakki

Gaggal

To Lahore

PUNJAB

To Amritsar

1

1A

To Jalandhar

Beas Dam

The trail crosses a series of alpine meadows to the *shepherd camp* at **Seikwas** (3430m) before ascending to this glacial lake with fine views of the summit ridges of Kolahoi.

Retrace the route to Lidderwat. The final stage from Lidderwat to Pahalgam can be completed in a long morning with time to catch the bus back to Srinagar the same day.

Sumbal & the Sindh Valley

Follow the previous route to reach **Tar Sar** and *camp* overnight at **Seikwas** (3430m). The next stage heads up an enclosed valley to the **Sonamous Pass** (3960m). There follows a steep and tiring descent (difficult under snow in early spring) to the Gujar settlement at **Sonamous** (3340m). An ill-defined trail descends through mixed forest to the outlying villages and fields of the Sindh Valley. It's then on to the rice paddies and cornfields of **Sumbal** village, where a bus goes to Srinagar or Sonamarg at the head of the Sindh Valley.

Amarnath Cave via Mahagunas Pass

From **Pahalgam**, follow a jeep track along the East Lidder Valley to the *campsite* at **Chandanwadi** (2900m). The next stage begins with a steep climb to the ridge known as **Pisu Top** (3390m) before heading across alpine meadows to **Sheshnag** (3720m), a glacial lake beneath the peaks of Vishnu, Shiva and Brahma. There are magnificent views of these peaks on the following stage as the trail ascends to **Mahagunas Pass** (4270m) before the long descent to **Panchtarni** (3450m).

From Panchtarni, it takes several hours to reach the **Amarnath Cave** (4050m), following the trail up the Amarvati Valley. The cave is set within a vast limestone cliff face in which a huge, ice stalagmite symbolises the power of Shiva. The return from Panchtarni to Pahalgam requires two days, camping at Chandanwadi.

Suru Valley (Ladakh) via Boktol Pass

From **Pahalgam**, the first two stages follow the route of the Amarnath pilgrimage as far as **Sheshnag** (3720m). The next stage involves a steep climb to the **Gul Gali** (4410m), with

The Amarnath Trek

The trek to Amarnath Cave is the most important pilgrimage in Kashmir. It is timed to coincide with the *Shavan* full moon (July–Aug). Despite the political unrest, about 20,000 Hindu pilgrims from all over India trek to the cave to see the ice statue that symbolises the presence of Shiva, Hindu god of destruction.

There are many legends regarding the discovery of the cave, but little historical fact. In all probability, it was discovered as shepherds searched the valley for new pastures. Not only is the cave an ideal refuge for meditation, it is also close to one of the sources of the Jhelum River, an important tributary of the Indus. According to legend, Lord Shiva related his theory of reincarnation to his consort Parvati in the cave on a full-moon night. A huge ice statue (or stalagmite) – said to wax and wane with the moon – formed in the cave. It represents the *lingam*, a symbol of Shiva, the source of creation. The huge size of the cave symbolises Parvati and the vast womb of the universe.

In recent years, the Indian government has made elaborate plans to ensure a safe pilgrimage. However, in late July 2000, gunmen indiscriminately shot more than 30 Hindu pilgrims and Kashmir villagers in Pahalgam shortly after the pilgrimage. This incident called for another review of the region's security.

fine views of the Himalaya Range. A steep descent leads to the shepherd encampment at **Permandal** (3610m).

Head down the upper reaches of the Warvan Valley before entering the Kanital Valley. Waterfalls and tiny birch groves line the route to **Humpet** (3400m). A short trek leads to the *shepherds encampment* at **Kanital** (3680m).

The trail from Kanital heads to the valley's true left and ascends the terminal moraine. The route to the pass is then quite straightforward across the glacier, although take care to avoid the crevasses just below **Boktol Pass** (4860m). A long haul leads down to the meadow at **Donara** (3780m) before a short stage to **Panikhar** (3350m) and the **Suru Valley**. Catch a bus or truck to Kargil or Padum.

Himachal Pradesh

Himachal Pradesh includes a variety of trekking possibilities. The treks out of Manali and the Kullu Valley, Dharamsala, Brahmaur and Kinnaur provide an opportunity to appreciate the culture of the hill states while exploring the Dhaula Dhar and Pir Panjal Ranges. From Lahaul, there are challenging treks over the Himalaya to the Zanskar, while in Spiti, there are treks to Kinnaur, with its cultural similarities to Tibet.

HISTORY

Himachal Pradesh (HP) is one of the youngest states in India. It is a composite of many hill kingdoms (including Kullu, Lahaul, Spiti, Chamba, Kangra and Kinnaur) that maintained a long history of independence until the mid-19th century. Following the Treaty of Amritsar in 1846, these kingdoms were annexed to British India and administered as part of the Punjab. In 1966 the Punjab was partitioned into the states of Punjab, Haryana and Himachal Pradesh. Himachal Pradesh was given formal recognition as a state in the Indian Union in 1971.

NATURAL HISTORY

Four main mountain ranges extend across Himachal Pradesh. The lowest is the Dhaula Dhar Range, which rises to an average elevation of 4500m to 5000m. To its north are the snowcapped ridges of the Pir Panjal Range, followed by the Great Himalaya Range, which separates Himachal Pradesh and Ladakh. Many of its peaks rise above 6000m, while the glaciated passes are above 5000m. Beyond this, the Zanskar Range forms the mountain divide between the Spiti Valley and the Tibetan Plateau and, further east, an impressive divide between Himachal Pradesh and Tibet. A short distance from the border with Tibet, the Sutlej River breaches the Zanskar Range, before heading southwest through the Great Himalaya and Dhaula Dhar Ranges en route to the Indian Plains.

See the 'Watching Wildlife' boxed text for animals you might see.

Highlights

KERRY LORIMER

A Gaddi shepherd leads his flock to higher pastures for the summer.

- Trekking in the magnificent conifer and oak forests of the Kullu Valley (p150)

- Trekking from the verdant Parbati Valley to the stark mountainscape of Spiti (p166)

- Savouring the views from alpine campsites en route to Bara Bhangal (p169)

- Witnessing the migration of the Gaddi shepherds (p175)

- Crossing the Kugti Pass (p182), with views of the Dhaula Dhar and Himalaya Ranges

- Visiting the Buddhist villages of Spiti on a trek to Kinnaur (p188)

CLIMATE

The valleys of Chamba, Kangra and Kullu come under the influence of the Indian monsoon. Pre-monsoon clouds build up by mid-June and the first heavy rainfall normally occurs by early July. The heaviest

Watching Wildlife

The drier, higher elevations north of the Himalaya, including Lahaul, Spiti and eastern Kinnaur, attract wildlife similar to that of Ladakh and the Zanskar. **Bharal** graze on the high ridges, while **snow leopards** have been sighted in the high, remote valleys in Kinnaur and the Pin National Park in Spiti.

Ibex live south of the Himalayan Range and on the high alpine pastures of the Pir Panjal, while **thar** are generally confined to the upper forest bands. Two members of the goat-antelope family – the **goral** and **serow** – are also found in this vicinity. Goral favour the grassy slopes, while serow tend to roam the higher cliffs. **Musk deer** inhabit the dense thickets towards the upper levels of the tree line.

Brown bears are confined to the alpine pastures where they forage for small rodents and roots in summer. In late autumn, before hibernation, they are often seen in birch copses near alpine meadows. **Black bears** are often found in the oak and conifer forests, along with **common leopards**, which stalk close to villages in search of stray domestic animals. **Marmots** are common in the mountain valleys, while troops of **langur** are often seen in the oak forests above the Kullu Valley and Dharamsala.

The **golden eagle, kestrel, lammergeier** and **Himalayan griffon** ascend to above 5000m in search of prey. Six of the seven pheasants in the West Himalaya can be found in the Great Himalaya National Park to the east of the Kullu Valley. The high-altitude meadows close to the Himalaya are also the habitat of the **brown** and **robin accentors** and **black-billed magpies**. The forests provide habitat for a variety of **woodpeckers, jays, rosefinches, Himalayan bulbuls, white-throated laughingthrush** and the distinctive **white-capped water redstart**. If you are spending time in hill resorts such as Manali and Dharamsala, you may spot **Indian** and **drongo cuckoos, scarlet minivets, white-browed fantails, Hume's warblers, rock thrush** and **yellow-breasted greenfinches**.

Himachal's temperate forests extend above the cultivated rice and cornfields to stands of **oak, chestnut** and **maple**. The **deodar** and **blue pines** are also present between 1800m and 3000m before giving way to mixed **oak** and **West Himalayan spruce, fir** and **rhododendron**, and a variety of **mosses, ferns** and **orchids**. A small band of **silver birch** defines the upper limit of the tree line. An ideal trek to see the relationship between elevation and forest bands is to descend from the alpine meadows of the Jagatsukh Valley to the Kullu Valley – a 2000m descent that can be tackled in a day.

The best time for **wildflowers** is July and August. A trek to the alpine slopes of the Hampta Valley; to the meadows above Kareri Lake; or close to Kugti Pass provide an exceptional array of species, including **aster, gentians, primula, euphorbia, delphinium, anemone, potentilla** and **saxifrage**.

Lahaul is an attractive alternative when other areas are subject to the monsoon. A trek to the Miyar Valley in July and August is particularly rewarding and the meadows near Chandra Tal display a variety of flowering plants. To the north of the Himalaya Range, there is less to see; the best 'flowering' areas are close to irrigation channels or along the banks of streams in the remote valleys.

rainfalls are in August, and continue until early September. Day temperatures vary considerably, rising to above 20°C, even at higher altitudes, and dropping below freezing during some of the worst storms, which deposit snow on the higher elevations.

The region of Lahaul experiences a modified monsoon climate, with most rain falling on the south side of the Pir Panjal Range. However, when the occasional storm breaks over Lahaul, it can cause heavy rainfall in July or August.

Spiti lies outside the influence of the monsoon and is not subject to heavy rainfalls.

The same holds for the Kinnaur region north of the Himalaya Range, although southern Kinnaur is subject to the monsoon rain in July and August.

The post-monsoon season (mid-Sept–late Oct) in Himachal is normally settled, with day temperatures between 15° and 20°C. Towards late October, the first of the permanent winter snows fall on the passes.

By late March, temperatures begin to rise and snows thaw. However, with the exception of the mountain passes south of Manali, most are snowbound until early June or the first monsoon rain in July.

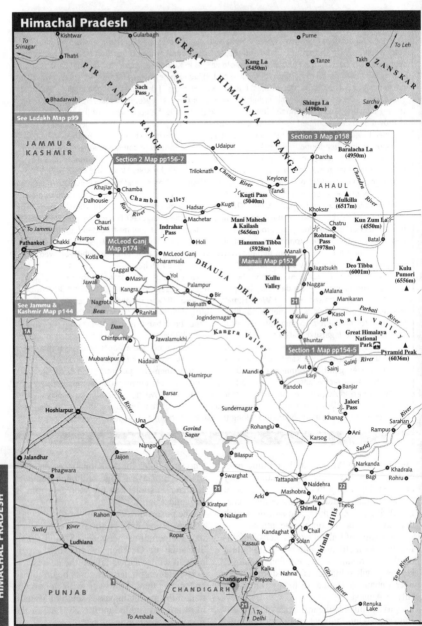

Himachal Pradesh

To Srinagar
Kishtwar
Gularbagh
Purne
To Leh
Thatri
GREAT
Kang La
(5450m)
Tanze
Takh
ZANSKAR
PIR
PANJAL
Sach
Pass
Panji Valley
HIMALAYA
Shinga La
(4980m)
Sarchu
Bhadarwah
RANGE
See Ladakh Map p99
Section 3 Map p158
JAMMU &
KASHMIR
Udaipur
Darcha
Baralacha La
(4950m)
Section 2 Map pp156-7
Triloknath
Chenab River
Keylong
Chamba
Khajiar
Chamba
Kugti Pass
(5040m)
Tandi
LAHAUL
Chandra River
Dalhousie
Valley
Hadsar
Kugti
Khoksar
Mulkilla
(6517m)
Chauri
Khas
Machetar
Mani Mahesh
Kailash
(5656m)
Chatru
Kun Zum La
(4550m)
To Jammu
Indrahar
Pass
Holi
Hanuman Tibba
(5928m)
Rohtang
Pass
(3978m)
Batal
Pathankot
Chakki
Nurpur
McLeod Ganj
Map p174
McLeod Ganj
Dharamsala
DHAULA
Manali
Manali Map p152
Jagatsukh
Deo Tibba
(6001m)
Kulu
Pumori
(6556m)
Kotla
Gaggal
Masrur
Yol
Palampur
DHAR
Kullu
Valley
Naggar
Malana
Jawali
Kangra
Bir
RANGE
Manikaran
See Jammu &
Kashmir Map p144
Nagrota
Beas
Ranital
Baijnath
Kullu
Jari
Kasol
Parbati
Valley
River
Dam
Jogindernagar
Kangra Valley
Bhuntar
Great Himalaya
National
Park
1A
Chintpurni
Jawalamukhi
Section 1 Map pp154-5
Pyramid Peak
(6036m)
Mubarakpur
Nadaun
Hamirpur
Mandi
Aut
Sainj
River
Sainj
Hoshiarpur
Barsar
Pandoh
Larji
Banjar
Jalori
Pass
Una
Sundernagar
Khanag
River
Sarahan
Jalandhar
Govind
Sagar
Rohanglu
Ani
Rampur
Phagwara
Nangol
Jaijon
Bilaspur
Karsog
Sutlej
Narkanda
Khadrala
Swarghat
Tattapani
Naldehra
Bagi
Rohru
Rahon
Sutlej
River
Arki
Mashobra
Kufri
22
Theog
Ludhiana
Ropar
Kiratpur
Nalagarh
Shimla
Chail
Shimla Hills
Kandaghat
Solan
Kasauli
Kalka
Nahan
Giri River
Tons River
PUNJAB
CHANDIGARH
Chandigarh
Pinjore
21
To Delhi
Renuka
Lake
To Ambala

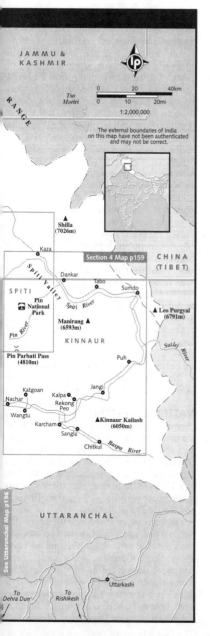

INFORMATION
When to Trek

The trekking season is from May to October, although November and December are pleasant times to undertake shorter treks and tour the region's many hill stations. The season coincides with the spring thaw, making it possible to traverse the lower passes across the Dhaula Dhar and the Pir Panjal from mid-May. The higher passes, including those over the Himalaya Range, are normally passable by the mid-June. Monsoon rain in July and August is experienced in many of the regions south of the Pir Panjal, including the Kullu, Kangra and lower Ravi Valleys. The first winter snows do not normally fall until mid-October, although storms and huge snowfalls have been known in mid-September.

The Rohtang Pass (linking Manali to Lahaul and Leh) is not normally open to vehicular traffic until June, while the Kun Zum La (linking Lahaul and Spiti) is normally open in July. The former Hindustan to Tibet highway linking Shimla to Kinnaur and Spiti is open for most of the year, although monsoon rain can cause landslides.

Maps

The Leomann 1:200,000 series and the US Military U502 1:250,000 series are useful for planning and trekking. See Planning for each trek for specific map requirements.

Books

To read about the region's history:

History & Culture of the Himalayan States Vol 2 by Sukhdev Charak is a good backgrounder.
Kulu: The End of the Habitable World, written by Penelope Chetwode in the 1960s, is the standard reference on the temples and treks out of Kullu.
Himalayan Circuit by GD Khosla details the trek from Manali to Lahaul in the 1950s.

For more contemporary recollections:

At Home in the Himalayas by Christina Noble provides a wealth of information for trekkers in the Kullu Valley.
Over the High Passes, also by Christina Noble, describes the lifestyle of the Gaddi shepherds.
Exploring the Hidden Himalaya by Soli Mehta and Harish Kapadia details climbing expeditions in the region.

HIMACHAL PRADESH

Information Sources

For general enquiries, contact the state tourist offices in Manali and McLeod Ganj. For roads information, contact the local Public Works Department (PWD) offices. For trekking information, visit the Mountaineering Institutes at Manali, McLeod Ganj or Brahmaur, or contact the local trekking agencies. See the town information for contact details.

Permits

While there are no special regulations or permits for trekking in Himachal, an Inner Line permit is necessary if travelling or trekking between Spiti and Kinnaur or close to Tibet on the Kinnaur Kailash trek. See the boxed text 'Inner Line Permits' (p191).

Manali & the Kullu Valley

The Kullu Valley is justifiably considered one of the most picturesque valleys in the West Himalaya. It is practically enclosed by snow-capped mountain ranges that give way to alpine meadows and conifer forests. At lower elevations, orchards, cornfields and rice paddies merge with an assortment of villages that stretch along the course of the Beas River.

Manali is a trading town and an important centre for travellers heading to Ladakh and the Indus Valley.

Treks out of Kullu Valley head east up the Hampta Valley and over the Pir Panjal Range to Lahaul. The ridges of the Pir Panjal give way to a series of high ridges, traversed when trekking from Naggar. A more demanding trek goes over the Pin Parbati Pass and the Himalaya Range to Spiti. West of Manali, the Kali Hind Pass and the Bara Bhangal Range are crossed before heading south over the Dhaula Dhar to the Kangra Valley.

HISTORY

The history of the Kullu Valley can be traced back to the 10th century when its capital was established at Jagatsukh. The local rajah ruled the upper part of the valley between Sultanpur (Kullu) and the Rohtang Pass. It was not until the 15th century that the boundaries of the kingdom extended south to Mandi. In later centuries both the Kullu rajahs and the Ladakhi kings laid claim to Lahaul. During the Moghul period the Kullu rajahs paid tribute to the emperor's court before a turbulent era when the Sikhs changed the balance of power in the West Himalaya. The Sikh armies invaded the Kullu Valley in 1840–1, and the conflict was not resolved until after the Sikh wars with the British and the Treaty of Amritsar in 1846. After the treaty, most of the hill states, including Kullu, were administered by the British.

In the latter half of the 19th century, many roads and forest trails in the Kullu Valley were upgraded. Forest areas were explored, and the PWD and Forest Department moved into the mountain regions. The system of *beggar* (forced labour) enabled the improvement of roads and living conditions in the more remote villages.

It was a time when many British families settled in the valley. Orchards were established and comfortable houses constructed in the local style. The first motorable road into the valley, up the Larji Gorge, was completed in 1927. For many settlers, this was the beginning of the end of their tranquil life in the valley and many families were on their way home to Britain well before 1947.

NATURAL HISTORY

Dominating the region's topography are the mountain ranges of Pir Panjal, Great Himalaya and Dhaula Dhar. The Great Himalaya National Park is east of the Kullu Valley and includes the upper sections of the Parbati Valley. The Manali Sanctuary extends to the upper elevations of the Bara Bhangal and the Pir Panjal Ranges.

The best chance of seeing wildlife is in the national parks and sanctuaries. The ibex and markhor tend to seek out the highest crags above alpine meadows, while serow, goral and musk deer graze in the more secluded forest slopes above the Kullu Valley. The brown bear is seen in the birch copses, while black bear and common leopard are found in the oak and conifer forest near villages.

Treks out of the Kullu Valley provide fine opportunities to appreciate wildflowers. These include the meadows in the vicinity of the Chandrakani Pass, the Kali Hind Pass, the Hampta Valley and the alpine pastures in the upper Jagatsukh Valley.

ACCESS TOWN
Manali
☎ 01902 • alt 2050m

The thriving town of Manali has always been an important trading centre linking the upper sections of the Kullu Valley with the rarefied heights of Lahaul and the Indus Valley. For some, Manali is a resting point before undertaking the two-day journey to Leh and Ladakh. For others, there are a number of trekking possibilities, which rank among the finest in the West Himalaya.

Information For reliable trekking information, contact the **Mountaineering Institute** *(☎ 52342, Naggar Hwy)*. The **HP Tourist Development Corporation** *(HPTDC; ☎ 52175, The Mall)* is helpful for general enquiries.

Supplies & Equipment There is a wide variety of fresh and tinned food in Manali. If trekking out of Naggar (on the Chandrakani Pass & Malana trek) or from Pulga (Pin Parbati & Spiti trek), bring supplies from Manali, although some fruit and vegetables may be available at the trailheads.

Trekking agents sometimes hire quality gear (sleeping bags, tents and insulated mats) to clients. If in doubt, bring your own gear. Cooking equipment such as stoves, pots and pans are available at local markets.

Trekking Agents Of the many agents in Manali, some of those recommended include:

Antrek Tours *(☎ 52292, fax 52786, ⓔ e_kaludia@ hotmail.com)* is just below the tourist office.
Chandratal Treks & Tours *(☎ 52665, fax 52665)* is close to bus station.
Himalayan Adventures *(☎ 52750, fax 52182)* is opposite the tourist office.
Himalayan Frontiers *(☎ 52750, fax 52182, ⓔ himfrontad@vsnl.com)* is opposite Chandratal Treks & Tours.
Himalayan Journeys *(☎ 52365, fax 53065, ⓔ himjourneys@del.vsnl.net.in, the Mall)* is one of the most established and reliable companies offering treks out of the Kullu Valley.
Tiger Eye *(☎ 54336, fax 52718, ⓔ tigereyeindia@ yahoo.com, Old Manali)* is 150m south of Manalsu Nala.

Most agencies offer trekking packages for around US$30 to US$40 per day per person for small groups. Discounts are usually available for groups of five or more.

Alternatively, agents can organise porters or horsemen. The rate for porters is around Rs 200 per day, plus a clothing, travel and location allowance. The Tourist Office sets the rates for pack horses each season. Budget for about Rs 200 per horse per day, with a discount if hiring more than five horses.

If you are making your own arrangements, it is also useful to check out the information boards at *Chopsticks* and *Mount View* restaurants in Manali and *Moon Dance Garden* and *Shiva Garden Cafe* in Old Manali.

Places to Stay & Eat Hotels recommended by trekkers in Old Manali include *Tourist Nest* *(☎ 56520)*, with doubles for Rs 300, and *Dragon Guest House* *(☎ 52790)*, charging from Rs 250 to Rs 300 for doubles.

Most accommodation in Manali is more expensive. *John Banon's Hotel* *(☎ 52335)* has large rooms for Rs 600. *Pinewood Hotel* *(☎ 52118)* is also run by the Banon family, with doubles for Rs 700. The *Sunshine Guest House* *(☎ 52320)* has doubles from Rs 400 to Rs 600.

There is no shortage of restaurants in Manali. Close to the Mall, *Mount View Restaurant* and *Chopsticks* are well established, as is *Mona Lisa*, opposite the bus station. *Johnson's Cafe*, uphill from the Mall, is set in a pleasant garden and is a good place to share a beer.

Getting There & Away Manali is well serviced with buses and taxis to/from most other towns in Himachal as well as Delhi.

Air The nearest airport is Bhuntar, 52km south of Manali and 10km south of Kullu. Daily flights go to/from Delhi with Alliance (US$135) and Jetair (US$137). A taxi from Manali to Bhuntar costs Rs 800 (two hours).

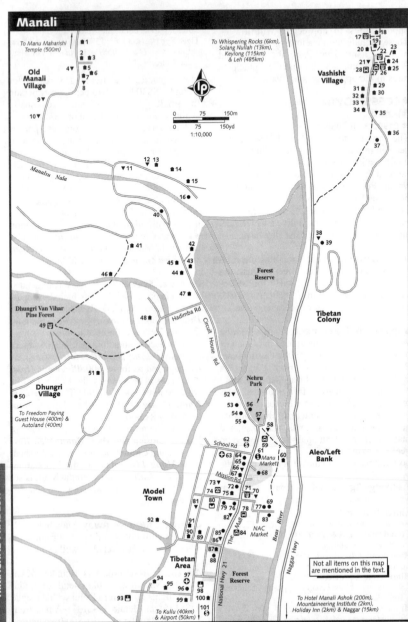

Manali

To Manu Maharishi Temple (500m)

Old Manali Village

To Whispering Rocks (6km),
Solang Nullah (13km),
Keylong (115km)
& Leh (485km)

Vashisht Village

| 0 | 75 | 150m |
| 0 | 75 | 150yd |

1:10,000

Manalsu Nala

Forest Reserve

Tibetan Colony

Dhungri Van Vihar Pine Forest

Hadimba Rd

Circuit House Rd

Dhungri Village

To Freedom Paying
Guest House (400m) &
Autoland (400m)

Nehru Park

Aleo/Left Bank

School Rd

Manu Market

Mission Rd

Model Town

The Mall

Beas River

NAC Market

Tibetan Area

Not all items on this map
are mentioned in the text.

Forest Reserve

National Hwy 21

Naggar Hwy

To Hotel Manali Ashok (200m),
Mountaineering Institute (2km),
Holiday Inn (2km) & Naggar (15km)

To Kullu (40km)
& Airport (50km)

HIMACHAL PRADESH

Manali

PLACES TO STAY
1 Krishna Guest House
2 Diplomat Guest House
3 Dragon Guest House
5 Tourist Nest
6 Veer Paying Guest House
7 Kishoor Guest House
13 Hotel Riverbank; Hotel Him View
14 Rising Moon; Riverside; Hema Guest House; Mamta Paying Guest House
15 Jungle Bungalow
18 Bodh Guest House
19 Dolath Guest House
20 Negi Guest House
23 Guest House Dharma; Amrit
24 Kalptaru
25 New Dharma
29 Anand Hotel; Travel Assistance Centre
30 Sonan; Prem
31 Surabhi Guest House & World Peace Cafe
32 Janta; Ganga
34 Hotel Valley View; Hotel Bhrigu; Basho Restaurant
36 Sita Cottage
41 Hotel Kalpana
42 Pinewood Hotel
43 Hotel Mayflower
44 Banon Resorts
45 Sunshine Guest House
46 Hotel Chetna
47 John Banon's Hotel
48 Hotel Rohtang Manalsu
51 Hotel Shrinagar Regency
60 Hotel Beas
67 Hotel Renuka
75 Su-Khiran Guest House
87 Hotel Ibex; Ibex Travels; Hotel Snow View; Underground Market; Tibetan Market

89 Premier Hotel
90 Hotel Diamond
91 Hotel Shishar; Lhasa Hotel
92 Mount View Hotel
94 Potala Hotel
95 Sunflower
99 Hotel Snow Drop
100 Samrat Hotel

PLACES TO EAT
4 Mount View Cafe
8 Little Tibet Cafe; Shiva Garden Cafe
9 Ish Cafe
10 Moon Dance Garden
11 River Music Cafe
12 Tibet Kitchen
21 Super Bake; Zodiac Cafe; Ranu Rooftop Cafe
33 Freedom Cafe
35 Rose Garden Inn
38 Phuntsok Coffee House
52 Johnson's Cafe
57 Sa-Ba
58 Juniper; Chandertal
66 Sher-e-Punjab
70 Mona Lisa
73 Swamiji's Madras Cafe; Sangam; Neel Kamal
81 Mona Lisa
82 Mount View Restaurant; Chopsticks; Himalayan Quest
86 Gozy Restaurant

OTHER
16 HPTDC Club House
17 Two-storey Temple
22 Vashisht Temple
26 Rama Temple; Public Baths; Rainbow Cafe
27 Taxi Stand
28 Bu152s Stand
37 HPTDC Hot Baths Complex

39 The Enfield Club
40 Tiger Eye
49 Dhungri Temple
50 Utopia Complex; Handicraft Museum
53 Ambassador Travels (Indian Airlines)
54 Himalayan Journeys
55 Jagson Airlines
56 Himachal Emporium
59 Him-Aanchal Taxi Stand
61 HPTDC Tourism Reception Centre; HPTDC Tourism Marketing Office; HPTDC Hotel Kunzam
62 UCO Bank
63 Mission Hospital
64 Himalayan Adventures; Bhuttico
65 Charitrust Tibetan Handicraft Emporium
68 Antrek Tours
69 Himalayan Frontiers
71 Temple
72 Swagtam Tours
74 Central Telegraph Office
76 Harison Travels
77 Bookworm
78 Bus Station
79 Delightful Things; Tibetan Food Corner
80 Main Post Office; Himalaya Internet
83 Chandratal Trek & Tours
84 Him-Aanchal Taxi Stand
85 North Face Adventure Tours
88 Tibetan Market
93 Gadhan Thekchokling Gompa
96 Inder Motors
97 Mentsikhang Clinic
98 Himalayan Nyingmapa Gompa
101 State Bank of India

Bus Regular public buses run to/from Prini (Rs 3), Jagatsukh (Rs 5) and Naggar (Rs 12).

Delhi There are a number of long-distance bus companies operating between Manali and Delhi. Most buses leave Manali at 5pm (Rs 520/380 deluxe/A class, 12 to 14 hours).

Leh Several daily buses operate to/from Leh (June–early Oct). It's a two-day drive; the A-class bus (Rs 1000 plus food & accommodation) halts overnight at the tented camp at Sarchu, while the B-class bus (Rs 400) stops overnight at Keylong.

Lahaul The Rohtang Pass links Manali and Lahaul (open mid-June–Oct). Several buses operate each day to/from Keylong (Rs 72, six hours).

Spiti The bus leaves Manali for Kaza at 6am daily (Rs 72, 12 hours). It only operates when the Kun Zum La is open (early July–Sept).

Other Destinations Buses to/from Dharamsala take eight hours (Rs 250/160 deluxe/public). It is six hours to/from Manikaran (Rs 180/42).

Taxi Long-distance taxis are available from the Mall. There is one rate for 4WDs, and one for the larger Tata Sumo. To Leh, budget for Rs 13,000/16,000 for a 4WD/Sumo; to Kaza, Rs 6800/7500; to Dharamsala, Rs 3750/4500; and to Manikaran, Rs 1100/1400. Other fares are Rs 100/150 to Prini; Rs 125/175 to Jagatsukh; and Rs 375/450 to Naggar.

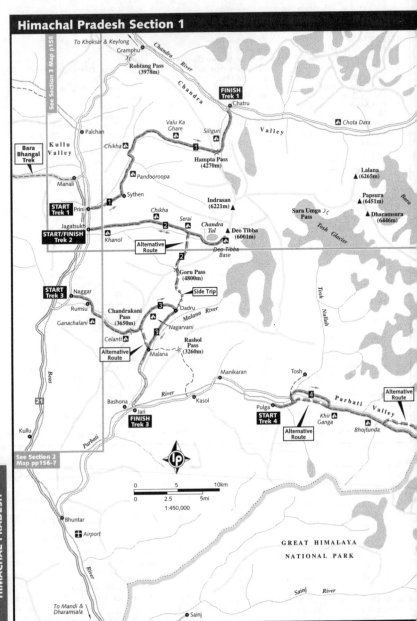

Himachal Pradesh Section 1

To Khoksar & Keylong

Gramphu

Rohtang Pass
(3978m)

Chandra River

Chandra

FINISH
Trek 1

Chatru

Chota Dara

Valu Ka
Ghare

Siliguri

Valley

Palchan

Kullu
Valley

Chikha

Pandooroopa

Hampta Pass
(4270m)

Manali

Sythen

Indrasan
(6221m)

Lalana
(6265m)

Papsura
(6451m)

Sara Umga
Pass

Dharamsura
(6446m)

START
Trek 1

Prini

Chikha

Serai

Chandra
Tal

Deo Tibba
(6001m)

Tosh Glacier

Bara

Jagatsukh

START/FINISH
Trek 2

Khanol

Deo Tibba
Base

Alternative
Route

Goru Pass
(4800m)

Side Trip

Tosh
Nullah

START
Trek 3

Naggar

Rumsu

Ganachalani

Chandrakani
Pass
(3650m)

Dadru

Malana River

Nagarvani

Beas

Celanti

Rashol
Pass
(3260m)

Alternative
Route

Malana

Manikaran

Tosh

Alternative
Route

Bashona

Jari

FINISH
Trek 3

River

Kasol

Pulga

START
Trek 4

Parbati Valley

Khir
Ganga

Bhojtunda

Kullu

Parbati

Alternative
Route

See Section 2
Map pp156-7

See Section 3 Map p158

Bara
Bhangal
Trek

0   5   10km
0   2.5   5mi
1:450,000

Bhuntar

Airport

GREAT HIMALAYA
NATIONAL PARK

To Mandi &
Dharamsala

Sainj River

Sainj

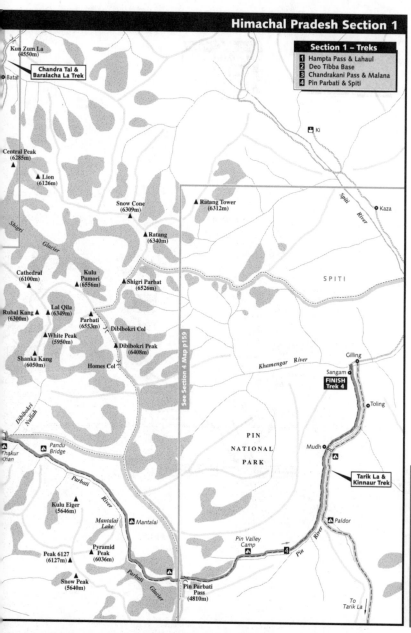

Himachal Pradesh Section 1

Section 1 – Treks
1 Hampta Pass & Lahaul
2 Deo Tibba Base
3 Chandrakani Pass & Malana
4 Pin Parbati & Spiti

Kun Zum La
(4550m)

Chandra Tal &
Baralacha La Trek

Batal

Ki

Central Peak
(6285m)

Lion
(6126m)

Snow Cone
(6309m)

Ratang Tower
(6312m)

Kaza

Shigri

Glacier

Ratang
(6340m)

SPITI

Spiti River

Cathedral
(6100m)

Kulu
Pumori
(6556m)

Shigri Parbat
(6526m)

Rubal Kang
(6300m)

Lal Qila
(6349m)

Parbati
(6553m)

Dibibokri Col

White Peak
(5950m)

Dibibokri Peak
(6408m)

Shanka Kang
(6050m)

Homes Col

Khamengar River

Gilling

Sangam

FINISH
Trek 4

Toling

Dibibokri Nullah

Pandu
Bridge

PIN

Mudh

Thakur
Khan

NATIONAL

Parbati

PARK

Tarik La &
Kinnaur Trek

River

Kulu Eiger
(5646m)

Mantalai
Lake

Mantalai

Paldor

Pin River

Peak 6127
(6127m)

Pyramid
Peak
(6036m)

Pin Valley
Camp

4

Snow Peak
(5640m)

Parbati

Glacier

Pin Parbati
Pass
(4810m)

To
Tarik La

See Section 4 Map p159

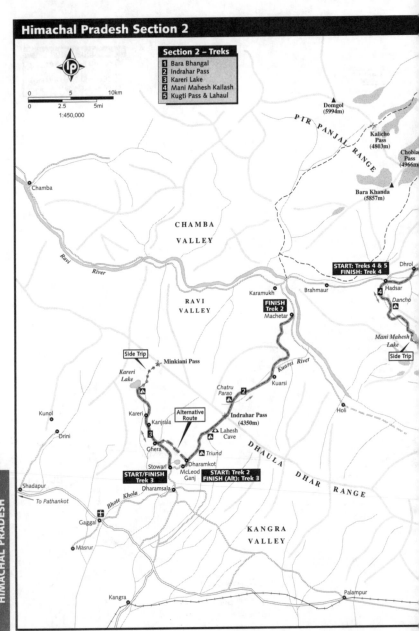

Himachal Pradesh Section 2

Section 2 – Treks
1. Bara Bhangal
2. Indrahar Pass
3. Kareri Lake
4. Mani Mahesh Kailash
5. Kugti Pass & Lahaul

0   5   10km
0 2.5 5mi
1:450,000

PIR PANJAL RANGE

Domgol (5994m)

Kalicho Pass (4803m)

Chobia Pass (4966m)

Bara Khanda (5857m)

Chamba

CHAMBA VALLEY

Ravi River

RAVI VALLEY

Karamukh

Brahmaur

START: Treks 4 & 5
FINISH: Trek 4

Dhrol

Hadsar

Dancho

FINISH Trek 2

Machetar

Mani Mahesh Lake

Side Trip

Side Trip

Minkiani Pass

Kareri Lake

Kuarsi River

Kuarsi

Kunol

Kareri

Kanjrala

Alternative Route

Indrahar Pass (4350m)

Holi

Drini

Lahesh Cave

Ghera

Triund

DHAULA DHAR RANGE

Stowari

Dharamkot

McLeod Ganj

START/FINISH Trek 3

START: Trek 2
FINISH (Alt): Trek 3

Shadapur

Dharamsala

To Pathankot

Bhote Khola

Gaggal

Masrur

KANGRA VALLEY

Kangra

Palampur

HIMACHAL PRADESH

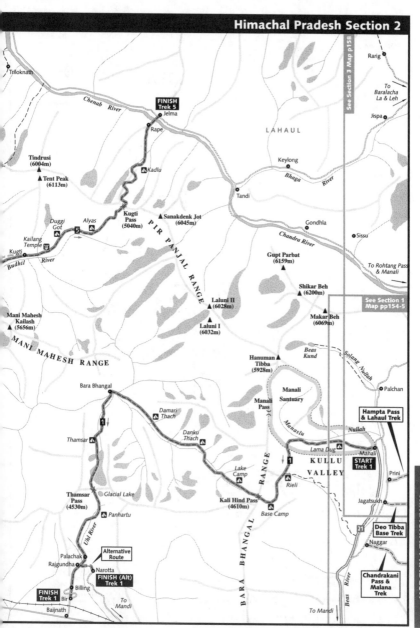

Rarig

See Section 3 Map p158

To Baralacha La & Leh

Triloknath

Jispa

Chenab River

FINISH Trek 5
Jelma

Rape

LAHAUL

Tindrusi (6004m)
Tent Peak (6113m)

Kadlu

Keylong

Bhaga River

Duggi Got
Alyas
Kugti Pass (5040m)
Sanakdenk Jot (6045m)

Tandi

Gondhla

Chandra River

Sissu

Kailang Temple

Kugti

Budhil River

P I R   P A N J A L   R A N G E

Gupt Parbat (6159m)

To Rohtang Pass & Manali

Mani Mahesh Kailash (5656m)

Laluni II (6028m)

Laluni I (6032m)

Shikar Beh (6200m)

See Section 1 Map pp154-5

M A N I   M A H E S H   R A N G E

Makar Beh (6069m)

Beas Kund

Hanuman Tibba (5928m)

Bara Bhangal

Damari Thach

Manali Santuary

Manali Pass

Manaslu

Solang Nullah

Palchan

Hampta Pass & Lahaul Trek

Thamsar

Danku Thach

Lama Dug

Manali

START Trek 1

KULLU VALLEY

Prini

Thamsar Pass (4530m)

Glacial Lake

Lake Camp

Rieli

B A R A   B H A N G A L   R A N G E

Base Camp

Kali Hind Pass (4610m)

Jagatsukh

Deo Tibba Base Trek

Panhartu

Uhl River

Palachak
Rajgundha

Alternative Route

Narotta

FINISH (Alt) Trek 1

Naggar

Billing

To Mandi

FINISH Trek 1
Bir

Baijnath

Beas River

To Mandi

Chandrakani Pass & Malana Trek

HIMACHAL PRADESH

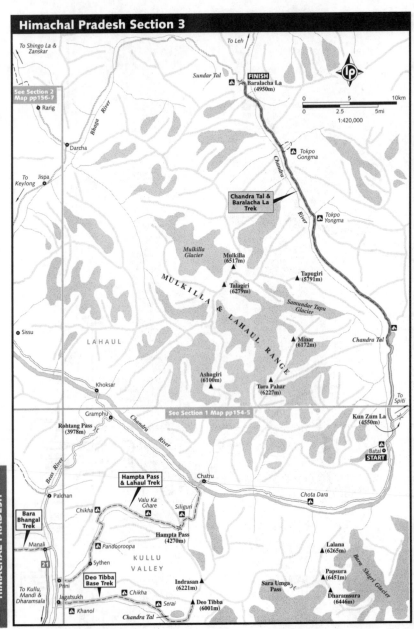

Himachal Pradesh Section 3

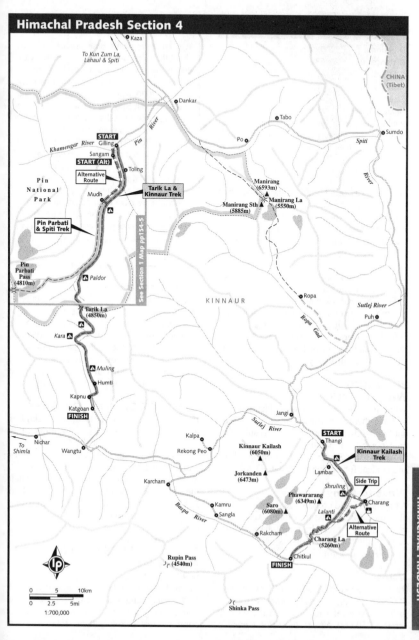

Hampta Pass & Lahaul

Duration	5 days
Distance	53km
Difficulty	moderate
Start	Prini
Finish	Chatru
Nearest Town	Manali (pp151–3)
Public Transport	yes

Summary An easily accessible trek ascending the verdant Hampta Valley and traversing the Pir Panjal Range to Lahaul.

You can be trekking within an hour of leaving your hotel in Manali. While the days are graded easy to moderate, at least three days should be spent acclimatising before crossing the Pir Panjal Range over the Hampta Pass.

The trek also provides an excellent opportunity to acclimatise and improve fitness before trekking over the Shingo La or Phitse La in Ladakh.

The trek leads through Sythen village and a number of Gaddi and Gujar encampments. It also affords fine views of the high peaks, including Deo Tibba (6001m), Indrasan (6221m) and Hanuman Tibba (5928m; on the far side of Kullu Valley).

PLANNING
When to Trek

While it is possible to cross the Hampta Pass in June, there is normally snow on the pass until mid-July. In July, the region is subject to monsoon rain, although the heaviest rains fall in August. By September the weather clears and is ideal for trekking until late October.

What to Bring

A tent, stove and cooking gear are essential, plus food for at least four days. An ice axe is useful for descending the Hampta Pass early in the season. A rope is necessary for fording the Indrasan River.

Maps

Refer to the Leomann series 1:200,000 *Sheet 5 (Kullu Valley, Parbati Valley & Central Lahaul).* Also refer to the US Military U502 series 1:250,000, *NI 43-16 ref Palampur.*

Warning

Two recent incidents pose serious questions about the safety of trekkers in the Kullu Valley. Both involved foreign tourists trekking alone or in small parties unaccompanied by a local crew.

In July 2000, two trekkers were robbed and shot while camping near Hampta Pass. One was killed and the other left for dead. Police made several arrests, and the ringleader later confessed to killing a number of Western trekkers reported missing in the past decade.

In August 2000 three trekkers were beaten in their tents at night. A women and her son were killed and another man left for dead.

While there have been no similar incidents since that time, it is not advisable to trek alone. There are no records of any foreigner being harmed while trekking with a local crew; for now, this arrangement is highly recommended.

Accommodation

There are a couple of *dhabas* (tea stalls or restaurants) at Sythen. Beyond Sythen, Gujar shepherds occasionally set up camps in the Hampta Valley for tea and snacks. However, do not rely on these for accommodation. There are a couple of dhabas at the trailhead at Chatru, where you can get a bed for around Rs 50. Otherwise, be prepared to camp.

GETTING TO/FROM THE TREK

From Manali, catch the local Jagatsukh bus as far as Prini village (Rs 3, 30 minutes). A 4WD will cost Rs 100 to Rs 150.

From Chatru, the bus from Spiti arrives around midday, continuing to Manali (Rs 50, 5½ hours). If heading to Darcha or Leh, catch the same bus to the junction of the Manali to Leh road (just above the village of Khoksar), from where onward buses go to Keylong.

THE TREK (See map pp154–5)
Day 1: Prini to Sythen & Pandooroopa
3–4 hours, 10km

From **Prini** village (1950m), ascend the trail to the small temple above the village before commencing a steep climb to the denuded conifer forest below Sythen. There are fine

Top: Chandra Tal, an alpine lake that marks the source of the Chandra River, in Himachal Pradesh.
Bottom: A classic Himalayan scene on Uttaranchal's Kuari Pass.

Village life in Uttaranchal. **Top Left:** Dancers in a wedding parade. **Top Right:** A spice salesman displaying tika powder, Rishikesh. **Middle:** Uttarkashi, the popular pilgrim town en route to Gangotri. **Bottom:** Breathtaking in its own right, Joshimath is the gateway to the Valley of the Flowers.

views down the Kullu Valley. Just below the village are a couple of *dhabas* from where you can appreciate the snowcapped ridges of the Bara Bhangal Range. **Sythen** (2710m) was established by villagers from Spiti several generations ago. The trail levels out before entering a narrow pine-forested valley. The *campsite* is 3km up the valley in a small clearing known as **Pandooroopa**.

Day 2: Pandooroopa to Chikha
3–4 hours, 10km

From camp, the trail crosses several side streams and meadows where Gujar herd buffalo and Gaddi shepherds graze flocks before descending to the Hampta River. Until mid-July there should be a snow bridge over the river. If the shepherds are crossing the bridge, you can follow; if not, continue on the true left bank for about 2km until the river widens and it is safe to cross. There may even be an improvised bridge to save you getting your feet wet. After crossing the river, the trail continues across a series of meadows before a short ascent to **Chikha** (3270m). The *campsite* is set beneath **waterfalls** and is covered in **wildflowers** as soon as the snow melts in June. A few sliver birch trees on the nearby ridges mark the upper limit of the tree line.

Day 3: Chikha to Valu Ka Ghare
3 hours, 8km

This comparatively short day is included for acclimatisation before the Hampta Pass. The trail winds high above the valley on its true right. There are side streams to cross before descending back to the main valley floor.

Valu Ka Ghare (3700m) is at the base of Hampta Pass. Early in the season it is an important grazing area for the Gaddi shepherds before they migrate to Lahaul.

Day 4: Valu Ka Ghare to Siliguri via Hampta Pass
7 hours, 15km

A short, steep climb leads over scree slopes to a plateau with views down the Hampta Valley and across to the peaks on the far side of the Kullu Valley. The trail climbs boulder fields to the valley's true right before the 200m to 300m climb to **Hampta Pass** (4270m). Enjoy

views of Lahaul Range and the peaks of Deo Tibba and Indrasan. (The history of climbing these peaks dates to 1912 when CG Bruce led a British team on the first ascent of Hanuman Tibba. The next ascent was not until 1966. The first ascent of Deo Tibba was in 1952. Indrasan was not climbed until 1962.)

A very steep descent leads to the valley floor. Early in the season the trail is under snow and an ice axe is useful. There is a choice of *campsites* on the true left of the Indrasan River at **Siliguri** (3750m).

Day 5: Siliguri to Chatru
3 hours, 10km

A river crossing is required before following the true right of the valley down through boulder fields. This earns views of the Chandra Valley – and the cliffs opposite do not lend themselves to easy trekking. Some Gaddi shepherds follow this route, but they are more sure-footed than the average mountain goat. Unless you are too, forget it.

Continuing to the valley floor, there may be a problem crossing the Indrasan River to reach Chatru. Gaddi shepherds are commissioned each year to build a bridge over the river but you can't rely on this, particularly if the bridge is swept away by storms. If there is no bridge, ford the river with a rope. Continue for about 1km to where the trail meets the road coming from Rohtang Pass.

Chatru (3360m) is really just a line of *dhabas* on the north side of Chandra River.

Deo Tibba Base

Duration	5 days
Distance	69km
Difficulty	easy
Start/Finish	Jagatsukh
Nearest Town	Manali (pp151–3)
Public Transport	yes

Summary Ascend the secluded Jagatsukh Valley to the flower-filled meadows beneath the glaciers of Deo Tibba.

Despite its proximity to Manali, this is one of the less popular routes. Perhaps this is

Environmental Watch

Although the past decade has seen a significant increase in tourist numbers (mainly domestic) to the hill resorts of Manali and McLeod Ganj, there has not been a proportionate increase in trekkers to Himachal Pradesh. Nevertheless, there are environmental concerns regarding certain trek routes.

The trails and campsites out of the Kullu Valley are a source of concern, particularly on the days to the Hampta and Chandrakani Passes. Nonbiodegradable rubbish has not been disposed of; toilet pits not covered; tent trenches have been dug indiscriminately; while ramshackle *dhabas* (tea stalls or restaurants) have been established across the alpine meadows. As in all areas of the Indian Himalaya, a more responsible attitude among trekkers will go a long way.

Of more particular concern is the pilgrim trail to Mani Mahesh Kailash. Huge amounts of garbage, including plastic sheets, tin cans and human waste, are evident. By the end of the season the area is nothing short of an environmental disaster zone, reflecting a lack of concern by pilgrims, dhaba owners and local authorities in protecting this magnificent corner of Himachal.

Legislation to protect the mountain flora and fauna has met with some success. There is evidence of rare wildlife species in the less frequented valleys, while in some of the national parks there has been a concerted effort to implement protective measures. Measures have also been adopted to stem the collection of rare plants and medicinal herbs in the Kinnaur region, and similar programs are underway in other regions. To help, contact organisations in New Delhi such as **World Wide Fund for Nature** (☎ 011-4627586) and the **Himalayan Environmental Trust** (☎ 011-6215635).

The cultural impact in the mountain villages is not as acute as elsewhere in the Himalaya. Remote villages such as Bara Bhangal, Kugti village (in the upper Ravi Valley) and many of the settlements in Kinnaur and Spiti have not yet been subject to large numbers of trekkers. However, it remains to be seen how the communities will adjust to developments that may undermine their traditional values.

Technological developments include the use of solar power in Spiti, Kinnaur and Lahaul. However, large-scale dam projects, particularly in the vicinity of the Kullu Valley, highlight the problem of meeting increasing energy demands in a fragile mountain environment. For example, the dam in the upper Parbati Valley has been the source of much debate.

Road developments are a priority for the state authorities. However, the construction of roads into wilderness areas, such as the new road to Chandra Tal in Lahaul, is a cause for environmental concern.

---

because it doesn't go over any passes and involves retracing several kilometres. However, the easy-to-moderate days, the sense of isolation and the spectacular views of Deo Tibba at the head of the valley make it a worthwhile trek.

An additional day at Chikha is recommended for acclimatisation, while extra days can be spent identifying the many wildflowers near the Serai campsite.

PLANNING
When to Trek

The Gaddi shepherds normally follow the trail from early June. The Jagatsukh Valley, like others in the region, is subject to monsoon rain in July and August, although this is an ideal time to see wildflowers. The

weather settles from September to mid-October, and is ideal for trekking.

What to Bring

Bring a tent, stove, cooking gear and food for the entire trek.

Maps

Refer to the Leomann series 1:200,000 *Sheet 5* (*Kullu Valley, Parbati Valley & Central Lahaul*). Also refer to the US Military U502 series 1:250,000, *NI 43-16 ref Palampur*.

Accommodation

Camping is unavoidable: there are a number of lodges in Jagatsukh and a dhaba at Khanol; however, there are no lodges or rest houses on the higher stages of the trek.

GETTING TO/FROM THE TREK

Regular buses run from Manali to Jagatsukh (Rs 5, one hour). A 4WD/Tata Sumo costs Rs 125/175. The last return bus to Manali departs around 5pm.

THE TREK (See map pp154–5)
Day 1: Jagatsukh to Khanol
2 hours, 5km

The town of **Jagatsukh** (1850m) was the capital of the Kullu Valley at a time when traders from Spiti and Lahaul still held influence over the region. The town's origins can be traced back to the 9th century; the original foundations of the **Sandya Devi Temple** date from then. The temple was rebuilt in the 15th century, and some of the carvings from that period can still be seen.

From Jagatsukh, the trail ascends gradually through a series of small villages to the *campsite* at **Khanol** (2280m), a small clearing where the local villagers graze cattle. Although this is a comparatively short day, there are no further campsites until Chikha.

Day 2: Khanol to Chikha
4–5 hours, 10km

The trail stays on the true right of the valley – at first through thickets and then across scree slopes. Ascend the side of the heavily forested gorge, lined with orchids and ferns. Avoid this steep climb in the heat of the day. In summer, a profusion of **wildflowers** line the trail as it climbs for almost 600m to the head of the gorge. The route enters the glaciated upper valley, and continues for several kilometres across open pastures to the *Gujar encampment* at **Chikha** (3100m).

Day 3: Chikha to Serai
4–5 hours, 12km

Continue along the true right of the valley, trekking through pastures and birch groves, and past tumbling waterfalls. After 4km to 5km, the valley turns to the north, revealing a series of hanging glaciers at the base of Deo Tibba. The trekking becomes progressively easier as the gradient levels out. **Serai** (3900m) is a particularly rich pasture where Gaddi shepherds graze their sheep from late June until September.

Day 4: Serai to Deo Tibba Base & Return
7 hours, 15km

This day may take considerably longer in spring before the snows have melted. Cross the Jagatsukh stream and ascend the grassy ridge to the true left of the waterfall. If you have any problem locating the trail, ask one of the shepherds to point it out.

The climb up the ridge takes about two hours before leading around the cliff top above the waterfall. From this vantage point, you gain excellent views across to the high ridges beyond the Kullu Valley; to the north is the impressive southwest face of **Deo Tibba** (6001m). The trek continues up the valley across the grassy slopes that lead to the terminal moraine at around 4800m.

Chandra Tal (not to be confused with the Chandra Tal in the nearby Chandra Valley) is a small glacial lake. Although marked prominently on some maps, it is not easy to find. On the high ridges opposite Deo Tibba, it has no significant outflow and virtually dries up later in the season.

Return to Serai by the same route.

Alternative Route: Serai to Dadru
3 days, 50km

This route links to the Chandrakani Pass & Malana trek (pp164–6). From Serai, take the trail opposite camp, which follows the side valley to the south.

After the first day, set up *camp* below Goru Pass (4800m) and ascend the pass the following day. From here, there is a steep descent to a glacier in the upper Malana Valley.

It is a further day down the valley to the settlement of Dadru where you can *camp* for the night or continue for two to three hours to Malana village (see the boxed text, p166). An interesting circuit can be made back to the Kullu Valley by crossing the Chandrakani Pass to Naggar.

Day 5: Serai to Jagatsukh
7–8 hours, 27km

The return to Jagatsukh can be completed in a day. During the descent the correlation between the altitude and various vegetation

HIMACHAL PRADESH

zones is evident. The lower elevation of birch trees is at about 3700m; the rhododendron trees at 3600m; conifers at 3500m; and holly oak at 2150m.

Chandrakani Pass & Malana

Duration	5 days
Distance	70km
Difficulty	easy
Start	Naggar
Finish	Jari
Nearest Town	Manali (pp151–3)
Public Transport	yes

Summary Climb to the pass for a bird's-eye view of the Kullu Valley and the snowcapped Pir Panjal Range en route to the ancient village of Malana.

The fit, acclimatised villagers from the Kullu Valley trek to Malana in a day. This is not surprising as they are unlikely to take more than a fleeting interest in the magnificent views that extend up the Kullu Valley to the snow-capped peaks of the Pir Panjal Range or the myriad peaks north of the Malana and Parbati Valleys that define the crest of the Himalaya.

For a more leisurely pace – and to acclimatise and enjoy the views – spend an additional day or two en route to Chandrakani Pass. Beyond the pass, a steep descent leads directly to the ancient village of Malana. However, if you have a tent, we recommend the longer (main) route, for a day or two exploring the upper Malana Valley.

The construction of the dam several kilometres below Malana will undoubtedly change the character of the valley. When construction is complete, the trek over Rashol Pass to the Parbati Valley will provide an attractive alternative.

PLANNING
When to Trek
Villagers from Malana normally cross the Chandrakani Pass from April until November. However, the regular trekking season extends from May through October. Monsoon rains come in July and August.

What to Bring
To fully appreciate the best campsites and retain flexibility, bring a tent, stove and cooking gear, plus food for at least two days.

Maps
Refer to the Leomann series 1:200,000 *Sheet 5* (*Kullu Valley, Parbati Valley & Central Lahaul*). Also refer to the US Military U502 series 1:250,000, *NI 43-16 ref Palampur*.

Accommodation
The trek can be completed without a tent if heading directly from the Chandrakani Pass to Malana village.

At Naggar, hotels include the **Alliance Guest House** (☎ 47763), with doubles for Rs 200 and Rs 300; **Hotel Ragini** (☎ 47855), charging Rs 400 to Rs 500; and **HPTDC Castle Hotel** (☎ 47816), with rooms/dorm beds from Rs 250/50.

At Ganachalani, a couple of dhabas provide meals and overnight shelter. There are also several dhabas and basic lodges, including the **Shiva Cafe**, on the meadows below the Chandrakani Pass. At Malana, lodges include the recently constructed **Malana Lodge**, with rooms for Rs 150 with meals, and **Renuka Lodge**, charging Rs 50.

GETTING TO/FROM THE TREK
From Manali, several buses run daily to Naggar (Rs 12, two hours). A 4WD will cost between Rs 375 and Rs 450. From Jari, buses go to Bhuntar (Rs 13, two hours). You may be able to get a seat on one of the direct private buses from Manikaran to Manali, which stop in Jari (Rs 150, six hours). The taxi stand at Jari charges Rs 350/1200 to Bhuntar/Manali. Alternatively, four or five daily buses go to Kullu, from where buses head to Manali.

THE TREK (See map pp154–5)
Day 1: Naggar to Rumsu & Ganachalani
5–6 hours, 15km
Naggar (1840m) was a former capital of the Kullu Valley and includes the 500-year-old **Naggar Castle**, steeped in legend and commanding an imposing position above the Kullu Valley. Below the castle are a number

of ancient **temples**, including the sandstone temple of Gauri Shankar that dates from the 11th century. Another attraction is the **Roerich Gallery**, displaying the work of famous painter and philosopher Nicholas Roerich. His reputation as one of the avant-garde, post-1917 Russian painters was enhanced during his stay in the Kullu Valley in the 1930s, when he made Naggar his home.

From Naggar, the trail leads past **Roerich's cottage** and along the main bridle path for 1km, before branching uphill to the village of **Rumsu** (2060m). There is a 4WD road to Rumsu but follow the foot trail to avoid the road for most of the 10km to the village.

Of particular interest in Rumsu is the ancient wooden **temple** with close ties to the temples dedicated to Jamlu in Malana. Leather boots or apparel is not permitted in the vicinity of the temple. Across the village square there is a thriving **cottage industry** where shawls and rugs are woven in winter.

From Rumsu, head up the ridge to the east of the village and follow a well-defined trail through a forest of deodar, pine and horse chestnut. There is a small *campsite* and stream after 3km; from here it is a further 2km to the meadow at **Ganachalani** (2700m).

Day 2: Ganachalani to Celanti
4–4½ hours, 12km

Beyond Ganachalani the trail ascends through the forest for 4km to a series of open meadows. The lowest meadow is around 3000m, where shepherds from the Kullu Valley graze their animals. From these alpine meadows, fine views extend up the Kullu Valley to Manali and the Pir Panjal Range, and across to the Bara Bhangal Range.

The trail heads through a small rhododendron forest to a series of alpine meadows. There is no shortage of campsites, including *Celanti* (3500m), a short distance below Chandrakani Pass.

Day 3: Celanti to Dadru via Chandrakani Pass
5½–6 hours, 15km

From the high camp, it is less than an hour to the ridge line and cairns that define the **Chandrakani Pass** (3650m). There are impressive

views to the north, including the Ghalpo peaks of Lahaul – Dharamsura (6446m) and Papsura (6451m) – and the other high peaks in the upper Tosh Valley, while the snow-capped ranges of the Himalaya extend to the head of the Parbati Valley. Completing the panorama, views to the south stretch across the endless ridges to the Shimla Hills.

The Chandrakani Pass extends north for 1km along the ridge line before the trail winds along the east face of the ridge for 2km, then splits. The lower trail (Alternative Route) heads steeply down the hillside and continues directly to Malana village. The higher trail to Dadru (described here) heads across the ridge to the meadows and summer settlements further up the valley.

The trail to Dadru remains about 100m below the ridge line for a further 2km to 3km. It descends to the meadow at Nagarvani. En route, the trail winds through a series of rock gullies, small alpine meadows and birch groves.

Nagarvani (3350m) is two to 2½ hours from the pass and an ideal *campsite*. From here the trail is less defined – descend to a side valley and cross a small tributary before winding through a forest of silver fir and oak to a second tributary, which flows immediately to the south of Dadru. After reaching the true left of this tributary, descend the trail to the highest of a series of settlements and fields tended by Malana villagers in summer.

Dadru (3000m) is one of the larger settlements, close to the confluence of the tributary and the Malana River. The village fields include barley and potatoes and an abundant cash crop of hemp. The best *campsite* is below the settlements alongside Malana River.

Side Trip: Upper Malana Valley
5–6 hours, 14km return

Ascending beyond Dadru gives fine views of the spectacular hanging glaciers and peaks of the upper Malana Valley. You can also view the terrain leading to the Goru Pass (4800m), which leads to the upper Jagatsukh Valley. To link with the Deo Tibba Base trek, see the Alternative Route (p163).

Day 4: Dadru to Malana

2½–3 hours, 8km

From Dadru, there is a choice of following the trail through the settlements or the horse trail alongside the Malana River. The trails meet after about 4km before winding down the valley. You will meet a bridge over the Malana River and the trail to Kasol village; this route leads to the Rashol Pass (3260m) and the Parbati Valley.

Continuing to Malana, it's a long gradual haul. Just before the village is a tributary and the direct route to Chandrakani Pass.

Malana (2650m) is an isolated village community with around 50 families. It has its own language, customs and laws, and is governed by village elders. It is said the village beliefs were determined by the god Jumla, who was pre-Aryan and independent of the Hindu gods who ruled the Kullu Valley.

The existence of Malana was recorded in Moghul times. Until recently the villagers resisted intrusion from the outside world; see the boxed text below. *Campsites* are at a premium; the best is close to the school, 1km beyond the village. Alternatively, there are a couple of *lodges* run by people from outside the Malana community.

Day 5: Malana to Jari

4–5 hours, 20km

From Malana, a newly constructed trail descends 500m to the valley floor. The electricity lines across the hillside indicate that Malana is about to receive further technological advances.

At the valley floor, a fairly level walk leads through beautiful forest for 5km to 6km, reaching the new dam on the Malana River. Cross the dam wall to the true left of the valley and continue along the road through a series of workers camps. Signs outline the joint Indian-Canadian construction consortium's environmental impact policy. The 12km trek from the dam wall to Jari can be completed in two to three hours, although a service vehicle may offer you a lift.

Jari (1520m) is just above the confluence of the Malana and Parbati Rivers, on the main road linking Manikaran and the Kullu Valley.

Malana Village

Malana is not the most inviting village in the Himalaya, even though its laws are not as strictly enforced as they were a generation ago. You are no longer required to take off your leather boots to walk through the village but you must not wear leather apparel in the vicinity of the Jamlu temple. You should not touch any of the walls, particularly near the temple. Also avoid touching any of the villagers as they still regard outsiders as unclean. Rules regarding photography have been relaxed, although check before taking any photographs of the villagers. In the past, breaking these rules incurred a fine; usually the purchase of a goat for around Rs 2000, although this is not likely to be enforced nowadays.

Until a few generations ago, people married within their community. The men still tend to stay in Malana, but women sometimes marry into families in the Parbati or Kullu Valleys.

Pin Parbati & Spiti

Duration	8 days
Distance	113km
Difficulty	moderate–demanding
Start	Pulga
Finish	Sangam
Nearest Towns	Manali (pp151–3), Kaza (p188)
Public Transport	yes

Summary A spectacular traverse from the forests and verdant meadows of the Parbati Valley to the Buddhist villages in the Trans-Himalaya region of Spiti.

This is a fine trek for the well-prepared trekker, following a rough and often ill-defined trail. Ascend the Parbati Valley to alpine meadows in the Great Himalaya National Park. Note that horses cannot cross the Pin Parbati Pass. Organise porters in Manali rather than Kaza.

Traversing the pass is difficult when it's under snow. Later in the season beware of hidden crevasses. Beyond the pass there is a complete change of geography, with the stark mountainscape of the Trans-Himalaya extending north towards the border of Tibet. There is also a change in culture from the Hindu villages of the Kullu Valley to the Buddhist villages of Spiti.

The construction of a dam opposite the meadow at Thakur Khan is a concern. It would be an environmental disaster if the project was to undermine the character of the upper Parbati Valley so close to the Great Himalaya National Park.

PLANNING
When to Trek
The route over the Pin Parbati Pass is normally open by mid-June, although it may be hard ascending the snow slopes below the pass. The Parbati Valley is subject to monsoon rains in July and August. The ideal time to trek is mid-September until mid-October before the winter snows settle on the pass.

What to Bring
A tent, stove, cooking gear and food supplies for the entire trek are required. An ice axe, karabiners and length of rope are also necessary.

Maps
Refer to the Leomann series 1:200,000 *Sheet 5 (Kullu Valley, Parbati Valley & Central Lahaul)*. Also refer to the US Military U502 series 1:250,000, *NI 43-4 ref Shimla* for the Parbati Valley section of the trek and *NI 44-1 ref Chini* for the Pin Valley section in Spiti.

Accommodation
There are a number of lodges and a Forest Rest House at Pulga. At Khir Ganga there is a dhaba, then there's nothing until Sangam. A tent is essential.

GETTING TO/FROM THE TREK
From Manali, two direct buses run to Manikaran each day (Rs 42, six hours). There is also a deluxe bus (Rs 180). From Manikaran, there are two buses to Pulga daily (Rs 10, 1½ hours).

From Sangam, the crowded bus leaves for Kaza at around 11am (Rs 28, two hours).

THE TREK (See map pp154–5)
Day 1: Pulga to Khir Ganga
4–5 hours, 12km
Pulga (2100m) is well served with *tea stalls* and *lodges* built in the apple orchards. The *Forest Rest House*, a popular retreat for foreigners escaping the pace of the Kullu Valley, is just above the village.

Follow the trail up the valley for 2km to 3km before crossing the bridge over the Parbati River. Follow the trail that crosses the Tosh Nullah before continuing through a number of small villages and recrossing the river about 4km below Khir Ganga.

There is an alternative route following a forest trail on the true left of the valley. It leads through coniferous forest and past several waterfalls and can be tiring, as fallen tree branches often block the trail. There is steep climb around a particularly impressive **waterfall** just before this trail meets the horse trail (main route). From there the trail is well defined for the last 4km to Khir Ganga.

The camp at *Khir Ganga* (2850m) is in an open meadow. The *dhabas* and **hot springs** are a further 100m up the meadow.

Day 2: Khir Ganga to Bhojtunda
5 hours, 12km
There is a steady ascent out of the gorge. The valley widens and the trail crosses several delightful pastures supporting a variety of **wildflowers** in summer. Several Gaddi shepherd encampments line the opposite bank, while on the true left bank there are Gujar encampments, where buffalo are grazed throughout the season. **Bhojtunda** (3200m) marks the lower limit of the silver birch trees. There is a *shelter hut* at Bhojtunda and fine alpine views down the valley. The **waterfalls** tumbling down the cliffs on the opposite side of the valley are impressive.

Day 3: Bhojtunda to Thakur Khan
4–5 hours, 11km
For the first few kilometres, the trail leads through birch groves and across a series of boulder fields covered in vegetation, which

can slow the pace. The trail is ill defined in places until it descends to the river. Here, there is a pulley bridge to assist workers on the nearby dam.

There is a choice of trails. If the pulley bridge is working, follow the trail (alternative route) on the true right of the valley. Recross over a shepherd bridge back to the true left at Thakur Khan. If the pulley bridge is not in service, there is little choice but to remain on the true left of the valley and ascend the trail across a number of rock sections. A length of rope would be useful for laden porters and less sure-footed trekkers.

The camp at **Thakur Khan** (3400m) is above the cliff section of the valley opposite the Dibibokri Nullah. This is the construction site for a dam, and Nepalese workers camp there throughout the season. Another *campsite*, a few kilometres up the valley from Thakur Khan, affords the first views of the snowcapped peaks near Pin Parbati Pass.

While the dam construction continues, there is an ongoing debate about how to reconcile the demand for electricity in the lower Kullu Valley with the need to preserve this beautiful area, particularly since the upper section of the Parbati Valley forms part of the Great Himalaya National Park.

Day 4: Thakur Khan to Mantalai
6–7 hours, 20km

Beyond Thakur Khan, the trail passes several Gaddi encampments before crossing a side river by a natural rock bridge, which leads back down to the Parbati River. Just above this crossing is the **Pandu Bridge**, another natural rock bridge over the Parbati River and a possible *campsite*. According to Hindu mythology, the bridge commemorates the retreat of the Pandava brothers to the region of Spiti, and Tibet. The climb to the top of the huge boulder can be made without difficulty before descending a rock staircase to the opposite bank. The trail climbs gradually through a series of flowered meadows interspersed with boulder fields.

To reach **Mantalai**, complete the 200m ascent over the boulder fields to a broad plateau (4070m). For much of the season, the lake is nothing more than a series of braided rivulets

blocked by the terminal moraine, which occasionally backfills to form a lake. There is a choice of grassy *campsites* just beyond here.

Day 5: Mantalai to High Camp
7 hours, 14km

Head to the true right of the valley and follow the trail through the terminal moraine. Locate the cairns that mark the route and follow the comparatively straightforward trail through the boulders. If the going gets tough and you need to clamber over boulders, it is imperative that you find the cairns again rather than waste energy here.

The Pin Parbati Pass is due east of the Parbati Glacier. After passing the second side valley on the glacier's true right, commence a steep 300m climb out of the main valley floor. The climb affords a bird's-eye view of Parbati Valley. Directly below, the Parbati River gushes out of the main glacier. The peaks on the far side of the valley also come into full view, including Pyramid Peak (6036m), Snow Peak (5640m) and an unnamed peak (6127m), the region's highest.

After scrambling over boulders and scree out of the main valley, the trail crosses a series of meadows before a steep 150m climb to the side valley that leads to Pin Parbati Pass. *Camp* here or continue to a higher camp at the base of the pass, which is under snow until mid-July.

To reach the high camp, continue up the side valley and ascend the lateral moraine. The trail is ill defined and it is a very tiring, two-hour ascent to the flat sandy *campsite* at 4550m. There are magnificent views of the surrounding peaks, including those on the far side of the Parbati Valley. There are a number of accessible snowfields, and a rest day could be spent ascending these to the base of the peaks along the main ridge line.

Day 6: High Camp to Pin Valley Camp via Pin Parbati Pass
5 hours, 12km

From the high camp, a steep 200m ascent leads over boulders to a large snowfield below the pass. The pass is a small col immediately south of the prominent rock monolith. The trek to the pass is straightforward across the snowfield, but you should rope up, particularly early in the season when the crevasses are concealed. The **Pin Parbati Pass** (4810m) is marked by cairns and prayer flags. The alpine views to the snow-capped ranges towards the Kullu Valley contrast with the barren mountain ridges stretching east towards Spiti.

The gradual descent from the pass heads over a snowfield. Maintain caution as crevasses are still a danger. To reach the Pin Valley, follow the trail over scree to the true right of the valley. It becomes very steep in places. At the confluence with a valley from the north, cross the side river and continue down the true left of the main valley for 2km to a grassy *campsite* (4550m).

Day 7: Pin Valley Camp to Mudh
8–9 hours, 20km

Continue down the true left of the valley. There is no trail for the first few kilometres, and it is advisable to stick close to the valley floor. Whichever route is followed, there is a fair amount of loose scree, which makes for a tiring start to the day. There are also some side streams to cross. After 5km to 6km, the route leads to a small plateau above the valley floor. This marks the upper limit of the grazing pastures for the shepherds from Mudh and the nearby villages.

This *campsite* is often used by groups trekking in the opposite direction, and marks the halfway point to Mudh. The trail down the valley is well defined, although there is a large torrent after 4km to 5km, which must be forded with care. Just below this crossing, the village of Mudh is visible beneath a huge cliff face. The outlying barley fields are tended by village children who are not yet familiar with the 'one pen' mantra chanted on the more popular trails in Ladakh. The *campsite* (3850m) is in a small enclosure before the main village of **Mudh**.

The catchment area of the Pin Valley, separating the Pin and Parbati Valleys, has been designated the **Pin National Park**. There have been reports of snow leopards roaming the upper stretches of the valleys, and of herds of bharal grazing the high pastures in summer.

Day 8: Mudh to Sangam
4–5 hours, 12km

Start early to ensure you reach Sangam in time for the daily bus to Kaza.

From Mudh, there is no need to cross the bridge, instead follow the trail on the true left of the valley. The trail skirts high above the river at some stages but is at present being upgraded and there are plans to eventually extend the road from Sangam to Mudh.

Sangam (3570m) is a substantial village with extensive fields of barley and a number of recently completed government buildings. The bridge over the Khamengar River has facilitated easier access to the village. Until recently the only way to cross the river was to use a harness and karabiner to haul yourself across on a wire; an exhilarating, if inconvenient, way to complete the trek!

Bara Bhangal

Duration	11 days
Distance	153km
Difficulty	demanding
Start	Manali
Finish	Bir
Nearest Town	Manali (pp151–3)
Public Transport	yes

Summary A remote trek traversing the Bara Bhangal and Dhaula Dhar Ranges. Visit the isolated settlement of Bara Bhangal and follow Gaddi shepherd trails to the Kangra Valley.

This trek covers one of the most remote corners of Himachal Pradesh. There are a number of demanding days so an extra day or two should be set aside for acclimatisation before crossing the first pass. The Kali Hind and Thamsar Passes are both complicated routes; a local guide is necessary.

Apart from the occasional Gaddi shepherds encampment, there are no settlements until Bara Bhangal – a substantial village cut off by high passes and deep snow for at least six months of the year.

The alpine campsites are particularly attractive. Extra time camping in the vicinity of the Kali Hind will provide a fine opportunity to explore the snowfields and glaciers that define the Bara Bhangal Range.

PLANNING
When to Trek
Heavy snow on the Kali Hind and Thamsar Passes precludes trekking until June. Even then, snow will remain until mid-July, when the monsoon rains begin. Mid-September to mid-October is ideal for trekking.

What to Bring
Bring a tent, stove and cooking gear plus food for at least ten days. Ice axes and rope should also be carried, although neither of the passes is heavily crevassed.

Maps
Refer to the Leomann series 1:200,000 *Sheet 4 (Chamba, Dhaula Dhar Passes, Pangi Valley & Western Lahaul)*. Also refer to the US Military U502 series 1:250,000, *NI 43-16 ref Palampur*.

Accommodation
Bara Bhangal, Rajgundha and Billing have Forest Rest Houses. Elsewhere, vacant shepherds huts may be the only option.

GETTING TO/FROM THE TREK
For travel to Manali, see Getting There & Away (pp151–3). From Bir, there is a bus to Baijnath (Rs 5, one hour, three a day). From Baijnath (on the Mandi-Pathankot highway), regular buses go to Dharamsala, McLeod Ganj and to Mandi and the Kullu Valley.

THE TREK (See map pp156–7)
Day 1: Manali to Lama Dug
4–5 hours, 12km
From **Manali** (2050m), follow the trail past the Hadimba Temple to the entrance of the **Manali Sanctuary**. Climb through the deodar forest for 3km to a rocky outcrop with a view of Manali. Just above this vantage point is a small meadow (2350m) before a steep 400m ascent through small pastures and conifer and oak forest. This section is particularly difficult after rain and can often reduce the first day to a continual mudslide – all the way to the large meadow of Lama Dug.

Lama Dug (2920m) is a lovely meadow ringed by maple, spruce and oak, while stands of silver birch are further up the hillside. The small stream flowing through the meadow is one of the sources of Manali's water supply.

Day 2: Lama Dug to Rieli
6–7 hours, 17km
Beyond Lama Dug, the trail ascends the meadow along the southern perimeter of the **Manali Sanctuary**. There are uninterrupted views north towards the Solang and Rohtang Valleys, while the prominent snowcapped peaks peering above the Pir Panjal Range provide a further reminder of the elevation.

The ascent across the higher pastures is long, gradual and exhilarating, with views opening up across to the Hampta Valley and Deo Tibba (6001m). The shepherd trails split and turn a number of times. The correct trail constantly ascends and does not veer towards the Manali Pass and the pastures to the north. If in doubt, check your directions at one of the many Gaddi encampments. It takes around four to five hours to reach the highest of the alpine ridges, which form a plateau at around 3800m.

From the grassy plateau, the trail heads south across a series of verdant ridges. A long descent follows, reaching an intermediate valley and a prominent side trail (from Katrain in the Kullu Valley). From this point, a gradual climb of 2km to 3km leads through a small oak forest to the meadow known locally as *Rieli* (3320m).

Day 3: Reili to Kali Hind Base Camp
5 hours, 12km
The trail winds above the upper river course before gradually descending to the valley floor. The location of the next camp can be appreciated, as can the route to Kali Hind Pass, on the crest of the Bara Bhangal Range. After about two hours, the trail crosses a bridge at 3270m to the true right of the valley. You climb a series of grassy ridges and pass a number of shepherd encampments to reach a choice of *campsites* at the base of the pass.

From camp – at around 3700m – there are fine views east towards the Chandrakani Pass and the peaks of the Himalaya Range.

Day 4: Base Camp to Lake Camp via Kali Hind Pass
4–5 hours, 10km

If the conditions are clear, an early start will not be a problem – the sun hits the campsite very early. The trail ascends a further grassy ridge (4000m) to a small plateau before ascending a series of moraine fields. Steep in sections, these fields lead to the base of Kali Hind Pass. The trail heads south for 500m before a steep ascent to a snowfield. Another short ascent on ice reaches the cairns and prayer flags of **Kali Hind Pass** (4610m). It takes three to four hours to reach the pass.

Enjoy impressive views to the north across a series of snowfields and hanging glaciers that form the crest of the Bara Bhangal Range. To the west, the Mani Mahesh Range is also in sight.

The initial descent from the pass avoids a large crevasse before heading across a snowfield that gradually descends to a series of glacial lakes (4350m). The time from the pass to *Lake Camp* is around one hour. If the weather deteriorates there is the option to descend to a small *campsite* about two hours further down the valley.

Day 5: Lake Camp to Danku Thach
5–6 hours, 14km

Peering down the valley from camp, the remarkable change of geography after crossing the pass is evident. It seems that the Bara Bhangal Range restricts the monsoon rain to the confines of the Kullu Valley, while the area is also beyond the influence of the rain extending up the Ravi Valley. The result is an arid region more similar to Ladakh than to this region of Himachal Pradesh.

The trail heads across a rocky plateau before descending steeply over scree and boulders to the valley floor. Initially the trail leads down the valley's true right. A *campsite* (3800m) is about two hours from camp.

The trail continues along the river course through boulder and scree gullies. It crosses the river numerous times before reaching a *Gaddi encampment* and the small Hindu temple **Danku Thach** (3500m).

Day 6: Danku Thach to Damari Thach
6 hours, 16km

Just beyond camp, cross the side river before continuing down the valley across flowered meadows and the occasional scree slopes above the river. The trail remains on the true right past several Gaddi shepherd encampments. Birch trees (to 3600m) and blue pine (to 3300m) reflect the upper limit of the monsoon rain in this remote valley.

There is a short, steep ascent to reach a meadow with two huge ancient maple trees. Continue climbing to reach a side valley from the north and a further river crossing. *Camp* here or continue for 3km or 4km to a large meadow known as *Damari Thach* (3550m).

Fine views reach down the Ravi Gorge below the village of Bara Bhangal. To the south, uninterrupted views extend to the hanging glaciers and snowcapped peaks that define the north ridge of the Dhaula Dhar.

Day 7: Damari Thach to Bara Bhangal
5–6 hours, 15km

The trail ascends a further alpine ridge to 3670m before crossing a series of pastures with a view down the valley. A long and gradual descent leads to the village of Bara Bhangal. The trail takes in silver birch trees, rhododendron and blue pine, and there are signs of brown bears having foraged in the grassy clearings. Snakes may also be seen, which is quite remarkable at elevations above 3000m.

The final 500m to 600m descent is steep and dusty in places to the outlying cornfields of **Bara Bhangal** (2350m). The village is spread over a number of kilometres and consists of 30 to 40 houses. In summer, villagers from the upper Kangra Valley live here; only some of the men remain throughout winter.

A look at the map might tempt the unwary to believe there is a more direct trail following the course of the Ravi River. While there is a trail of sorts, by the time it

HIMACHAL PRADESH

enters the gorge it is extremely difficult for all but the most sure-footed villager to follow. There are plans to extend the road from Chamba all the way up the gorge to Bara Bhangal, a big task for even the most ambitious road builder.

Day 8: Bara Bhangal to Thamsar
6–7 hours, 15km

Cross the bridge over the river flowing from the Kali Hind Pass and commence a steep 400m ascent of the valley leading to the south. Continue on the true left for 3km to a broad glacial valley before crossing to the true right. There follows a gradual ascent across open meadows and scree slopes, and past Gaddi encampments to reach the base of an impressive **waterfall**. Ascend the trail to the true right of the waterfall before crossing the river to a series of meadows referred to as *Thamsar* (3750m). This is by far the best campsite before Thamsar Pass, a further four- to five-hour trek. There are fine views of Mani Mahesh Kailash and the impressive Pir Panjal Range.

Day 9: Thamsar to Panhartu via Thamsar Pass
7–8 hours, 14km

The trail gradually climbs on the true left of the valley, passing a prominent side valley and glacier to the east. After 3km to 4km, negotiate the scree and boulder fields to reach a **glacial lake** at 4100m. Look for the rock cairns en route. The trail winds above scree slopes on the true right of the lake. This leads to another **glacial lake** (4380m) and the base of the pass.

Crossing the snowfield leads to a prominent ridge line – the crest of the Dhaula Dhar Range and the **Thamsar Pass** (4380m). The pass is marked by Hindu tridents and prayer flags. There are impressive views north to the Pir Panjal Range. To the south, the alpine ridges extend towards the Indian Plains.

The initial, steep descent from the pass reaches a large glacial lake at 4370m. Continue to a series of alpine pastures (and potential *campsites* if coming from the opposite direction) between 3900m and 4200m. There follows a steep descent to the meadow at

Panhartu (3390m). It takes around three hours to reach camp from the pass.

The meadows in the vicinity of Panhartu attract many Gaddi shepherds on their spring migration to the high pastures beyond the Bara Bhangal. The meadow is at the confluence of the river flowing from the Thamsar Pass and two other streams that form the upper reaches of the Uhl River, which eventually flows into the Beas River at Mandi.

Day 10: Panhartu to Rajgundha
6 hours, 16km

From Panhartu, the trail initially follows the true right of the valley. It descends across a series of permanent snow bridges for 2km to 3km to reach a well-defined trail on the true left of the valley. The trail leads through a mixed forest of rhododendron, spruce and oak down to the *dhabas* and a *Forest Rest House* at **Palachak** (2500m).

Just below Palachak, cross the concrete bridge to the true right of the valley. Continue through a forest of spruce and oak to the fields of corn, beans and potatoes near **Rajgundha** (2400m). There is a *campsite* beside the *Forest Rest House*.

An alternative is to cross the bridge over the Uhl River (about 1km above Rajgundha) and continue to the village of Narotta. A recently introduced bus service links the area to Mandi and the upper Kangra Valley.

Day 11: Rajgundha to Bir
5–6 hours, 12km

While it is possible to catch the bus from Narotta, the final day of the trek affords fine views across the north Indian Plains.

From Rajgundha, the trail continues on the true right of the Uhl Valley through spruce, oak and rhododendron forest. After 4km to 5km, there are fine views to the Indian Plains before the trail heads around contours and alpine ridges to **Billing** (2200m).

From Billing, there is a 14km 4WD road to Bir that has not been maintained. However, the distance is shortened considerably by taking many of the shortcuts down the forest trail; you could reach **Bir** (1450m) in about two hours.

McLeod Ganj & the Kangra Valley

Although Dharamsala is the district headquarters of the Kangra region, this section focuses on nearby McLeod Ganj at the foot of the snowcapped Dhaula Dhar. Its commanding views above the Kangra Valley – combined with the presence of the 14th Dalai Lama and his government in exile – have contributed to its popularity among trekkers keen to explore the trails across the Dhaula Dhar.

The region offers varied trekking: from forested ridges and alpine meadows en route to Kareri Lake; to uninterrupted views from the Indrahar Pass north to the Pir Panjal and Mani Mahesh Ranges.

HISTORY

The ancient town of Kangra, 20km south of Dharamsala, is an important indicator of the region's early history. Once in a position of great strategic importance, it gave credence to the local saying 'he who holds the fort holds the hills'. This factor was to determine the history of Kangra and many of the other Himalayan kingdoms.

During the Moghul period, the local rajahs paid tribute to the emperor's court. Following the decline in Moghul rule, the famous rajah Sanser Chand sought to establish a huge Himalayan empire that extended far beyond the Kangra Valley. An era of expansion followed until the Sikhs exerted their control over the Punjab Himalaya.

After the Treaty of Amritsar in 1846, the British established administration of Kangra, Kullu and Lahaul at Dharamsala, which it held until 1947. In those times, the hill tracks provided a delightful walk between Dharamsala and Shimla, while the colonial buildings in Dharamsala and McLeod Ganj provide a fitting testimony to the era.

NATURAL HISTORY

The Dhaula Dhar Range dominates the region. Another major feature is the Ravi River. Its course can be viewed, as can the Bara Bhangal Range, separating the Ravi's upper tributaries from the Kullu Valley.

Wildlife in the region includes black bear, common leopard, serow, goral and kakor, which are found at lower forest elevations. Brown bears may be spotted foraging close to the alpine meadows.

Birds of prey, including the golden eagle, kestrel and lammergeier, soar above the ridges of the Dhaula Dhar. The forests and glades above McLeod Ganj attract a variety of birdlife that migrates each summer from the Indian Plains.

Wildflower enthusiasts may be attracted to the meadows beneath the Indrahar Pass or close to Kareri Lake, although large herds of goats and sheep heavily graze these pastures.

ACCESS TOWN
McLeod Ganj
☎ 01892 • alt 1980m

McLeod Ganj was originally established as a British garrison in the 1850s before being gradually developed as a hill station and an attractive alternative to Dharamsala. However, it wasn't until the 14th Dalai Lama and his exiled government settled here, together with many Tibetan refugees, that a steady flow of trekkers and travellers started to visit this delightful region.

Information For general enquiries, visit the **HPTDC Tourist Office** opposite Bookworm.

Supplies & Equipment You can purchase a wide selection of food supplies in McLeod Ganj before commencing a trek. Cooking stoves, pots and pans can be bought in the bazaar. Quality camping gear is generally not available and, even if undertaking an inclusive trek with one of the local agents, it is worth bringing your own sleeping bag, tent and insulted mat.

Trekking Agents With information on treks out of the Kangra and Chamba Valleys, the **Regional Mountaineering Centre** (*☎ 21787, Dharamkot Rd; closed Sun*) also has maps and copies of *Treks & Passes of the Dhaula Dhar & the Pir Panjal*, written by the centre director SR Sani.

HIMACHAL PRADESH

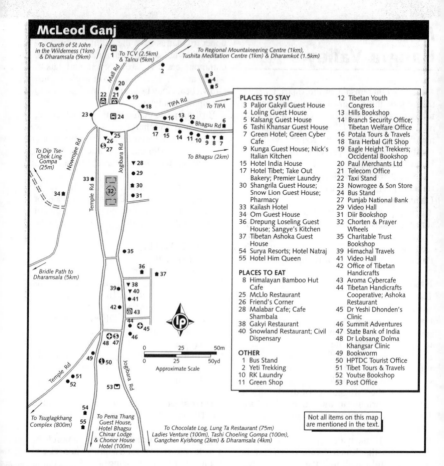

McLeod Ganj

To Church of St John
in the Wilderness (1km)
& Dharamsala (9km)

To TCV (2.5km)
& Talnu (5km)

To Regional Mountaineering Centre (1km),
Tushita Meditation Centre (1km) & Dharamkot (1.5km)

Mall Rd

TIPA Rd — To TIPA

Bhagsu Rd

To Bhagsu (2km)

Nowrojee Rd

To Dip Tse-
Chok Ling
Gompa
(25km)

Jogibara Rd

Temple Rd

Bridle Path to
Dharamsala (5km)

0   25   50m
0   25   50yd
Approximate Scale

To Tsuglagkhang
Complex (800m)

To Pema Thang
Guest House,
Hotel Bhagsu
Chinar Lodge
& Chonor House
Hotel (100m)

To Chocolate Log, Lung Ta Restaurant (75m)
Ladies Venture (100m), Tashi Choeling Gompa (100m),
Gangchen Kyishong (2km) & Dharamsala (4km)

PLACES TO STAY
3 Paljor Gakyil Guest House
4 Loling Guest House
5 Kalsang Guest House
6 Tashi Khansar Guest House
7 Green Hotel; Green Cyber Cafe
9 Kunga Guest House; Nick's Italian Kitchen
15 Hotel India House
17 Hotel Tibet; Take Out Bakery; Premier Laundry
30 Shangrila Guest House; Snow Lion Guest House; Pharmacy
33 Kailash Hotel
34 Om Guest House
36 Drepung Loseling Guest House; Sangye's Kitchen
37 Tibetan Ashoka Guest House
54 Surya Resorts; Hotel Natraj
55 Hotel Him Queen

PLACES TO EAT
8 Himalayan Bamboo Hut Cafe
25 McLlo Restaurant
26 Friend's Corner
28 Malabar Cafe; Cafe Shambala
38 Gakyi Restaurant
40 Snowland Restaurant; Civil Dispensary

OTHER
1 Bus Stand
2 Yeti Trekking
10 RK Laundry
11 Green Shop

12 Tibetan Youth Congress
13 Hills Bookshop
14 Branch Security Office; Tibetan Welfare Office
16 Potala Tours & Travels
18 Tara Herbal Gift Shop
19 Eagle Height Trekkers; Occidental Bookshop
20 Paul Merchants Ltd
21 Telecom Office
22 Taxi Stand
23 Nowrogee & Son Store
24 Bus Stand
27 Punjab National Bank
29 Video Hall
31 Diir Bookshop
32 Chorten & Prayer Wheels
35 Charitable Trust Bookshop
39 Himachal Travels
41 Video Hall
42 Office of Tibetan Handicrafts
43 Aroma Cybercafe
44 Tibetan Handicrafts Cooperative; Ashoka Restaurant
45 Dr Yeshi Dhonden's Clinic
46 Summit Adventures
47 State Bank of India
48 Dr Lobsang Dolma Khangsar Clinic
49 Bookworm
50 HPTDC Tourist Office
51 Tibet Tours & Travels
52 Youtse Bookshop
53 Post Office

Not all items on this map
are mentioned in the text.

Eagle Height Trekkers (☎ 21330, ☎ 21938, ⓔ *prem.sagar@eudoramail.co, Dharamkot Rd*) is just above the bus stand. It's run by two friendly brothers, Prem and Daya Shagar, who can organise guides and porters. Inclusive treks cost US$30 to US$40 per person per day.

Yeti Trekking (☎ 21060, *Dharamkot Rd*) is the oldest agency in McLeod Ganj. They can organise porters for Rs 250 and guides for Rs 400.

Summit Adventures (☎ 21679, ⓔ *summit65@yahoo.com, Jogibara Rd*) offers porters and inclusive treks.

Places to Stay & Eat There is no shortage of hotels and plenty of variety here.

The **Green Hotel** (☎ 21200, *Bhagsu Rd*) is popular, with rooms from Rs 100 to Rs 250, as is **Om Guest House** (☎ 24313), on a path leading down from the bus station, with similar rates. Also recommended is **Snow Lion Guest House** (☎ 21289, *Jogibara Rd*), charging from Rs 200.

There are a number of upmarket hotels. Doubles at **Hotel Tibet** (☎ 21587, *Bhagsu Rd*) cost Rs 600 to Rs 900. **Pema Thang Guest House** (☎ 21871), on the road past the tourist office, offers fine views to Dharamsala and the Indian Plains. Rooms cost Rs 700 to Rs 900.

HIMACHAL PRADESH

Recommended eating places include the central *McLlo Restaurant*, near the bus station, and *Hotel Tibet*. Both offer a range of Tibetan, Chinese and Indian cuisine.

Getting There & Away McLeod Ganj has bus services to/from most major towns in northern Himachal Pradesh. The airport at Gaggal, 15km from Dharamsala, provides convenient flights to/from Delhi.

Air Indian Airlines operates flights from Delhi to Gaggal (US$145, three per week). The flight arrives from Delhi around 1pm and returns to Delhi around 3pm. From Gaggal, a taxi to McLeod Ganj costs Rs 250.

Bus A number of agencies in McLeod Ganj book buses to Delhi (Rs 350/250 deluxe/public, 12 hours). Most leave around 6pm.

Regular buses travel to/from Dharamsala (Rs 6, 30 minutes), Pathankot (Rs 60, four hours) and Chandigarh (Rs 130, nine hours). Daily buses go to/from Chamba (Rs 130, 10 hours) and Brahmaur (Rs 170, 12 hours). Deluxe buses service Manali (Rs 250, eight hours) and Dehra Dun (Rs 280, 11 hours).

Taxi Prices vary depending on whether you use the minivan or the larger Tata Sumo. A minivan taxi to/from Dharamsala/Pathankot costs around Rs 90/1000. Expect to pay around Rs 4000/4500 to Manali/Chandigarh.

Indrahar Pass

Duration	5 days
Distance	62km
Difficulty	moderate
Start	McLeod Ganj
Finish	Machetar
Nearest Town	McLeod Ganj (pp173–5)
Public Transport	yes

Summary A spectacular traverse of the Dhaula Dhar Range following Gaddi shepherd trails to the Ravi and Chamba Valleys.

The ridges over the Dhaula Dhar do not lend themselves to easy trekking. This trek over the Indrahar Pass is no exception, even though it follows one of the more established trails used by Gaddi shepherds en route to their summer grazing pastures in the upper Ravi Valley and Lahaul.

The ascent to the Indrahar Pass involves a continual climb, often over scree or boulders. The views compensate: to the south, there are spectacular views of the Indian Plains; to the north is the sacred peak of Mani Mahesh Kailash and the snowcapped Pir Panjal Range. Beyond the pass, an ill-defined trail leads through Hindu villages and temples to the upper Ravi Valley. There is the opportunity to extend the trek to Mani Mahesh Kailash or over the Kugti Pass to Lahaul.

PLANNING
When to Trek
If you are prepared to trek on snow, it is possible to cross the Indrahar Pass in early May. By June the snow begins to melt at higher elevations and the Gaddi shepherds set out on their summer migration. In July and August, the region takes the full brunt of the monsoon rain. September and October are ideal trekking months, with settled conditions occasionally lasting into November.

What to Bring
A tent, stove and cooking gear ensure a flexible alternative to staying in shelter huts and village temples. Food supplies for a minimum of three days should be carried; you can pick up food at Triund and Machetar.

Maps
Refer to the Leomann series 1:200,000 *Sheet 4 (Chamba, Dhaula Dhar Passes, Pangi Valley & Western Lahaul)*. The relevant map of the US Military U502 series 1:250,000, *NI 43-15* is hard to obtain and may be classified due to its proximity to India's border with Pakistan.

Accommodation
You could get by without a tent. There are comfortable rooms for Rs 300 at Triund's Forest Rest House; book in advance at the **Forest Office** (☎ 245887) in Dharamsala. Lahesh has a huge rock overhang for shelter,

while at Chatru Parao you may be fortunate to find an empty shepherds hut. The village temple at Kuarsi can provide shelter for the night and there is a Forest Rest House at Machetar. A tent would be a good back-up.

GETTING TO/FROM THE TREK

For travel to McLeod Ganj, see Getting There & Away (p175). From Machetar, several buses each day travel to Chamba (three to four hours, Rs 35). However, be warned that the early morning bus reaches Machetar around 7am and is crowded even by Indian standards. The 'air-con' seats on the roof may be the only option until Karamukh, where many villagers change buses to Brahmaur.

THE TREK (See map pp156–7)
Day 1: McLeod Ganj to Triund
3–4 hours, 10km

Turn left at the Mountaineering Institute and continue past the *tea stall* at **Dharamkot** to the ridge known as Galu Devi, where there is a small **temple**. From here the trail is well defined to Triund. An early start from McLeod Ganj is recommended, since the trail faces south and offers little shade. It tends to be warm by mid-morning and there are few, if any, springs to quench the thirst. The final few kilometres up to the meadow are steep, but it is worth the effort to savour the views to the south across the Beas Dam to the Indian Plains. To the north, the snowy ridges of the Dhaula Dhar provide an impressive backdrop.

There is a comfortable *Forest Rest House* at **Triund** (2975m) and there are some good *camping spots* nearby – an ideal place to spend a day or two.

Day 2: Triund to Lahesh Cave
3–4 hours, 9km

The time required for this stage will depend largely on fitness. The trail follows the ridge behind the prayer flags above the Gaddi encampment. It climbs gently through oak and conifer forests and across open meadows to the encampment at **Laka Got** (3350m). This is an ideal place to rest before commencing the ascent through scree to the true right of the main gully, which leads to Indrahar Pass.

It is a tiring scramble for 200m to 300m to **Lahesh Cave** (3600m), a huge rock overhang, which can serve as *shelter* for the night. Nearby are a few level grassy ridges on which to *pitch a tent*. There is a small stream in the main gully. The cave is distinguished by brown and black markings, and is big enough to house a large party of porters, trekkers and shepherds.

Day 3: Lahesh Cave to Chatru Parao via Indrahar Pass
6–7 hours, 12km

The ridges of the Dhaula Dhar do not offer easily defined passes. In June the snow plod is very tiring, while in September and October the rock scramble to the pass will take around four hours. Watch for the rock cairns to avoid unnecessary detours. The search for gullies and footholds over boulders, although by no means technical, is not easy.

During the climb, the route remains on the true right of the main gully. At the higher elevations, there is a steep 300m to 400m ascent towards the crest of the Dhaula Dhar, before a 1km traverse just below the ridge to the **Indrahar Pass** (4350m). Panoramic views reward your efforts: to the south, the Indian Plains stretch as far as the eye can see; to the north, the snowcapped ridges of the Pir Panjal Range are impressive. The peak of Mani Mahesh Kailash (5656m) is visible to the east, while the depths of the Ravi Valley can be appreciated in the middle foreground.

The descent from the pass is initially very steep, down a gully strewn with loose boulders. The terrain levels out across a plateau marked with huge boulders. However, under snow, these boulders make for difficult trekking. The trail down to **Chatru Parao** is often muddy and slippery, and very tiring at the end of a long day. The *camp* (3700m) consists of a few shepherds huts set in an open meadow.

Day 4: Chatru Parao to Kuarsi
7 hours, 15km

The trail, little more than a goat track in places, follows the true left of the valley for the first few kilometres. Early in the season, it would be worthwhile abandoning the trail,

The Gaddi Shepherds

The Kangra and Chamba districts are the home of the Gaddi – Hindu shepherds who tend their flocks on the Dhaula Dhar and the Pir Panjal Ranges in summer.

Their traditional routes across the mountain passes follow a seasonal migration. In spring they take their flocks to the Kangra foothills and slowly ascend to the pastures below the Dhaula Dhar. The time to cross the first pass is determined by the snowmelt, but is not normally until early June. After spending time in their traditional meeting centre at Brahmaur, they head to the rich pastures below the Pir Panjal. A further, often demanding, traverse leads to the summer pastures in Lahaul. The pastures in the Miyar Valley are a typical destination, where they remain for a couple of months before heading back to Brahmaur and the Kangra Valley in early September.

Alternative routes to Lahaul include migrations via the Kullu Valley and over either the Rohtang or Hampta Passes before ascending to pastures in the vicinity of the Baralacha La, on the border between Jammu and Kashmir State and Himachal Pradesh.

The Gaddi can be distinguished by the *chola* – a warm knee-length cloak of natural wool, spun and woven by hand – which they wear tightened at the waist by a black woollen cord.

The Gaddi trace their origins to when the Rajput settlers made their way to the Himalayan foothills, although it was not until the late Moghul period that families chose to settle in Brahmaur and Chamba. The annual Gaddi migration, like that of other shepherd groups in the West Himalaya, means that bridges are reconstructed and mountain trails maintained. This helps to ensure their own safe passage over the passes, and is greatly appreciated by anyone trekking in their footsteps.

and descending across the snow bridges on the main valley floor. After about two hours, the track crosses the valley on a permanent snow bridge, and ascends steeply to an open meadow. There is a **spring line** here, and an ideal rest spot. Continue down the true right of the valley on a trail more suitable for goats than trekkers. The trail peters out in places, particularly across a series of meadows, before finally descending to **Kuarsi** (2730m).

There is a *campsite* above the main spring line in the village. Continue for 10 minutes to a secluded *camp* by the main river.

Day 5: Kuarsi to Machetar
6 hours, 16km

Make an early start to tackle the climb out of the valley and over the ridge to the trailhead. After descending to the valley floor and crossing the bridge, the 700m trek up the hill can be very hot and sticky. The trail ascends through high grassland and forest to a **spring line** about three-quarters of the way up the hill. Here, the trek becomes easier, reaching a pass marked with tridents and cairns.

The views from the top of the ridge extend across the whole region. To the south, the

Dhaula Dhar is seen from a new angle. To the northwest, is the Pir Panjal, and to the east are the snowcapped ridges of the Mani Mahesh Range. There is a long, steady descent for a couple of hours through barley fields and forest to the Ravi Valley. Just above the road is the *Forest Rest House* at **Machetar** (1800m).

Kareri Lake

Duration	4 days
Distance	56km
Difficulty	easy
Start/Finish	Stowari
Nearest Town	McLeod Ganj (pp173–5)
Public Transport	yes

Summary A short, accessible trek through Hindu villages to Kareri Lake and the spectacular ridges of the Dhaula Dhar Range.

This is an ideal alternative to the Indrahar Pass trek, as it does not cross any passes. The Hindu villages reflect the traditional values of the Kangra Valley, while the forests and meadows provide a further dimension.

HIMACHAL PRADESH

Kareri Lake is an ideal base for ascending the upper ridges of the Dhaula Dhar (see the Side Trip). Views across the Indian Plains are unrivalled at these higher elevations.

On the return, consider an alternative route (see p179) via Dharamkot or perhaps spend a few days camping at Triund before returning to McLeod Ganj.

PLANNING
When to Trek
September through October is ideal for trekking. However, to witness the migration of Gaddi shepherds to Kareri Lake, you would need to trek in May. By June most of the snow in the vicinity of the lake has melted. The region is subject to heavy monsoon rain from July to early September.

What to Bring
A tent, stove and cooking gear are required. Carry food supplies for the entire trek.

Maps
Refer to the Leomann series 1:200,000 *Sheet 4 (Chamba, Dhaula Dhar Passes, Pangi Valley & Western Lahaul)*. Be aware that the ridge profiles and river courses in the vicinity of this trek are inaccurate on this map.

Accommodation
There is a Forest Rest House above Kareri village and a temple alongside Kareri Lake for possible shelter. It is possible, but not recommended, to do this trek without a tent.

GETTING TO/FROM THE TREK
From the bazaar at McLeod Ganj, it is a 6km walk or taxi ride (Rs 100) to the trailhead at Stowari. A three-wheel scooter will charge around Rs 20 for the trip, depending on your baggage. From Stowari, walk to Dal Lake, from where scooters go to McLeod Ganj.

THE TREK (See map pp156–7)
Day 1: Stowari to Kareri Village
5 hours, 15km
From Stowari, follow the bridle track that descends through the chir forest for 5km to the Bhote Khola and the small bazaar at **Ghera** (1350m). The trail ascends above the

dam site for about 2km before commencing a steady ascent to the village of **Kanjrala**. The trail heads across the hillside, crossing a couple of small tributaries to reach **Kareri village**, which spreads for several kilometres along the hillside. The *Forest Rest House* is on the main trail above the village.

Day 2: Kareri Village to Kareri Lake
5–6 hours, 13km
From the Forest Rest House, follow the main trail that ascends above Kareri village through a holly oak and spruce forest. The trail remains on the true left of the valley before crossing a stone bridge over the river. The ascent is not steep, and winds through mixed forest and small secluded meadows.

After about 3km, the trail recrosses the river flowing from the lake to the true left of the valley. It is a 5km ascent through rhododendron and oak forest to the shores of **Kareri Lake** (2900m).

There is a Hindu temple and *shelter*, maintained by the villagers and Gaddi shepherds, to the south of the lake. There are many *campsites* in the vicinity of the lake.

Side Trip: Towards Minkiani Pass
5–6 hours, 10km return
From Kareri Lake, you can ascend the alpine meadows beneath the Dhaula Dhar. If heading directly above the lake, there is no established trail and you will have to pick your way along goat trails through oak, rhododendron and silver birch to reach the first of a series of alpine ridges that eventually lead to the Minkiani Pass. How far you ascend depends on your endurance and capacity to absorb the spectacular views that extend across the Indian Plains. At higher elevations, the views to the north extend across the Dhaula Dhar and Pir Panjal Ranges to the 6000m peaks of the Kishtwar Himalaya.

Days 3 & 4: Kareri Lake to Stowari
Retrace the route for Days 1 and 2. The return to Kareri village takes three to four hours. If you leave from the lake early, it is possible to reach Stowari and McLeod Ganj in one day.

Alternative Route: McLeod Ganj via Dharamkot
2 days, 25km

Consider trekking down to the Bhote Khola and *camping* alongside the river. The following day, head up the valley and across the wooded ridges to Dharamkot. From here, descend to McLeod Ganj. Camping at Triund or in the vicinity of the meadows at the base of the Indrahar Pass is also worthwhile. See the Indrahar Pass trek (pp175–7).

Brahmaur & the Ravi Valley

Few travellers make their way to this isolated corner of Himachal Pradesh. It consists of Chamba, the district headquarters, and the ancient capital of Brahmaur. It is enclosed by the snowcapped Pir Panjal and Dhaula Dhar Ranges, and drained by the headwaters of the Ravi River. The region is well suited for trekking, and includes the important Hindu pilgrimage to Mani Mahesh.

Trekking over the Pir Panjal affords fine views north towards the Himalaya Range and the upper sections of the Chandra Valley. To the south are the peaks of the Mani Mahesh Range and the glaciers and snowfields of the Dhaula Dhar.

HISTORY

Historical records indicate that the Chamba state has maintained an uninterrupted cultural tradition since the 9th century. Prior to that the capital was at Brahmaur, where the well-preserved temples today reflect the cultural highpoints of this era. In spite of its important strategic position, Chamba paid only a nominal tribute to the Moghuls and at times its borders extended well beyond the Ravi Valley.

Following the wars with the British in the 1840s, the Sikhs were granted all the country between the Ravi and Indus Rivers. However, it was agreed that the Chamba region, which then included the nearby Pangi Valley and Lower Lahaul, would be under British administration.

In 1868 the hill station of Dalhousie was founded. Chamba had hopelessly inadequate roads and forest trails, which were upgraded and surveyed as British PWD and forest departments extended into the region. Even today the occasional sign remains, outlining the stages (in miles) between Kashmir and Kullu prior to 1947.

NATURAL HISTORY

Treks out of Brahmaur lead north over the rugged passes of the Pir Panjal Range. The route to the Kugti Pass leads through a mixed forest of oak, blue pine and cedar before giving way to birch groves and alpine meadows noted for their wildflowers. Above the meadows are extensive terminal moraine fields below the glaciers and peaks that guard the passes.

Wildlife in the area includes black bears and common leopards in the forests above the villages. At higher elevations, there is the chance of spotting serow and goral, while markhor and brown bears may be seen close to the alpine meadows.

Birds of prey such as lammergeier and kestrel are seen at high altitudes. A variety of dippers, minivets, thrushes and woodpeckers are found in the mixed forests.

Wildflower enthusiasts may elect to spend extra days camping in the vicinity of the alpine meadows en route to Mani Mahesh. The pastures in the valleys near Kugti Pass are also very attractive, particularly in July and August.

ACCESS TOWN
Brahmaur
☎ 01899 • alt 2195m

The town of Brahmaur sits above the Ravi River. The well-preserved Hindu temples here are some of the finest in northern India. The dramatic setting beneath the Dhaula Dhar and Pir Panjal Ranges provides a further attraction. It is also the departure point for many thousands of pilgrims who make the annual trek to Mani Mahesh Kailash.

Supplies & Equipment Fresh fruit and vegetables are available, along with a limited assortment of tinned food. Nuts, raisins and other luxuries should be purchased from Chamba or Dharamsala. Supplies are limited beyond Brahmaur, except during the peak periods of the Mani Mahesh pilgrimage.

Equipment such as cooking stoves, pots and pans can be purchased in the Brahmaur bazaar. Quality camping gear such as sleeping bags, tents and insulated mats are not available for hire.

Trekking Agents There are no trekking agents in Brahmaur. Make arrangements from McLeod Ganj (pp173–4). In Chamba, **Hills & Treks** (☎ 22253) is recommended. It is managed by a local trekker, Navneet Chowfla, who also works at the PWD office in Brahmaur.

If making your own arrangements, you can hire porters in Hadsar. Budget for around Rs 200 per porter per day, plus a transport, accommodation and relocation allowance (around Rs 300).

Places to Stay & Eat On the lower of the two roads leading up from the bus stand, the **PWD Rest House** (☎ 25023) has double rooms for Rs 350. There are also a number of small hotels. **Rajdhani Guest House** (☎ 25307) is good value, with rooms from Rs 200 to Rs 250. **Chamunda Guest House** (☎ 25056) has rooms with shared bathrooms for Rs 200. **Sonam Guest House** (☎ 25155), near the Mountaineering Institute, charges Rs 200 to Rs 250.

The **guesthouses** can provide basic Indian dishes, while there is an assortment of **dhabas** near the bus station.

Getting There & Away Regular buses and taxis connect Brahmaur with Chamba, Pathankot, Dharamsala and Hadsar.

Bus There is a bus service from 5.30am to 5.30pm to/from Chamba (Rs 38). From Chamba, onward buses depart every hour to Pathankot. There is one direct bus (Rs 85) between Brahmaur and Pathankot; it leaves Brahmaur at 8.30am. There is a direct service to/from Dharamsala (Rs 170), departing Brahmaur at 5.30pm. At other times, the fastest option to/from Dharamsala is to travel via Pathankot. There are also four or five buses from Brahmaur to Hadsar (Rs 10, one hour). A bus service to Kugti will commence within the next few seasons when the road is completed.

Taxi A 4WD to Chamba costs Rs 500 and to Hadsar, Rs 150.

Mani Mahesh Kailash

Duration	3 days
Distance	40km
Difficulty	easy
Start/Finish	Hadsar
Nearest Town	Brahmaur (pp179–80)
Public Transport	yes
Summary	Follow the pilgrim trail to Mani Mahesh Lake and the sacred peak of Mani Mahesh Kailash.

Many thousands of Hindu pilgrims complete the trek to Mani Mahesh Lake each season. While the historic origins of the trek are obscure, it would have evolved because Mani Mahesh Kailash (5656m) is close to a main source of the Ravi River – one of the five main tributaries of the Indus.

Prior to the main pilgrimage in late August, a fair is held in Brahmaur with folk dances and festivities attended by villagers and a sizeable gathering of Gaddi shepherds. Following the ceremony, the high priests lead the pilgrims from Brahmaur to the shores of Mani Mahesh Lake – although nowadays many other pilgrims travel by bus or 4WD to the trailhead at Hadsar.

Beyond Hadsar the well-defined trail and large numbers of dhabas en route make this an easy trek. It is not advisable to stay overnight at Mani Mahesh Lake (4100m) unless you are well acclimatized.

While the pilgrimage is one of the most important in the Hindu calendar, it is unfortunate that the trekking route is an environmental disaster. The huge amount of garbage and human waste is a poor reflection on the local administration (see the 'Environmental Watch' boxed text, p162).

PLANNING
When to Trek
The trek can be completed from the end of May, although the lake will be under snow until at least mid-June. July and August bring monsoon rain, although this is the time when most pilgrims trek. Mid-September to mid-October is ideal for trekking.

What to Bring
Walking boots, a reliable windproof and waterproof jacket and appropriate warm clothing are essentials. There are many dhabas, allowing the trek to be completed without a tent.

Maps
Refer to the Leomann series 1:200,000 *Sheet 4* (*Chamba, Dhaula Dhar Passes, Pangi Valley & Western Lahaul*). Also refer to the US Military U502 series 1:250,000, *NI 43-16 ref Palampur*.

Accommodation
There are dhabas every few kilometres between Hadsar and Mani Mahesh Lake, together with basic pilgrim shelters. These are often crowded during the main pilgrimage in August.

GETTING TO/FROM THE TREK
There are three or four buses a day from Brahmaur to Hadsar (Rs 10, one hour). A 4WD costs Rs 150.

THE TREK (See map pp156–7)
Day 1: Hadsar to Dancho
3–4 hours, 10km
Before commencing the pilgrimage from **Hadsar** (2150m), ascend the stone steps above the bazaar and follow the trail to the small **temple** where offerings are made. The well-defined trail descends alongside the Mani Mahesh River before winding up through oak, pine, beech and elder forest to the first of a series of meadows.

After 5km cross the bridge to the true right of the valley and ascend 2km to the *dhabas* and *shelters* at Dancho. There is also a small *campsite* about 1km before **Dancho** (3000m) in a meadow above the river.

Dancho offers inspiring views back down the valley towards the hanging glaciers and snowfields of the Dhaula Dhar. To the east, the impressive ridge of the Pir Panjal provides a further backdrop.

Day 2: Dancho to Mani Mahesh Lake & Return
7 hours, 20km
Cross the bridge over the Mani Mahesh River to the true left of the valley. Continue for 2km before recrossing over a wooden bridge to the true right bank. There follows a long ascent with many switchbacks as the trail ascends through flowered meadows. The birch trees on the opposite side of the valley provide a reminder of the gain in altitude.

Two hours after leaving camp, there is a line of *dhabas* (3600m) from where the trail to Mani Mahesh Lake is visible. It is a further hour across scree slopes and meadows to the impressive **waterfall** flowing from the lake. The trail ascends steeply to an open valley ringed by snowcapped peaks. A variety of *dhabas* and *shelters* are here, where pilgrims prepare for the final stage to the lake.

It is a further 1.5km ascent (about 30 minutes) across grassy ridges to **Mani Mahesh Lake** (4100m). In terms of size and depth, the lake is not particularly impressive. However, its location – directly opposite the peak of Mani Mahesh Kailash and a host of other peaks and hanging glaciers – would inspire even the least devout pilgrim.

There is a small Hindu **temple** dedicated to Lakshmi Devi beside the lake, where pilgrims pay their respects and priests cut the hair of any newborn sons. The descent to Dancho takes about three hours.

Side Trip: Beyond Mani Mahesh Lake
2 hours, 5km return
Climb the grassy ridge directly above the lake for even finer views of the mountains. It's also a chance to view the initial stages of the trek around the base of Mani Mahesh Kailash, a 50km, three-day *kora* (pilgrimage). The first day is to a meadow on the far side of the mountain, the second to Kugti village, and the third returning to Hadsar.

HIMACHAL PRADESH

Day 3: Dancho to Hadsar
3 hours, 10km

The return trek to Hadsar can be completed in the morning, with ample time to return to Brahmaur and Chamba.

Kugti Pass & Lahaul

Duration	5 days
Distance	70km
Difficulty	moderate–demanding
Start	Hadsar
Finish	Jelma
Nearest Town	Brahmaur (pp179–80)
Public Transport	yes

Summary Ascend the Gaddi shepherd trails through Hindu villages and flowered meadows before completing a rugged traverse of the Pir Panjal Range to Chandra Valley and Lahaul.

While the Kugti Pass is the most regularly crossed pass over the Pir Panjal between Brahmaur and Lahaul, it is by no means easy! Even the Gaddi shepherds regard the pass with caution and will not lead their flocks across until the weather is clear and settled.

While the route over the pass is not technically demanding, trekkers should be sure-footed, not afraid of the occasional rock scramble and physically prepared for a long day. Bearing that in mind, the views of Mani Mahesh Kailash, the Dhaula Dhar and the Himalaya Range are well worth it.

On the trek to the pass, the trail winds through Hindu villages and past Gaddi shepherd encampments. The alpine meadows are carpeted with wildflowers. These offer ideal spots for rest and acclimatisation before completing the traverse to Lahaul and the Chandra Valley.

PLANNING
When to Trek

Depending on snow conditions, Gaddi shepherds normally cross the Kugti Pass by mid-June. The monsoon rain extends to this region in July and August so the ideal trek time is from mid-September until mid-October, before the first snows settle on the Pir Panjal.

What to Bring

A tent, stove, cooking gear and food supplies for at least four days are necessary. An ice axe and rope should also be carried. Each person should carry a good supply of water as there are few places to get water when crossing the pass.

Maps

Refer to the Leomann series 1:200,000 *Sheet 4 (Chamba, Dhaula Dhar Passes, Pangi Valley & Western Lahaul)*. Also refer to the US Military U502 series 1:250,000, *NI 43-16 ref Palampur*.

Accommodation

Accommodation in Hadsar is restricted to a couple of lodges in the main bazaar and the PWD dormitory. Beds are Rs 50 per night, but bargain hard to ensure that you do not have to pay for all the unoccupied beds.

Kugti has a comfortable Forest Rest House, with doubles for Rs 300. Beyond Kugti, there is a large rock overhang above Duggi Got and basic shepherds huts (not always unoccupied) at Alyas.

GETTING TO/FROM THE TREK

For travel to Brahmaur, see Getting There & Away (p180). From Brahmaur, there are three or four buses to Hadsar (Rs 10, one hour). In the next couple of seasons, the road from Hadsar to Kugti will be completed and a bus service will commence.

Buses from Udaipur (Lahaul) stop in Jelma on the way to Keylong (Rs 20, two hours, three per day). For the same price, you could get a seat in one of the many trucks that drive this route.

From Keylong, there is transport to Manali or Leh; see Getting There & Away (p185).

THE TREK (See map pp156–7)
Day 1: Hadsar to Kugti Village
5 hours, 13km

During the shelflife of this edition, a road will be completed linking Hadsar and Kugti village. However, it can be avoided for the first few kilometres of the trek.

Follow the trail on the true left of the Budhi River. This involves a number of ascents and descents as you follow the course of the river. After 5km to 6km, cross a bridge to the true right of the valley. Here the trail meets the road from Hadsar (under construction) and the going is rough to the settlement at **Dhrol** (2350m).

For a further 6km, the trail winds through a mixed forest of oak, blue pine and cedar, and across meadows to **Kugti** (2640m). There is a good *campsite* alongside the Budhil River about 2km Kugti. The *Forest Rest House* is above the trail just before the village.

From Kugti there is a demanding three- to four-day trek to the village of Bara Bhangal. A trek to the base of Mani Mahesh Kailash is briefly outlined on p181 (see Side Trip). The initial route from Kugti for both treks is to backtrack for 2km before crossing the Budhil River and ascending the valley heading south.

Day 2: Kugti Village to Duggi Got
4–5 hours, 15km

Ascend the outlying fields and meadows beyond Kugti village. After 2km the trail splits. Follow the upper trail and commence the climb (steep in places) to Kailang Temple. This stage should take around two hours.

Kailang Temple (3050m) is steeped in local and Gaddi tradition. Inside the main temple is a statue of Kartik (son of Vishnu and Shiva). There are also Naga statues in deference to Kailong Nag – a benevolent serpent said to ensure the safety of the flocks of sheep and goats that pass this way each season.

From the temple, the trail winds through a forest of cedar and dwarf rhododendron. Small stands of silver birch are also seen on the hills en route to the extensive meadows known as **Duggi Got** (3100m). The meadow is covered in **wildflowers** from July to September. There is a profusion of aster, gentians, primula, euphorbia, delphinium, anemone, potentilla, saxifrage and many other species' that could keep a botanist occupied for many days.

Day 3: Duggi Got to Alyas
4–5 hours, 14km

Follow the well-defined shepherds trail across a boulder field. There is a huge rock overhang 2km beyond the side river known as **Duggi Cave** (3200m), a popular shelter for Gaddi shepherds in spring.

The trail ascends the true right of the river across meadows where cattle from Kugti village graze in summer. The trail splits 3km beyond Duggi Cave. The lower trail heads straight up the valley. Follow the higher trail, which winds up pastures to a side valley to the north. Another ascent, steep in places, leads to the grassy plateau of **Alyas** (4100m).

There are a couple of *Gaddi shepherds huts* in the meadow and many *campsites*. Camp here or continue for 1km towards the terminal moraine at the base of the pass (4150m). With binoculars, it is possible to identify the cairns on top of Kugti Pass.

Day 4: Alyas to Kadlu via Kugti Pass
8–9 hours, 18km

Ascend the terminal moraine field along a trail that heads to the true left of the glacial stream. The trail through boulders and scree is marked by rock cairns, reaching a **plateau** (4500m) at the snout of the glacier flowing from below the pass.

The route heads west and ascends a ridgeline to around 4800m. There are dramatic views of the north face of Mani Mahesh Kailash and the adjoining peaks of the Pir Panjal.

After reaching a substantial cairn, the route heads across a broad rock band between the ridge and the pass. Take care with hand and foot holds, particularly in the early morning when the rocks are icy. Be sure not to miss the cairns that lead around to a point just above the pass. The route then winds down to the tridents and cairns that mark the **Kugti Pass** (5040m). The time from camp to the pass is around five hours.

From the Kugti Pass, there are spectacular views north to the Himalaya Range. The drier valleys and ridges of Lahaul are a reminder of the change in geography ahead.

The route drops to a lower pass before heading west across an extensive scree slope, under snow until July. The trail winds high above the glacial floor, leading to the true left of the glacier before gradually descending for 3km or 4km to the lateral moraine on the main glacier. Trek towards the centre of the glacier before veering to the true left across the extensive glacial moraine.

Follow the trail down the scree slope towards the meadow of **Kadlu** (3720m). Cross the braided river flowing from the snout of the glacier to a *campsite* marked by Gaddi flags and tridents. The time from the pass to camp is around four hours.

Day 5: Kadlu to Jelma
3 hours, 10km
The trail from Kadlu is nothing more than a goat track as it descends across scree slopes on the true right of the valley. After 5km the trail crosses the river over an improvised bridge. It then follows the course of an irrigation channel to the outlying fields of the village of **Rape** (3000m). Descend further to the bridge over the Chenab River and complete the short ascent to the trailhead and the nearby village of **Jelma** (2850m).

Keylong & Lahaul

Lahaul is wedged between the alpine reaches of the Kullu Valley and the windswept terrain of Ladakh. Upper Lahaul includes the Chandra and Bhaga valleys, and Lower Lahaul has the Chenab Valley. For many the region is a gateway to trekking in the Zanskar and Ladakh. Aside from the following two treks, treks in this chapter that visit Lahaul are the Hampta Pass & Lahaul trek (pp160–1) and Kugti Pass & Lahaul trek (pp182–4).

HISTORY
Lahaul's history can be traced back to the wanderings of many sages. This includes Padmasambhava in the 7th century, who is credited with popularising Buddhism in the region. In the 10th century, upper Lahaul was united with Spiti and the Zanskar as part of the Lahaul–West Tibet kingdom of Guge.

Although political alliances changed over the centuries, it was Ladakh's defeat by the Mongol-Tibetan armies in the 18th century that led to the division of Lahaul. Upper Lahaul came under the influence of Kullu, while Lower Lahaul became Chamba territory. Trade agreements between Kullu and Ladakh considered Lahaul neutral territory.

William Moorcroft and George Trebeck were among the first Europeans to cross the Baralacha La during their epic journeys in the 1820s. By 1847 Lahaul was under British administration. Under the *beggar* system (forced labour), trails were upgraded and bridges constructed along the main trading routes. Trade between Lahaul and Kullu prospered, with the Hakurs of Lahaul securing many valuable agreements in the Kullu Valley. Many of the Hakurs set up bases in the Kullu Valley, where many remain today.

NATURAL HISTORY
The mountainous region of Lahaul is one of the most complex in the West Himalaya, with the Himalaya Range merging with the Lahaul and Pir Panjal Ranges.

Lahaul is drained by the tributaries of the Chenab River. The Bhaga flows from the west side of the Baralacha La, the Chandra from the east. Both tributaries create impressive gorges as they surge through the main axis of the Himalaya Range.

Forest and vegetation bands vary considerably. The lower (western) regions of Lahaul come under the influence of the monsoon. The heavier rainfall is reflected in the verdant meadows and oak and conifer tree bands that begin to peter out in the vicinity of Udaipur. Further up the Chenab Valley, there is a marked decline in rainfall. This region is noted for its barren mountainscape, where poplar and willow trees thrive along the irrigation channels and cypress and blue pine grow on the hillsides.

Wildlife is confined to the remote valleys and ridges, including those in the Miyar Valley and also the area north of Chandra Tal. To have a chance of spotting any, including brown bears or wild sheep and goats, trek in the late spring, well before the snow melts on the alpine pastures.

Birdlife is similar to Ladakh, with alpine choughs, snowfinches, black-billed magpies, lammergeiers and golden eagles. A far greater variety of species are found in the mixed forest in the western regions.

ACCESS TOWN
Keylong

☎ 019002 • alt 3068m

Keylong is the administrative centre of Lahaul. For most it is a place to complete last-minute preparations before a trek to the Zanskar; an overnight stop en route from Manali to Leh; or a transit point before commencing a trek from Chandra Tal. One of the main attractions is the **Khardung gompa** (Tibetan Buddhist monastery) on the far side of the Bhaga Valley. It is a one-hour hike to the oldest gompa in the region, servicing many of the smaller gompas in Lahaul.

Supplies & Equipment Fresh vegetables and fruit from the Kullu Valley are available in the local market, as is a variety of tinned food. Bring other luxury items with you from Manali. If you're heading to the Chandra Tal & Baralacha La trek from the Kullu Valley, it is not necessary to travel via Keylong; bring all supplies from the Kullu Valley.

Pots and pans, stoves and cooking gear can be purchased in the market. However quality camping gear is not available for hire or purchase.

Trekking Agents Numerous offices along the Mall in Keylong claim to be travel and trekking agents, but most simply cater for onward travel arrangements to Leh and the Indus Valley. Prearrange an inclusive trek in Manali. If you plan to trek independently to the Zanskar, allow a few days for horses to materialise in Darcha (around Rs 200 per horse). If trekking out of Batal, arrange horses in Manali.

Places to Stay & Eat Peacefully situated above the Mall, *Snowland Hotel (☎ 22219)* has doubles for Rs 300. *Hotel Tashi Deleg (☎ 22450)* has recently upgraded its rooms (some with cable TV), with doubles from Rs 450. The *HPTDC Tourist Bungalow (☎ 22247)* has dorm beds for Rs 55; singles/doubles cost Rs 290/350.

Hotel Tashi Deleg has a comprehensive menu (good for breakfast), while the restaurants in *Hotel Lamayuru* and *The Gyespa* offer a variety of Indian and Chinese dishes.

Getting There & Away Regular buses link Keylong with other towns in Lahaul and the Kullu Valley, and Leh in Ladakh.

Bus There is a regular local service to/from Manali (Rs 72, six hours) and Darcha (Rs 35, 3 per day). If undertaking or completing a trek from the Baralacha La, get a lift on a truck en route to Leh (around Rs 100); buses to and from Leh are normally fully booked. Buses also go to/from Udaipur (Rs 60, six hours, two per day). The early morning bus to Spiti goes via Batal (Rs 50) en route to Kaza.

Taxi The taxi stand is beside the bus stand. Rates are around Rs 12,000 to Leh, Rs 3800 to Manali and Rs 900 to Darcha.

Chandra Tal & Baralacha La

Duration	4 days
Distance	60km
Difficulty	moderate
Start	Batal/Chandra Tal
Finish	Baralacha La
Nearest Town	Keylong
Public Transport	yes
Summary	A wilderness trek from Chandra Tal to the alpine pastures near the Baralacha La.

The recent construction of the 4WD road to Chandra Tal (4250m) will undoubtedly alter the character of the upper Chandra Valley. Unless the numbers driving to the lake are regulated, it will have a detrimental impact on the fragile environment.

People driving direct from the Kullu Valley will suffer from the effects of altitude. Indeed this trek should not be undertaken from Batal or Chandra Tal without spending a few days in Keylong or after completing a trek out of the Kullu Valley. The Hampta Pass & Lahaul trek (pp160–1) from Manali to Chatru is a good option.

Beyond Chandra Tal, the trek follows Gaddi shepherd trails across summer grazing pastures. Preparation, care and a length of rope are needed for river crossings.

HIMACHAL PRADESH

PLANNING
When to Trek

Heavy winter snows in Lahaul prevent trekking before early July. However, the region is outside the influence of the monsoon rain, and the trek can be completed from July until mid-October.

The 4WD road to Chandra Tal is unlikely to be open until at least mid-July.

What to Bring

Trekking parties must be self sufficient with a tent, stove, cooking gear and food. A length of rope is also essential.

Maps

Refer to the Leomann series 1:200,000 *Sheet 5 (Kullu Valley, Parbati Valley & Central Lahaul)*. Also refer to the US Military U502 series 1:250,000, *NI 43-16 ref Palampur*.

Accommodation

There are a number of dhabas at Batal where you can overnight. It is also likely that tented accommodation and food will be available at Chandra Tal from the time the road opens until mid-September. Beyond Chandra Tal there is no shelter until the trailhead at the Baralacha La.

GETTING TO/FROM THE TREK

From Manali or Keylong, catch the daily bus to Spiti that takes around six hours to reach Batal. From Batal to Chandra Tal there is no public transport. To hire a 4WD you will need to make prior arrangements in Keylong or Manali.

The public bus from Leh to Keylong passes the Baralacha La. However, it is unlikely that there will be spare seats. Hitching a ride on a truck is the best option to reach Keylong (Rs 70, 3 hours).

THE TREK (See map p158)
Day 1: Batal to Chandra Tal
6–7 hours, 18km

This stage is included as the 4WD track is unlikely to be cleared of snow and landslides until mid-July. From then, it is a matter of choice whether you commence the trek from Batal or Chandra Tal.

Batal (3950m) is a small, grassy campsite a short distance from the road. In summer it is often occupied by geology students studying the mountains. The area is particularly significant geologically as the Pir Panjal Range, the main Himalaya and the Baralacha Range merge in the vicinity of the nearby Kun Zum La (4550m).

From Batal, cross the road bridge over the Chandra River and head up the road to the Kun Zum La. After a few kilometres, the 4WD track diverts up the Chandra Valley. The trekking here can be hot and dusty but the views back down the valley compensate. Mountains in view include Lalana (6265m), Papsura (6451m) and Dharamsura (6446m). They tower above the Bara Shigri Glacier – one of the largest glaciers in the West Himalaya.

After several kilometres the Chandra River enters a gorge. The trail to Chandra Tal cuts away from the river valley and gradually ascends through boulder fields before meeting the stream coming from the lake. The trail becomes steeper, passing over grassy ridges towards a fertile plateau. The plateau divides the main Chandra Valley and the side valley fed by the stream from Chandra Tal.

As you climb higher, the peaks of the Lahaul Range become visible, including Minar (6172m), Talagiri (6279m), Tara Pahar (6227m), and also Mulkilla (6517m), the highest peak at the head of the Samundar Tapu Glacier.

Chandra Tal (4250m) is a welcome relief from a strenuous day's trek. Follow the Gaddi trails around to the many *campsites* at the head of the lake, where you can appreciate the spectacular scenery.

Day 2: Chandra Tal to Tokpo Yongma
6 hours, 15km

Trek up the valley across a series of scree slopes, where the constant, abrupt ascents and descents will take their toll on the leg muscles. The trail runs along a high bank above the Chandra River. Wildflowers on the banks of the side streams provide welcome relief from the otherwise dun-coloured scenery. The *campsite* beside **Tokpo Yongma** (lower river) at 4350m is the most suitable, particularly in order to cross the river early the following morning.

Day 3: Tokpo Yongma to Tokpo Gongma
6–7 hours, 15km

The time required for this stage depends on how easily you cross the Tokpo Yongma. Until early July, the snow bridges should be in place, but from then to late August the river can be a problem. Seek the assistance of the local Gaddi to find the best crossing points. A rope is also essential, and it is not advisable to attempt to cross alone.

After the river crossing, the trail is well defined, with a steady ascent through boulder landscape. After about five hours, a raging side stream requires care in selecting the best crossing. Ropes are again essential.

There is a small *campsite* just beyond this side stream; or you can continue to the confluence with the next large side river, the **Tokpo Gongma** (upper river) at 4650m.

Day 4: Tokpo Gongma to Baralacha La
4 hours, 12km

Cross the Tokpo Gongma with care. Seek help from the Gaddi shepherds if the water level is high. From the riverbank, the trail climbs a steep scree slope before the country opens out. The trail is well defined by a series of rock cairns as it crosses the open meadows that lead gradually to the pass.

The **Baralacha La** (4950m) is a double pass. It marks the divide between the Himalaya and Lahaul Ranges, and also between the Himalaya and the Baralacha Range that extends north to the Zanskar. The mountains provide an impressive backdrop.

Kaza & Spiti

On the borderlands close to Tibet, the Trans-Himalaya region of Spiti provides an attractive alternative to Ladakh. The gompas and ancient Buddhist heritage set amid the stark, windswept mountainscape make it an ideal destination for trekking.

HISTORY
The historical background of both Lahaul and Spiti runs parallel to that of Ladakh. In the 10th century Spiti was united with Lahaul and the Zanskar as part of the vast Lahaul–West Tibet kingdom of Guge. Pilgrims and sages wandered the passes, including the Kun Zum La linking Spiti and Lahaul.

Political allegiances changed over the centuries, with Spiti paying tribute to Ladakh and extending its trading relations with West Tibet. Even during the times of the Gurkha and Sikh expansion, Spiti's cultural ties with Ladakh remained. In 1846, along with Ladakh, it became part of the Maharajah's state of Jammu and Kashmir.

In 1849 it was exchanged for other territories and came under British administration. Yet Spiti continued to trade with Tibet until Tibet's borders were closed in the 1950s. The ancient trade routes, from Kinnaur to Spiti over the Manirang La, and from the Kullu Valley over the Pin Parbati Pass, were followed. Other trails, including that over the Tarik La, were also crossed by villagers from Spiti stocking up on wood and building materials.

Spiti was to remain off limits to foreigners until 1990 and even today an Inner Line permit (see the boxed text, p191) is required to trek to Kinnaur.

NATURAL HISTORY
The average elevation of the valleys in Spiti is around 3500m. This, and its location north of the Himalaya Range, ensures that the region is one of the driest in the West Himalaya.

Trekking over the glacial passes of the Himalaya from Spiti to the Kullu Valley or Kinnaur reveals a remarkable change in landscape. The barley fields, willow and poplar groves in the depths of the valleys in Spiti suddenly give way to verdant alpine meadows and forested valleys.

To the north of Spiti is the Zanskar Range, a formidable range of barren peaks rising above 6000m and dividing Spiti and the Tibetan Plateau. This region is drained by the Sutlej, the only river in the West Himalaya that runs through the Trans-Himalaya and Himalaya Ranges to the Indian Plains.

Villagers in the Pin National Park claim regular sightings of the snow leopard in winter. Packs of wolves are also present, while chiru are found close to the Tibetan Plateau.

Birdlife on the sparse mountainside includes alpine choughs, black-billed magpies, Hume's groundpeckers, Tibetan snowcocks and chukar partridges. Birds of prey, including lammergeiers, kestrels and golden eagles, soar amid the Himalaya's peaks.

ACCESS TOWN
Kaza
☎ 01906 • alt 3640m

Kaza is the administrative centre of Spiti and the base to visit some of the outlying gompas, including the ancient Tabo gompa, Ki gompa, and the small gompa at Kibber. The gompas maintained close cultural ties with Tibet until a generation ago.

Kaza is also the most convenient base to prepare for a trek from Spiti, whether it be to Kinnaur, the Kullu Valley, or over the Parang La to Ladakh (a route that is currently restricted to Indian trekkers).

Supplies & Equipment Fruit and vegetables are transported from Shimla and the Kullu Valley during summer. Other food supplies, including most tinned items, can be in short supply; bring these from Shimla or Manali. There are limited food supplies at Gilling at the trailhead and beyond that there is nothing until Kinnaur.

Pots and pans, stoves and food containers can be purchased from the market. However, quality camping gear is not available and should be brought with you.

Trekking Agents There are no trekking agents in Kaza so inclusive treks will need to be prearranged in Manali (p151). For the Tarik La & Kinnaur trek, horse attendants can be hired at the trailhead (around Rs 200 per horse per day). For the Pin Parbati & Spiti trek (in reverse if it is undertaken from Sangam, near Kaza; see pp166–9), horses cannot cross the Pin Parbati Pass and porters are not readily available in Spiti. Organising the trek in Manali and starting from the Parbati Valley is a better option.

Places to Stay & Eat One of Kaza's most popular hotels is *Sakya Abode* (☎ 22254), with rooms from Rs 250 to Rs 500. There is also the *Snow Lion* at the top end of town, with doubles from Rs 200, and the *Milarepa Guest House*, charging Rs 200 to Rs 300. The *HPTDC Tourist Lodge* offers dingy rooms for Rs 440 and tented accommodation during peak season.

Tibetan-style meals are available at most of the hotels, while the *Layul Cafe* in the old town has been recommended for its soup and *momo* (Tibetan steamed spring roll) dishes.

Getting There & Away Regular buses link Kaza to Kinnaur and Shimla and also to the Kullu Valley in summer.

Bus Services link Kaza and Manali (Rs 125, 12 hours); the bus to Manali leaves at 4am. Buses also go to/from Rekong Peo in Kinnaur (Rs125, 10 hours); to Rekong Peo it departs at 7.30am. Direct buses run to/from Shimla (Rs180/144 overnight/day). The bus to Gilling leaves at 9am (Rs 23, two hours).

Taxi The 4WD taxi stand near the bus station services Gilling for Rs 900 and Manali for Rs 2200.

Tarik La & Kinnaur

Duration	5 days
Distance	71km
Difficulty	moderate
Start	Gilling
Finish	Katgoan
Nearest Town	Kaza
Public Transport	yes
Summary	A traverse over the Himalaya Range from the Buddhist villages in Spiti to the verdant valleys and forests of Kinnaur.

This trek has been followed by many generations of villagers. As with most passes over the Himalaya Range the change in scenery is marked – from the stark ridges of Spiti to the meadows and forests of Kinnaur. The culture also changes: from Buddhist to Hindu.

The initial stages are in the Pin National Park, although there are no checkpoints or facilities for paying park fees. You need an Inner Line permit, which is issued in Kaza and will be inspected at Kapnu.

Acclimatisation is necessary before the trek; a few days in Kaza visiting the ancient gompas is recommended. You may also consider this trek as an extension of the Pin Parbati & Spiti trek (pp166–9) for a challenging double traverse of the Himalaya Range.

The trail over the Tarik La is not demanding. Although there are a few small crevasses south of the pass, these are easily avoided.

PLANNING
When to Trek
The Tarik La can be traversed from mid-June to mid-October. If undertaking the trek after visiting the Kullu Valley, it should be noted that the Kun Zum La – the road pass linking the Kullu Valley and Lahaul to Spiti – is not normally open until mid-July. If trekking early in the season, it would be necessary to either drive to Spiti via Kinnaur or trek in the reverse direction from Kinnaur to Spiti.

The region of Kinnaur sees the monsoon rain, although this should not preclude trekking in July and August. September until mid-October is ideal for trekking.

What to Bring
A tent, stove and cooking gear is essential. All food supplies should also be carried.

Maps
Refer to the Leomann series 1:200,000 *Sheet 6 (Kalpa-Kinnaur, Spiti & Shimla)*. Also refer to the US Military U502 series 1:250,000, *NI 43-4 ref Shimla* and *NI-44.1 Chini*, which cover most of the trek.

Accommodation
Apart from the odd shepherds hut, there is no accommodation until Kapnu, which has some dingy dhabas. However, there is a comfortable PWD Rest House at Katgoan. Rooms cannot be booked but are available subject to the resident Engineer's approval. Doubles with hot showers cost Rs 500 and provide a comfortable break before the next journey.

GETTING TO/FROM THE TREK
The daily bus from Kaza to Gilling leaves at 9am (Rs 23, two to three hours). There is a minibus service between Kapnu and Wangtu. However, the most convenient connection to Shimla is the early morning bus from Katgoan (Rs 135, seven to eight hours).

THE TREK (See map p159)
Day 1: Gilling to Mudh
5 hours, 14km
From the road at **Gilling** (3500m), descend to the Pin River and cross the bridge, from where horses can be loaded. A steep 150m ascent climbs to a vantage point high above Sangam and the confluence of the Pin and Khamengar Rivers. The trail passes a lone settlement before heading up the true right of the valley. It undulates for several kilometres across scree slopes and light vegetation to the village of **Toling** (3700m).

From Toling, the trail descends to a gully and crosses a side river before ascending the Pin Valley. A series of ups and downs follow for 6km until you reach a position opposite the village of **Mudh** (3850m). Cross the bridge to the village or remain on the true right of the valley for a further 2km. There's a *campsite* beside an irrigation channel.

Alternative Route: Gilling to Mudh via Sangam
4–5 hours, 12km
Catch the bus to the trailhead 3km after Gilling and cross the bridge over the Khamengar River to **Sangam** (3550m). The trail remains on the true left of the valley to the village of **Mudh**. It is suitable for porters but not at present for horses, although it is being upgraded with a view to eventually extending the road to Mudh. See Day 8 of the Pin Parbati & Spiti trek (p169) for more information on this route.

Day 2: Mudh to Paldor
5 hours, 14km
From camp, remain on the true right of Pin Valley. This is part of the Pin National Park, where the upper reaches of Pin Valley and the nearby Khamengar Valley are reputed to contain bharal, wolves and snow leopards.

HIMACHAL PRADESH

The trail up the valley leads through scree and the occasional meadow, where villagers from Mudh often graze their animals. On the far side of the valley, you can see the trail leading towards the Pin Parbati Pass.

About 2km below Paldor, the Pin River splits into two tributaries – one flowing from the east from the Tarik La, the other from the Pin Parbati Pass. The trail ascends steeply in places to the meadow at **Paldor** (4050m) and a good *campsite* with a spring line.

Day 3: Paldor to Base Camp via Tarik La

7 hours, 15km

An early start is recommended to complete the tiring trek to the Tarik La. The first 5km involves an ascent (steep in places) over scree and boulder fields before crossing the river flowing from the pass. There's a potential *campsite* here at 4450m. Once on the true left of the valley, a steady ascent leads across scree slopes, which become progressively steeper on the last 250m below the pass.

The **Tarik La** (4850m) forms part of the Himalaya Range. Striking views extend to the north across the barren ridges of Spiti, while to the south are the snowcapped peaks of Kinnaur.

The initial descent from the pass is steep for 200m to a broad snowfield riddled with small crevasses. These are not a major problem providing you stick to the trail on the true left of the valley. Beyond the snowfield, watch out for rock cairns marking the trail across a series of boulder fields. A long, steep descent follows to a series of alpine pastures at 4050m. It is advisable to *camp* here, although fit parties may elect to continue down the valley for a further 5km to 6km to the meadow at **Kara**.

Day 4: Base Camp to Muling

3–4 hours, 13km

This is a comparatively easy day after crossing the pass, with a chance to appreciate the array of wildflowers that flourish in the upper reaches of the valley. Follow the shepherds trail that descends the alpine pastures for 3km or 4km. The river flowing from the Tarik La meets a larger river flowing from the east. Cross the river coming from the Tarik La and remain on the true right of the valley for a further 2km to the large meadow at **Kara** (3500m).

From Kara, remain on the valley's true right to reach a vantage point of the meadows of Muling and the Kinnaur Kailash Range. There is a short steep descent to the river and a bridge to the true left of the valley. Continue past birch, elm and hemlock trees to **Muling** (3100m). There's a choice of idyllic *campsites* where shepherds graze their animals.

Day 5: Muling to Katgoan

4 hours, 15km

From Muling, cross the lower pastures before a short ascent to a large rock adorned with prayer flags. The trail winds through a mixed forest of elm, pine and spruce to the small settlement of **Humti** (2690m). There follows a short steep descent to the river. Cross the bridge to the true right of the valley and continue through the outlying fields to the dam construction above the village of **Kapnu** (2450m).

There is a police checkpoint at Kapnu, where you will be required to show your Inner Line permit; see the boxed text. There are also a few fly-blown *dhabas* at the trailhead. Wait here for a minibus or truck, or complete a further 3km to the substantial village of **Katgoan** (2250m).

Rekong Peo & Kinnaur

Kinnaur's mountainous terrain amid the stunning backdrop of the Himalaya and Kinnaur Kailash Ranges lends itself to trekking. The spectacular valleys above the Sutlej River extend to the borderlands of Tibet, however, unlike Spiti and Lahaul, much of its cultural heritage is not derived from Tibet.

Kinnaur offers many fine trekking possibilities, including the route over the Tarik La and the Kinnaur Kailash trek over the Charang La. Treks over the Dhaula Dhar linking Kinnaur with the Tons Valley are covered in the Uttaranchal chapter.

Inner Line Permits

Permits have been required to travel close to the Indo-Tibetan (Chinese) border since the Indian-Chinese war in 1962. While regulations have been relaxed in recent years, you still need a permit for travelling between Kinnaur and Spiti. This includes trekking, whether over the Tarik La from Spiti to Kinnaur or crossing the Charang La on the Kinnaur Kailash trek. (A permit is not required on the Pin Parbati & Spiti trek.) There have been rumours circulating for years that these restrictions will be dropped but it hasn't happened yet.

In theory, permits can be obtained from the District Magistrates in Shimla, Rekong Peo, Keylong, Kullu and Chamba; or the Sub-Divisional Magistrates in Kaza, Rampur and Nichar. In reality, Shimla, Rekong Peo and Kaza are by far the easiest places to get a permit.

Officially you need a minimum group of four to travel but this rule no longer seems to be enforced. You need three passport-sized photographs, a photocopy of your passport (including your personal details and the page with your Indian visa), an application form from the Magistrate's office and plenty of patience.

A standard permit is issued regardless of whether you are trekking or travelling by road. The permit details your route along the highway from Kinnaur to Spiti, and lists restrictions (ie, no camping at non-designated places and no photography). These restrictions are not enforced, although be careful not to photograph any sensitive or military areas. Do not worry that the permit does not mention trekking. The standard Inner Line permit is acceptable to the police and at checkpoints. All you need to do is show your passport and register your itinerary.

HISTORY

Kinnaur is historically linked with Shimla and the adjoining hill states, rather than the vast and powerful rulers of West Tibet and Guge. While the neighbouring regions of Lahaul and Spiti have been interdependent on Tibet, Kinnaur has not paid a similar tribute.

In the 19th century, the region came under Gurkha rule and later British administration. *Beggar* was introduced here, as elsewhere in the West Himalaya, to upgrade local roads and trails. This included the Hindustan-Tibet road that was to establish the trade mission in Gar and facilitate trade between British India and Tibet. Agreements were also made leasing forests to the British, evident in the many Forest Rest Houses built in the remote mountain valleys to accommodate forest officers on their tours of duty.

Following prolonged protests, *beggar* was abolished in 1920–1. In 1960 Kinnaur became a district of Himachal Pradesh. Initially Kalpa was the administrative capital. This was transferred to nearby Rekong Peo a few years later.

NATURAL HISTORY

The rugged mountain terrain of Kinnaur is characterised by the Himalaya and Kinnaur Kailash Ranges.

The Sutlej River, flowing from the Tibetan Plateau, drains the region. The river is a classic example of antecedent drainage, its waters forming impressive gorges as they surge through the Zanskar and Himalaya Ranges. Its main tributaries include the Spiti River to the north and the Sangla River to the east.

Forest and vegetation bands are determined by the extent of the monsoon. The conifer forests just north of Marang and on the trek to the Charang La indicate how far the rains penetrate up the Sutlej Gorge. A comparison between the upper reaches of the Charang Valley and the verdant Sangla Valley – with its oak and conifer forests, apple orchards and lush pastures – further demonstrates the effects of monsoon rain.

Wildlife varies considerably. In the forested regions, there are black bears, serow and goral, while ibex and the Himalayan thar are found at higher elevations. In the regions immediately north of the Himalaya, including the Tirung Valley leading to Charang, there are bharal, snow leopards, brown bears and the occasional pack of wolves.

Birdlife is also diverse. A variety of species are attracted to the verdant meadows south of the Tarik La and in the lower Sangla Valley. To the north are birds more common to the Trans-Himalaya and the Tibetan Plateau.

ACCESS TOWNS
Rekong Peo & Kalpa
☎ 01786

Rekong Peo (2290m) is spectacularly located high above the Sutlej River, opposite the snowcapped peaks of Kinnaur Kailash. This is the place to get Inner Line permits (see the boxed text, p191) and a base for visiting the impressive **Kalachakra Celestial Palace** (or Mahabodhi gompa), inaugurated by the Dalai Lama in 1992.

If you are spending more than one night, the town of Kalpa (2960m; 7km away) is a far nicer place to stay.

Supplies & Equipment Fresh fruit and vegetables and most tinned foods are available at Rekong Peo. Luxury items should be brought from Shimla or Delhi.

Pots and pans and cooking gear can be purchased at Rekong Peo. It is not possible to hire or purchase sleeping bags and tents.

Trekking Agents There are no agents in Rekong Peo so arrange your porters and crew at Thangi. Hotel Reena is a good contact point. Budget around Rs 150 per day for porters plus a relocation allowance.

Places to Stay & Eat Rekong Peo's *Fairyland Guest House* (☎ 22477) is close to the bus stand. Rooms with a view cost Rs 200.

In Kalpa, the *Auktong Guest House* (☎ 26019) has pleasant rooms for Rs 200. The nearby *Sivalik Hotel* (☎ 26158) offers rooms for Rs 200 to Rs 300. The *HPTDC Hotel Kinnaur Kailash* (☎ 26159) has a range of rooms from Rs 500 to Rs 800; the manager and his local associates are keen to offer advice on trekking in the region.

The *Manish Bhojnayla* in the centre of Rekong Peo is a small Tibetan-run restaurant serving soup and momos. The other rudimentary hotels in the vicinity offer a basic selection of Indian food.

Kalpa's hotels offer a selection of Indian, Chinese and European food.

Getting There & Away From Kalpa, regular bus services go to other parts of Kinnaur and also to Spiti and Shimla.

Bus Buses run to/from Shimla (Rs 170, nine hours) and to/from Spiti and Kaza (Rs 125, 10 hours). The bus from Kaza to Rekong Peo departs at 7.30am. There are several buses each day between Rekong Peo and Kalpa (Rs 5, one hour). From Rekong Peo, the bus to Thangi travels twice a day (Rs 25, two hours). There is also a service to Sangla (Rs 30, two hours).

Taxi A 4WD to Thangi or Sangla will cost around Rs 800 to Rs 1000, depending on whether the driver can get a return fare. For taxis from Rekong Peo to Kalpa, expect to pay around Rs 200.

Kinnaur Kailash

Duration	4 days
Distance	46km
Difficulty	demanding
Start	Thangi
Finish	Chitkul
Nearest Town	Rekong Peo (p192)
Public Transport	yes

Summary Trek close to the Tibetan border on the pilgrimage route over the Kinnaur Kailash Range to the verdant Sangla Valley.

This remarkable trek follows the route of the annual August pilgrimage when many villagers from Kinnaur complete the challenging kora around the sacred peak of Kinnaur Kailash (6050m).

Although comparatively short, this is a demanding trek and extra days should be reserved before crossing the Charang La. The traverse involves a long haul over terminal moraine and scree slopes that become progressively steeper near the pass.

Top: The view from Darjeeling includes stunning Kangchenjunga. **Bottom Left:** This Darjeeling tea estate shows there's plenty to see before setting off on a trek. **Bottom Right:** Trekking staff on the trail through rhododendron forest, north of Tsoska, Sikkim.

CHRIS BEALL

RICHARD I'ANSON

RICHARD I'ANSON

Sikkim scenes. **Top:** Climb above Dzongri for a view of Kangchenjunga (in the distance, on the left). The closer mountain to the right is Pandim. **Bottom Left:** A Lepcha attends to prayer flags near Dzongri. **Bottom Right:** A waterfall between Bakhim and Yuksam.

PLANNING
When to Trek
Shepherds and villagers cross the Charang La in early June, although the snow on the pass does not normally melt until at least mid-July. While the region is subject to monsoon rain, it is not as heavy as elsewhere in Himachal. It is possible to do the trek in July and August, while September until mid-October is ideal.

What to Bring
A tent, stove and cooking gear plus food supplies for at least three days is recommended. An ice axe and rope are also necessary. Due to the proximity of the Tibetan border, you need an Inner Line permit (see the boxed text, p191).

Maps
Refer to the Leomann series 1:200,000 *Sheet 6 (Kalpa-Kinnaur, Spiti & Shimla)*. Also refer to the US Military U502 series 1:250,000, *NI 44-1 Chini*.

Accommodation
This trek could be completed without a tent, although it is not recommended. *Hotel Reena* at Thangi charges Rs 250 for a room with four beds. Meals can also be arranged. There is a dhaba at Lambar, a PWD Rest House at Charang and a couple of houses may also offer beds for the night.

Lalanti has a basic pilgrim shelter but it's usually in a poor state of repair prior to the pilgrimage. Chitkul has a couple of lodges, including the *Amar Guest House*, charging Rs 100 to Rs 150. There is also a comfortable PWD Rest House; doubles with hot shower cost Rs 400.

In Sangla, en route to Rekong Peo or Shimla, lodges include *Rupin View* and *Highlands Guest House* (☎ 42285). Rooms cost Rs 100 to Rs 250 (prices are seasonal).

GETTING TO/FROM THE TREK
There are two buses a day from Rekong Peo to Thangi (Rs 25, two hours). From Chitkul, there are two buses at 7am and 2pm to Sangla and Rekong Peo (Rs 40, three hours). To reach Shimla, take the direct bus from Sangla (Rs 160, 10 hours).

THE TREK (See map p159)
Day 1: Thangi to Lambar
3 hours, 11km
The village of **Thangi** (2660m) is located about 200m above the road. It has around 30 dwellings that reflect a mixture of Buddhist and Hindu cultures. The checkpoint where you need to register is on a small hill to the east of the village.

The road from Thangi is currently being extended towards Lambar. Follow the road until it reaches the foot trail that winds high above the gorge. After 4km to 5km, the foot trail descends to the valley floor, reaching a conifer plantation and a bridge over the river. Remain on the true right bank for 2km before crossing a wooden bridge to the true left.

The trail continues for 2km before a bridge returns you to the true right. Complete the final 2km to a *campsite*, and the checkpoint opposite the settlement of Lambar.

To visit **Lambar** (2930m), cross the bridge and follow the trail up the hill to the village's six or seven houses. Note the solar panels – also found at Charang village – and the use of irrigation channels to water the barley fields.

Day 2: Lambar to Shruling
3–4 hours, 10km
Continue on the true right of the Tirung Valley through a narrow gorge. After 1.5km the gorge widens. Sometimes the trail follows the course of the boulder-strewn riverside while at other times it is hewn out of the cliffside.

The blue pines on the hillside gradually give way to juniper and wild roses, while the intermediate meadows support a variety of anemone and primula.

After about 8km (2½ to three hours from camp), the trail leads over a wooden bridge to the true left of the valley. It continues for a further 2km across an extensive meadow known as **Shruling** (3370m) to the confluence of the river flowing from the Charang La. There is a *campsite* and a checkpoint here.

Side Trip: Charang Village & Gompa
4–5 hours, 12km return
Charang is one of the most attractive villages in this region of Kinnaur. It is a substantial

Buddhist village, dramatically located beneath the snowcapped ridges and glaciers of the Himalaya Range.

From Shruling, cross the small bridge over the tributary flowing from near the Charang La and remain close to the Charang River for 1km. The trail ascends gradually for a further 3km to the village of Charang.

Charang (3500m) has a school and a medical centre. The ancient gompa is 2km beyond the village. Access to the gompa must be arranged at Charang as there is no resident monk. Take your passport and Inner Line permit with you to show at the checkpoint next to the gompa. Retrace the route to Shruling.

Alternative Route: Lalanti via the Ridge Southeast of Charang
5–6 hours, 13km

An alternative to the Day 3 trek is to overnight at the **PWD Rest House** in Charang after visiting the gompa. The following day, ascend the grassy ridge to the south of Charang and climb another ridge to the Lalanti Valley. The climb to the ridge top is quite steep before a narrow trail leads down to the river. The trail continues on the true right of the valley (difficult in places across the many rock gullies) before crossing the Lalanti River just opposite Lalanti.

Day 3: Shruling to Lalanti
3–4 hours, 10km

Cross the Lalanti River and head up the true left of the valley. After climbing for about 3km there is an open meadow (3650m). From here a narrow trail ascends steeply to a larger meadow (3950m) and the grazing pastures for zhos, sheep and goats during summer. It is a further 3km up the valley to the meadows at **Lalanti** (4200m).

At Lalanti there is a basic *pilgrim shelter* and plenty of good *campsites*. Magnificent views to the north showcase the Zanskar Range and the high passes leading into Tibet.

Day 4: Lalanti to Chitkul via Charang La
8–9 hours, 15km

The trail follows the true left of the valley across pastures and scree slopes. After 5km,

you will find yourself at a **glacial lake** and a possible *campsite*.

To reach the base of the pass, continue across the extensive moraine fields, taking care not to miss the rock cairns before gradually descending to the valley floor. Cross the glacial river close to its source and ascend a moraine field on the true right of the valley. This leads to the base of the pass at 4700m. The view from here is impressive, with the upper valley enclosed by the peaks and hanging glaciers of the Kinnaur Kailash Range.

The 500m climb to the pass is steep. In spring and early summer, the scree slopes are under snow and an ice axe and rope is essential. Later in the season, the climb is equally difficult and great care must be taken not to dislodge loose boulders onto other members of your party. Whatever the season, there is little in the way of a trail. Ascend directly for the first 350m before heading across towards the pass. The upper sections include slopes of 50- to 55-degree angles that lead to the flags, tridents and cairns atop the **Charang La** (5280m). The time from Lalanti to the pass is around five hours.

The pass offers superb views along the Kinnaur Kailash Range. To the south are the spectacular peaks and glaciers of the Dhaula Dhar Range.

It's a long descent to the Sangla Valley and Chitkul. The first, very steep stage is to a plateau at 4650m. The next, 300m descent reaches another plateau that is a potential *campsite* for anyone trekking from the opposite direction.

Take care descending the next scree slope; it is very unstable and prone to rock slides. An ill-defined trail leads to the true left of the valley and a series of alpine pastures. From here, the village of Chitkul can be seen way down the valley.

The trail gradually veers across to the true right of the valley before descending for nearly 1km to the outskirts of Chitkul. Cross the bridge over the stream coming from the pass before heading through the barley fields to the trailhead at **Chitkul** (3450m). The descent from the pass takes 3½ to four hours – a tiring but exhilarating day.

Uttaranchal

This recently created state of the Himalayan regions of Uttar Pradesh was granted autonomy in 2000 and has administrative headquarters at Dehra Dun. In February 2002 elections were held for the first time.

Uttaranchal's formidable terrain, characterised by deep valleys, gorges and mountains, was conducive to the establishment of small kingdoms separated by high mountain ridges. Many kingdoms maintained their independence by establishing a *garh* (fortress), from which to guard against neighbours and invading armies from northwest India. The terrain was gradually divided into two regions: Garhwal to the west, as far as the Tons River; and Kumaon to the east, extending to the Kali River and the present-day border of India and Nepal.

Nanda Devi (7816m) is the highest mountain entirely within India, and forms part of the main axis of the Great Himalaya Range. To the south of the Himalaya Range, the Kali River and the main tributaries of the Ganges form rugged gorge country before cutting through the Siwalik Hills, where the peaks rarely exceed 3000m.

Uttaranchal is also a source of spiritual inspiration and has been the scene of countless pilgrimages since the time of the early Aryan settlers. The sources of the Ganges River – Yamunotri, Gangotri, Kedarnath and Badrinath – are visited by many thousands of Hindus each year. Gangotri is recognised as the actual source of the Ganges, though the stream actually emerges from the snout of an impressive glacier at nearby Gaumukh (at the base of the Bhagirathi peaks). Yamunotri is the source of the Yamuna River, a main tributary of the Ganges. Kedarnath is recognised as one of the divine resting places of Lord Shiva, while Badrinath is assigned to Vishnu.

The trekking possibilities in Uttaranchal are among the best in the Himalaya. Treks, such as Source of the Ganges (pp215–17) and Hem Kund & Valley of the Flowers (pp220–2) follow routes that attract thousands of pilgrims each year. However, many

Highlights

A campsite en route to Rup Kund, a popular trek in the Garhwal.

GARRY WEARE

- Following pilgrim trails to the sacred source of the Ganges (p215)

- Spending time in the Valley of the Flowers (p220) and other high-altitude meadows renowned for wildflowers

- Viewing the distinctive twin peaks of Nanda Devi – the highest mountain in India – while ascending to the Kuari Pass (p222)

- Ascending trails through pristine bamboo, rhododendron, oak and conifer forest to the mysterious lake of Rup Kund (p226)

- Visiting villages near the Milam Glacier (p234) where the legendry Pundits were recruited for early exploration in Tibet

only attract a handful of trekkers; one reason being that few want to travel the long distances – sometimes two full days by road – before starting to trek. The effort required is easily outweighed by the untouched and spectacular mountain trails on offer.

Uttaranchal

HIMACHAL PRADESH

Sumdo

Manirang
(6593m)

CHINA
(TIBET)

Puh

Jangi

Section 1 Map p204

See Himachal Pradesh Map pp148-9

Karcham   Kinnaur
               Kailash
Sangla   (6050m)

Chitkul

0   20   40km
0 10 20mi
1:2,500,000

Govind National   Har Ki Dun
Park
Taluka
Sankri   Harsil   Gangotri
Janki Chatti   Yamunotri   Kedar   Gaumukh   GREAT HIMALAYA RANGE
Hanuman Chatti   Tal   Tapovan
Purola   Dodi   Jaonli   Gangotri Glacier   Bhagirathi 1   Kanet   Mana
                Tal   (6630m)   (6856m)   (7756m)   (7272m)
Barkot   Uttarkashi Bhatwari Kedarnath   Section 2 Map p205
               Dunda   (6940m)   Nilkanth
                                   Kedarnath   (6596m)   Valley of Flowers
Mussoorie   Gaurikund   Madmaheshwar   Badrinath   National Park
                GARHWAL   Thati   Sonprayag   Malari
Mussoorie Map pp200-1   Kathur   Rudranath Govind   Hem
                 Ghamsali   Ghuttu   Ghat   Kund   Milam
Tehri   Ukhimath   Anasya   Glacier
Dehra Dun   Devi   Joshimath
                                   Gopeshwar   Auli   Nanda Devi   Milam
Narendranagar   Alaknanda   Nandprayag Chamoli   Kuari Pass (7816m) Chiring We
                Deoprayag   Ramni   (3640m)   Nanda Devi East (6559m)
Rajaji   Srinagar   Ghat   Trisul   (7434m)
National   Pauri   Rudraprayag Karnaprayag   (7120m)   Pindari Glacier
Park   Rishikesh   Adi Badri   Tharali Maiktoli   Nanda Kot
Haridwar   Chilla   Rup   (6803m)   (6861m)   Panch Chuli
                                              Kund   Phurkiya (6904m)
                UTTARANCHAL   Mundoli   Pindari River   KUMAON   Munsyari
                                   Gwaldam   Section 3 Map pp206-7
Lansdowne   Baijnath   Song   Kapkot
                Chaukhutiya   Garur   Sarju Bageshwar   Dharchula
Kotdwar   Kausani   Didihat
                Dwarahat   Takula Sallya River   Gangolihat
        Ramganga   Ranikhet   Jageshwar   Pithoragarh   NEPAL
        Reservoir   Kosi   Almora   Rameshwar   Askot
Najibabad   Corbett   Muktehwar
Bijnor   National   Champawat
Nihtaur   Kalagarh Park   Kosi River   Bhowali
                Ramnagar   Naini Tal Bhimtal
Seohara   Naini Tal Map p230 Naukuchiyatal
        Thakurdwara   Kaladungi Kathgodam   Champawat
Chandpur   Kashipur   Haldwani
UTTAR PRADESH   Tanakpur
                              To Delhi   Gola   Nanak
Bhojpur   (210km)   River   Sagar Banbassa To Nepalganj
Bachhraon   Amroha   To Moradabad (15km)   & Kathmandu
                  & Delhi (215km) Rampura Sitarganj Khatima Mahendranagar

CLIMATE

With the exception of the remote valleys north of the Himalaya Range, the Uttaranchal region is subject to the monsoon. The pre-monsoon months are May and June, with monsoon rains falling in July. By mid-September, settled conditions return.

Winter snows start to fall by late October. This also marks the end of the pilgrimage season. Heavy snowfalls on the Himalaya Range preclude any thoughts of trekking in winter. In early May snows melt sufficiently to reopen the main trails into the mountains.

South of the Himalaya Range some valleys, including the Har ki Dun, enjoy milder climates. At lower altitudes the snowfall is not so heavy and the trails between the villages are passable even during winter.

INFORMATION
When to Trek

There are two distinct trekking seasons: pre-monsoon (May & June) and post-monsoon (mid-Sept–Oct). The beginning of the pre-monsoon season is dependent on the spring snowmelt, although you may encounter snow on the high passes well into July. During this period, expect day temperatures to rise to 20°C, although they can still fall well below freezing during an occasional storm.

In July and August the monsoon rain does not fall incessantly and if well prepared you can trek. Day temperatures rise to the mid-20°Cs. However, expect delays getting to and from the trailhead, as landslides blocking the highways are a regular feature.

Maps

The Leomann 1:200,000 series and US Military U502 1:250,000 series are useful for planning as well as trekking. The Ground Survey of India trekking map series are also available from the Uttaranchal Tourist Office (p258) in Delhi. See Planning for each trek for specific map requirements.

The detailed aerial survey *Garhwal Himalaya* (1:150,000) was published in 1992 by the Swiss Foundation for Alpine Research (SFAR). The two sections (east and west) are based on Survey of India maps and drawn by Ernst Huber.

Books

The Nanda Devi Affair by Bill Aitken is an enjoyable account of the author's exploits in the area.

Mountain Delight, also by Bill Aitken (English Book Shop, Dehra Dun, 1994), recounts his travels in Uttaranchal over the past 30 years.

Sacred Waters by Stephen Alter is an entertaining stroy of a modern-day pilgrimage to the Garhwal.

Beautiful Garhwal by Ruskin Bond (Dev Dutt Pt Ltd, 1988) gives an appreciation of the Garhwal from one of the region's most prolific writers.

Nanda Devi by Eric Shipton is included in *Eric Shipton – The Six Mountain-Travel Books*.

The Ascent of Nanda Devi by HW Tilman is included in *HW Tilman – The Seven Mountain-Travel Books*.

The Valley of Flowers by Frank Smythe provides an account of his climbs in the region in 1937.

Exploring the Hidden Himalaya by Soli Mehta and Harish Kapadia is the reference for climbing in the Indian Himalaya, including Uttaranchal.

High Asia – An Illustrated History of 7000 Metre Peaks by Jill Neate (1989) includes a comprehensive section on Uttaranchal.

Bookshops in the region include the **Cambridge Book Depot** *(The Mall, Mussoorie)*, stocking a range of local titles.

Information Sources

Trekking information is available from the trekking divisions of the GMVN and KMVN (both are state-owned organisations). The head office of the **GMVN** *(☎ 0135-746817, fax 746847, 74 Rajpur Rd)* is in Dehra Dun, with offices in Rishikesh, Uttarkashi and Joshimath. The head office of the **KMVN** is at Naini Tal. The **Nehru Mountaineering Institute** in Uttarkashi is invaluable for advice on challenging treks. Alternatively, contact the trekking agencies in Rishikesh, Mussoorie, Uttarkashi, Joshimath or Naini Tal for further information. The local Public Works Department (PWD) in each region will provide information on roads leading to the treks. Look under the relevant town information for the contact details of these offices.

Permits

There are no permits needed or special regulations to observe for treks in this chapter. Carry your passport and do not cross the Inner Line borders close to the Tibet border.

Watching Wildlife

Although the subtropical forest in the Corbett National Park is renowned for its **tigers**, the highest recorded sighting was at around 3200m in the Garhwal! **Common leopards** are found in the lower temperate forests of Uttaranchal. However, there are no contemporary records to compare with the famous man-eater of Rudraprayag that killed 125 people before being shot by Jim Corbett in May 1926.

Serows and **gorals** live in the upper reaches of temperate forests, where **musk deer** may also be spotted. To provide safer breeding grounds for these endangered species, a number of sanctuaries have been established, including one near Kedarnath. **Brown bears** frequent the caves and ledges above high alpine slopes. **Black bears** are seen at lower elevations in summer, near village cornfields.

Bharal and **ibex** are restricted to the high alpine pastures. Mountaineers and trekkers in the Nanda Devi Sanctuary in the 1970s were taken aback by the tame bharal, while there were frequent sightings of **snow leopards**. Today the ibex and bharal are confined to remote regions such as the Govind National Park, the alpine meadows beneath Khatling Glacier and the upper reaches of the Milam Valley.

As with Himachal Pradesh, the huge geographic contrast favours a wide variety of species. Birds of prey include **golden eagles**, **lammergeiers** and **Steppe eagles**. **Sparrowhawks** are also seen swooping on small birds at lower altitudes. **Koklass** and **kalij pheasants** are regularly seen in the forested regions bordering the alpine pastures, as are **cheer pheasants** and the impressive **satyr tragopan**. In the mixed forest, expect to see the distinctive **white-capped water redstart**, **blue whistling thrush**, **leaf warblers**, **yellow-breasted greenfinches**, **Himalayan** and **scaly-bellied woodpeckers**, **white-tailed nuthatch** and **spotted forktails**. **Eurasian** and **black-headed jays** are found at lower altitudes, as are **dwarf kingfishers**, **black-throated tits**, **flycatchers**, **Himalayan woodpeckers**, **Indian** and **Drongo cuckoos**, **barn swallows** and **winter wrens**.

Extensive **chir** forests extend from 1500m to 2300m across the many hill regions. Above the chir pine are temperate regions of **horse chestnut**, **yew** and **sycamore**, which give way to **blue pine**, **bamboo** and **rhododendron**. Birch groves are found in the upper regions to the west of the state. To appreciate the striking relationship between vegetation and elevation, consider the trek days from Bedni Bugyal down to the village of Loharjang (Rup Kund trek, pp226–8) or from the alpine meadows of Har ki Dun to the trailhead at Sankri (Har ki Dun & Ruinsara Lake trek, pp210–13). Both can be completed in a day.

This region offers an exceptional range of wildflowers. The Bhyundar Valley, known as the **Valley of the Flowers** is the most famous location but there are many other areas of interest. Any high alpine meadow in Uttaranchal is worth visiting during the monsoon. Earlier in the season the wildflowers are particularly attractive in the Har ki Dun Valley.

Garhwal

The Garhwal was described by many inter-war British travellers and mountaineers as the most beautiful region of the Himalaya. The snowcapped peaks (including Nanda Devi), flowered meadows and ancient pilgrim trails provided an idyllic combination for anyone heading for the hills. Today, the attractions for trekkers are still diverse, from the mysterious Rup Kund to the Valley of the Flowers.

The treks are accessible from the hill station of Mussoorie or the pilgrim towns of Rishikesh, Uttarkashi and Joshimath.

HISTORY

In the early 16th century, the powerful Panwar dynasty united many of the independent hill kingdoms to form the Garhwal. In 1517 it established its capital at Srinagar, where it administered an impressive area, including much of the terrain from the Yamuna River to Nanda Devi.

During the time of the Moghuls, the various rajahs paid tribute to the Moghul court. However, it was a flexible arrangement, with the Moghul emperors having little desire to establish absolute rule over the region.

In 1790 the Gurkhas attacked, as a part of their ambitious plan to form a Himalan kingdom as far as the Sutlej River. This attracted the attention of the British East India Company, which was wary of the Gurkhas and the Sikhs joining forces to form a vast Trans-Himalaya empire. The British wanted to maintain a neutral Himalayan territory between the two powers to protect their trade with Tibet. When the local rajahs asked the British to intervene, the East India army fought a number of wars with the Gurkhas, which resulted in the Treaty of Siliguri in 1817. This treaty brought Nepal's western borders back to the Kali River.

After the Treaty, the British ruled Dehra Dun and the eastern districts of Garhwal. The western region was restored to the local rajah, Sadarshan Shah, who established his capital at Tehri (known as Tehri Garhwal).

Hill stations were built to accommodate the British officials, notably at Mussoorie. The British districts in the Garhwal were initially administered by the Residency of Bengal before becoming part of the North-West Frontier Province, and finally part of the United Provinces. In 1947, after India's independence, the region became part of the state of Uttar Pradesh, while the ruler of the Tehri Garhwal, Maharajah Manvedra Shah merged his kingdom with Uttar Pradesh on 1 May 1949.

Further administrative developments in 1968 ensured that Chamoli, Dehra Dun, Pauri Garhwal, Tehri Garhwal and Uttar-kashi were administered from Pauri. A line running northeast from the town of Gwal-dam up the Pindar Valley and along the east ridge of the Nanda Devi Sanctuary is the accepted division between the Garhwal and Kumaon regions.

NATURAL HISTORY

The Himalaya Range forms the backbone of the Garhwal region. In western Garhwal, it includes the Swargarohini Range (some-times regarded as an extension of the Dhaula Dhar Range) and the Bandarpunch Range. The latter forms the main divide between the headwaters of the Yamuna and the Bhagi-rathi Rivers.

The Himalaya Range extends to the Gangotri region, where a huge concentration

of peaks almost encloses the Gangotri Gla-cier. At the head of the glacier, the Chau-khamba Range provides an impressive divide between the headwaters of the Bhagirathi and Alaknanda Rivers. The peaks near Nanda Devi Sanctuary further define the Himalaya Range.

Central Garhwal is different from other regions of the West Himalaya. There are no intermediary ranges between the Himalaya and the north Indian Plains to temper the geography or climate. Instead, an incredible series of gorges mark the passage of the headwaters of the Ganges as they forge their way south to the plains.

Wildlife sightings are becoming increas-ingly rare outside of the national parks and sanctuaries. However, this region is home to black bears, common leopards, serow, goral, Himalayan thar and musk deer. Brown bears may are seen on the meadows close to the tree line, while on the higher ridges snow leopards stalk bharal. Closer to the villages are langur, jungle cats and porcupines.

Birdlife includes many warblers, owls, cuckoos, woodpeckers, magpies and mini-vets in the forested regions. Pheasants are also found in forest clearings. Birds of prey, including the lammergeier and golden eagle, soar above the high alpine pastures.

An obvious attraction is the Valley of the Flowers, (see the boxed text, p222). How-ever, Har ki Dun, the Khatling Glacier and the many *bugyals* (high-altitude meadows) throughout the Garhwal also offer a profu-sion of wildflowers.

ACCESS TOWNS
Mussoorie
☎ 0135 • alt 1921m

The hill station of Mussoorie is an impor-tant gateway to the Garhwal. Its ridge-top location offers commanding views south across the Siwalik foothills and the Indian Plains and north to the Himalaya Range. Since it was established in the 1820s, many trekkers have set out to explore the forests, ridges and variety of hill cultures. Today the town retains some of its former charm and a few relaxing days can be spent here before or after a trek.

Information For general information try the **UP Tourist Office** (☎ *632863, The Mall*). There is also a **GMVN office** (☎ *632984; Hotel Garhwal Terrace, The Mall*).

Supplies & Equipment There is no shortage of fresh fruit and vegetables in the local markets, along with a wide variety of tinned food and luxury items. Beyond Mussoorie there are several towns from where you can purchase further supplies before reaching the trailheads.

If you need to hire camping equipment, contact the **GMVN office** (☎ *0135-476817*) in Dehra Dun, although there is sometimes a shortage of quality gear. Cooking equipment can be purchased in the market.

Trekking Agents The local option is **Trek Himalaya** (☎ *630491, Upper Mall*). **Garhwal Treks & Tours** (☎ *627769; 151 Araghar Rd, Dehra Dun*) is the most established agency in the region.

Trekking agents closer to the trailhead include **Himalayan Trekkers** at the head of the bazaar in Sankri, who can organise porters for around Rs 200 per day. Guides/cooks are also available for around Rs 400/300.

Places to Stay & Eat There is a wide range of accommodation in Mussoorie, although it is more expensive than other hill stations. *Hotel Broadway* (☎ *632243, Kulri Bazaar*) has doubles from Rs 250. *Valley View Hotel* (☎ *632324, Lower Mall*) has doubles from Rs 600 to Rs 800. Raj-style *Hotel Clarks* (☎ *632393, Kulri Bazaar*) has doubles from Rs 900 to Rs 1800. *Hotel Padmini Nivas* (☎ *632793*), off the Mall about 500m east of Gandhi Chowk, provides an oasis of comfort and rooms with a view from Rs 900.

In Gandhi Chowk, there is *Whispering Windows* and *Swiss Cafe*. Both offer a variety of European, Chinese and Indian dishes. In Kulri Bazaar, *The Tavern*, *Kwality Restaurant* and *Madras Cafe* are popular. Downhill from Hotel Clarks is *The Rice Bowl*, serving inexpensive Tibetan food such as *momos* (steamed spring rolls) and *thukpa* (noodle soup).

Getting There & Away From Mussoorie, there are bus services to the mountain regions of the Garhwal. Regular services go to/from Dehra Dun, which has train connections to/from Delhi.

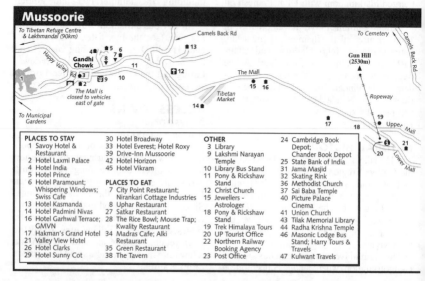

Mussoorie

To Tibetan Refuge Centre & Lakhmandal (90km)

Camels Back Rd

To Cemetery

Happy Valley

Gandhi Chowk

Rd

The Mall is closed to vehicles east of gate

To Municipal Gardens

The Mall

Tibetan Market

Gun Hill (2530m)

Ropeway

Camels Back Rd

Upper Mall

Lower Mall

PLACES TO STAY		OTHER	
1 Savoy Hotel & Restaurant	30 Hotel Broadway	3 Library	24 Cambridge Book Depot;
2 Hotel Laxmi Palace	33 Hotel Everest; Hotel Roxy	9 Lakshmi Narayan Temple	Chander Book Depot
4 Hotel India	39 Drive-Inn Mussoorie	10 Library Bus Stand	25 State Bank of India
5 Hotel Prince	42 Hotel Horizon	11 Pony & Rickshaw Stand	31 Jama Masjid
6 Hotel Paramount; Whispering Windows; Swiss Cafe	45 Hotel Vikram	12 Christ Church	32 Skating Rink
	PLACES TO EAT	15 Jewellers - Astrologer	36 Methodist Church
13 Hotel Kasmanda	7 City Point Restaurant; Nirankari Cottage Industries	18 Pony & Rickshaw Stand	37 Sai Baba Temple
14 Hotel Padmini Nivas	8 Uphar Restaurant	19 Trek Himalaya Tours	40 Picture Palace Cinema
16 Hotel Garhwal Terrace; GMVN	27 Satkar Restaurant	20 UP Tourist Office	41 Union Church
17 Hakman's Grand Hotel	28 The Rice Bowl; Mouse Trap; Kwality Restaurant	22 Northern Railway Booking Agency	43 Tilak Memorial Library
21 Valley View Hotel	34 Madras Cafe; Alki Restaurant	23 Post Office	44 Radha Krishna Temple
26 Hotel Clarks	35 Green Restaurant		46 Masonic Lodge Bus Stand; Harry Tours & Travels
29 Hotel Sunny Cot	38 The Tavern		47 Kulwant Travels

Bus There are many buses running between Mussoorie and Dehra Dun (Rs 22, 1½ hours). To Delhi, there are overnight deluxe buses (Rs 180) departing at around 8.30pm. There are several daily buses to/from Hanuman Chatti (Rs 90, seven hours) and a daily service to/from Sankri (Rs 100, nine hours), although you may have to change at Nowgaon.

Train At the Kulri Bazaar end of the Lower Mall, the **Northern Railway Booking Agency** (☎ 632846) has a small quota of tickets for trains out of Dehra Dun. You will need to give 24 hours notice to make a booking. The most convenient connection to/from Delhi is the *Shatabdi Express* (chair seat Rs 495). It departs Dehra Dun at 5pm and arrives in New Delhi at 10.40pm.

Taxi A taxi to Dehra Dun will cost about Rs 350; to Rishikesh Rs 700; to Uttarkashi Rs 1700; to Hanuman Chatti Rs 3000; and to Sangla Rs 3400.

Rishikesh
☎ 0135 • alt 335m
Rishikesh is a popular pilgrim and meditation centre and also the gateway for the Char Dham to the sacred sources of the Ganges. Each year many thousands of Hindu pilgrims congregate on the banks of the Ganges at Haridwar and camp at Rishikesh before undertaking their journey. It is not surprising that there are many trekking agencies here, some offering extended treks beyond Mussoorie, Uttarkashi and Joshimath.

Information For local information, try the **UP Tourist Office** (☎ 430209, *Train Station Rd; closed Sun)*. The **GMVN Tourist Office** (☎ 430799; fax 430372; *Lakshman Jhula Rd, Muni-ki-Reti; closed Sun)* is also helpful. In the same office, the **GMVN Trekking & Mountaineering Centre** (☎ 430799, ℮ *gmvn@nda.vsnl.net.in)* can hire gear. For Char Dham inquires call ☎ 431783.

Supplies & Equipment Fresh fruit and vegetables and a wide assortment of supplies can be purchased at Rishikesh, although for treks out of Mussoorie, Uttarkashi and Joshimath it is advisable to buy bulky items such as rice and flour closer to the trailhead.

The **GMVN Trekking & Mountaineering Centre** (see Information) has gear for hire. A substantial deposit is required, along with your passport details and proposed itinerary. The rates for two-person tents/sleeping bags/insulated mattresses are Rs 65/25/6 per day. Other items, such as windproof jackets, gaiters and mittens, are also available.

Trekking Agents At the **GMVN Trekking & Mountaineering Centre** (see Information), a comprehensive selection of treks are offered, lead by experienced guides. Prices start from Rs 1500 per person per day plus transport.

There are about a dozen local agents in the immediate vicinity of the GMVN office, although most are geared to the Char Dham market. It is difficult to recommend a particular agency as the local guides may not be a permanent fixture. Contact a few agents before making a booking, including:

Garhwal Himalaya Exploration (☎ 433478, fax 431654, ℮ *Himalayas@vsnl.com)*
Himalayan Adventure Holidays (☎ 442267, ℮ *fx_carbon@hotmail.com)*

```
                    0    100    200m
                    0    100    200yd
                       1:13,000
              30
                    31
Kulri              C
Bazaar      32      33
       29         34              To Tehri Bus Stand (1.5km)
23   24   28    35    39          & Dhanoltri (25.5km)
22
   25  27             40    41
        37   38
26      36 Picture
           Palace            The Mall is closed to
                             vehicles west of gate
                    43
                    42
              44              47
                          46
       45
                    To Dehra Dun (34km)
Not all items on this map
are mentioned in the text.
```

Places to Stay & Eat Close to the trekking agents, the *GMVN Tourist Bungalow (☎ 433002, Haridwar Bypass Rd)* is in pleasant surroundings. Rates vary from Rs 180 to 420 per double. If spending extra time in Rishikesh, consider the Lakshman Jhola area. The popular *Hotel Divya (☎ 434 938)* has double rooms for Rs 150. *Laxman Jhola Guest House (☎ 435720)* charges from Rs 100.

The restaurant at the *GMVN Tourist Bungalow* offers excellent Indian food. *Devraj Coffee Corner*, above the bridge in Lakshman Jhola, has good snacks and a well-stocked bookshop. *Neelam Restaurant*, just south of the bridge in a lane off Haridwar Rd, offers a good selection of Indian and Italian dishes.

Getting There & Away There are many buses linking Rishikesh with Haridwar and Dehra Dun. There are also regular services to the mountain areas, including Ghuttu, Uttarkashi and Joshimath.

Bus Regular buses go to/from Haridwar (Rs 14, one hour), from where there are hourly buses to/from Delhi (Rs 95, five hours). There is also a service every half hour to/from Dehra Dun (Rs 19, 1½ hours). Several buses a day run to/from Uttarkashi (Rs 92, seven hours), Joshimath (Rs 140, eight hours) and Hanuman Chatti (Rs 160, eight hours). There is one daily direct service to Ghuttu (Rs 110, seven hours), while many buses go to Tehri (Rs 45, seven hours), from where there are connections to Ghuttu (Rs 45, three hours).

Taxi A 4WD to Ghuttu is Rs 1800; to Uttarkashi Rs 1000; to Mussoorie Rs 700; and to Joshimath Rs 2500.

Uttarkashi
☎ 01374 • alt 1158m

Uttarkashi is an important pilgrim centre in the picturesque Bhagirathi Valley. It is visited by thousands of pilgrims as they make their way from Hanuman Chatti (and Yamunotri) on the second day of the Char Dham to Gangotri. It is also an important gateway for trekking in the Garhwal, including treks out of Gangotri and the nearby trails to Dodi Tal and Hanuman Chatti.

Information The GMVN office (☎ 22290) is in the GMVN Tourist Bungalow just off Bhatwari Rd. It can provide travel information to Gangotri and book accommodation in other GMVN hotels.

Supplies & Equipment The market sells vegetables and fruit, tinned milk, oatmeal, soup packets, and nuts and raisins. If trekking out to Dodi Tal, buy all supplies here. If trekking out of Gangotri, vegetables, fruit, rice and flour are available there.

Although Uttarkashi has numerous trekking agents, there is a limited amount of good gear for hire. Your best bet is **Mount Support** (☎ 22419), which has a stock of sleeping bags, tents and insulated mats, plus cooking tents, stoves and associated cooking items. Other cooking gear is available in the market.

Trekking Agents The **Nehru Mountaineering Institute** (☎ 23647), 3km outside of Uttarkashi, is well worth a visit. There is a museum and an information office (closed Tues; call ahead for current hours) that can assist with mountaineering and high-altitude trekking enquiries.

The trekking agents in Uttarkashi are on Bhatwari Rd. Many of the guides here were trained at the Nehru Institute. The following agents are well established:

Crystal Holidays (☎ 22271, e crystalnature@ rediffmail.com)
Mount Support (☎ 22419)
Peak & Pine Adventure (☎ 23966)

Places to Stay & Eat Off Bhatwari Rd, the *GMVN Tourist Bungalow (☎ 22271)* offers double rooms from Rs 240 to Rs 680 and dorm beds for Rs 60. There are many hotels along Bhatwari Rd, including *Hotel Mandakini (☎23377)*, with doubles from Rs 250, and *Hotel Relax (☎22893)*, charging Rs 250 to Rs 350.

Most hotels serve good vegetarian Indian food. On Bhatwari Rd, *Preeti Restaurant* and *Bhandari Restaurant* serve Indian and Chinese cuisine.

Getting There & Away For most, Uttarkashi is an important stop en route to Gangotri. There are regular bus services to Gangotri and also to/from Rishikesh, Dehra Dun and Haridwar.

Bus Many buses operate to/from Gangotri (Rs 80, four hours) and Rishikesh (Rs 65, eight hours).

Taxi There are many share taxis operating in this region of the Garhwal. They are an especially good option for large groups. The fares are not much higher than the bus and they can be hired close to the bus station. Full taxi rates are around Rs 800 to Gangotri, Rs 1200 to Rishikesh.

Joshimath
☎ 01389 • alt 1845m

Close to Nanda Devi, Joshimath has had a long association with trekking and mountaineering. Although the route into the Nanda Devi Sanctuary has been closed since 1983, there are many other fine treks here. Joshimath is also near Govind Ghat and the important Sikh pilgrimage to Hem Kund and the *Valley of the Flowers*. Thousands of Hindu pilgrims stop at Joshimath before completing the final stage of the Char Dham to Badrinath.

Information The GMVN Tourist Office (☎ 22226) is in the new GMVN Rest House above the main bazaar. The office can give advice about travel arrangements and treks in the vicinity.

Supplies & Equipment Fruit and vegetables are available in the market, along with most food supplies. While there are basic supplies available at the trailheads at Auli and Govind Ghat, make your purchases at Joshimath. However, bring items such as porridge, and tinned cheese and fish from Rishikesh or Delhi.

There is no trekking gear for hire in Joshimath. Cooking items such as pots, pans and stoves can be purchased in the market. Cooking tents may be hired from the local agents if they are making other arrangements for you.

Trekking Agents Agents in Joshimath include the established **Nanda Devi Mountain Travel** (☎ 22170), who are keen to promote new treks in the region, and **Garhwal Adventure Sports** (☎ 22288). Both are in the Hotel Nanda Devi in the main bazaar (and are often staffed by the same person!). They organise inclusive treks from around Rs 1500 per person per day. For the Kuari Pass trek (pp222–5), budget for around Rs 250 per porter per day.

If you are doing the Hem Kund & Valley of the Flowers trek (pp220–2), pack horses and porters can be organised at the trailhead at Govind Ghat. Both are at a premium in May and June so allow for at least a few hours at Govind Ghat before heading off. Budget for around Rs 200 for porters per day and Rs 400 for pack horses for the day to Ghangaria.

Places to Stay & Eat There are two *GMVN Tourist Rest Houses* in Joshimath. The *New Rest House* (☎ 22226) above the main bazaar is the better of the two, with doubles/dorms costing Rs 460/130. The *Old Rest House* (☎ 22118, main bazaar) was something of an institution for climbers prior to 1983. Doubles/dorms cost Rs 260/130. *Hotel Nanda Devi* (☎ 22170, main bazaar) has basic doubles from Rs 100.

Along with the *GMVN Tourist Rest Houses*, there are many dhabas and restaurants in the main bazaar. *Paradise Cafe* serves affordable Indian and European dishes.

Getting There & Away Regular buses and 4WDs service Joshimath.

Bus Buses go every day to/from Rishikesh (Rs 142, 10 hours) and Haridwar (Rs 170, 12 hours); from Joshimath, they leave early in the morning. Several buses run to/from Badrinath each day (Rs 25, two hours), stopping at Govind Ghat (Rs 10, one hour). Three buses go to/from Auli (Rs 12, 1½ hours).

UTTARANCHAL

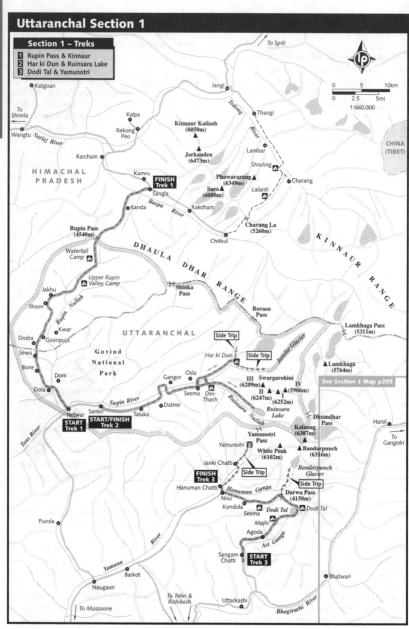

Uttaranchal Section 1

Section 1 – Treks
1. Rupin Pass & Kinnaur
2. Har ki Dun & Ruinsara Lake
3. Dodi Tal & Yamunotri

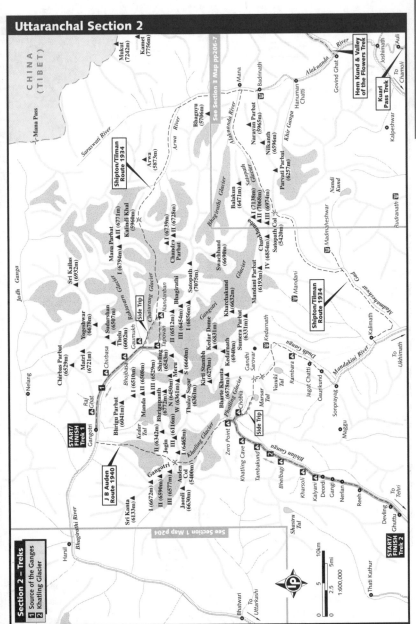

Uttaranchal Section 2

CHINA
(TIBET)

Mana Pass

Mukut (7242m)

Kamet (7756m)

Saraswati River

Hem Kund & Valley of the Flowers Trek

Kuari Pass Trek

To Chamoli

Auli

To Joshimath

Alaknanda River

River

Govind Ghat

Mana

Badrinath

See Section 3 Map pp206-7

Haruman Chatti

Kalpeshwar

Khir Ganga

Jadh Ganga

Nelang

Chirbas Parbat (6529m)

Sri Kailas (6932m)

Yogeshwar (6678m)

Matri (6721m)

Sudarshan (6507m)

Mana Parbat I (6794m) ▲ II (6771m)

Kalindi Khal (5960m)

Arwa River

Bhagyiru (5716m)

Shipton/Tilman Route 1934

Arwa (5873m)

Chandra Parbat I (6739m)
▲ II (6728m)

Abkashank River

Narayan Parbat (5965m)

Nilkanth (6596m)

Parvati Parbat (6257m)

Nandi Kund

Rudranath

Balakun (6471m)

Satopath I (7138m)
▲ II (7068m)
▲ III (6974m)

Chaukhamba I (7138m)
▲ II (7068m)
▲ III (6974m)
▲ IV (6854m)

Satopath Col (5420m)

Satopath Glacier

Gangotri Glacier

Chaturang Glacier

Nandanban

Bhagirathi I (6512m) ▲ II (6454m) ▲ III (6856m)

Gangotri Glacier

Swachhand (6690m)

Mandani Parbat (6193m)

Madmaheshwar

Shipton/Tilman Route 1934

Madmaheshwar Gad

To Kalimath

Chirbasa

Bhojbasa

Thelu (6002m)

Shyling (6543m)

Tapovan

Meru

Kharchakund (6632m)

Sumera Parbat (6331m)

Mandini

Mandakini River

To Ukhimath

Kedar Dome (6831m)

Kedarnath (6940m)

Kedar (6941m)

Gandhi Sarovar

Kedarnath

Manda I (6510m)
▲ II (6508m)
▲ III (6529m)

Bhrigupanth (6772m)

N (6450m)

Meru W (6361m)

Thalay Sagar S (6660m)

Bharte Khunta (6578m)

Kirti Stambh (6270m)

Phating Glacier

Vasuki Tal

Rambara

Gaurikund

Jagat Chatti

Bhrigu Parbat (6041m)

Kedar Tal

Bhrigupanth (6342m)

Jogin II (6308m)

Jogin III (6116m)

Chobha

Marsur Tal

Side Trip

Zero Point

Khatling Glacier

Khatling Cave

Tambakund

Sonprayag

Maggu

START/FINISH Trek 1

Gangotri

Gangotri

J B Auden Route 1940

I (6672m)
▲ II (6590m)
▲ III (6577m)

Jaonli (6630m)

Auden Col (5400m)

Sri Kanta (6133m)

Bhelbagi

Kharsoli

Kalyani

Deodri

Gangi

Nerlan

Reeh

Devling

Ghuttu

To Tehri

START/FINISH Trek 2

Thati Kathur

Bhatwari

To Uttarkashi

Harsil

Bhagirathi River

Shastru Tal

See Section 1 Map p204

Bhilangna Ganga

Raj Ghat

Section 2 – Treks
1 Source of the Ganges
2 Khatling Glacier

10km
5mi
0 2.5 5
1:1,600,000

UTTARANCHAL

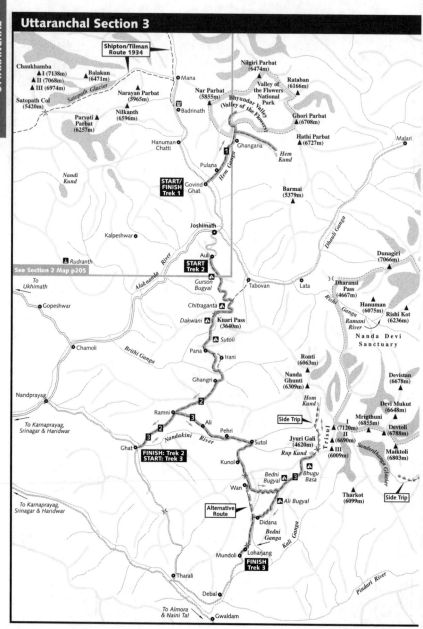

Uttaranchal Section 3

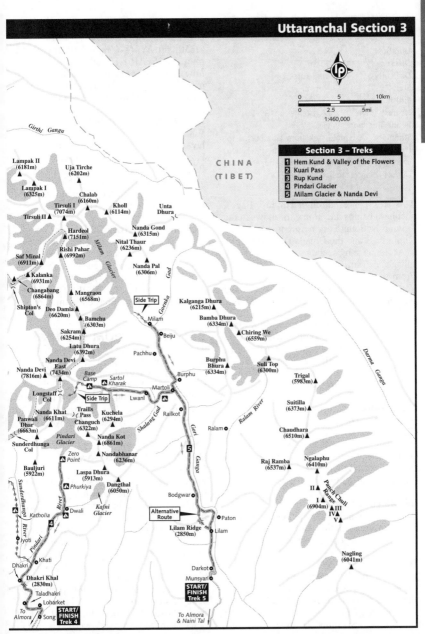

Uttaranchal Section 3

CHINA
(TIBET)

0   5   10km
0   2.5   5mi
1:460,000

Section 3 – Treks
1 Hem Kund & Valley of the Flowers
2 Kuari Pass
3 Rup Kund
4 Pindari Glacier
5 Milam Glacier & Nanda Devi

Girthi Ganga

Lampak II
(6181m)
Uja Tirche
(6202m)
Lampak I
(6325m)
Chalab
(6160m)
Kholl
(6114m)
Tirsuli I
(7074m)
Unta
Dhura
Tirsuli II
Hardeol
(7151m)
Nanda Gond
(6315m)
Rishi Pahar
(6992m)
Nital Thaur
(6236m)
Saf Minal
(6911m)
Nanda Pal
(6306m)
Kalanka
(6931m)
Changabang
(6864m)
Mangraon
(6568m)
Kalganga Dhura
(6215m)
Shipton's
Col
Deo Damla
(6620m)
Bamchu
(6303m)
Bamba Dhura
(6334m)
Chiring We
(6559m)
Sakram
(6254m)
Beiju
Latu Dhura
(6392m)
Pachhu
Burphu
Bhura
(6334m)
Suli Top
(6300m)
Trigal
(5983m)
Nanda Devi
East
(7434m)
Nanda Devi
(7816m)
Base
Camp
Sartol
Kharak
Burphu
Martoli
Suitilla
(6373m)
Longstaff
Col
Side Trip
Lwanl
Panwali
Dhar
(6663m)
Nanda Khat
(6611m)
Trails
Pass
Kuchela
(6294m)
Railkot
Chaudhara
(6510m)
Changuch
(6322m)
Ralam
Sunderdhunga
Col
Zero
Point
Pindari
Glacier
Nanda Kot
(6861m)
Nandabhanar
(6236m)
Raj Ramba
(6537m)
Ngalaphu
(6410m)
Bauljuri
(5922m)
Laspa Dhura
(5913m)
II
Phurkiya
Dangthal
(6050m)
I
(6904m)
III
Dwali
Kafni
Glacier
IV
V
Jyoti
Kathola
Bodgwar
Dhakri
Khati
Alternative
Route
Paton
Nagling
(6041m)
Dhakri Khal
(2830m)
Lilam Ridge
(2850m)
Lilam
Taladhakri
Loharket
To
Almora
Song
START/
FINISH
Trek 4
Darkot
Munsyari
START/
FINISH
Trek 5
To Almora
& Naini Tal

Milam Glacier
Gorenka Gad
Goriganga
Gori Ganga
Shalang Gad
Ralam River
Darma Ganga
Panch Chuli Ridge
Sunderdhunga River
Pindari River

UTTARANCHAL

Rupin Pass & Kinnaur

Duration	6 days
Distance	93km
Difficulty	moderate
Start	Netwar
Finish	Sangla
Nearest Town	Mussoorie (pp199–201)
Public Transport	yes

Summary A remote trek from Uttaranchal to Himachal Pradesh, following trails through Hindu villages and across the snowcapped ridges of the Dhaula Dhar to the Sangla Valley.

This trek passes through Hindu villages, shepherd camps and alpine meadows in the Govind National Park before traversing the Rupin Pass and the Dhaula Dhar Range.

Acclimatise by spending extra days in the villages or camping in the alpine meadows. From the campsites at the base of the pass, you can explore the extensive snowfields and glaciers beneath the crest of the Dhaula Dhar.

Views to the north of the pass include the impressive peaks of the Kinnaur Kailash Range, while to the south endless verdant ridges stretch towards the Indian foothills. This trek links with the Kinnaur Kailash trek in Himachal Pradesh (pp192–4), which starts in Chitkul near Sangla.

PLANNING
When to Trek
The Rupin Pass can normally be crossed from late May through June. The settled post-monsoon season (mid-Sept–mid-Oct) is the best time to trek, before the first winter snows fall on the high ridges.

What to Bring
A tent, stove and food supplies for at least five days are essential. A rope is also handy for crossing the upper sections of the pass.

Maps
Refer to the Leomann series 1:200,000 *Sheet 6 (Kalpa-Kinnaur, Spiti & Shimla)* for the northern sections of the trek and *Sheet 7 (Gangotri, Har ki Dun & Mussoorie)* for the southern sections. However, the trail

route on the south side of the pass needs correction. The US Military U502 series 1:250,000 *NI 44-1 ref Chini* covers the route. The SFAR 1:150,000 *Garhwal Himalaya (West Section)* is by far the clearest map (based on the US 502 series), although the trails marked for this trek are inaccurate.

Local Trekking Agents
While there are no agents in Netwar, **Himalayan Trekkers** at the head of the Sankri bazaar can arrange porters/guides for around Rs 200/300 per day. For each guide/porter, also budget for an allowance; this should include clothing, food and accommodation for two days and return travel.

Accommodation
There is little in the way of accommodation in Netwar, so it is best to head down to the river and camp. Camping is the only option en route, except for at Dola, where there are double rooms for Rs 70; the Forest Rest House at Jakhu; and basic accommodation at Kanda.

GETTING TO/FROM THE TREK
The bus to Netwar (Rs 100, eight to 10 hours) stops just below (not actually in) Mussoorie. A 4WD from Mussoorie to Netwar costs Rs 2000.

There is a direct bus from Sangla to Shimla (Rs 150, 10 hours). The bus from Sangla to Rekong Peo (Rs 30) takes 1½ to two hours.

THE TREK (See map p204)
Day 1: Netwar to Sewa
5–6 hours, 17km
From Netwar (1400m) descend to the Tons River and cross the main bridge. The trail heads up the true left of the Rupin River through mixed oak and conifer forest. A number of Gujar settlements here supply fresh milk and cheese to the villages in the upper Tons Valley. Cross the bridge over the river to a cluster of houses and a small bazaar at **Dola** (1610m).

The trail remains on the true right of the valley. After 3km the valley widens and the trail splits. The lower fork of the trail descends to the river and over the bridge to the substantial village of **Doni**. However, take the upper trail that gradually winds above the river before a short, steep ascent to the settlement of **Borie** (2030m). It is a further 4km through rhododendron forest to the outlying potato and barley fields of **Sewa** (2000m).

Sewa, high above the Rupin River, is spread out across the hillside over a couple of kilometres. There is a good *campsite* just below the main trail about halfway through the village. Just to the north of the village is a distinctive two-storey **Hindu temple** constructed in a style merging local and Kinnaur traditions. This is not surprising so close to the state boundaries of Uttaranchal and Himachal Pradesh – reflecting the period when the kingdom of Kinnaur extended beyond the crest of the Dhaula Dhar and south towards the Tons Valley.

Day 2: Sewa to Jakhu

7 hours, 20km
Follow the trail past the temple before descending to the banks of the Rupin River. At the first side valley, a substantial wood pile marks the geographic boundary between Uttaranchal and Himachal Pradesh, although the Uttaranchal government administers the villages in the vicinity.

There are several beehives nearby. The large villages on the far side of the Rupin River reflect the comparative prosperity of the valley.

Remain on the true right of the river before ascending (steeply in places) past a series of houses to **Jikson** (2320m). High above the confluence of the Rupin and Nurgang Rivers, Jikson has a *village store* and even a post office.

It is a further 3km to **Jakhu** (2650m). This includes a steep descent to a tributary, followed by an equally steep ascent to the highest village in the valley. Houses are set amid walnut, apricot and deodar trees. The *campsite* is just above the village and also doubles as the childrens playground, so don't expect tranquillity until evening. The water supply is limited during the day, but available in the late afternoon and early morning. There is also a *Forest Rest House* just below the campground.

Day 3: Jakhu to Upper Rupin Valley Camp

5–6 hours, 18km
Ascend the well-defined trail through the fields before entering a magnificent blue pine and maple forest. The forest track gradually descends to the Rupin River before crossing a shepherds bridge to the valley's true left. The time to the bridge is around 1½ hours.

A trail of sorts follows the course of the boulder-strewn riverbed before heading away from the river through rhododendron and silver birch forest to a series of alpine meadows. The peaks and glaciers of the Dhaula Dhar enclose the upper valley while an impressive **waterfall** in the centre of the valley marks the route towards the pass.

There are many *campsites* en route and a wide array of wildflowers, including edelweiss and blue poppies, adorn the meadows. This is also the summer grazing area from May to September.

Day 4: Upper Rupin Valley Camp to Waterfall Camp

3 hours, 10km
Remain on the true left of the valley across the meadows to the base of the large **waterfall** (3500m) in the centre of the valley. From here, the trail ascends the true left bank over scree to reach a grassy plateau about 150m above the main valley floor. The shepherds trail is not easy to follow as it winds across to the true right of the valley, fording the main stream above the lowest waterfall. It is a steep ascent towards the prominent rock cliffs before the trail winds around to a beautiful meadow just above the highest waterfall. The *campsite* (3950m) is marked by stone cairns and affords panoramic views: the Tons Valley to the south, the rugged peaks and snowfields of the Dhaula Dhar to the north.

Day 5: Waterfall Camp to Kanda via Rupin Pass

6 hours, 18km
The trail heads up the hillside for 250m, gaining impressive views of hanging glaciers, snowfields and the route to the pass. The route heads across boulder fields to a wide gravel plain at the base of the pass.

From the base, it is a further 100m climb over boulders to a narrow gully and a final 200m ascent to the pass. Take care not to dislodge any rocks that could endanger group members below you. In spring, until early July, the gully will be under snow and a length of rope may be useful. The time from camp to the pass is 2½ to three hours.

The **Rupin Pass** (4540m) affords uninterrupted views of the Kinnaur Kailash Range, including Jorkanden (6473m), Saro (6080m) and the peaks near the Charang La.

The descent from the pass is gradual, first over scree (snow early in the season), then across alpine pastures with no shortage of *campsites* (ideal, if coming from the other direction). A steady descent past shepherd encampments and grazing meadows takes you to the outskirts of **Kanda** (3400m), where villagers from Sangla tend to their fields and animals in summer. There are many *campsites* above the settlement. A deserted Forest Rest House is just above the village.

Day 6: Kanda to Sangla
3 hours, 10km

Enjoy bird's-eye views of Sangla Valley before descending through blue pine, deodar and oak forest to the main bridge over the Baspa River. Cross it and complete the short ascent to the bazaar at **Sangla** (2650m).

Har ki Dun & Ruinsara Lake

Duration	6 days
Distance	96km
Difficulty	easy–moderate
Start/Finish	Sankri
Nearest Town	Mussoorie (pp199–201)
Public Transport	yes

Summary Trek through Hindu villages to the verdant pastures of Har ki Dun and Ruinsara Lake, sitting beneath the peaks and glaciers of the Dhaula Dhar Range.

This trek crosses no pass. The well-defined trail in the Govind National Park is renowned for wildflowers. Plan an additional day or two for acclimatisation before ascending to Har ki Dun, from where there are opportunities to explore the peaks and glaciers of the Swargarohini Range.

PLANNING
When to Trek
The trail is mostly clear of snow by early May, and the wildflowers bloom in May and June. Mid-September until mid-October provides the ideal climate for trekking.

What to Bring
If not trekking to Ruinsara Lake, it is possible to get by without a tent, while meals can be cooked by the *chowkidar* (caretaker) at the GMVN hotels.

Maps
Refer to the Leomann series 1:200,000 *Sheet 7 (Gangotri, Har ki Dun & Mussoorie)*. Also refer to the Survey of India Trekking map series 1:250,000 *Gangotri – Yamunotri*. The SFAR 1:150,000 *Garhwal Himalaya (West Section)* is the best available section for this trek. The US Military U502 series 1:250,000, *NI 44-1 ref Chini* also covers the route.

Local Trekking Agents
At the head of the bazaar in Sankri, **Himalayan Trekkers** can organise porters and guides. See Local Trekking Agents (p208) for prices.

Accommodation
The GMVN hotels at Sankri, Taluka, Seema and Har ki Dun provide reasonably priced accommodation. In theory, the rooms can be booked from the **GMVN office** (☎ 011-3326620) in Delhi but there is no guarantee that the chowkidar will have your reservation when you arrive. Arrive early in case the rooms have been overbooked. Doubles/dorms cost Rs 380/120 (May–Oct). Hotels and lodges can be crowded during the school holidays in May and June.

GETTING TO/FROM THE TREK
The bus to Sankri (Rs 100, eight to 10 hours) stops just below Mussoorie. Alternatively,

catch the bus from Mussoorie to Purola, from where there are connections to Sangri. From Mussoorie, a 4WD will cost around Rs 2000.

From Sankri, the bus to Mussoorie leaves at 7am but check the time the night before. There are 4WDs from Sankri to Taluka for Rs 25 per seat. A full 4WD costs Rs 300.

THE TREK (See map p204)
Day 1: Sankri to Taluka
3–4 hours, 12km

A 4WD road connects **Sankri** (1450m) to Taluka. However, it is better to walk as the road is sometimes blocked and the ride uncomfortable. Besides, the walk through the forest gives you time to appreciate the wild roses and irises, bamboo, and chestnut, sycamore and deodar trees that line the trail. There is a *campsite* beside a beautiful stream about 2km below Taluka, which might be useful if you leave Sankri late in the day.

The village of **Taluka** (1800m) is devoid of charm. It is centred on a concrete fish-breeding pond that is complemented by the imposing concrete structure of the *GMVN hotel*. It's a pity the state government did not draw on the traditional wood and stone *pahari* construction found in nearby villages in the Har ki Dun Valley. To complete the tale of woe, the *dhabas* (small food stalls) are among some of the most fly-blown anywhere in northern India.

To shorten Day 2, trek past Taluka to one of many *forest camps*.

Day 2: Taluka to Seema
5–6 hours, 14km

From Taluka, the trail descends to the river valley and continues through the forest on the true left of the valley. In spring, there are plenty of Gujar encampments established as the Gujar travel to the head of the valley. After 2km to 3km, the trail winds below **Datmir** (1950m). A few kilometres past the turn-off to Datmir, the main trail crosses the river via a substantial bridge before crossing back to the true left about 1km further. There is a *campsite* just above the second bridge.

The trail continues to climb on the true left of the valley, winding through barley and wheat fields, and apple orchards. After

several kilometres, **Osla** village (2560m) appears on the opposite side of the valley.

The main trail does not divert to Osla but leads through a row of *dhabas* and a *Forest Rest House* at **Seema** (2500m). There is a *GMVN hotel* managed by a lively and obliging chowkidar (until he found we weren't staying!). As with the GMVN hotel at Taluka, the construction is less than sympathetic to the traditional styles of the local village houses.

There is a *campsite* 3km up the valley en route to Har ki Dun and close to a small spring line.

Day 3: Seema to Har ki Dun
4–5 hours, 12km

From Seema, cross the main bridge directly above the village. The trail remains on the true right of the valley all the way to Har ki Dun. There is a gradual ascent through the fields as the trail winds high above the valley floor. After 3km, there is a higher bridge (the Day 4 route).

The trail splits 1km beyond the higher bridge. Take the upper trail and continue up a steep section, which winds above wheat fields. These fields are tended by the villagers living in the two highest houses in the valley. The trail ascends above the confluence of the Har ki Dun and Ruinsara Rivers to a vantage point of the snowcapped ridges of the Dhaula Dhar. It is a further 3km or 4km to the *campsite* – just follow a trail through pine forest and a series of meadows (villagers from Osla graze their cattle here in summer). **Har ki Dun** (3510m) is beyond the confluence of the two alpine valleys.

Side Trip: North of Har ki Dun
2 hours, 6km return

From Har ki Dun, trek north across the flowered meadows towards the peaks and ridges of the Dhaula Dhar Range. There are excellent views back down the valley, while the route towards the Borasu Pass and the Sangla Valley is also in view.

Side Trip: Towards Swargarohini
6 hours, 15km return

A second option is to trek up the alpine valley to the north of the Swargarohini Range,

Environmental Watch

One of the most pressing environmental problems in the mountain regions of Uttaranchal is the Char Dham – the pilgrimage to the sacred sources of the Ganges. This pilgrimage is undertaken by domestic tourists in numbers estimated between 200,000 and 250,000 each year. Environmental damage in terms of unauthorised developments, garbage disposal, and the impact on forest and water resources has been the subject of wide debate. Since 1995 the Gangotri Environmental Project – operated by the Himalayan Environmental Trust (HET) and with the assistance of local nongovernment organisations – has made significant efforts to improve the pilgrimage trail to Gaumukh. Clean-up operations; the introduction of low-propane gas to the *dhabas* (small food stalls); the establishment of toilet facilities on the trail; and reforestation projects are some of the adopted measures. However, further funding is needed to introduce similar projects to the other *Char Dham* sites at Yamunotri, Kedarnath, and Badrinath, and the trail to Hem Kund visited by thousands of Sikh pilgrims each year. Contact the offices of the **Himalayan Environmental Trust** (☎ 011-6215635; Legend Inn, New Delhi).

Other trails, including those to Har ki Dun, the Kuari Pass and the Pindari Glacier, are also in need of attention. Overused campsites, indiscriminate garbage disposal, deforestation and inappropriate buildings (including those constructed by the state governments) are a cause for concern. Trekkers can help by demonstrating and encouraging clean trekking practices.

Wildlife protection, although high on the list of government priorities, is still in need of funding. Projects in the Govind and *Valley of the Flowers* National Parks require further resources to preserve and protect endangered animals and plants. By contrast, there are no current plans to reopen the Nanda Devi Sanctuary – subject to a significant flow of mountaineers and trekkers until it was closed in 1983 for protection. In 2001 an environmental research group carried out a survey in the Sanctuary. Their findings may determine the direction of the state's national-park programs. Contact the **Wildlife Institute of India** (☎ 0135-620910; PO Box 18, Dehra Dun, Garhwal).

As with other regions of the Himalaya, the use of solar panels and the introduction of micro hydroelectric schemes have helped to satisfy local energy demands. However, larger developments, including the current dam construction on the Sutlej and Bhagirathi Rivers, are the subject of continued environmental concern.

---

including Swargarohini I (6252m). This peak is famous in Hindu legend, being the gateway to heaven taken by the Pandava brothers. It is a day trek to reach the snout of the Jamdar Glacier and return to the Har ki Dun camp.

Day 4: Har ki Dun to Dev Thach
3 hours, 10km

It is from this stage on that you will require a tent. This is a short stage, returning to the Gujar meadow above Seema. Do not take any shortcuts here. Local porters may point out a log bridge across two huge boulders just above the confluence of the Har ki Dun and Ruinsara Rivers but this crossing is dangerous. Instead, go back down the trail as if returning to Osla and Sankri. En route the large meadow on the opposite side of

the valley – **Dev Thach** (3000m) – can be appreciated. Cross the higher of the two bridges above Seema and climb 3km to *camp* in the meadow. Local Gujar shepherds graze buffalo here in summer.

Day 5: Ruinsara Lake Circuit
7 hours, 18km

From Dev Thach, pass the Gujar huts and take the trail that descends steeply to the bridge over the Ruinsara River. Cross the river and begin a gradual ascent. The trail leads through mixed forest and meadows of forget-me-nots and buttercups. Early in the season, residual snowfields cover the trail, and there are several stream crossings, none of which pose any problem. The trail also passes under some impressive **waterfalls** before ascending above the conifer forest.

At about the halfway mark to the lake, the valley widens and the trail crosses flowered meadows where shepherds graze flocks in summer. There are also some delightful birch copses and juniper – a sure sign that you have ascended above 3000m.

Ruinsara Lake (3350m) is considered sacred by the villagers in the Har ki Dun Valley. It is above the main valley floor on the true right, surrounded by alpine pastures and low rhododendrons, beneath the impressive Swargarohini Range. From the lake, it is a two- to three-hour descent to Dev Thach.

Day 6: Dev Thach to Sankri
8 hours, 30km

The return to Sankri can be completed in a day. It is a one-hour trek from Dev Thach to Seema, followed by up to four hours from Seema to Taluka. From Taluka, you may be fortunate enough to find a 4WD or truck. If not, it's a further three hours to Sankri.

Dodi Tal & Yamunotri

Duration	4 days
Distance	52km
Difficulty	easy
Start	Sangam Chatti
Finish	Hanuman Chatti
Nearest Town	Uttarkashi (pp202–3)
Public Transport	yes
Summary Easily accessible but uncrowded, this trek over the Darwa Pass to a pilgrim town affords inspiring views of the Dhaula Dhar.	

This is an ideal introduction to trekking in the Garhwal. The days include a comparatively easy traverse over the Darwa Pass, with fine views of the Gangotri peaks to the east. To the north, uninterrupted views of the Dhaula Dhar provide a constant backdrop throughout the long descent to the pilgrim town of Hanuman Chatti.

There are interesting side trips, including a foray to the Bandarpunch Base Camp and a trek along the pilgrim trail to Yamunotri – the first of the Char Dham stages followed by thousands of Hindu pilgrims each year.

PLANNING
When to Trek

The Darwa Pass can be crossed by mid-May. The spring trekking season extends to late June before the monsoon rain. September and October are ideal and afford the clearest mountain views.

What to Bring

A tent and stove are essential, with a minimum of two days food for the stages between Dodi Tal and Hanuman Chatti.

Maps

Refer to the Leomann series 1:200,000 *Sheet 7* (*Gangotri, Har ki Dun & Mussoorie*) and the Survey of India Trekking map series 1:250,000 *Gangotri – Yamunotri*. The SFAR 1:150,000 *Garhwal Himalaya (West Section)* is the best available section for this trek. The US Military U502 series 1:250,000 *NI 44-5 ref Dehra Dun* also covers the route.

Accommodation

There are a couple of lodges and a Forest Rest House near Agoda. At Dodi Tal there is a Forest Rest House with double rooms for Rs 200. However, they may be fully booked by Indian trekkers, so the basic shelter and food at one of the dhabas beside the lake may be the only option. Beyond Dodi Tal there is no accommodation other than camping until Hanuman Chatti.

GETTING TO/FROM THE TREK

There are three buses each day from Uttarkashi (Rs 7, one hour) to the trailhead several kilometres below Sangam Chatti. A 4WD will cost Rs 400.

From Hanuman Chatti, there is a bus to Mussoorie (six hours, Rs 80) and Dehra Dun (two hours, Rs 100). Three buses go each day to Uttarkashi (six hours, Rs 50). The last bus leaves around 2pm – handy for porters returning to Uttarkashi.

THE TREK (See map p204)
Day 1: Sangam Chatti to Agoda
2–3 hours, 7km

From Uttarkashi, it is 4km to the 4WD track leading up the Asi Ganga Valley. From the turnoff, the road continues for about 10km towards **Sangam Chatti** (1350m). Buses and 4WDs come this far from Uttarkashi. However, the road is subject to landslides and this should be taken into account when planning the first day.

Sangam Chatti consists of several *dhabas* beside a tributary of the Asi Ganga. Cross the bridge over the side stream and follow the trail on the true right of the valley leading to Agoda. It is a steady ascent through deciduous to semitropical forest. As it approaches the village, the trail is lined with rose bushes and hedgerows. The spring wheat crop is harvested in May, allowing time for a second crop by autumn.

Agoda (2250m) consists of 20 to 30 two-storey, slate-roofed houses, each with a stone courtyard. There is a *Forest Rest House* at the far end of the village. Just beyond the village, there are some small *hotels–cum–tea stalls* run by the local villagers, where meals are also available.

Day 2: Agoda to Dodi Tal
6 hours, 16km
The trail gradually ascends through the forest high above the Asi Ganga before entering a side valley leading to Dodi Tal. Gujar shepherds follow this trail regularly as they carry buffalo milk and produce to the market at Uttarkashi. There is a substantial Gujar settlement at **Majhi** (3150m) about 5km before Dodi Tal, on a ridge that affords a glimpse of Bandarpunch (6316m). The *campsite* here could be convenient if you have made an early start from Uttarkashi and do not want to spend half a day at Agoda.

From Majhi, it is a pleasant trek through rhododendron, oak, pine and bamboo forest around the hillside to **Dodi Tal** (3310m). The lake is set in forest and is about 500m wide. There is a recently constructed temple at its southern end. There are a couple of *dhabas* and a *Forest Rest House* here. There are *camping spots* next to the rest house and at the far side of the lake.

Fishing is banned in the lake, although trekkers are not necessarily deterred. When questioned about this flagrant breaking of the rules, the fishing inspector gave an assurance

that it didn't matter, as he had never seen an amateur angler catch anything!

Day 3: Dodi Tal to Seema via Darwa Pass
6–7 hours, 17km
The trail to the Darwa Pass ascends the valley at the far end of the lake. It crosses the stream flowing into the lake several times before the valley widens. Follow the true right valley that heads towards the pass. It's a pleasant climb through flowered meadows – the rows of rhododendrons here remain in bloom until mid-June. The final climb up the alpine meadows to the pass is short and steep.

The climb from Dodi Tal to the **Darwa Pass** (4150m) can be completed in two to three hours and could be a day walk out of Dodi Tal. However, an early start is imperative if you are to appreciate the range of peaks stretching beyond Gangotri as far as Nanda Devi. To the north of the pass, the peak of Bandarpunch dominates the upper part of the valley. To the northwest, Swargarohini I (6252m) rises above the Har ki Dun Valley.

From the pass, a further climb heads along the ridge to the south. This ridge is under snow until mid-June. The narrow trail continues for 3km to 4km, commanding views of Bandarpunch and the Himalaya Range. For the remainder of this stage, the trail leads across the alpine ridges just above the tree line. A number of idyllic *camping spots* can be seen from the high trail. These include the magnificent campsite at **Seema** (3450m) – a beautiful meadow with rhododendron bushes dotting the pastures, framing Bandarpunch and the nearby snowcapped peaks.

Side Trip: The Base of Bandarpunch
3 days, 30km return
From the Darwa Pass, a steep descent leads through meadows and forest to the Hanuman Ganga. Cross the river by a birch bridge (of sorts) and continue up the true right of the valley. The trail follows the valley floor for 1km before ascending a low ridge and leading through a series of meadows and rhododendron forests to the upper valley. The time from the pass to the *alpine camp* (3700m) is

two to three hours. From the camp, it is a day walk to the snout of the Bandarpunch Glacier.

Retrace the route to Darwa Pass.

Day 4: Seema to Hanuman Chatti
4 hours, 12km

The trail drops steeply – in fact, very steeply in places – past a series of meadows to the settlement at **Kondola** (3050m). It is a short descent to the first village of **Nisu** (2700m). The trail is well maintained from here to Hanuman Chatti. Cross a bridge across a tributary of the Hanuman Ganga and continue for about 1km to **Hanuman Chatti**. Join the pilgrim trail into the main bazaar (2400m).

Side Trip: Yamunotri
2 days, 24km return

This trek to an ancient temple at the source of the Yamuna River is the first stage of the Char Dham, undertaken each season by many thousands of Hindu pilgrims.

From the main bazaar of **Hanuman Chatti**, the trail crosses the bridge over the Hanuman Ganga to the Yamunotri Valley. The first day of the trek is to the village of **Janki Chatti** (2650m), which has many *hotels*, *dhabas* and *rest houses*. There is also a *campsite* on the far side of the valley. As it takes three to four hours (7km) to reach the village, the rest of the day can be spent appreciating the spectrum of Indian society undertaking the pilgrimage. Rich families hire horses and some people are even carried on a *dandy* (wooden platform) supported by four or five porters. The less affluent make their way with the aid of a walking stick.

On the second day, the pilgrims leave early to reach Yamunotri before returning to Hanuman Chatti. From Janki Chatti, the trail starts to steepen and there are plenty of switchbacks as you enter a narrow gorge. It takes about two hours to trek the 5km to **Yamunotri** (3185m). The temple is in the centre of the valley, enclosed by high, snowcapped ridges.

The return to Hanuman Chatti takes three to four hours, depending on the number of pilgrims and horses on the trail.

Source of the Ganges

Duration	5 days
Distance	48km
Difficulty	easy–moderate
Start/Finish	Gangotri
Nearest Town	Uttarkashi (pp202–3)
Public Transport	yes

Summary Follow the pilgrim trail to Gaumukh before ascending to the meadow of Tapovan beneath the sacred summit of Shivling.

The initial days of the trek to Gaumukh are followed by thousands of Hindu pilgrims en route to the sacred source of the Ganges. The pilgrims normally stay overnight at Bhojbasa and depart early the next morning to offer their *darshan* (prayers) at Gaumukh before returning to Gangotri. Other pilgrims on horseback complete the journey there and back in a day, as do those carried on a *dandy*, a wooden platform supported by a team of porters who charge around Rs 3000 for the day.

Acclimatisation is essential before ascending to Tapovan (4450m). Reserve at least two days before ascending to Bhojbasa.

Beyond Gaumukh, the established trail gives way to a poorly defined route across scree and boulder fields to Tapovan. This meadow offers uninterrupted views of the Bhagirathi peaks, which define this part of the Himalaya Range.

Experienced trekkers may also consider the Gangotri Glacier side trip (p217) before returning to Gangotri.

PLANNING
When to Trek
The trail is normally open by early May and is regularly followed until late June. The monsoon rain in July and August can (as elsewhere in the Garhwal) lead to landslides across the trail. Mid-September until mid-October is ideal for trekking.

What to Bring
A tent and stove are essential when trekking above Gaumukh. Also bring food supplies for the time above Gaumukh.

Maps

Refer to the Leomann series 1:200,000 *Sheet 7 (Gangotri, Har ki Dun & Mussoorie)*. Also refer to the Survey of India Trekking map series 1:250,000 *Gangotri – Yamunotri*. The SFAR 1:150,000 *Garhwal Himalaya (West Section)* is the best available section for this trek. The US Military U502 series 1:250,000 *NI 44-5 ref Dehra Dun* also covers the route.

Accommodation

Gangotri has many small hotels, including the GMVN Rest House, with doubles/dorms for Rs 400/100. There is no shortage of dhabas offering food and a bed for the night en route to Gaumukh. There is also a GMVN hotel at Bhojbasa with doubles/dorms for Rs 200/80. However, these are all heavily booked, particularly in May and June. At Tapovan, basic dhaba accommodation run by *sadhus* (wandering Hindu holy men/women) may be available. Check with the dhaba owners before leaving Gaumukh as they will know what is available.

GETTING TO/FROM THE TREK

There are regular buses from Uttarkashi to Gangotri (Rs 60, five to six hours). After the trek, the last bus to Uttarkashi normally leaves Gangotri at around 2pm.

THE TREK (See map p205)
Day 1: Gangotri to Chirbasa

4 hours, 9km

From **Gangotri** (3050m), the trail passes the Gangotri Temple on the true right of the valley. Just beyond the temple, concrete steps lead up to the main trail. The trail is well defined with stone markers every kilometre. After the first 4km, there are *dhabas* at **Raj Ghat** (3250m), where a tributary flows into the valley. The former pilgrim trail can be seen following the valley floor in places. The present trail has only been upgraded in the past 20 to 30 years.

Beyond Raj Ghat the glacial valley begins to widen. Just before Chirbasa you will gain the first views of the Bhagirathi peaks, including Bhagirathi I (6856m), at the head of the valley.

At **Chirbasa** (3600m), dhabas line the trail. There is a sheltered *campsite* below the trail close to the river.

Day 2: Chirbasa to Bhojbasa

2–2½ hours, 5km

Just beyond Chirbasa, the trail passes the last of the silver birches, which frame the Bhagirathi Range and the upper section of Shivling (6543m). To the south, the peak of Bhrigu Parbat (6041m) looms high above the valley.

The trail gradually ascends the next 5km to Bhojbasa. Here, it is above the tree line, although juniper bushes are scattered up the otherwise barren hillside. Just below Bhojbasa, the trail leads through an extensive boulder field – a hot and dusty section on a warm day.

Bhojbasa (3790m) is a rather desolate camp with a crowded *GMVN hotel* and a shelter for the less affluent pilgrims. A small **temple** and a potential *campsite* are down towards the river.

Day 3: Bhojbasa to Tapovan

5–6 hours, 10km

From Bhojbasa, trek for 1½ hours to reach the dhabas below Gaumukh. This is as far as the porters and the horses go. It is a further 2km to **Gaumukh** (3890m). The trail leads through moraine, and boulders deposited by many landslides. It is hard going, particularly for those pilgrims who until now have been on horseback or carried on a *dandy*. The proposed construction of a bridge over the river just before Gaumukh will avoid most of the route across the terminal moraine, and shorten this day by at least an hour.

The final 500m to the **source of the Ganges** follows a trail along the riverbank. The pilgrims conduct their darshan as close as possible to where the river flows from the ice wall (the Cow's Mouth) beneath the terminal moraine.

The trail (main route) to Tapovan diverts from the main pilgrim trail (beside the last dhabas), just before the final 500m to Gaumukh. It ascends the terminal moraine of the Gangotri Glacier for about 1km before splitting. The trail to the true right of the valley leads to Nandanban (see Side Trip), while the trail on the true left (the south side of the valley) leads to Tapovan. Even with the stone cairns marking the trail, the route is not easy to follow, and the services of a local guide are essential.

The trail traverses the terminal moraine above Gaumukh before rising abruptly up the side ridge to Tapovan. Take great care not to dislodge rocks and boulders onto trekkers below.

Tapovan (4450m) is a very pleasant surprise. It is a large meadow complete with bubbling streams, wildflowers and *campsites* beneath the imposing peak of Shivling. On the far side of the glacier the Bhagirathi peaks, including Bhagirathi I, Bhagirathi II (6512m) and Bhagirathi III (6454m), provide an equally impressive backdrop. It is little wonder that sadhus choose this spot for extended meditation during the long summer months.

Side Trip: Gangotri Glacier to Nandanban & Gaumukh
7 hours, 14km
From Tapovan, there is the option of crossing the Gangotri Glacier to the camp at **Nandanban** (4340m). Groups with no previous experience of crossing glaciers should not proceed without an experienced guide.

The route from Tapovan leads from the upper section of the meadow down and onto the glacier. It will take three to four hours to cross the Gangotri Glacier. Plan for an additional hour to scramble up the scree to the Nandanban *campsite*.

From Nandanban, it is a two-hour trek (6km) down to the lateral moraine on the far side of the valley to Gaumukh.

Days 4 & 5: Tapovan to Gangotri
2 days, 24km
It takes a couple of hours to descend directly to Gaumukh before following the pilgrim trail to Chirbasa for the night. The following morning it should take no more than three hours to return to Gangotri, with time to catch onward transport the same day.

Khatling Glacier

Duration	7 days
Distance	119km
Difficulty	easy–moderate
Start/Finish	Ghuttu
Nearest Town	Rishikesh (pp201–2)
Public Transport	yes

Summary Trek through Hindu villages, mixed forest and flowered meadows to an impressive range of peaks and glaciers above the spectacular Khatling Glacier.

Although Ghuttu is marked as a small and rather insignificant village on most maps of the Garhwal, it is the starting point for one of the finest treks in Uttaranchal. The trek is alongside the Bhilan Ganga, an important tributary of the Ganges, flowing from the extensive snowfields of the Khatling Glacier.

The trek to the Khatling Cave is easy. However, beyond the cave, there are more strenuous sections over scree and boulders to reach the snout of the glacier. There are also a couple of river crossings en route to the alpine meadow of Chobia.

From Chobia, a side trip leads to Marsar Tal. It's possible to continue across the high ridges to Kedarnath and Gaurikund.

PLANNING
When to Trek
May and June are ideal to appreciate the wildflowers and rhododendrons before the monsoon rain. Mid-September until mid-October is a further opportunity to trek before the onset of winter snows.

What to Bring
A tent, stove and appropriate warm clothing is essential. Food is difficult to obtain from the villages; carry all supplies.

Maps
Refer to the Leomann series 1:200,000 *Sheet 7 (Gangotri, Har ki Dun & Mussoorie)* and the Survey of India Trekking map series 1:250,000 *Gangotri – Yamunotri*. The SFAR 1:150,000 *Garhwal Himalaya (West Section)* is the best available section

for this trek. The US Military U502 series 1:250,000 *NI 44-5 ref Dehra Dun* also covers the route.

Local Trekking Agents

While there are no trekking agents in Ghuttu, the chowkidar at the Forest Rest House can put you in touch with local porters. They charge around Rs 150 per day.

Accommodation

Ghuttu has a Forest Rest House, which has double rooms for Rs 300. The GMVN Rest House at Reeh and Forest Rest House at Gangi both offer rooms/dorm beds for Rs 200/60. Beyond Gangi there is no accommodation except for the rock shelter at Khatling Cave.

GETTING TO/FROM THE TREK

There is only one direct bus from Rishikesh to Ghuttu (Rs 70, eight hours), which leaves early in the morning. Alternatively, change buses at Tehri. A 4WD from Rishikesh to Ghuttu will cost around Rs 1800. From Ghuttu, the 7am bus goes direct to Rishikesh, while the last bus to Tehri (with onward connections) departs at 2pm.

THE TREK (See map p205)
Day 1: Ghuttu to Reeh
3½–4 hours, 10km

Beyond Ghuttu (1520m) follow the village trail on the true right of the river to **Devling** before a gradual ascent through chir pine, rhododendron and bamboo. There is a split in the trail after about 7km. Take the lower trail following the course of the river to the village of **Reeh** (2130m), which has a well-appointed *GMVN Forest Rest House*.

Day 2: Reeh to Gangi
3½–4 hours, 12km

Cross the bridge over the tributary just beyond Reeh and commence a steady 500m ascent to a series of meadows high above the valley. From the top of the ridge, fine views extend back down the valley to the ridge of Panwali Kantha and the region south of Ghuttu. The trail continues through oak and rhododendron forest to **Nerlan** (2550m).

Trek for a further 4km to **Gangi** (2590m), one of the largest villages in the Bhilan Ganga valley. Along with its 30 or so houses, there is a Hindu **temple** just before the village and a *Forest Rest House* just beyond the village.

Day 3: Gangi to Kharsoli
6 hours, 15km

The trail descends through forest to the valley floor and **Deordi** (2450m), the last village in the valley. The trail follows the Bhilan Ganga for a further 2km to the meadows of **Kalyani**. Here the trail splits, with the upper trail, and the trek route, winding up to **Shastru Tal**.

This trek takes the lower trail along the riverbank. It is well marked, through rhododendron and spruce forest. An occasional tiring climb is necessary to avoid areas where the floodwaters of the Bhilan Ganga have swept away the trail. There are intermittent views of the wall of snowcapped peaks at the head of the valley.

The meadow of **Kharsoli** (2890m) is a great *campsite*, just beyond the confluence of the substantial side river flowing into the Bhilan Ganga.

Day 4: Kharsoli to Khatling Cave
4–5 hours, 12km

The trail follows the river before entering a forest of oak, spruce and silver birch. The impressive **waterfalls** on the opposite side of the valley provide an additional attraction on the 3km to 4km trek to the shepherd encampment at **Bhelbagi** (3100m). Here, the local villagers graze their sheep, goats and cattle during summer.

From Bhelbagi the trail winds past stands of silver birch. A steep ascent leads across a scree slope to another encampment, **Tambakund**. The time required to trek from Kharsoli is around three hours.

From the open meadow at Tambakund, the trail winds through alpine meadow, juniper and silver birch to the **Khatling Cave** (3650m). There is a sheltered *campsite* a few minutes beyond the cave, although the porters tend to favour staying in the cave.

Shipton & Tilman: The 1934 Badrinath-Kedarnath Traverse

The remote mountain trails linking the sacred sources of the Ganges have been the subject of myth and legend since the earliest pilgrims ventured into the Himalaya. The high, remote trails linking Gangotri, Kedarnath and Badrinath were the particular focus of attention for a number of expeditions during the 1930s, including that of the legendry British mountaineers Shipton and Tilman. During their epic expedition to Nanda Devi and its environs in 1934, they explored the possibility of crossing the watersheds linking Badrinath, Gangotri and Kedarnath. Although pilgrim folklore maintained that such routes existed, the demands of climbing high and remote glaciers led Shipton and Tilman to think otherwise.

After forging their way up the Rishi Ganga to the Nanda Devi Sanctuary in May 1934, the team of Shipton, Tilman and three Sherpas turned their attention to the Badrinath-Gangotri crossing. From Badrinath, they headed up the Arwa Valley, exploring several side glaciers before crossing the Kalindi Khal (5960m), the pass marking the watershed between the Alaknanda and the Bhagirathi river systems. Beyond the pass the team descended to the Gangotri Glacier and Gaumukh. Returning via the same route, the group seemed ideally prepared for the next challenge – the crossing from Badrinath to Kedarnath.

The party prepared for a week's trekking and set out on 5 August, immediately encountering the full force of the monsoon. Incessant rain obliterated views of even the most impressive peaks as well as the route for the days ahead. They ascended the Satopath Glacier before negotiating a formidable icefall leading to the pass.

It took five long and demanding days to reach the Satopath Col (5420m), marking the watershed between the Alaknanda and the Mandakini river systems. The thick monsoon clouds prevented any view of the heavily forested terrain leading towards Kedarnath, or of the steep icefall below the pass. When the team finally made it down to the upper forest level, their supplies were almost exhausted and their gear was soaked.

On 12 August, after travelling only a small distance down the gorge, they reached a side river flowing from the slopes of the Chaukhamba Range. It took two days to find a crossing point. They were reduced to living off the land, while doing their best to protect themselves from the rain. On a typical day they would travel no more than 2km, existing on a diet of wild fungus and the ubiquitous bamboo. On 18 August they finally reached the established pilgrim trail to Kalimath.

In view of the exceptional terrain, it is not surprising that the route was not successfully completed again until 64 years later. In 1998 a small joint British/Indian expedition (whose party included Eric Shipton's son John) completed the route. Refer to the 1999 *Himalayan Journal* for a full description of the 1998 crossing. For the complete account of the 1934 traverse, read *Nanda Devi* by Eric Shipton, now published in *The Six Mountain-Travel Books*.

Day 5: Khatling Cave to Khatling Glacier & Chobia

6 hours, 18km

This can be a tiring day. The trail descends steeply to the riverbank before ascending boulder and scree slopes beside the Bhilan Ganga. The trail remains on the true right of the river for around 3km before reaching a wide glacial fan extending from the terminal moraine of the Khatling Glacier. The trekking becomes easier from here to **Zero Point** (3710m), where the river emerges from the glacier.

The views up the glacier include the Jogin peaks, while to the north are impressive hanging glaciers. To the east, another range of 6000m peaks complete an almost 360-degree mountain panorama.

To reach Chobia, cross the river flowing from the Khatling Glacier to reach the true left of the valley. One option is to climb above Zero Point and traverse across the snout of the glacier. This takes at least two hours. The alternative is to select a place to cross the braided river, which will mean getting your feet wet.

Once on the true left the valley, head towards the terminal moraine of the Phatling Glacier. There is no trail across the moraine and a short steep ascent is necessary before descending to **Chobia** (3400m). This alpine meadow has many good *campsites* and is ideal for a rest day or two. It is also a convenient base for the side trip to Marsar Tal.

Side Trip: Marsar Tal
9 hours, 22km return
From Chobia, cross the stream flowing from the east and ascend the alpine ridges on the true left of the valley. Follow the ill-defined shepherds trail (steep in places) across boulder fields; be prepared for the occasional rock scramble. The views are magnificent: across the upper sections of the Khatling Glacier and towards the high pass – the Auden Col (5400m) – leading to Gangotri. The Jogin peaks are in view, as is Jaonli (6630m). Thalay Sagar (6361m), Kirti Stambh (6270m) and Bharte Khunta (6578m) rise above the Phatling Glacier.

The last 2km leads across high alpine pastures and scree slopes to the serene waters of **Marsar Tal** (4590m), which is frozen until at least mid-June. Retrace the outward route to Chobia.

The ridge immediately to the east of Marsar Tal defines the route to **Vasuki Tal** and **Kedarnath**. It is a one-day trek to Vasuki Tal and a further day to Kedarnath, with time to follow the pilgrim trail to the trailhead at Gaurikund.

Days 6 & 7: Chobia to Ghuttu
2 days, 52km
Allow two days to return to Ghuttu. The first day, trek back down the valley to Gangi. The trail down to Reeh and along the forest trail to Ghuttu can easily be completed the following day.

From Chobia, it's about a 3km trek back to Khatling Cave. Avoid returning to the glacier by choosing a safe place to cross the Bhilan Ganga. A tiring climb to the cave follows. Check whether the shepherds have reconstructed the bridge about 1km south of the meadow, as this will avoid fording the river and the climb.

Hem Kund & Valley of the Flowers

Duration	4 days
Distance	55km
Difficulty	easy
Start/Finish	Govind Ghat
Nearest Town	Joshimath (p203)
Public Transport	yes

Summary Follow the Sikh pilgrims to the sacred Hem Kund and take day treks to the renowned Bhyundar Valley – the *Valley of the Flowers*.

Thousands of Sikh pilgrims trek this route each year, while the Valley of the Flowers has been an attraction for botanists worldwide ever since it was 'discovered' in 1931. The trail to the Valley of the Flowers branches off the main pilgrim trail just beyond Ghangaria – camping in the national park is not permitted so each night you need to return to Ghangaria.

While the well-defined trails suit the novice trekker, acclimatisation is a major problem, particularly as most trekkers ascend to Hem Kund (4330m) within a day of leaving Govind Ghat (1830m). Few pilgrims would return to Govind Ghat without at least getting a headache.

PLANNING
When to Trek
The trail is usually open from May until mid-October. In May the upper stages of the trek will be under snow, while the monsoon rain falls in July and August.

In spring, visit the Valley of the Flowers as soon as the winter snows melt in May. The wildflowers are best in July and August. Unfortunately, this is also when the mountain roads to Govind Ghat are subject to landslides.

What to Bring
It is not necessary to bring a tent, stove and cooking equipment if you intend to stay in one of the many hotels in Ghangaria, where you return to every day. There are also dhabas on every twist and turn of the trail

so there is no need to bring food, except snacks for day walks in the Bhyundar Valley.

Maps

Refer to the Leomann series 1:200,000 *Sheet 8* (*Pindari Glacier, Badrinath & Nanda Devi*). Also refer to the Survey of India Trekking map series 1:250,000 *Badri – Kedar*. The US Military U502 series 1:250,000 *NI 44-6 ref Nanda Devi* covers the route. You may also consult the SFAR 1:150,000 series *Garhwal Himalaya* but you will need both the east and west sections.

Accommodation

There are many hotels in Govind Ghat at the trailhead. Ghangaria has a GMVN hotel with doubles/dorms for Rs 400/80. There are also many private hotels, charging from Rs 100 to Rs 500 depending on the season (high season is May, June & Sept).

GETTING TO/FROM THE TREK

There are regular buses between Joshimath to Govind Ghat (Rs 10, one hour). A 4WD will cost Rs 300. From Joshimath, most buses continue to Badrinath.

THE TREK (See map pp206–7)
Day 1: Govind Ghat to Ghangaria
5–6 hours, 14km

Govind Ghat (1830m), on the true right bank of the Alaknanda River, has hotels, dhabas, pilgrim shelters and ritual bathing areas, along with vendors selling colourful bangles and combs.

Cross the suspension bridge over the Alaknanda River and commence the steady ascent on the concrete path to the village of **Pulana** (2100m).

Beyond Pulana continue along the well-defined trail that leads through a mixed forest of oak, rhododendron, spruce and silver fir before winding down to the bridge over the Hem Ganga. The trail ascends steeply at first though the forest before gradually winding across the meadows to Ghangaria. En route there are many *dhabas*.

Ghangaria (3050m), also known as Govind Dham, is a large pilgrim complex, including a *gurdwara* (Sikh temple), small *guesthouses* and a *GMVN hotel*. The more impeccably dressed pilgrim may like to visit the village Tailor & Drycleaner.

The *camping ground* is about 2km below Ghangaria near the helicopter landing pad. Above the Hem Ganga it provides a modicum of serenity after a hectic day on the pilgrim trail.

Day 2: Hem Kund Day Trek
5–6 hours, 12km

Cross the bridge above Ghangaria over the Hem Ganga. The trail ascends steeply at first before crossing a series of meadows to the stands of silver birch marking the upper tree line at around 3500m. The trail is well defined and after each major switchback there is a *dhaba* serving tea and snacks.

While the stone steps that mark the final 300m to Hem Kund may appear inviting, they are considerably more tiring than the long and gradual switchbacks followed by the horse attendants.

On arrival at **Hem Kund** (4330m), most pilgrims wash themselves in the icy waters of the lake before visiting the gurdwara, built around 20 years ago. The lake was 'discovered' in 1930 by a teacher from a Sikh religious centre who set out to identify where the Sikh guru Gobind Singh meditated in a former life. The description of the locality in the Sikh holy book *Dasam Granth* fits Hem Kund – a remote lake surrounded by seven snowcapped peaks.

The return to Ghangaria is by the same route. The exhilaration of visiting the lake, together with the downhill, ensures that most pilgrims are back to Ghangaria within a couple of hours.

Day 3: Valley of the Flowers Day Trek
5–6 hours, 15km

From Ghangaria, recross the bridge over the Hem Ganga and commence the climb to the entrance of the Bhyundar Valley. The checkpoint just above the crossing charges an entrance fee to the Valley of the Flowers National Park (Rs 100 for foreigners, Rs 15 for Indian trekkers).

Valley of the Flowers

The Bhyundar Valley was first brought to the attention of mountain enthusiasts and botanists by Frank Smythe in 1931 after a successful climb on Kamet. The team crossed the Bhyundar Pass in the lashing rain and mist, intent on forging a new route through the mountains back to Joshimath. As they descended into the shelter of the valley, the clouds lifted and revealed alpine meadows carpeted with wildflowers. They were greeted with the sight of primula, saxifrage, red potentillas, geraniums, asters, gentians, anemones, delphiniums, blue corydalis and wild roses. The many hundreds of flowering species lead Smythe to refer to the Bhyundar Valley as the Valley of the Flowers.

While Smythe was justifiably enthusiastic about the great range of flowers he saw, it is a matter of debate as to whether the Bhyundar Valley is the best place for appreciating Uttaranchal's wildflowers. There are many *bugyals* (high-altitude meadows) that are equally attractive. Also on treks in this chapter, these include the bugyals en route to the Kuari Pass, and the meadows above Dodi Tal and near the Khatling Glacier. The alpine meadows beneath the Rupin Pass or those in the upper Har ki Dun Valley are also worthy of a visit.

Wherever you choose to trek, bring a copy of Polunin and Stainton's *Flowers of the Himalaya*. Reprints of Frank Smythe's *The Valley of the Flowers* are available in Delhi.

About 2km to 3km beyond the checkpoint, the trail crosses the stream flowing from the Bhyundar Valley and continues on the true right. The 5km climb is more gradual than the one to Hem Kund. On the ascent, the trail enters a gorge before the valley widens. There is a permanent snow bridge over one of the larger side streams. This marks the entrance to the valley.

The Bhyundar Valley is a glacial valley about 10km long and 2km wide, at an altitude of between 3650m and 3950m. It is characterised by alpine glades, silver birch trees and rhododendrons, and is enclosed by the peaks of Nar Parbat (5855m), Nilgiri Parbat (6474m), Rataban (6166m) and Ghori Parbat (6708m).

Well-marked trails lead to meadows supporting a profusion of wildflowers. Plan to spend at least three days appreciating the multitude of species. Since 1983, grazing has been banned in the park and there is debate about the (detrimental) effect on the variety of wildflowers.

Return to Ghangaria via the same route.

Day 4: Ghangaria to Govind Ghat
5 hours, 14km

The return trek to Govind Ghat can be completed in a morning, allowing time to return to Joshimath the same day.

Kuari Pass

Duration	5 days
Distance	75km
Difficulty	moderate
Start	Auli
Finish	Ghat
Nearest Town	Joshimath (p203)
Public Transport	yes

Summary Ascend through alpine meadows to the Kuari Pass and gain impressive views of the Great Himalaya and Zanskar Ranges before continuing through mixed forest and traditional Hindu villages.

Trekking over the Kuari Pass affords some of the finest views of the Himalaya – including the many peaks near Nanda Devi. This trek was a favourite of the British trekkers. The pass was often referred to as the Curzon Pass because of former Viceroy George Nathaniel Curzon's love for the region, although he never crossed the pass; his party turned back after an attack by a swarm of bees!

Although the Kuari Pass (3640m) is not high by Himalayan standards, take an additional day for acclimatisation, particularly if considering camping near the pass.

Beyond the pass the trail leads through a number of valleys with plenty of ascents and descents. The trek can also be extended to Rup Kund (see pp226–8) for an exhilarating 10- to 12-day expedition.

PLANNING
When to Trek
The trail can normally be followed from mid-May until late October, although expect residual snow on the upper sections early in the season. Mid-September to mid-October is an ideal time to trek.

What to Bring
A tent, stove and cooking gear are necessary, as are food supplies for the whole trek.

Maps
Refer to the Leomann series 1:200,000 *Sheet 8 (Pindari Glacier, Badrinath & Nanda Devi)*. Also refer to the Survey of India Trekking map series 1:250,000 *Badri – Kedar*. The US Military U502 series 1:250,000 *NI 44-6 ref Nanda Devi* includes most of the trek. The SFAR 1:150,000 *Garhwal Himalaya (West Section)* includes only the days up to and near the Kuari Pass.

Accommodation
There is a GMVN hotel at Auli, followed by camping until Ghangri, which has a Forest Rest House. There are some lodges at Ramni and a few guesthouses at Ghat. You could continue to the comfortable Tourist Rest House at Nandprayag, with rooms for around Rs 200 and a hot shower.

GETTING TO/FROM THE TREK
There is a regular bus service from Joshimath to Auli (Rs 10, one hour). From Ghat, there are 4WDs to Nandprayag available on a per seat basis (Rs 30, one to 1½ hours). From Nandprayag, regular buses go to Srinagar and Dehra Dun. For the porters, the last bus to Joshimath departs around 4pm.

THE TREK (See map pp206–7)
Day 1: Auli to Chitraganta Meadow
6–7 hours, 15km
Auli (2750m) is a small settlement that has recently developed into a thriving ski resort.

It also supports a sizeable army camp. The distinctive summit of Nanda Devi can be seen at the head of the sanctuary.

The trail heads up the hillside beyond the ski lift before reaching a small oak and holly forest. A small **temple** is passed before the trail emerges at the base of the extensive series of meadows of **Gurson Bugyal**. The shepherd routes split on these initial stages but this trek follows the trail heading up towards the grazing meadows. Once you are through the forest, there are many views of the classic route up the Rishi Ganga into the Nanda Devi Sanctuary, where the trail via Lata and Lata Kharak to the Dharansi Pass (4667m) can be appreciated on the far side of the valley.

The trail beyond Gurson Bugyal is steep in places, before crossing a rocky outcrop to a small lake. Alongside the lake is a well-constructed trail from Tabovan village.

Continue through a hemlock, oak and rhododendron forest for 2km to 3km before a short descent to the *meadow* at **Chitraganta** (3310m). The impressive snowcapped ridge includes Chaukhamba I (7138m), II (7068m), III (6974m) and IV (6854m), and can be seen beyond Joshimath.

The shepherds living in the meadows here and nearby are mostly from Rishikesh or Hardiwar, and graze flocks of sheep and goats here in summer. There is a small spring line at the head of the meadow for replenishing your water supply.

Day 2: Chitraganta to Dakwani via Kuari Pass
4–5 hours, 14km
Ascend the ridge above Chitraganta. Cairns mark the track, which is being upgraded by the villagers from Tabovan. Just below the pass the trail leads through a large meadow affording spectacular views of the Himalaya and Zanskar Ranges. North of Joshimath is the Chaukhamba Range, while the summits of Mana (7272m), Kamet (7756m) and Abl Gamin (7355m) extend to the Tibet border. In the middle foreground, a number of spectacular peaks including Dunagiri (7066m) and Changabang (6864m) enclose the Nanda Devi Sanctuary.

Nanda Devi Sanctuary

Nanda Devi (7816m) is the highest peak completely within India. It is surrounded by a huge circle of mountain walls with only one outlet, where the Rishi Ganga forges a route through deep, almost impenetrable gorges before flowing into the Alaknanda River. Given these natural defences, it was not until 1934 that the first mountaineers were finally able to reach the base of Nanda Devi.

In the 1830s GW Traill, the first Commissioner of Kumaon, explored the glacial systems to the south and east of the sanctuary. He ascended the Pindari Glacier and crossed the Pindari Kanda (known also as Traills Pass) to the Gori Ganga. However, neither he nor the parties that also took this route in the following decades attempted to enter the sanctuary.

In 1883 WW Graham attempted a route following the course of the Rishi Ganga. The small expedition managed to make its way over the Dharansi Pass (4667m) before heading down the slippery slopes to the Rishi Ganga. Here they discovered that there were two sanctuaries; inner and outer. They had reached the outer sanctuary, with access to the north up the Ramani Glacier to Changabang and Dunagiri, while to the south a huge glacier flowed from the base of Trisul. However, the inner sanctuary and the base of Nanda Devi were further up the Rishi Ganga through a formidable gorge.

In 1905 the British mountaineer Dr GT Longstaff explored a possible route to the east of the sanctuary, climbing a pass (the Longstaff Col) south of Nanda Devi East (7434m). This route proved to be unfeasible, with steep ice cliffs falling away into the inner sanctuary. Longstaff returned in May 1907. This time he followed the route over the Dharansi Pass but was defeated by the spring snow. Undeterred, the small party headed north to the Bagini Glacier and over the Bagini Pass (6128m), a high pass between Dunagiri and Changabang. The party descended the Ramani Glacier to the Rishi Ganga, to the point reached by WW Graham's party in 1883. Faced with the same difficulty of finding a route

---

There are many *campsites* nearby. In fact, a short day from Chitraganta could be combined with a trek along the adjoining ridge that heads towards the Nanda Devi Sanctuary. Here there are possible vantage points for Nanda Devi's distinctive profile, including the twin peaks of the main summit (7816m) and the East summit (7434m).

The **Kuari Pass** (3640m) is by no means demanding – just a small col in a grassy ridge. Looking south, there are impressive views across the forest ridges, while Dakwani can also be spotted. The initial, steep 200m descent is difficult at the best of times, and especially tricky if wet and slippery. On the true right of the gorge, the route heads past a small shepherd encampment to a clearing at **Dakwani** (3300m), suitable for a *campsite*. This marks the upper limit of the mixed oak and pine forest.

Day 3: Dakwani to Ghangri
7 hours, 16km

The forest trail descends to a small wooden bridge over the river flowing from the Kuari Pass. After crossing, there is a short ascent to a small ridge before a long descent to an impressive **waterfall**. It is a long and gradual ascent through oak, hemlock, silver birch and rhododendron forest to **Sutoli** meadow (2980m). If you plan to head to Sutoli direct from the Kuari Pass, allow approximately four hours.

The shepherds from the nearby villages tend their buffalo here during summer. There are clear views back to Dakwani and the Kuari Pass, while the tips of the peaks beyond Joshimath peep above the ridge to the west of the valley. From the meadow, the trail rounds a wooded ridge (3020m) with views of Nanda Ghunti (6309m) on the western rim of the Nanda Devi Sanctuary.

There are some *campsites* on the gradual descent to the prosperous village of **Pana** (2450m). After the village, the trail crosses a small tributary via a concrete bridge. The trail splits 1km beyond here: the upper route leads to Irani village, the district headquarters; the lower trail (main route) goes direct to Ghangri. The descent to the Brithi

Nanda Devi Sanctuary

up the Rishi Gorge, the party explored the outer sanctuary. Longstaff made the first ascent of Trisul (7120m) later that season.

In 1932 Hugh Ruttledge attempted to reach the inner sanctuary via a pass at the head of the Sunderdhunga Glacier. He was unsuccessful, with reports of a huge 3000m ice wall at the glacier's head.

In 1934 HW Tilman and Eric Shipton, together with three Sherpas, attempted the route up the Rishi Ganga. They forged through the Rishi Gorge to become the first party to enter the inner sanctuary and reach the base of Nanda Devi. Later that season they returned to recce a climbing route up Nanda Devi before heading south over the Sunderdhunga Col and Sunderdhunga Glacier. This drew unqualified applause from the climbing circles of the day.

In 1936, while Shipton was engaged on Everest, Tilman and a group of American mountaineers made the first successful ascent of Nanda Devi, before exiting via the Longstaff Col to the Gori Ganga. In June 1939 a Polish expedition made the first ascent of Nanda Devi East (7434m), via the Longstaff Col.

It was not until the post-war years that increasing numbers of expeditions began to enter the sanctuary. The lifting of Inner Line restrictions in 1974 resulted in a large number of climbing expeditions and trekkers making their way up the Rishi Ganga. Within a few seasons the large herds of bharal and musk deer were forced from their natural habitat, and there was wholesale destruction of birch trees – either cut down for bridge construction or for camp fires when groups returned to base camp.

Increasing environmental pressure finally led the Uttar Pradesh government to close the sanctuary in 1983. Since then the forest guards at Lata have not permitted expeditions, or local shepherds with their flocks, inside the sanctuary. Whatever the future plans of the government, it is unlikely that the inner sanctuary will be reopened in the near future.

Ganga is steep and steamy in places with bamboo, tropical undergrowth and the occasional troop of langurs. Cross the large suspension bridge over the river before a 200m ascent to Ghangri.

Ghangri (2000m) is a small village at the entrance to the upper Brithi Ganga Valley. The well-maintained *Forest Rest House* is immediately above the village. Alternatively you may spend the night at the *schoolhouse*, set in a garden of marigolds.

The villagers at Ghangri usually take a full day to trek down the valley to Chamoli. The trail is cut off by snow between December and late February.

Day 4: Ghangri to Ramni
5–6 hours, 15km

Climb for 450m through the forest to a small clearing. Cross the clearing before a further ascent to a wooded ridge at 2900m, marking the watershed between the Brithi Ganga and the Nandakini valleys. The trek from Ghangri village to the ridge should take about four hours. There is a cairn on top

of the ridge, just below is a *campsite* with views back to Pana.

A gradual descent takes you through pastures and forests where villagers from Ramni graze their animals in summer. After about 4km, the trail crosses an open meadow with views of Kunol village and the route to Wan and Rup Kund. To the north, the snowcapped ridges of the Chaukhamba Range are easily recognisable beyond Joshimath. There is also a small spring line, which makes the spot an ideal *campsite*. **Ramni** (2550m) includes a few shops serving the outlying villages, some *dhabas* and a couple of *lodges*.

Day 5: Ramni to Ghat
4–5 hours, 15km

From Ramni, the trail leads through the village fields and houses below Ramni for 4km before descending, steeply in places, through a conifer and oak forest to the Nandakini River. Remain on the true right side of the valley until the bridge over the Nandakini River leads to the bazaar and *dhabas* at **Ghat** (1330m).

Rup Kund

Duration	7 days
Distance	101km
Difficulty	moderate
Start	Ghat
Finish	Mundoli
Nearest Town	Joshimath (p203)
Public Transport	yes

Summary Trek through traditional Hindu villages and ascend through mixed forest and alpine meadows to the mysterious lake of Rup Kund.

For many years, Rup Kund has attracted attention because of the human skeletons clearly visible at the bottom of the shallow lake. Pilgrims and trekkers ascend the extensive bugyals to the small and often snowbound lake set beneath the impressive backdrop of Trisul (7120m).

The trek can be completed either from Ghat or Mundoli, although extra time should be reserved for acclimatisation if trekking from Mundoli. This trek can also be combined with the Kuari Pass trek (pp222–5).

PLANNING
When to Trek
The higher stages of the trek to Rup Kund are under deep snow until early June. Even in June there is likely to be considerable snow above Bedni Bugyal. The ideal time to trek is from mid-September until mid-October.

What to Bring
Carry a tent, stove, cooking gear and food for at least two or three days.

Maps
Refer to the Leomann series 1:200,000 *Sheet 8* (*Pindari Glacier, Badrinath & Nanda Devi*). Also refer to the Survey of India Trekking map series 1:250,000 *Badri – Kedar*. The US Military U502 series 1:250,000 *NI 44-6 ref Nanda Devi* covers the sections between Ramni and Rup Kund.

Accommodation
It is possible to get by without a tent, providing you are prepared to stay in very basic huts on the higher days of the trek. There is a comfortable Tourist Rest House at Nandprayag before commencing the trek. Ramni has a couple of private lodges and a village store, and there is a similar set-up at Sutol. At Wan there is a GMVN hotel, with rooms for Rs 400 per double. There are basic pilgrim huts at Bedni Bugyal and Bhugu Basa. There is a GMVN hotel at Loharjang just before the trailhead at Mundoli.

GETTING TO/FROM THE TREK
From Nandprayag, 4WDs are available on a per-seat basis to Ghat (Rs 30, one to 1½ hours). Regular buses go to Nandprayag from Joshimath, Srinagar and Dehra Dun.

After the trek, there is a bus from Mundoli to Debal (Rs 18, two hours). Shared 4WDs are also available (Rs 30 per seat). From Debal, there are buses to Karnaprayag, with onward connections to Srinagar and Dehra Dun. There is also a direct overnight bus to Delhi (Rs 200).

Alternatively, take the local bus to Tharali and catch an onward bus via Gwaldam to Almora (Rs 60, seven to eight hours). From Almora, many buses go to Naini Tal and overnight buses head direct to Delhi.

THE TREK (See map pp206–7)
Day 1: Ghat to Ramni
7 hours, 15km

From **Ghat** (1330m), cross the bridge over the Nandakini River and ascend to Ramni. The well-defined trail through conifer forest is steep in places before crossing a small ridge, the Bota Khal, leading to the fields and houses below **Ramni** (2550m). Stay at one of the *lodges* or *camp* about 1km above the village to gain views of the peaks beyond Joshimath.

Day 2: Ramni to Sutol
6–7 hours, 16km

A well-defined trail leads high above the river along the true right of the Nandakini Valley. **Ali** (2350m) is the first of a number of well-maintained and friendly villages. Some of the more prosperous houses have commissioned ornate woodcarvings above their doors, such as statues of Ganesh (the elephant-headed god). From Ali, the trail gradually ascends to the small village of **Pehri** (2500m) before descending to a tributary. From the bridge, it is a further 5km to **Sutol** (2200m). There is an excellent *campsite* beside the river, and a couple of *lodges* and a *store* in the village.

Day 3: Sutol to Wan
5 hours, 14km

The forest trail ascends to Kunol. Steep in places, the trail is lined with orchids and luxuriant ferns, as it passes through one of the finest mixed forests in Garhwal. Barking deer have been seen in the forest clearing, while the heavy, spiked collars worn by the shepherd dogs indicate the need for protection from leopards.

The village at **Kunol** (2650m) has an idyllic location with views of the high peaks north of Joshimath. It has a *Forest Rest House*. Above the village, the rhododendron trees remain in full bloom from April until early June.

To reach Wan, there is a small ridge pass (2900m) to cross. The pass is not demanding and the views of the main Himalaya to the north are complemented with impressive views south towards the Indian Plains. Immediately below the pass is the village of **Wan** (2450m). If continuing to Rup Kund, don't descend to the village. There is a *Forest Rest House* about 100m above Wan, and a *GMVN hotel* run by a helpful chowkidar. The village **temple** is just above the Forest Rest House.

Alternative Route: Wan to Mundoli
3–4 hours, 10km

From Wan, it is a four-hour trek down the valley to the trailhead at Mundoli. For trekkers coming from Mundoli, this distance can easily be completed in a morning.

Day 4: Wan to Bedni Bugyal
5 hours, 11km

From the Forest Rest House, follow the trail down the valley for 1km. Here the trails diverge, with the upper trail leading to Bedni Bugyal. Ascend this trail for 2km to reach an open meadow and a small **temple** with views of Trisul at the head of the valley. This is an excellent *campsite* with a good water supply.

From the meadow, there is a short descent to a small tributary, before the long ascent to Bedni Bugyal. The trail through the forest is steep in places. Jungle cats climbing the tallest oak trees are common here. Oaks persist to around 3000m, and the pines and rhododendrons thin out at 3200m. This marks the upper limit of the forest, as there are no silver birch trees in this region of Garhwal. The 800m climb through the forest takes around three hours. It is a further 3km across the meadows to Bedni Bugyal.

The *alpine campsite* at **Bedni Bugyal** (3350m) rivals the best in the Himalaya. To the west and northwest, views of the Himalaya Range stretch as far as the peaks near Gangotri, while the Chaukhamba Range and the peaks beyond Joshimath are also visible. To the northeast, the peaks of Trisul and Nanda Ghunti rise above the alpine ridges. The wildflowers in these meadows remain in bloom until mid-September and are, by all accounts, magnificent during the monsoon in July and August.

Just above the meadow is a small **temple** where pilgrims make their offerings en route to Rup Kund. There are a few *huts* for shelter nearby. Unfortunately, the ugly concrete pillars used to support pilgrim shelters scar the meadow.

Day 5: Bedni Bugyal to Bhugu Basa
4–5 hours, 10km

There is a gradual climb up and along the northeast ridge towards Trisul. After one to 1½ hours, the trail reaches a cairn overlooking Bedni Bugyal. To the north, uninterrupted views of Trisul and Nanda Ghunti can be appreciated. Here, the trail splits: a route to the west leads eventually to Sutol, while the higher trail heads north towards Rup Kund.

The Rup Kund trail follows the contours for about 3km before ascending steeply in places to a small **temple** on the ridge. This ridge is an extension of the one crossed between Sutol and Wan, and marks the divide between the catchments of the Bedni Ganga and the Nandakini River. After making an offering at the entrance to the temple and ringing the temple bell, descend gradually to Bhugu Basa.

Compared to the beauty of Bedni Bugyal, it is hard to imagine a more desolate, boulder-strewn *campsite* than that of **Bhugu Basa** (4100m). It is exposed to icy northern winds that whip around the stone *shelter huts*. If you choose to stay in the small, sheltered *campsite* about 500m beyond the huts, you'll need to retrace your steps to the limited water supply.

Day 6: Bhugu Basa to Rup Kund & Return to Bedni Bugyal
7–8 hours, 18km

After savouring the panoramic views of the Himalaya, the 500m climb to the sacred, eerie waters of Rup Kund should take around two to three hours. The trail is often under snow until mid-July, and the route can be difficult to follow. Even in the post-monsoon season, there are some steep, rocky sections just before Rup Kund that may require a bit of scrambling.

Rup Kund (4450m) is 50m below the trail at the head of the valley. It has no outflow. The human bones visible beneath the surface are probably the remains of a party of pilgrims who were trapped by bad weather in the 14th century.

From Rup Kund, it takes about 1½ hours to return to Bhugu Basa and a further 2½ to three hours back to Bedni Bugyal.

Side Trip: Jyuri Gali & Hom Kund
7 hours, 12km return

From Rup Kund, the onward climb to the pass of **Jyuri Gali** (4620m) is steep and requires a few handholds in places. The pass offers superb views of Trisul and Nanda Ghunti. It also marks the divide between the headwaters of Rup Kund and Hom Kund, the main sources of the Nandakini River. **Hom Kund** (4060m) is on the far side of the opposite valley. The trek takes three to four hours one way. *Camp* overnight and return via the same route.

Day 7: Bedni Bugyal to Mundoli
6–7 hours, 17km

Follow the trail to the south of Bedni Bugyal and cross the alpine grazing meadows to **Ali Bugyal**. The views are again magnificent.

The trail from Ali Bugyal splits in places, and a local shepherd may have to point you in the direction of the route. Descend steeply through the forest to the village of **Didana** (2450m). A further descent to the substantial bridge over Bedni Ganga meets the main trail coming from Wan. A gradual ascent through pine, fir, oak and bamboo forest and past cascading side streams takes you to the ridge-top *dhabas* and the *GMVN hotel* at **Loharjang** (2150m). It is a short descent to the trailhead at **Mundoli** (1970m).

Kumaon

The Kumaon region, close to the border of western Nepal, is often overlooked by trekkers. Yet the impressive trails here offer many opportunities to appreciate the spectacular peaks stretching to the borderlands of Tibet.

The hill station of Naini Tal is a convenient centre for trekkers, before travelling to the trailheads at Song and Munsyari.

HISTORY
Kumaon's history can be traced to the Chand dynasty that united many of the small hill states in the 16th century. The unification of the region became particularly apparent during the time of the Moghuls, when the various rajahs paid tribute to the Moghul court and, in return, were able to maintain a semblance of independence.

In 1790 Chand kingdoms, together with the Garhwal, were attacked by the Gurkhas. When the local rajahs asked the British to intervene, the East India army fought a number of wars with the Gurkhas, resulting in the Treaty of Siliguri in 1817. This treaty brought Nepal's western borders back to the Kali River. The British were anxious to exercise their authority over the region and established direct rule over the Kumaon, including the districts of Almora and Naini Tal. Hill stations were built to accommodate the British officials, notably at Naini Tal and Ranikhet.

In 1947, after India's independence, the region became part of the state of Uttar Pradesh. In 1968 the Kumaon region, including Almora, Naini Tal and Pithoragarh, was administered from Naini Tal.

NATURAL HISTORY

Nanda Devi (7816m) – the highest peak in India – defines the northern boundary between the Garhwal and Kumaon. Significant peaks to the south include Nanda Ghunti (6309m), Trisul I (7120m), Devtoli (6788m) and Nanda Kot (6861m). Northeast of Nanda Devi, the Himalaya is defined by many more impressive peaks, including Hardeol (7151m), Tirsuli I (7074m) and Rishi Pahar (6992m), which enclose the Milam Glacier.

Southeast of Nanda Devi is the Panch Chuli Range (6904m), which forms the mountain divide between the Gauri Ganga and the Kali River – the border between India and Nepal.

Wildlife sightings in Kumaon are similar to the Garhwal: black bears, common leopards, serows, Himalayan thar and musk deer. Snow leopards and bharal are found on the outlying ridges of the Nanda Devi Sanctuary.

Wildflower enthusiasts will not be disappointed with the alpine meadows close to the Himalaya Range, while the upper Milam Valley is particularly attractive in July and August.

Many of the birds found in Kumaon are also found in western Nepal. They range from brightly coloured bulbuls, flycatchers and babblers in the lower foothills, to the pheasants found in the upper forests, to kestrels, lammergeiers and golden eagles across the high alpine pastures.

ACCESS TOWN
Naini Tal
☎ 05942 • alt 1938m

This attractive hill resort is one of the main gateways for trekking in the Kumaon region. The town is centred around the large lake or *tal*, hence the name Naini Tal. In 1839 the town was selected as a retreat for British people wanting a reminder of the Lake District in northern England. Yet Naini Tal could offer far more, for besides the lake and the forest walks the surrounding ridges provide fine views of the Himalaya.

Nowadays the dramatic increase in the number of domestic tourists has put increasing strain on the local resources. Strict environmental guidelines have been drawn up to ensure that the lake is protected from further pollution, that there are no additional inappropriate developments and that the surrounding forests are not denuded.

It is a further day's drive (usually via Almora) to trailheads at Song or Munsyari, or to reach the Garhwal and Joshimath. These long distances are one reason why the superb trekking possibilities here only attract a handful of foreign trekkers each season. It's also an opportunity for you to enjoy a unique trekking experience.

Information The **KMVN Tourist Office** (☎ 35337, the Mall) provides travel information. There are also many agents, including **Parvat Tours** (☎ 35656) run by the KMVN, at the Talli Tal end of the Mall.

The **KVMN Trekking & Mountaineering Office** (☎ 36043), at Sukha Tal on the outskirts of Naini Tal, is the best place for specific trekking information.

Supplies & Equipment Fruit, vegetables and a wide range of food items are available at Naini Tal. If trekking out of Song, bring all your food supplies from Naini Tal or Bhageshwar. If trekking out of Munsyari, fruit, vegetables, rice and cooking oil are available there, although bring luxury and tinned items with you.

The **KMVN Trekking & Mountaineering Office** (see Information) has sleeping bags, tents and insulated mats for hire. For rates, see Hiring Gear in India (p67). A substantial deposit is necessary, together with passport and itinerary details.

Quality gear is often in short supply, particularly in May and June. Bring your own gear if possible. Cooking gear, including stoves, can be hired from the office or purchased in the market.

UTTARANCHAL

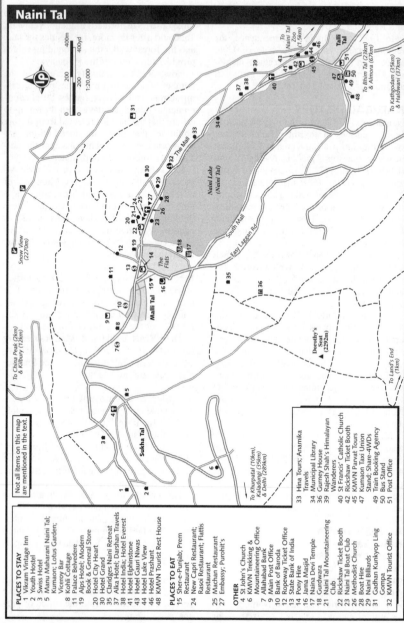

Naini Tal

To China Peak (2km)
& Kilbury (12km)

Snow View (2270m)

Sukha Tal

To Khurpatal (10km),
Kaladung (35km)
& Delhi (289km)

The Flats

Malli Tal

Naini Lake
(Naini Tal)

The Mall

South Mall

Easy Laggan Rd

Dorothy's
Seat
(2292m)

To Land's End
(1km)

To Naini Tal
Zoo (1.5km)

Talli
Tal

To Bhim Tal (23km)
& Almora (67km)

To Kathgodam (35km)
& Haldwani (37km)

0   200   400m
0   200   400yd
1:20,000

PLACES TO STAY
1 Vikram Vintage Inn
2 Youth Hostel
3 Swiss Hotel
5 Manu Maharani Naini Tal;
   Kumaon; Lotus Garden;
   Viceroy Bar
8 Kohli Cottage
11 Palace Belvedere
19 Alps Hotel; Modern
20 Book & General Store
30 Hotel City Heart
35 Hotel Grand
37 Claridges Naini Retreat
38 Alka Hotel; Darshan Travels
41 Hotel India; Hotel Everest
43 Hotel Elphinstone
44 Hotel Gauri Niwas
46 Hotel Prashant
48 KMVN Tourist Rest House

PLACES TO EAT
15 Sher-e-Punjab; Prem
   Restaurant
24 New Capri Restaurant;
   Rasoi Restaurant; Flattis
   Restaurant
25 Machan Restaurant
27 Embassy; Purohit's

OTHER
4 St John's Church
6 KMVN Trekking &
   Mountaineering Office
7 Allahabad Bank
9 Main Post Office
10 Bank of Baroda
12 Ropeway Ticket Office
13 State Bank of India
14 Pony Hire
16 Jama Masjid
17 Naina Devi Temple
18 Gurdwara
21 Naini Tal Mountaineering
   Club
22 Rickshaw Ticket Booth
23 Naini Tal Boat Club
26 Methodist Church
28 Boat Hire
29 Naini Billiards
31 Gadhan Kunkyop Ling
   Gompa
32 KMVN Tourist Office

33 Hina Tours; Anamika
   Travels
34 Municipal Library
36 Gurney House
39 Rajesh Shah's Himalayan
   Wanderers
40 St Francis' Catholic Church
42 Rickshaw Ticket Booth
45 KMVN Parvat Tours
47 Kumaon Taxi Union
   Stand; Share-4WDs
49 Train Booking Agency
50 Bus Stand
51 Post Office

Not all items on this map
are mentioned in the text.

Trekking Agents Consider the following agents:

Rajesh Shah's Himalayan Wanderers (☎ 35119, ✉ sam@corbett-trails.com, Headingly Cottage) is near St Francis Church.
Adventure Links (☎ 47022; ✉ adventure_links @hotmail.com; No 5 Bungalow, Bhim Tal) is run by the highly experienced Guari Rana.

There are also trekking agents in Almora, who offer inclusive arrangements with guide, porters, food and accommodation for around Rs 1000 per person per day. However, unless the guides are outstanding and the agents have a means of contacting the rest houses in advance, it is debatable whether there is any advantage to this arrangement.

At the trailhead at Song (for the Pindari Glacier trek), there is no shortage of porters. The going rate is around Rs 150 per porter per day. In Munsyari (for the Milam Glacier & Nanda Devi trek, pp234–9), there are many reports of porters renegotiating on deals. Employ one of the local agents to make the arrangements for you. Budget for around Rs 200 to Rs 250 per porter per day.

Places to Stay & Eat Naini Tal is not a cheap place to stay in high season (May, June, mid-Sept–mid-Oct). The following rates are an indication of high-season prices.

Most budget hotels are south of the Mall. **Hotel Lake View** (☎ 35632, Ramji Rd) has doubles from Rs 300 to Rs 600. The **KMVN Tourist Rest House** (☎ 35570), on the southeast end of the Mall at Talli Tal, has dorm beds from Rs 40 and doubles from Rs 550. The **Alps Hotel** (☎ 35317), at Malli Tal on the northeast end of the Mall, has retained its character. Rooms cost Rs 200 to Rs 300.

At the other end of the scale, a number of renovated hotels still have charm and character. They include **Hotel Grand** (☎ 35406), in Malli Tal, with doubles from Rs 1500 to Rs 1800, and **Swiss Hotel** (☎ 36013, fax 35493), about ten minutes walk beyond the Mall. Comfortable doubles cost from Rs 1500.
The **New Capri Restaurant** (the Mall) is popular, with a range of Indian and Chinese cuisine. **Embassy** and **Machan Restaurant** offer a similar range. There is no shortage of restaurants in the larger hotels or dhabas to the south end of the lake.

Getting There & Away Regular buses connect Naini Tal with other towns, including Delhi, and the relevant trailheads.

Bus Many private companies offer deluxe buses to/from Delhi, most leave Naini Tal in the evening (Rs 250 to Rs 350). Public buses leave Naini Tal early morning or late afternoon (Rs 142, 10 hours). Half-hourly buses run to/from the railway at Kathgodam (Rs 20, 1½ hours) and to/from the nearby regional bus station at Haldwani. Regular buses go to/from Almora (Rs 42, three hours) and on to Bageshwar, Song and Munsyari.

Train Kathgodam (35km south of Naini Tal) is the nearest railway station. The **Train Booking Agency** in Talli Tal has a small quota of tickets; book as far in advance as possible, particularly in peak season. Overnight trains to Delhi including the *Ranikhet Express*, leaving Kathgodam at 8.45pm and arriving in Old Delhi at 4.45am (sleeper/two-tier Rs 129/550). However, there are plans for a *Shatabdi* service (now operating on Sundays) to provide a daytime alternative.

Taxi A 4WD to Almora will cost Rs 650.

Pindari Glacier

Duration	7 days
Distance	94km
Difficulty	easy
Start/Finish	Song
Nearest Town	Naini Tal (pp229–31)
Public Transport	yes
Summary	One of the most popular treks in Uttaranchal; ascend through Hindu villages, mixed forests and open meadows to view the peaks and passes above the Pindari Glacier.

This trek offers well-defined trails with only one minor pass crossing en route to the Pindari Glacier. The views from the pass – the Dhakri Khal (2830m) – are particularly impressive and include the many snow-capped peaks that form the southern rim of the Nanda Devi Sanctuary. The views from above the Pindari Glacier are also striking, particularly for the first-time trekker.

The route is very popular with Indian students during the school holidays in May and June and many of the lodges and dhabas are full. However, there are very few pilgrims. This is surprising considering that the Pindari River is one of the main tributaries of the Ganges.

Acclimatisation is essential. Spend an additional night at Dwali (2650m) before ascending to Phurkiya (3250m) and the Pindari Glacier. There is also a side trip to the nearby Sunderdhunga Glacier.

PLANNING
When to Trek

The trail is open from May though October. However, if trekking in May, expect some residual snow on the final stage to the Pindari Glacier. Mid-September through October is normally clear, with ideal conditions for trekking.

What to Bring

While you can get by without them, having your own tent, stove and cooking gear gives you the flexibility to camp in more serene settings when the huts and lodges are busy. In May, a ski pole or ice axe will be helpful on the ascent to the Pindari Glacier.

Maps

Refer to the Leomann series 1:200,000 *Sheet 8 (Pindari Glacier, Badrinath & Nanda Devi)*. Also refer to the Survey of India Trekking map series 1:250,000 *Kumaon Hills*. The US Military U502 series 1:250,000 *NI 44-6 ref Nanda Devi* covers the trek. The SFAR 1:150,000 *Garhwal Himalaya (East Section)* also covers the route.

Accommodation

This trek can be done without a tent. Song has a number of basic lodges. There is a KMVN Rest House just above Loharket, and a number of lodges that can also assist with hiring porters. There are KMVN Rest Houses at Dhakri, Khati, Dwali and Phurkiya, and PWD Rest Houses at Khati and Dhakri. Many other private lodges and dhabas are along the trail.

However, in May and June, many of the rest houses and lodges are booked out by student groups. Arrive early to ensure you get accommodation.

The rates for the lodges vary from Rs 100 per person plus food at the KVMN Rest Houses to Rs 200/100 per bed for foreign/domestic trekkers at PWD Rest Houses. There are also basic dorms that charge Rs 50 for a bed. Food is available at all the rest houses, and costs around Rs 30 for a meal of rice, *dhal* (lentil-based soup or main dish) and vegetables.

GETTING TO/FROM THE TREK

From Naini Tal, it's a long day's drive to Song, normally requiring a change at both Almora and Bageshwar. The bus to Almora takes around three hours (Rs 42), onward to Bageshwar a further five hours (Rs 129), and Song is another two hours away (Rs 20). A shared 4WD (Rs 40 per seat) from Bageshwar to Song may save lots of time.

THE TREK (See map pp206–7)
Day 1: Song to Dhakri
6–7 hours, 16km

The small bazaar at **Song** (1400m) provides the usual trailhead scene, although 4WDs can follow the switchbacks up the hillside for a further 4km or 5km to the village of Loharket.

From above the main bazaar in Song, a well-marked stone trail ascends the 2km to **Loharket** (1600m). This trail meets the trailhead near the ***Rest House***. There is a ***campsite*** close to the stream that flows through the village.

From Loharket the trail is being upgraded (in places) into a 4WD track. This track passes through an evergreen forest of oak and horse chestnut before ascending to the small Hindu temple at **Taladhakri** (2300m). This is the halfway point on the ascent to the Dhakri Khal. There is a ***campsite*** 1km beyond the temple (a good stopping point if you leave Song in the middle of the day).

Beyond Taladhakri the trail ascends through meadows and rhododendron forest that bloom by late April. The gradient lessens towards the Dhakri Khal and there is a welcome *tea stall* just below the pass.

The impressive views from the **Dhakri Khal** (2830m) include Trisul, Devtoli, Maiktoli and Nanda Khat along the southern rim of the Nanda Devi Sanctuary. Nanda Kot rises high above the Pindari Glacier. You can also gain uninterrupted views of the Himalaya.

Reach higher vantage points by ascending the forested ridge southwest of the pass. This leads to a series of bugyals where shepherds graze their flocks in summer. The one-hour ascent is well rewarded with fine views of the Himalaya from Joshimath to the Panch Chuli Range beyond Munsyari.

The meadow of **Dhakri** (2680m) lies just below the pass. A number of huts, including the *KMVN Rest House* and the *PWD Rest House*, are in the centre of the meadow, with three or four other lodges. These buildings are an eyesore, and the nearby forest is being destroyed for construction and cooking. The water supply is immediately west of the meadow, where there are alternative *campsites*.

Day 2: Dhakri to Dwali
6–7 hours, 16km

The trail descends steeply in places past settlements and fields of potato and barley. Views up the Sunderdhunga Valley are impressive, including the huge ice wall at the head of the valley. After 3km or 4km, the trail diverts east and follows the contours through beautiful forest and meadow glades to **Khati** (2250m), the largest village in the region. Most houses here have solar panels, which will eventually be introduced to the other villages in the upper Pindari Valley. Khati is also the trekking-off point to the Sunderdhunga Valley (see Side Trip).

The forest trail passes a *KMVN Rest House* 1km beyond Khati before winding high above the Pindari River. After 5km the valley widens and the trail drops down to the valley floor. There are a few *tea stalls* beside a well-constructed wooden bridge

over the Pindari River. Cross to the true right of the valley and continue for 4km to **Dwali** (2650m).

Dwali is above the confluence of the Pindari River and the river flowing from the Kafni Glacier. Cross the Pindari River via the wooden bridge just above the confluence of the two rivers and ascend to the *PWD Rest House*. A comfortable *campsite* is immediately below the rest house, beside the river.

Side Trip: Sunderdhunga Glacier
3 days, 54km return

From **Khati**, the trail heads steeply down to the Pindari River (2100m). There are two bridges to cross: the first over the Pindari River just above the confluence of the Pindari and Sunderdhunga Rivers; the second over the Sunderdhunga River. The trail remains on the true right of the valley, ascending through mixed forest to the village of **Jyoti** (2450m).

Beyond Jyoti the trail winds above the river through forest and meadows to the *campsite* and meadow at **Katholia**, alongside the river. The following day, follow the course of the river for 7km to view the tumbling **Sunderdhunga Glacier** and the spectacular summit of Maiktoli (6803m). Return to *camp* at Katholia and head back to the main route the next day.

Day 3: Dwali to Phurkiya
2½–3 hours, 7km

This short day is ideal for acclimatisation before continuing to the Pindari Glacier.

The trail ascends through mixed forest, past tumbling waterfalls, across snowfields (which remain until late July) and through flowered meadows. The peak of Nanda Khat appears at the head of the valley, while the tip of Nanda Devi East can just be seen.

Phurkiya (3250m) has a *PWD Rest House* and a *KMVN Rest House* on the tree line. It is also where the valley widens to a broad U-shape that extends to the Pindari Glacier.

Day 4: Pindari Glacier (Zero Point) Day Trek
5–6 hours, 16km

Beyond Phurkiya the trail gradually ascends across meadows beneath the impressive

UTTARANCHAL

flanks of Nanda Khat. The trail crosses some side streams. After the spring snowmelt, flocks of sheep and goats from the villages lower down the Pindari Valley are herded to these high pastures, where they remain until mid-September.

The main shepherd encampment is about 3km below the snout of the **Pindari Glacier** and is known as **Zero Point** (3650m). A *PWD Rest House* and some *lodges*, including one occupied by a friendly and informative sadhu who spends most of the year in this remote locality, are 1km below Zero Point.

From the huts, the trail to Zero Point extends beside lateral moraine to where the Pindari River emerges from the glacier. From this vantage point, view the route to Traills Pass as well as the peaks of Nanda Khat (6611m), Changuch (6322m) and the formidable Nanda Kot (6861m) at the head of the glacier.

Days 5 to 7: Phurkiya to Song
3 days, 39km

The return to Song takes three days. Head back to Dwali on the first and Dhakri on the second. On the third day, reach the trailhead, in time to continue by 4WD or bus to Bageshwar and Almora.

Milam Glacier & Nanda Devi

Duration	10 days
Distance	142km
Difficulty	moderate
Start/Finish	Munsyari
Nearest Town	Naini Tal (pp229–31)
Public Transport	yes

Summary Follow the ancient trade route from the land of the Pundits to within striking distance of Tibet, before completing a foray to the spectacular Nanda Devi East Base Camp.

This fine trek explores a remote corner of Kumaon, close to the borders of Tibet and Nepal. Follow one of the former trading routes to west Tibet via an impressive trail

where the Gori Ganga surges through the main axis of the Himalaya Range.

While there are no pass crossings, the terrain is rugged in places, particularly en route to the Nanda Devi East Base Camp. There are spectacular views of the east face of Nanda Devi from the base camp but the distinctive twin-peak profile is best appreciated from opposite Pachhu (Day 4). From Martoli, there are impressive views of the peaks beyond the Milam Glacier, while an ascent to the Lilam Ridge on the return trek will afford uninterrupted views of the Panch Chuli Range. For the experienced trekker, there are many exhilarating possibilities – to the Longstaff Col or to the crest of the Traills Pass – while the many valleys to the east of the Panch Chuli Range provide unrivalled opportunities for true exploration.

PLANNING
When to Trek
The trail is open from May to late October, although the region south of the gorge is subject to monsoon rain in July and August. September and October are ideal months for trekking.

What to Bring
Essentials include a tent, stove and cooking gear, along with food supplies for at least seven days.

Maps
Refer to the Leomann series 1:200,000 *Sheet 8 (Pindari Glacier, Badrinath & Nanda Devi)*. Also refer to the Survey of India Trekking map series 1:250,000 *Kumaon Hills*. The US Military U502 series 1:250,000 *NI 44.6 ref Nanda Devi* covers the trek, as does the SFAR 1:150,000 *Garhwal Himalaya (East Section)*.

Local Trekking Agents
There are a number of agents in Munsyari, concentrated in and around the main bazaar. **Panch Chuli Trekking** (*☎ 059612-2327*) is recommended and also organise porters. Rates are set by the local magistrate and are calculated in terms of *paraos*, the local term for a trek stage. However, some *paraos*

involve just a few hours walking. Budget for around Rs 90 per *parao* for carrying loads up to 20kg (although just to complicate it a bit more, some *paraos* are now Rs 150 per day). Add the commission to the local agent on top of this, and you can be in for a comparatively expensive trek.

Permits

In spite of literature to the contrary, current regulations do not require trekkers to be part of a group or for arrangements to be made through an agency. Neither do foreign trekkers need to apply through the local magistrate in Munsyari. All you need is your passport, which is inspected at the various Indo-Tibetan Border Police (ITBP) checkpoints, including the one in Milam.

However, Indian trekkers and staff from outside the Munsyari region will require a special permit from the magistrate to trek. These permits are also checked at the ITBP checkpoints.

Accommodation

The past few years have seen a number of new hotels constructed above Munsyari's main bazaar. These include the *KMVN hotel* (☎ 059612-2339), with doubles/dorm beds for Rs 420/50.

The highly recommended *Martoli Family Guest House* (☎ 059612-2287) in Sartoli village, just north of Munsyari, has rooms from Rs 250 to Rs 350. It is run by a former police officer, a mine of local information who can also assist with hiring porters.

There are a number of lodges on the initial stages of the trek. There are also PWD Rest Houses at Bodgwar and Milam, but that is about it. Beyond Lilam there is nowhere to buy basic food supplies, while the settlements between Martoli and Milam are often deserted.

GETTING TO/FROM THE TREK

There is a direct bus between Almora and Munsari (Rs 120, 10 hours). If hiring a 4WD to Munsyari expect to pay around Rs 2000 from Almora and Rs 2500 from Naini Tal.

From Munsyari the road is being extended towards Darkot and 4WDs are available to the trailhead. Budget for around Rs 400, although most 4WDs will also operate on a per seat basis.

THE TREK (See map pp206–7)
Day 1: Munsyari to Lilam
4 hours, 16km

From the main bazaar at **Munsyari** (2290m), follow the road heading northeast towards the Johar Valley. This road is currently unsealed, while an alternative trail provides some shortcuts to the trailhead just above the village of **Darkot** (1800m).

From Darkot, it is a steady descent to the Gori Ganga. The well-defined trail follows the true right of the river past a series of small villages. Some houses are constructed of bamboo; this provides some respite from the humid summer temperatures, which reach the mid-30°Cs in the pre-monsoon season. There are also several *dhabas* en route to **Lilam** (1850m), where you will find *camping* options.

Day 2: Lilam to Bodgwar
5–6 hours, 15km

At Lilam do not cross the bridge over the Gori Ganga. The trail to Bodgwar continues on the true right of the valley high above the surging waters of the Gori Ganga. After 5km the trail passes the confluence of the Ralam River and the Gori Ganga.

Above the river confluence, the trail enters a spectacular gorge where the waters of the Gori Ganga echo and thunder through an incredible series of rapids. The narrow trail is often congested as shepherds lead their huge flocks of sheep or goats to the summer grazing pastures near Milam. The goats are laden with saddlebags carrying potatoes, rice and seeds, and even cement for construction.

About 3km above the confluence of the rivers, the trail passes a small meadow and side stream, where there is a *dhaba*. Here the trail from Lilam Ridge meets the valley floor (see the Day 9 Alternative Route on p239). Continue through conifer, chestnut and bamboo forest for 4km to the meadow of **Bodgwar** (2500m), nothing more than some shanty huts, an ITBP checkpoint and a *PWD Rest House*. If *camping*, continue for 1km past the huts to a grassy ridge close to the main river.

Day 3: Bodgwar to Martoli
5–6 hours, 14km

Follow the Gori Ganga through a series of narrow gorges. There is a **Hindu temple** beneath a rock overhang 3km past Bodgwar. The trail crosses a series of snow bridges that remain for most of the season. Impressive **waterfalls** cascade down the cliff walls.

The gorge begins to widen 4km or 5km later and, after rounding a small meadow, the trail splits for about 1km. The upper, more substantial trail skirts high above a steep rock wall and is suitable for horses; the lower trail, carved directly out of the rock face, is suitable only for trekkers and porters. This marks the upper limit of the Gori Ganga Gorge.

The next section of the trail crosses open meadows extending 3km or 4km to **Railkot** (3100m). The valley veers to the north and 2km beyond Railkot, the first of the high mountain peaks beyond Milam come into view, giving a taste of the scenes to come.

Martoli village (3430m) is on a grassy plateau high above the confluence of the Gori Ganga and the Lwanl Gad, flowing from Nanda Devi East. In its heyday, the village would have supported several hundred people and included a school and shops. At this time there was a thriving trade with Tibet – this ended in 1962 when the border was closed following the war between India and China.

Nowadays Martoli, like so many other villages in the upper Johar Valley, is practically deserted, its stone houses falling into total disrepair. Only a handful of villagers travel up the valley from Munsyari and the surrounding villages to spend the summer in Martoli or the other villages between there and Milam.

Just above Martoli there is a small stone **temple** dedicated to Nanda Devi. The temple commands a view up the Lwanl Valley to the tip of Nanda Devi East (7434m) and the peak of Nanda Kot. To the north, the peaks of Hardeol and Tirsuli can be seen.

Outside the temple is an impressive row of bells hanging from climbing rope attached to a prayer wall. The bells are donated by climbing expeditions or by groups of devotees from Munsyari to placate the goddess of the high mountains. The *Martoli Family Guest House* is in nearby Sartoli.

Beyond the temple there are several acres of conifers planted by the Forestry Department. Other reforestation projects are also being undertaken, as much of the surrounding hillside suffered deforestation well before the borders with Tibet were closed.

Day 4: Martoli to Milam
4 hours, 11km

This short and easy day offers spectacular views of the Himalaya, including the main peak of Nanda Devi.

From Martoli, descend steeply to the bridge over the Lwanl Gad. The trail remains on the true right of the valley for a further 2km until it is opposite **Burphu** (3350m). Cross the solid wooden bridge over the Gori Ganga. Although the trail skirts below Burphu, it is well worth detouring up the hillside to visit the village, one of the most active in this part of the Johar Valley.

Beyond Burphu, several settlements dot the opposite side of the valley. These are only occupied by a handful of shepherds from the Munsyari district from June until late September. Opposite the settlement of **Pachhu**, there are magnificent views of the unmistakable profile of **Nanda Devi**. Continue past **Beiju**, from where it is a further 3km to Milam (*Mi Lam* means man road). The main settlement is just beyond the confluence of the Gori Ganga (which flows from the Milam Glacier) and the Goenka Gad, which flows from the northeast.

Milam (3450m) was the home of a number of the renowned Pundit explorers (see the boxed text 'The Pundits of the Johar Valley', opposite). It is also the last major settlement before Tibet. (A one-day trek up the Goenka Valley reaches the base of the Unta Dhura pass, a further day's trekking, after a series of three pass crossings – the Unta Dhura, Jainta Dhura and Kangri Bingri La – a trader or shepherd could be in Tibet.)

The Pundits of the Johar Valley

The increasing Russian presence in Central Asia and Tibet in the 1860s made it imperative for the British to compile accurate surveys and gather political intelligence about the northern barriers of India and beyond, including the vast expanses of Tibet. However, there was no way that Imperial China would permit British survey officers to enter Tibet, let alone survey it. The Great Trigonometrical Survey of India Office (GTS), based in Dehra Dun, came up with the idea of training Indians who lived close to the Tibetan border – and were familiar with Tibetan customs and language – to undertake the survey work on their behalf.

The villagers of the Johar Valley fitted the bill. They had maintained trading relations with Tibet for many generations and knew the border regions well. In 1863 Nain Singh ('Chief Pundit' or 'No 1') and his cousin Mani Singh were trained in survey techniques. For two years the men were primed in the use of the sextant and the compass and taught to measure altitude by recording the temperature of boiling water. To calculate distance they were drilled to take exact steps and after every 100 steps to drop a bead in a modified Buddhist prayer wheel, which contained 100 rather than the traditional 108 beads. The prayer wheel was also modified to conceal their notes and calculations.

Nain Singh set off from Kathmandu in March 1865 disguised as a Ladakhi trader. He surveyed southern Tibet, including the Tsangpo Valley, Lhasa, Kailash and Manasorwar, before returning to Dehra Dun in June 1866. In 1867, he was commissioned to return to Tibet with Mani Singh and another Pundit, Kailan Singh (code-named 'GK'). They left India by way of Badrinath and the Mana Pass, disguised as horse traders, and wandered in near Kailash, confirming the source of the Indus and Sutlej Rivers. This notable achievement gained due recognition for the Pundits and the Survey's work both in India and in the UK.

Nain Singh's objective on his last journey in July 1874 was to survey the Tsangpo River. Setting out from Leh he crossed southern Tibet and the lower course of the Tsangpo as far as Assam, completing a journey of more than 2000km. Although he was not able to completely ascertain the lower course of the Tsangpo, it was a commendable effort.

Kishen Singh ('AK'), another of Nain Singh's cousins from the Johar Valley, also played an important role in the Survey. He embarked on his first important journey in 1872, exploring between Shigatse and the north of Lhasa. In April 1878 he returned to Tibet, travelling via Sikkim and Bhutan to Lhasa, before heading north to Mongolia. He returned south by a difficult route along the lower course of the Tsangpo, before returning to Lhasa and eventually to Darjeeling in November 1882, after his family and the Survey had given him up for dead.

A question mark still remained about whether the Tsangpo and the Brahmaputra in India were the same river. The formidable terrain between the known course of the Tsangpo and the Brahmaputra had been the subject of considerable speculation, and was the objective for a number of Pundits, including the remarkable Kinthup, from Sikkim.

Leaving Sikkim in October 1878, Kinthup undertook an epic journey through Tibet that included twice being sold into slavery. In spite of these rigours, he described the course of the Tsangpo as it rounded the huge peak of Namche Barwa (7745m) and the deep gorge country to within a short distance of the Indian foothills. However, on his return to India four years later, the lack of authentic details discredited his report. It was not until 1912, when the Tsangpo Gorge was finally explored, that Kinthup's report was finally given the recognition it deserved, just a few months before he died.

For more detailed accounts of the work of the Pundits, Indra Singh Rawat, a local surveyor from the Johar Valley, wrote the detailed *Indian Explorers of the 19th Century*, published by the government of India in 1970. Interested parties are trying to establish a museum in Munsyari to record the travels of the famous Pundits from Milam. For details and to make donations, contact Mr US Martolia (a retired police officer), c/- Post Office Munsyari, Pithoragarh, Uttaranchal.

In spite of the close association the villagers of Milam have with Tibet, they are anxious not to be called *Bhotia* (people from Tibet). The villagers trace their ancestry to the Rajput tribes who migrated from Rajasthan in the 12th century to settle in the hills of Uttaranchal. In the 16th century they moved to the Munsyari region and established trading relations with Tibet. Grains such as wheat, barley and rice were exchanged for salt, hardy Tibetan ponies and wool until 1962.

Limited trade has now resumed between Milam and Tibet, and one of the main roles for the ITBP in Milam is to prevent the smuggling of goods.

Side Trip: Towards Milam Glacier
2–3 hours, 6km return

Milam is as far as you are permitted to trek at present, although the ITBP will allow you to continue past the village for 3km to a vantage point at 3500m. Here, you can marvel at the sheer size and extent of the Milam Glacier. This trail leads you through high meadows dotted with sage, juniper, briar roses and miniature gorse high above the terminal moraine.

Looking towards the head of the glacier, the peaks you will see include Rishi Pahar (6992m), Hardeol (7151m) and Tirsuli I (7074m). The prominent peaks along the northeast rim include Kholl (6114m), Nanda Gond (6315m), Nital Thaur (6236m) and Nanda Pal (6306m).

Day 5: Milam to Camp (near Lwanl)
5 hours, 14km

It is a steady descent back to **Martoli**. The trail to the Nanda Devi East Base Camp heads west along the true right of the Lwanl Gad. The trail winds above the river for 3km until it is opposite the small settlement of Lwanl (3500m). This point is high above the confluence of the Lwanl Gad and the tributary flowing in from the southwest (the Shalang Gad), which is fed by the snows on the southern ridges of Nanda Kot. There are plenty of *campsites* nearby.

Day 6: Camp (near Lwanl) to Nanda Devi East Base Camp
6 hours, 12km

The trail diverts along the true right of the Shalang Gad. Early in the season cross the snow bridge over the tributary. Later, when the snow bridge collapses, villagers from Martoli and Lwanl construct a log bridge. Continue on the true left of the valley to the settlement of Lwanl.

Continue up the Lwanl Valley before entering spectacular gorge country. The trail skirts around side gullies and past rhododendron copses, which remain in bloom until late May. Descend (via the trail) to the river's edge to avoid rocky overhangs. After 4km to 5km, the valley widens and offers views of Nanda Kot. The trail passes a series of moraine fields until it is opposite the meadow of **Sartol Kharak** (3650m), a possible *campsite*. Cross the Lwanl Gad here to the true left of the valley (early in the season there is a snow bridge; later, a log bridge).

The trail continues to the meadow at **Naspanpatti** (3850m). A herd of bharal have been spotted on the cliffs above this meadow so (by association) there is the chance of sighting elusive snow leopards late in the season. The trail ascends high above the terminal moraine engulfing the main valley floor before crossing some scree slopes just below the base camp.

Nanda Devi East Base Camp (4150m) is a delightful series of meadows. There are many *campsites* from which to appreciate the peaks and the high snow ridges that virtually enclose the upper valley. To the south, a snow ridge links the imposing summit of Nanda Khat (6611m) to Changuch (6322m). The lowest point on the ridge, northwest of Changuch, is **Traills Pass** (5312m). West of Traills Pass, the snowcapped ridge merges with the one striking north from Nanda Khat before gradually rising to the imposing summit ridge below Nanda Devi East (7434m), the highest peak in the vicinity. Along this ridge lies the **Longstaff Col** (5910m), accessible only by a technical climb, from where it is possible to peer into Nanda Devi Sanctuary.

Side Trip: Nanda Devi East
3–4 hours, 3km–4km return

A scramble up the snow ridges southeast of Nanda Devi East offers unrivalled views of the gullies leading to the Longstaff Col and also the route leading to Traills Pass, the heavily crevassed pass linking the upper Lwanl Valley with the Pindari Valley.

Day 7: Nanda Devi East Base Camp to Martoli
5–6 hours, 15km

The return trek to Martoli can be completed in a long morning, with time to savour final views of the peaks near Nanda Devi East and the summits beyond Milam.

Days 8 to 10: Martoli to Munsyari
3 days, 45km

The return to Munsyari takes three days. Head back to Bodgwar on the first day, Lilam on the second (see Alternative Route), and finally to Munsyari. You may be able to shorten the third day if there is vacant 4WD or truck at the trailhead.

Day 9 Alternative Route: Bodgwar to Lilam via Lilam Ridge
7–8 hours, 17km

This alternative offers spectacular views. From Bodgwar, continue to the split in the trail (see Day 2, pp235–6) and take the upper trail leading to Lilam Ridge.

The trail ascends through a forest of rhododendron and conifer, and across open meadows to a ridge high above the Ralam River. There are fine views east of the Panch Chuli Range and north up the Gori Ganga towards Martoli.

Climb to the **Lilam Ridge** (2850m) before completing a long descent to the small settlement of **Upper Lilam**. There are impressive views down the valley and across to Munsyari, while the village supports a small Hindu **temple** and a number of *dhabas*. The trail winds down the hillside to Lilam.

Darjeeling

Darjeeling is part of the state of Bangla (West Bengal) but is administered locally by the Darjeeling Gurkha Hill Council (DGHC), which has a certain measure of control over its affairs.

For most travellers, Darjeeling consists of the large township that sprawls along the ridges of the Darjeeling Hills. Yet the outlying regions of the district provide fine opportunities for trekking and remarkable views of Kangchenjunga.

HISTORY

Darjeeling was part of Sikkim until the beginning of the 19th century. In 1780 the Gurkhas invaded Sikkim as part of their plan to establish a vast Trans-Himalayan empire. The British East India Company was drawn into the conflict, leading to the Gurkha wars. This resulted in the 1817 Treaty of Siliguri: territory lost to the Gurkhas was restored to the rajahs of Sikkim, on the condition that the British took control of their external affairs. It was during a local border dispute in 1828 that two British officers visited Darjeeling and recognised its potential as a hill station. This information was not lost on the authorities in Calcutta; in 1835, they pressured the rajah to grant them Darjeeling in exchange for an annual payment.

However, the rajah was not totally comfortable with the agreement. In 1849 matters came to a head when the British Superintendent of Darjeeling and the renowned botanist Dr Joseph Hooker were arrested by authorities while touring Sikkim. The British took this as an affront and, after the release of the prisoners, temporarily withdrew the rajah's stipend and annexed the area between the Sikkim border and the Indian Plains. This effectively redrew the borders of Sikkim, cutting it off from the plains except through British territory, while giving Darjeeling direct access to the rest of British India.

The development of Darjeeling was rapid. The newly completed road from the plains was upgraded and the settlement expanded.

The administrators from the East India Company were inspired by the magnificent views of Kangchenjunga. The tea plantations also thrived and a large number of workers were hired from across the border in Nepal. The Tea Planters' Club was established in 1868, and the narrow-gauge railway was completed in 1882.

Darjeeling remained part of Bengal after 1947. However, in 1985, the Gurkhas and Nepalese mounted their own political group with the aim of making Darjeeling an independent hill state. A compromise was reached

Darjeeling Region (Bangla Hills)

The external boundaries of India on this map have not been authenticated and may not be correct.

CHINA (TIBET)

SIKKIM

Gangtok
Rumtek
Kupup

Dentam
Singali La
Gezing
Rangpo

BHUTAN

Singalila Ridge & Phalut p247 Namchi
Sombare Jorethang
Sandakphu Raman River
Kali Pokhari Kalimpong Teesta Bazar
Darjeeling Map p244 Darjeeling Tiger Hill ▲(2590m)
Ghoom Darjeeling Hills
Chhukha
Dorokha
See Sikkim Map p250
Matiali

Mirik Kurseong
Samthar Plateau
Mongpong
Samtse

Pankhabari
Jaigaon Buxa Tiger Reserve

NEPAL
BANGLA
Kalchini

Bagdogra Siliguri
Ramshai
Birpara
Rajabhat-Khawa

To Kakarbhitta
Kathmandu Paniktanki
New Jalpaiguri
Bangabandhu
Teesta River
Jaldhaka Chuu
Jalpahara Wildlife Sanctuary
Falakata
Alipur Duar

Mahendra Hwy
31
Dhupagari
Mainaguri

Bhadrapur
Tetulia
Jalpaiguri

Cooch Behar

Chopra
Panchagarh
Haldibari
Patgram
Matabhanga

Pothia Atwari
Chilahati

BIHAR
Islampur
BANGLADESH
Sitalkuchi
Dinhata

Ruhea Boda
To Purnia & Malda
To Dinajpur
Domar

0 10 20km
0 5 10mi
1:1,500,000

DARJEELING

in 1988, which gave the DGHC a large measure of autonomy.

NATURAL HISTORY

The hill station of Darjeeling (2134m) is on the southeast rim of the Singalila Ridge that forms part of the Darjeeling Hills.

To the northwest of Darjeeling, the Singalila Ridge constitutes the impressive Himalayan divide between Sikkim and Nepal. As it extends south, the ridge forms the border between Darjeeling and Nepal.

Darjeeling's border with Sikkim is defined by the course of the Raman River. The river's headwaters flow from just below the Singali La – the lowest point on the Singalila Ridge.

CLIMATE

Day temperatures in April and May rise to around 20°C. In late May, huge clouds build up, signalling the onset of the monsoon. By early June, Darjeeling experiences the first continuous monsoon rain. July, with more than 800mm, sees the highest rainfall, a pattern that continues until mid-September.

In the post-monsoon season (Oct & Nov), day temperatures sit around 10°C and the settled conditions are ideal for trekking. Winter

Watching Wildlife

You don't have to trek to see the wildlife that is very close to the town of Darjeeling! In the forest, below the town and close to the Tibetan refugee camp, there have been sightings of **serow**, **wild boars**, **black bears**, **leopards** and **barking deer**. However, a trek to Phalut in the Singalila National Park will provide additional rewards, including an outside chance of sighting the **red panda**.

Birdlife includes pheasants such as **monals** and **tragopans** on the upper forest level, while birds of prey include **lammergeiers** and **golden eagles**. Snow and **rock pigeons** may also be seen at the higher elevations, together with the **Himalayan snowcock**. A variety of **redstarts**, **forktails**, **finches** and **owls** are found in the **mixed conifer** and **oak** forests.

While there is evidence of denuded forest along the Singalila Ridge, there are extensive forests on the eastern slopes away from the villages. These include the temperate broad-leafed forest that extends to around 2700m before giving way to **mixed conifer**, including fine stands of **silver fir**. **Rhododendron** is common at higher altitudes (to around 3800m), while **roses**, **ferns** and **orchids** provide a further attraction.

Wildflowers in the alpine meadows and yak-grazing pastures include a range of **anemone**, **iris**, **primulae** and **saxifrage**. These thrive on the margins of the snowmelt and bloom throughout the monsoon.

temperatures fall to near-freezing. Snowfall is common on the ridges from December to March, or April at higher elevations.

PLANNING
Maps

For treks out of Darjeeling, the Air India trekking maps provide a useful outline of the area's ridges and rivers. These are available from the Government of India Tourist Office in Delhi; see Tourist Offices (p258).

Books

Useful guidebooks for off-the-trail activities include:

Sikkim, Darjeeling & Kalimpong by Wendy Brewer Lama (1993).
An Introduction to the Hill Stations of India by Graeme Westlake (1993).

Bookshops include **Oxford Bookshop** in Chowrasta, which stocks local titles and a range of books for the trekker.

Information Sources

The **DGHC Tourist Office** (☎ *0354-54214, Chowrasta*) has a limited supply of basic maps and trekking information. Consult one of the trekking agents regarding the condition of trails out of Darjeeling.

Permits

No permits are necessary to complete the trek in this chapter. However, before commencing your trek, you will have to give your passport details at the registration office at Mana Bhanjang. You should also contact the office at Rimbik before returning to Darjeeling.

ACCESS TOWN
Darjeeling
☎ 0354 • alt 2134m

Surrounded by tea plantations and straddling a ridge with uninterrupted views of Kangchenjunga, Darjeeling is one of India's most famous hill stations. Its popularity can be traced from the mid-19th century, when it was established as a rest and recreation area for British troops. The climate and soil were also ideal for tea cultivation, leading to the production of a world-famous variety of tea. The views of Kangchenjunga also attracted attention. When the hill station was established, Kangchenjunga was regarded (until the survey of K2 and Everest) as the highest mountain in the world.

For information, see Information Sources.

Supplies & Equipment There is a variety of fruit and vegetables in the markets, plus items such as tinned meat, fish, cheese, drinking chocolate, nuts and raisins. If you intend staying in lodges on your trek, food is provided. However, stock up on chocolate bars to keep you going during the day. If camping, buy all supplies here. Pots and pans and cooking gear are also available in the market.

To hire gear, contact the **Tenzing Norgay Youth Hostel**; the warden Mrs Moktan has a limited amount of trekking gear for hire through her agency **Moktan Mountain Tours & Travel**. This includes sleeping bags (Rs 25 per day), down jackets (Rs 25) and rucksacks (Rs 15). A deposit and passport details are required. The **Himalayan Mountaineering Institute** does not hire out its climbing and trekking gear.

Trekking Agents There are hundreds of travel and trekking agents in Darjeeling, which can organise treks out of Darjeeling and also in Sikkim. They include:

Himalayan Tours & Travels (☎ 54544, 18 Gandhi Rd) is managed by the indefatigable KK Gurung.
Tenzing Himalayan Expeditions (☎ 54778, 10 Toong Song Rd) is run by Tenzing Norgay's eldest daughter, Pem Pen Tsering.
Moktan Tours & Travels (☎ 56794, Tenzing Norgay Youth Hostel)

Places to Stay & Eat The best budget accommodation is at the *Tenzing Norgay Youth Hostel* (☎ 56794, Dr Zakir Hussain Rd), with dorm beds/double rooms for Rs 40/120. The

Warning

Lonely Planet recommends that trekkers do not use fires as a means of heating hotel rooms, unless there is excellent ventilation (as there is in most top-end hotels). A number of deaths from carbon-monoxide poisoning have occurred. Under no circumstances should you burn charcoal or other fuels that give off toxic fumes.

Darjeeling Club, better known as *The Planters* (☎ 54349, above Nehru Rd), is for nostalgia buffs only. The rooms have seen better days and cost Rs 600 to Rs 2000. The *Pineridge Hotel* (☎ 54074, Chowrasta) offers good-value rooms from Rs 550 to Rs 700, while *Hotel Seven Seventeen* (☎ 547170, HD Lama Rd) has doubles priced from Rs 900 to Rs 1100; avoid the rooms in the annexe.

There is no shortage of impressive hotels, including the *New Elgin* (☎ 54114, HD Lama Rd), with singles/doubles for US$90/100, and the *Windamere Hotel* (☎ 54041, Chowrasta), charging US$100/140. Above the town, with great views of Kangchenjunga, *Cedar Inn* (☎ 53598, Jalaphar Rd) charges US$90/100.

Glenary's (Nehru Rd) is justifiably popular for its coffee and cakes. It has a separate restaurant serving Indian and Chinese cuisine. Many of the hotels have good restaurants. On HD Lama Rd, a number of *Tibetan restaurants* serve simple cuisine, while there

Environmental Watch

To some extent, the establishment of the Singalila National Park has protected the environment from the demands of villagers living on the Singalila Ridge. While legislation outlaws the clearing of more forest areas for cultivation, evidence remains of trees being cut for construction and fuel. This needs to be addressed as recent surveys in the national park indicate the presence of endangered flora and fauna, including the Himalayan red panda. For more information and ways to help, contact the Wildlife Warden at the Himalayan Zoological Park in Darjeeling, or the Wildlife Forest Officer in the Bengal Natural History Museum in Darjeeling.

The network of lodges and huts along the Singalila Ridge has put increasing pressure on the environment. Wood fires are the norm for cooking (rather than LPG or kerosene stoves), while there is little evidence of garbage disposal, particularly in Sandakphu and Phalut. A concerted clean-up campaign by the trekking agents in Darjeeling or the introduction of a trekking fee to fund such efforts may provide a short-term solution. In the meantime, it is the responsibility of all trekkers to help clean up the areas in the vicinity of the lodges and to encourage the lodge staff to do likewise.

DARJEELING

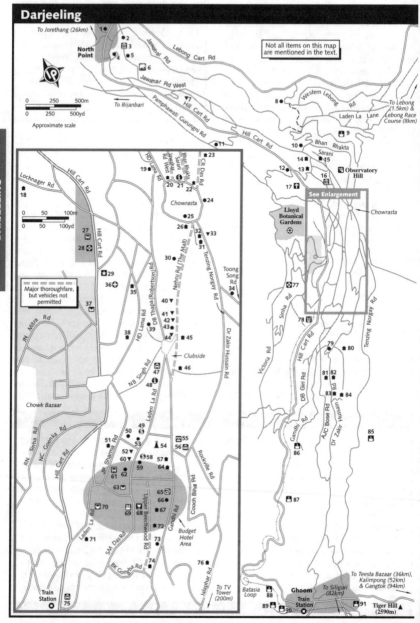

Darjeeling

Not all items on this map are mentioned in the text.

To Jorethang (26km)

North Point

To Bijanbari

To Lebong (1.5km) & Lebong Race Course (8km)

Observatory Hill

Lloyd Botanical Gardens

See Enlargement

Chowrasta

Major thoroughfare, but vehicles not permitted

Chowk Bazaar

Clubside

Budget Hotel Area

To TV Tower (200m)

Train Station

Batasia Loop

Ghoom Train Station

To Teesta Bazaar (36km), Kalimpong (52km) & Gangtok (94km)

To Siliguri (82km)

Tiger Hill (2590m)

are plenty of *Indian eateries* in the vicinity of Hotel Seven Seventeen.

Getting There & Away Convenient gateways to/from Darjeeling include Delhi, Kolkata and Kathmandu. To make travel arrangements in Darjeeling, contact:

Dorjee Ling Tours & Travel (☎ *56794, Hotel Seven Seventeen*)
Clubside Tours & Travels (☎ *54646, JP Sharma Rd*)
Pineridge Travels (☎ *53912, Chowrasta*) is adjacent to Pineridge Hotel.

Air From Delhi or Kolkata, the likely landing point is Bagdogra, near Siliguri, about 90km from Darjeeling. From Delhi, Jet Airways fly daily and Indian Airlines fly three times a week. Both airlines charge US$190. From Kolkata (US$65), Indian Airlines flies four times a week and Jet Airways twice a week.

Bus/Train From New Jalpaiguri – the main station for trains to/from Kolkata and Delhi – there is a *Toy Train* service to Darjeeling. However, it takes at least eight hours and is for train enthusiasts only. Most travellers take the train to New Jalpaiguri and catch an onward bus to Darjeeling. For information about trains to New Jalpaiguri, see p92 for Delhi; p97 for Kolkata.

Several buses connect New Jalpaiguri with Darjeeling (Rs 45, three to four hours). Taxis or shared 4WDs are a convenient alternative (Rs 100, two to three hours); they have a stand at the railway station.

Regular bus services run from Darjeeling to Gangtok (Rs 80, six to seven hours) and Kalimpong (Rs 42, three to four hours).

To/From Kathmandu By far the easiest (and most expensive) way to get to Kathmandu is to hire a taxi that has a special permit to cross the border into Nepal to the airport at Bhadrapur. The travel agents in Darjeeling can book this, together with the onward air ticket to Kathmandu (US$109). As most of the Nepalese air carriers fly from Kathmandu to Bhadrapur around midday and return early afternoon, you can leave Darjeeling mid-morning and be in Kathmandu that afternoon.

DARJEELING

If travelling in the opposite direction, you can leave Kathmandu around midday and be in Darjeeling that afternoon.

There are also several bus companies in Darjeeling that operate daily services to Kathmandu (Rs 250). However, you have to change buses at Kakarbhitta, the Nepalese border town. Alternatively, catch the local bus to Siliguri and another bus to the border. After completing Indian customs, hire a rickshaw that will take you to Kakarbhitta, where many buses leave in the late afternoon to Kathmandu. The total cost for this option is around Rs 150 to Rs 200.

There is no Nepalese consulate in Darjeeling but a 15-day visa can be issued at the border (US$25) and can be extended in Kathmandu.

Singalila Ridge & Phalut

Duration	5 days
Distance	76km
Difficulty	easy
Start	Mana Bhanjang
Finish	Rimbik
Nearest Town	Darjeeling (pp242–6)
Public Transport	yes

Summary A spectacular trek along the Singalila Ridge, travelling through Nepalese villages and alpine meadows and rewarding trekkers with magnificent views of Kangchenjunga.

Convenient access from Darjeeling and the network of lodges along the Singalila Ridge make this an easy trek to organise.

While the crest of the Singalila Ridge marks the border between India and Nepal, most of the villagers you'll encounter on the trek will be Nepalese. Indeed, at times you may believe this trek would be more appropriate in a guide on trekking in Nepal!

Acclimatisation is important. At least one extra day should be spent on the trail before ascending to Sandakphu (3620m). Also consider shorter trekking options, including descending directly from Molley to Sri Khola and Rimbik or following the direct trail from Sandakphu to Rimbik.

Whichever trek you choose, there are stunning views of Kangchenjunga. On the trails in Singalila National Park, you can enjoy the rhododendrons (in full bloom in May) and the extensive forests close to the Sikkim border.

PLANNING
When to Trek

The trekking season in Darjeeling is very similar to that in eastern Nepal. The post-monsoon season (Oct & Nov) brings clear days and warm temperatures, particularly in the valleys. Day temperatures drop to around 0°C in December and January, although trekking from lodge to lodge is still possible. Spring (Mar–May) has many attractions. The days are longer and the rhododendrons are in bloom until early June.

What to Bring

A good sleeping bag is essential. You only need a tent and insulated mat if you intend to camp. The weather on the higher ridges can deteriorate even during summer, so appropriate clothing and footwear is necessary.

Accommodation

There are a number of Trekkers Huts run by the DGHC, together with many private lodges on the trek. At Meghma, the *Sailung Tea House* has beds for Rs 35. There is a Trekkers Hut at Tonglu with beds for Rs 40, while there are several lodges at Tumling. At Jaubari, there is the *Teachers Lodge* and the *Indira Lodge*, while there is a Trekkers Hut at Gairi Bas. At Kali Pokhari, there is the *Singalila Lodge*, *Kangchenjunga Lodge* and *Chewang Lodge*; all with beds for around Rs 40. At Sandakphu, the Trekkers Hut charges Rs 100 per room; the privately run *Sherpa Chalet* and *Sherpa Tensing Lodge* offer similar rates.

There are well-maintained Trekkers Huts at Molley and Phalut. Dorm beds/rooms cost Rs 40/100. There are a number of private lodges at Gorkhey, while at Raman there is a Trekkers Hut and the *Hotel Sherpa*.

At the road head at Rimbik, privately run lodges include the *Sherpa Tensing Lodge* and *Hotel Sherpa*. Both charge Rs 50/100 per bed/room and have small restaurants.

DARJEELING

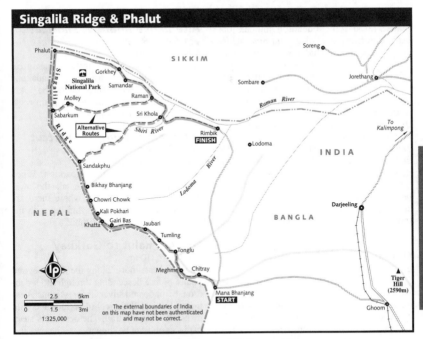

Singalila Ridge & Phalut

DARJEELING

GETTING TO/FROM THE TREK

From Darjeeling, take the bus to Rimbik that stops en route at Mana Bhanjang (Rs 25, two hours) For the same fare, a shared taxi is more convenient and faster.

From Rimbik, the bus (Rs 50, five hours) and shared 4WDs (Rs 70, three hours) leave at around 6.30am. The last bus leaves at 1pm.

THE TREK
Day 1: Mana Bhanjang to Tonglu
4–5 hours, 14km

Mana Bhanjang (2130m) is literally the *mani* (*stupa* – Buddhist religious structure like a chorten) on a *bhanjang* (ridge) – a village on the border of India and Nepal. After showing your passport at the registration office, walk through the bazaar to the trailhead.

The trail initially ascends to the ridge above the village. Cross the 4WD road a number of times to reach the *gompa* (Tibetan Buddhist monastery) at **Chitray** (2480m).

Beyond Chitray, the trail ascends through bamboo, rhododendron and oak forest,

complete with magnolias and wild roses. It passes a number of small settlements before reaching **Meghma** (2900m).

The village of **Tonglu** (3100m) is 2km beyond Meghma, with fine views towards Darjeeling. A short climb up the hill immediately north of the settlement affords clear views of Kangchenjunga and the adjacent peaks. From this vantage point, the forest ridge to Sandakphu can also be appreciated.

Day 2: Tonglu to Sandakphu
6–7 hours, 17km

The village of **Tumling** is about 1km above Tonglu. This is the entrance to the **Singalila National Park**. The checkpoint provides literature on the park, while the entrance fee is Rs 20/10 for foreign/Indian trekkers.

The well-defined trail continues through a number of villages, including **Jaubari** (2900m), **Gairi Bas** (2625m) and **Khatta** (2850m), each 2km to 3km apart.

The climb to **Kali Pokhari** (3100m) involves a further ascent, which is steep in places, through rhododendron and oak forest. Colourful prayer flags and *mani walls* (walls carved with Buddhist prayers) greet you as you reach the top – and the vicinity of the small lake. An overnight stay here in one of the *private lodges* is recommended if you are not already fully acclimatised.

Beyond Kali Pokhari, the trail winds along the ridge for 2km to **Chowri Chowk**. Fine views of the valleys extend deep into eastern Nepal. However, the slopes are heavily denuded of timber, reflecting the needs of many generations of Nepalese villagers. It is a further climb to the settlement of **Bikhay Bhanjang** (3200m) before a steady ascent through sliver fir forest to Sandakphu (3620m). The trek from Kali Pokhari to Sandakphu takes 2½ to three hours.

Day 3: Sandakphu to Phalut
6–7 hours, 17km

From Sandakphu, there are magnificent views of Kangchenjunga and the many peaks along the upper Singalila Ridge in Sikkim. The trail heads north through a forest of silver fir and rhododendron. About 3km beyond Sandakphu the trail splits. Take the trail that heads east along one of the most spectacular stages of the walk, with uninterrupted mountain views. The other trail returns directly to Rimbik (see Alternative Route 1).

A gradual climb reaches the deserted shepherds hut at **Sabarkum** (3530m). To stay on the main route, follow the higher (signposted) trail to Phalut. The lower trail descends for 2km to the Trekkers Huts at **Molley** (3420m; see Alternative Route 2).

From Sabarkum, the trail straddles the ridge across the extensive alpine meadows for 7km to the *Trekkers Huts* at **Phalut** (3590m). This is the high point of the trek, with panoramic views extending south into Nepal and east to Darjeeling and Kalimpong. To the north, the views include Pemayangtse in Sikkim and the huge flanks of Kangchenjunga.

To gain further views of Kangchenjunga, ascend the alpine pastures to the immediate west of Phalut. Take the time to appreciate this remote corner close to the borders of Nepal and Sikkim.

Alternative Route 1: Shortcut via Shiri River
5 hours, 15km

Although you would miss some great scenery, a trail to the east – after Sandakphu – shortens the trek to three days. The 15km shortcut from Sandakphu to the main route (Day 5) crosses the Shiri River.

Alternative Route 2: Shortcut via Molley
5½ hours, 15km

Another shortcut is after Sabarkum. When the main route continues north, take the lower trail. Molley is 2km east, where there are *Trekkers Huts*. At Raman, link up with the Day 5 route to finish in Rimbik.

Day 4: Phalut to Gorkhey
3–4 hours, 10km

The trail heads north along the ridge beyond Phalut before descending through rhododendron, bamboo and silver fir forest (much destroyed by fire). A variety of orchids and wild roses also line the trail. The descent is steep in places and can be slippery after heavy rainfall. It is also advisable *not* to follow the porter shortcuts unless you are very surefooted. At lower elevations, there is evidence of black bears foraging in the lower conifer forest. Forest leopards are also common.

Just above Gorkhey, the trail splits. The upper trail goes directly to Samandar, while the lower trail descends through potato and pea fields to **Gorkhey** (2390m), a pleasant village alongside the Raman River.

Day 5: Gorkhey to Rimbik
6 hours, 18km

From Gorkhey, ascend to **Samandar** (2500m) and the village school and football ground. Continue for a further 2km to a side stream before the trail gradually ascends for 4km through oak and blue pine forest to **Raman** (2530m). The *Trekkers Huts* are about a 10-minute hike above the main trail. From Raman, it is a 6km trek along the forest trail before a long descent to **Sri Khola** (2100m). Ascend the trail that winds high above the Raman River before joining the road for the last few kilometres to **Rimbik** (2290m).

DARJEELING

Sikkim

The Himalayan state of Sikkim was incorporated into the Indian Union in 1975. Since then the Indian government has maintained tight control over its border regions with Tibet (China). While travel restrictions on the areas north of Gangtok have been relaxed recently, the only area currently open to foreign trekkers is in the vicinity of Yuksam in southern Sikkim. There are plans to open other areas of the Kangchenjunga National Park, including the Zemu Glacier and the wild and desolate Lhonak Valley to the north of the state. This will make it possible to trek to the eastern flanks of Kangchenjunga.

HISTORY
The Lepchas, a tribal people thought to have migrated from Assam in the 13th century, originally populated Sikkim. They were essentially nature worshippers, moving from one forest clearing to the next throughout Sikkim. With the migration of the Tibetans to Sikkim during the 17th century, the Lepchas were forced to move to more remote regions.

In 1641 the 5th Dalai Lama in Lhasa appointed Phuntsog Namgyal the first ruler of Sikkim. At this time, Sikkim included part of eastern Nepal; part of the Chumbi Valley in Tibet; some of the western valleys of Bhutan; and, to the south, Darjeeling, Kalimpong and the territory down to the Indian Plains.

Boundaries were altered as a result of the wars with Bhutan between 1717 and 1734. Sikkim lost Kalimpong, on the India-Tibet trade route, and much of the southern foothills. More territory was lost after 1780, after the Gurkha expansion in Nepal. However, when the British East India Company won the Gurkha Wars, the Treaty of Siliguri (1817) returned the territory to the rajah of Sikkim. In exchange, the British were granted control over Sikkim's external affairs, including trade with Nepal, Tibet and Bhutan.

After the British annexation of Darjeeling (see p240), further expansion led to the 1861 declaration of Sikkim as a British protectorate. However, the Tibetans were becoming

Highlights

CHRIS BEALL

A Trekkers Hut at Dzongri in the Kangchenjunga National Park.

- Being awed by views of Kangchenjunga from the yak pastures of Dzongri

- Appreciating the multitude of blooms in some of the Himalaya's finest rhododendron forests

- Visiting indigenous Lepcha settlements and newly established Tibetan villages

increasingly suspicious of the British expansion and in 1886 they invaded Sikkim. The British resisted, and in 1890 a separate treaty declared Sikkim a semi-independent state, administered by the rajah under the guidance of a British Political Officer. It was not until 1902 that a Boundary Commission was established to determine the current borders between Sikkim and Tibet.

The British were keen to develop the country and encouraged workers from Nepal to settle in Sikkim. This continued after 1947, when India became independent and Sikkim

SIKKIM

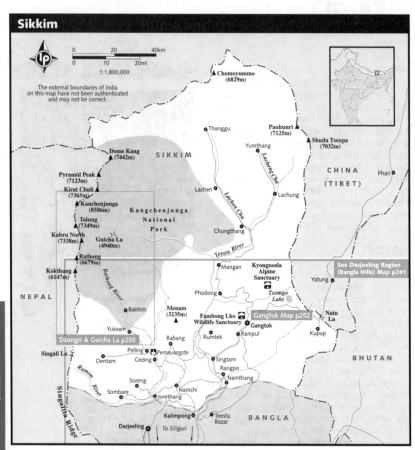

Sikkim

became a protectorate within the Indian Union. Indeed, in the early 1960s, the Nepalese constituted 75% of Sikkim's population. During this time, Sikkim's rajah upheld a policy to prohibit further immigration and to restrict the rights of Nepalese to gain citizenship. Demonstrations followed and the rajah sought refuge in India. India intervened, the rajah abdicated in 1975 and Sikkim became the 22nd state of the Indian Union.

NATURAL HISTORY

The Kangchenjunga massif is on the main axis of the Singalila Ridge – the mountain range forming the geographic divide between Nepal and Sikkim. The massif includes the main peak (8586m), the central peak (8482m) and the south peak (8476m). To the east, it is flanked by the Zemu Glacier, which feeds into the Zemu Chu and the Lhonak Chu, two of the main tributaries of the Teesta River.

North of the Kangchenjunga massif, the Singalila Ridge extends to Sikkim's northern border with Tibet. It includes Nepal Peak (6910m), Kirat Chuli (7365m), Pyramid Peak (7123m), Dome Kang (7442m), Jongsang (7483m) and Lhonak Peak (6710m), close to the borders of Nepal, Sikkim and Tibet.

South of the Kangchenjunga massif, the Singalila Ridge is equally impressive. It includes the main peak of Talung (7349m) at the head of the Talung Glacier, which feeds into the Talung Chu, another major tributary of the Teesta River. Immediately south of the Talung peaks are Kabru North (7338m), Kabru South (7317m), Rathong (6679m) and Kokthang (6147m), while on a subsidiary ridge are Kabru Dome (6600m) and Forked Peak (6108m). These peaks provide an impressive mountain wall, which encloses the Rathong Glacier and the Rathong River flowing south to Yuksam.

CLIMATE

Southern Sikkim is under the influence of the northeast monsoon. In particular, the region south of Kangchenjunga and the Himalaya Range is subject to heavy rainfall from early June to early September. The region experiences some of the heaviest rainfall in the Indian Himalaya, with up to 700mm per month falling in July and August.

The post-monsoon season extends from early October until mid-November. Although the day temperatures rarely average more than 5°C, at altitudes above 3500m, the settled conditions are ideal for trekking.

The first of the winter snows fall from mid- to late November and continue until early March. From mid-March, the snows begin to melt on the passes and the day temperatures rise to between 10° and 15°C. Monsoon clouds form by early May, with intermittent storms which last for a day or two. However, the mornings are generally clear and clouds do not build up until mid-morning.

INFORMATION
Maps

For treks out of Yuksam, the Air India trekking maps provide a useful ridge and river outline of the area. These are available from the Government of India Tourist Office in Delhi; see Local Tourist Offices (p258).

Books

Sikkim & Bhutan by Claude White (reprint 1984) gives historical background at the turn of the century.

Sikkim – A Travellers Guide by Sujoy Das and Arundhati Roy (Permanent Black, 2001) is exceptionally well illustrated.

For details of climbing expeditions in the region refer to:

Abode of Snow by Kenneth Mason (reprint 1987)
Exploring the Hidden Himalaya by Soli Mehta and Harish Kapadia (1990)
Himalayan Odyssey by Trevor Braham (1974)

Information Sources

The **Government of Sikkim Tourist Office** *(☎ 22064; MG Marg, Gangtok)* has a limited stock of maps and literature on trekking. Visit the reliable trekking agents (p253) for up-to-date information on trail conditions.

Permits

A permit is necessary to visit Sikkim. This allows you to visit most of southern towns, including Gangtok, Rumtek, Phodong and Pemayangtse. A special endorsement allowing foreigners to also visit Khecheopari Lake and Yuksam can be issued on the spot from the Tourist Office in Gangtok. An additional permit to visit Yumthang, in the north, is also necessary; a local travel agent in Gangtok can arrange a five-day permit.

Permit requirements for trekking out of Yuksam are gradually changing. For now, trekking permits can be obtained by your agent for a minimum of two people trekking together. If you plan to trek elsewhere in the state, you will need to apply to the **Ministry of Home Affairs** *(Lok Nayak Bhawan, Khan Market, Delhi 11003)*. Applications must be made at least three months before travelling and are unlikely to be granted. Alternatively, get your trekking agent in Gangtok to apply locally as the state authorities are keen to promote tourism and also gain some autonomy in their own affairs.

There are two entry/exit points for Sikkim: Jorethang (if travelling to/from Pelling) and Rangpo (if travelling to/from Gangtok). At Jorethang, you will need to organise a permit in advance; at Rangpo, you can get a free (two-day) permit at the border that must be extended within two days at Gangtok.

Basic travel permits take a day or two to issue. You will need photocopies of your

SIKKIM

passport details and one passport sized photo. There is no fee. Permits are normally valid for 15 days from the specified date of entry and can be extended for up to 45 days. Note that re-entry into Sikkim within three months is not possible, even if you leave before your 15-day visa expires.

Permits can be obtained at the following locations:

New Sikkim House (☎ *011-6116346; 14 Panchseel Marg, Chanakyapuri, Delhi*)
Office of the District Magistrate (*Hill Cart Rd, Darjeeling*)
Sikkim Tourist Information Centre (☎ *0353-432646; SNT Colony, Hill Cart Rd, Siliguri*)
Sikkim Tourist Information Centre (☎ *033-2468983; 4C Poonam Bldg, 5/2 Russell St, Kolkata*)

ACCESS TOWN
Gangtok
☎ 03592 • alt 1676m

Gangtok, the capital of Sikkim, is on a ridge above the Ranipul River. Spectacular views reach across to Kangchenjunga and the peaks on the Singalila Ridge between Nepal and Sikkim. Spend time wandering forest trails beyond the town or visiting Namgyal Institute of Tibetology, established in 1958 to promote the language and cultural traditions of Tibet. The library is stocked with manuscripts brought from Tibet in 1959 and many valuable *thangkas* (Buddhist religious paintings).

Rumtek's *gompa* (Tibetan Buddhist monastery) is the seat of the Gyalwa Karmapa, head of the Kargyupa sect of Tibetan Buddhism, is a further attraction. It is 24km away by road on the far side of the valley.

For tourist information, see Information Sources (p251).

Supplies & Equipment Fresh vegetables and fruit and a wide range of tinned items are available in Gangtok. However, most arrangements (including food) are made by a local agent. All you need to buy are some extra snacks for the trek.

It is difficult to hire sleeping bags, tents or down jackets. Check carefully with your trekking agent as to what exactly is provided and gear yourself up accordingly.

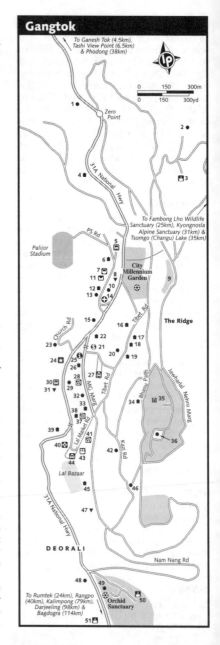

Gangtok

Gangtok

PLACES TO STAY

4 Hotel Superview Himalchuli; Yak & Yeti Travels Office
6 Hotel Lha Khar & Restaurant
12 Hotel Tibet; Charitrust Tibetan Handicraft Emporium
16 Hotel Sonam Delek; Oyster Bar & Restaurant
17 Hotel Heritage
18 Modern Central Lodge & Restaurant
19 Hotel Lhakpa & Restaurant
22 Gangtok Lodge
26 Green Hotel & Restaurant; Silk Route Tours & Travels Office
33 Hotel Golden Pagoda & Restaurant
34 Hotel Pomra
38 Hotel Orchid; Orchid Cafe
39 Hotel Central
45 Hotel Tashi Delek

PLACES TO EAT

8 Tibet Cafe
31 Hotel Hungry Jack; Tripti's
47 Oberoi's Barbique Restaurant

OTHER

1 Directorate of Handicrafts & Handlooms
2 Telecommunications Tower
3 Enchey Gompa
5 SNT Bus Station; Railway Reservation Counter
7 4WD Station
9 Flower Exhibition Centre; Ridge Park
10 Siniolchu Tours & Travels; Potala Tours & Travels
11 Main Post Office
13 Tibetan Souvenir & Handicrafts Stores
14 STNM Hospital
15 Jainco Booksellers
20 Namgyal Tours & Treks Office
21 State Bank of India
23 Sikkim Tours & Travels Office
24 Police Station
25 Sikkim Tourist Office; Blue Sheep Restaurant; Wisdom Tours & Travels Office
27 Old Children's Park Taxi Station

28 Gokul (Internet Centre); RNC Enterprises; Parivar Restaurant; Khan Khazana
29 Tashila Tours & Travels Office
30 Private Bus & Taxi Station
32 Good Books; Rural Artisans Marketing Centre
35 Palace
36 Tsuk-La-Khang (Royal Chapel)
37 Sip 'n' Surf
40 Supermarket Complex; Vajra Adventure Tours
41 Logon.com
42 Foreigners Registration Office
43 Denzong Cinema
44 Lal Bazaar Taxi Stand
46 Tashi Ling (Home Office)
48 Forest Department Office
49 Namgyal Institute of Tibetology; Orchid Sanctuary
50 Do-Drul Chörten & Gompa
51 Guru Lhakhang Gompa

Bring your own sleeping bag and waterproof jacket.

Trekking Agents In general, trekking agents in Gangtok are knowledgeable about the mountain regions and aware of environmental considerations. Rates per day for trekking are in the vicinity of US$40 to US$45 per person.

Recommended agents include:

Namgyal Tours & Treks (☎ 23701, Tibet Rd) is opposite Hotel Lhakpa. The agent gained extensive experience organising treks in Nepal before returning to Sikkim a decade ago.

Sikkim Tours & Travels (☎ 22188, Church Rd) is run by a keen trekker and photographer.

Vajra Adventure Tours (☎ 22446; e slg_vato urs@sancharnet.in; Hotel View Point, Arithang Rd) is a professional operation run by an experienced agent.

Yak & Yeti Travels (☎ 24643; e yakyeti@ mailcity.com; Hotel Superview Himalchuli, Zero Point, 31A National Hwy) is run by enthusiastic Satish Bardewa.

Places to Stay & Eat Most trekking agents will book accommodation for you as part of

their travel package, with competitive rates for most hotels. At **Modern Central Lodge** (☎ 24670, Tibet Rd), doubles cost Rs 180 to Rs 250. **Hotel Lha Khar** (☎ 25708, PS Rd) is opposite the SNT bus station, and charges Rs 200 to Rs 300 for doubles. Midrange accommodation includes **Hotel Sonam Delek** (☎ 22566, Tibet Rd), with doubles from Rs 550 to Rs 800; and **Hotel Superview Himalchuli** (☎ 24643, 31A National Hwy), well located with fine views and rooms from Rs 400 to Rs 775. The best of the top-end hotels is the popular and very comfortable **Hotel Tashi Delek** (☎ 22991, MG Marg), charging Rs 1300 to Rs 1800.

Tibet Cafe (National Hwy 31A) offers Tibetan and Chinese cuisine. **Blue Sheep Restaurant**, above the tourist office, serves good-value Indian and Chinese dishes. There are many good, inexpensive restaurants in the hotels, including **Modern Central Lodge**, **Hotel Lha Khar** and the **Green Hotel** (MG Marg).

Getting There & Away Regular buses run to/from Darjeeling, Kalimpong and Siliguri.

Watching Wildlife

The Kangchenjunga National Park constitutes around 25% of Sikkim's land. Within its boundaries, it supports a range of wildlife, including the **Himalayan red panda** (Sikkim's state animal), **leopards**, **black bears**, **musk deer** and **barking deer**. Goral and **serow** may also be sighted in the forest clearings. The elusive **clouded leopard** is confined to the most remote forest regions.

On higher elevations, there are **Himalayan Tahr**, **Nayan** or **Great Himalayan sheep**, plus **bharal** and **snow leopards**. While the chance of sighting even **wild sheep** and **goats** is small, they have been known to descend rapidly to lower altitudes after unseasonal snowfall.

Birdlife includes the **blood pheasant** (the state bird), and the **monal** and **tragopan** at higher forest elevations. Birds of prey include **lammergeiers**, **eagles**, **falcons** and **hawks**. **Tibetan snowcocks** and **snow partridges** are found in alpine meadows.

There is also a possibility of viewing migratory wildfowl, including the **bar-headed goose**, **eastern goosander**, **brown-headed gull**, and even the **black-necked crane** that settles in the high lakes of northern Sikkim.

The forests of Sikkim are generally more luxuriant than in Darjeeling. The temperate broad-leafed forest with its many varieties of **oak**, **maple** and **magnolia** gives way to mixed conifer with **fir** and **spruce**. More than 50 flowering **rhododendron** species bloom from April to mid-May, providing a highlight of any trek in southern Sikkim. A number of **dwarf rhododendrons** and **juniper**, along with many flowering species of **iris**, **anemone** and **delphinium** are found in alpine meadows.

There are connecting services to Yuksam and other outlying regions of Sikkim.

Air The nearest airport is at Bagdogra, near Siliguri. See p245 in the Darjeeling chapter for details.

Bus Sikkim Nationalised Transport (SNT) is the main bus operator to/from Gangtok. Several buses each day connect Gangtok with Siliguri (Rs 55, five hours); Darjeeling (Rs 83, 6½ hours, one daily); and Kalimpong (Rs 55, 3½ hours, one daily). Catch a bus to Rumtek (Rs 17, 1½ hours) or Pelling (Rs 70, 5½ hours) for connections to Yuksam. Private buses also operate on most routes. They cost a little more but are faster and more comfortable.

Taxi It is likely that your trekking agent will organise a share or private taxi from Gangtok to Yuksam. Otherwise, go to the private bus and taxi station on 31A National Hwy for rides to Darjeeling (Rs 100, five hours), Siliguri (Rs 90, four hours), Bagdogra (Rs 120, four hours), Kalimpong (Rs 65, three hours) and Kakarbhitta (Rs 120, five hours).

Dzongri & Guicha La

Duration	7 days
Distance	104km
Standard	easy–moderate
Start/Finish	Yuksam
Nearest Town	Gangtok (pp252–4)
Public Transport	yes

Summary Trek through rhododendron forests and across yak pastures to the snowcapped peaks and glaciers below the awesome summit of Kangchenjunga.

Although there are plans to open up other areas for trekkers, at present this is the only trek that can be undertaken in Sikkim. The stages to Dzongri are graded as easy, while those to the Guicha La are moderate, mainly due to altitude. At least one additional day is necessary to acclimatise before ascending to Dzongri (4020m). Beware of any agent's itinerary that specifies otherwise. An extra day at Dzongri is also recommended to do the side trip to the Dzongri La and Rathong Valley.

Essentially this is a wilderness trek through the southern region of the Kangchenjunga

National Park, although there is a small Lepcha encampment at Bakhim, a Tibetan village at Tsoska and the occasional yak herder on the alpine pastures.

In May, the rhododendrons are at their finest and a week or two could be spent appreciating the many varieties in the forest above Tsoska. The array of orchids and ferns in the subtropical forest and the wildflowers on the meadows above Dzongri provide a further attraction.

Be well prepared as inclement weather can occur with remarkable frequency when ascending towards the Guicha La.

PLANNING
When to Trek
The Kangchenjunga region is subject to monsoonal rain from June until late September. There are two distinct trekking seasons: pre-monsoon season (early April–mid-May) and post-monsoon season (early Oct–mid-Nov). Pre-monsoon season is best for the rhododendrons, while post-monsoon season normally provides clearer views. Snowstorms can develop rapidly at higher altitudes in both seasons.

What to Bring
Your agent will supply a tent and insulated mat, along with most of the other trekking gear. However, check exactly what is supplied; if in doubt, at least bring your own sleeping bag.

Accommodation
Accommodation will be included as part of the trekking package provided by your agent in Gangtok. Determine whether your trek is tent-based or lodge-based. If it is lodge-based, be prepared for basic facilities in the trekkers huts at Tsoska, Dzongri, Thansing, and Samiti Lake. These huts together with the Forest Rest House in Bakhim may also be occupied by Indian students during the May/June school holidays. There is a choice of private lodges at Tsoska with comfortable rooms and food. The rooms cost around Rs 100 per night.

There are a number of comfortable lodges in Yuksam at the entrance to Kangchenjunga

National Park. These include *Hotel Demazong* and *Hotel Wild Orchid*, with rooms from around Rs 100. At the upmarket *Hotel Tashi Gang*, well-furnished rooms cost around Rs 1000.

GETTING TO/FROM THE TREK
It is likely that your agent will organise your transport arrangements for you. If not, several buses travel between Yuksam and Pelling (Rs 20, two hours), and Pelling and Gangtok (Rs 70, 5½ hours). Alternatively, you could take one of the shared 4WDs to Pelling (Rs 20) and catch the onward bus to Gangtok; the same service applies for travel from Gangtok to Yuksam.

THE TREK
Day 1: Yuksam to Bakhim
5–6 hours, 16km
Two warnings apply for this day: firstly, protect yourself from midges by wearing long trousers and applying insect repellent;

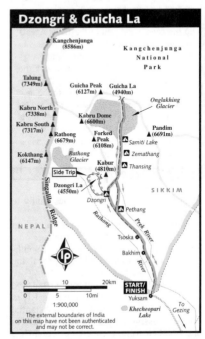

Environmental Watch

In the past decade, the trekking agents in Sikkim have adopted an environmental code of conduct to limit the impact of trekkers in Kangchenjunga National Park. This was of particular concern as the only area open for trekkers is the Yuksam/Dzongri region to the south of the national park.

Several seasons ago the trails from Yuksam to Dzongri left much to be desired. Discarded tin cans, plastic wrappings and other non-biodegradable rubbish littered the area. Campsites were scarred with toilet and tent trenches, and dwarf rhododendron and juniper were cut for fires.

A stricter adherence to the park regulations combined with the concerted actions of the agents has helped reverse the trend. Clean-up programs at the end of each season; an education program for local guides and crew; and support from the Himalayan Mountaineering Institute in Darjeeling have also ensured that appropriate measures are maintained.

To ensure that the operators are able to keep up the good work, contact the **Travel Agents Association of Sikkim** (PO Box 15, Gangtok) to donate. For more information about Kangchenjunga National Park policies, visit the **Wildlife & Forest Office** on the National Hwy 31A just south of Gangtok. A visit to the new **Sikkim Development Foundation** (☎ 29276; Chungyal Complex, MG Marg, Gangtok) is also recommended. The foundation is concerned with all aspects of conservation; donations and support are appreciated.

secondly, keep a box of matches handy to burn off the abundant leeches.

Yuksam (1760m), a former capital of Sikkim, is now no more than a village on a plateau with commanding views of southern Sikkim. It also marks the entrance to the Kangchenjunga National Park.

The trail heads north entering an oak and pine forest high above the Rathong River. The trail is well defined, with substantial bridges crossing the side rivers. Apart from one small clearing, there are no settlements en route. Just beyond the confluence of the Rathong and Prek Rivers (the latter comes from the Guicha La) the trail descends steeply to a substantial bridge. There follows a 600m ascent to the small settlement of **Bakhim** (2750m), occupied by a family of Lepcha farmers. There is a *Forest Rest House* and a *campsite*, complete with a small spring, just below the settlement. From Bakhim, enjoy commanding views down the Rathong Gorge to Yuksam.

Day 2: Bakhim to Pethang
4–5 hours, 12km

The trail from Bakhim heads up past the first rhododendron and magnolia trees to **Tsoska** (3050m).

Tsoska is a comparatively new village, founded in the early 1960s when the Sikkim government granted this tract of land to Tibetan refugees who had fled over the border in 1959. The village consists of a dozen or so houses, a gompa, and rows of *chortens* (reliquaries or shrines to the memory of a Buddhist saint) lining the trail.

Just above the village, the trail splits. A small trail diverts towards the Rathong Valley, while the main trail continues up the ridge. Steep in sections, it passes through magnificent **rhododendron forests**. The forest trail is well defined, with wooden boards over the potentially muddy sections.

Pethang (3650m) is a small clearing for camping. The water supply is about 200m down the side trail leading to the Prek Valley.

Day 3: Pethang to Dzongri
2–3 hours, 7km

From Pethang a steep ascent leads to the upper limit of the conifers and the top of the ridge separating the Prek and Rathong Valleys. Wonderful 360-degree views extend south down the valley and across the ridges beyond Yuksam; northeast to the sacred peak of Pandim (6691m) on the far side of the Prek Valley; west, beyond the Rathong Valley, to the Singalila Ridge; and north to the south face of Kangchenjunga (8586m), the world's third-highest peak.

The route along the ridge is covered with dwarf rhododendron bushes and leads to the open, grazing meadows at **Dzongri** (4020m). The ***Trekkers Huts*** are just below the main grazing area, while the best ***campsites*** are 1km further in an open meadow. Dzongri is a vast, windswept area where yaks from Yuksam and the surrounding villages graze from late March until early October.

From Dzongri, the views include Kokthang, Rathong and Kabru South, while Pandim is the highest peak on the east side of the Prek Valley. The nearby **Dzongri Peak**, about 300m above the camp, is the best vantage point to view Kangchenjunga and the surrounding peaks. Climb the peak early in the morning for the best views.

Side Trip: Dzongri La & Rathong Valley
3–4/6–7 hours, 10km/13km return
The trail heads to the **Dzongri La** (4550m), a small pass to the west of Kabur Peak. The 1½- to two-hour trek, with a steady ascent just before the pass, is rewarded by fine views across to the Rathong Glacier and the peaks that enclose Rathong Valley: Rathong, Kabru South, Kabru North, Kabru Dome and Forked Peak.

Return directly to camp or continue for one to 1½ hours to the Rathong Valley – for finer views of the spectacular peaks at the head of the valley. The trail then heads down the valley before commencing a steep ascent back to Dzongri. Take a local guide, as the trail is difficult to follow in places.

Day 4: Dzongri to Samiti Lake
6 hours, 16km
Head east from Dzongri to a series of cairns above the Prek Valley. You can view Kangchenjunga and the entire Prek Valley as far north as the Guicha La. From the ridge, a steep descent though rhododendron forest leads to the riverbed. Head up along the boulder-strewn riverbed to a bridge over the Prek River. The trail leads to the meadows at **Thansing** (3930m).

From Thansing, it is a two-hour climb up the valley to Samiti Lake. The gradual ascent heads across grazing meadows to the huts at Zemathang and the terminal moraine

of the Onglakhing Glacier. This is the base for climbing attempts on Pandim. It also marks the beginning of the climb up the moraine to **Samiti Lake** (4200m) – the sacred source of the Prek River.

Day 5: Samiti Lake to Guicha La & Return to Thansing
7–8 hours, 18km
From Samiti Lake, it will take three to four hours to reach the Guicha La. The pass is often shrouded in mist and cloud not long after sunrise, so an early start is necessary.

The trail heads along the far side of the lake and through moraine before crossing a sandy section alongside the Onglakhing Glacier. From here, you can see the pass at the head of the valley. However, the trek through the lateral moraine is tiring – more so if there has been a recent snowfall.

From the **Guicha La** (4940m), marked with fluttering, colourful prayer flags, there are uninterrupted views of the awe-inspiring east ridge of Kangchenjunga, high above the Talung Glacier. At present this is as far as you are permitted to trek. The return trek via Samiti Lake to Thansing will take three to four hours.

Day 6: Thansing to Tsoska
6–7 hours, 17km
From Thansing, follow the trail back down to the Prek River to recross the bridge. Descend through the boulder field to the base of the climb back up to Dzongri. Here, the trail divides. It is clearly signposted: the upper trail leads to Dzongri and the lower trail (main route) heads directly to Pethang.

The lower trail is too narrow for laden yaks, so if they are accompanying your group they will have to return via Dzongri and descend the ridge to Pethang. For this option, return along the Days 3 and 4 route.

Day 7: Tsoska to Yuksam
5–6 hours, 18km
This stage is often hot and muggy after the rarefied climes of the Guicha La. It can be completed in a long morning with time to arrange onward transportation.

Travel Facts

TOURIST OFFICES
Local Tourist Offices

The Government of India Tourist Office (GITO) branches in Delhi and Kolkata provide general travelling information. As with the state tourist offices, they provide helpful travelling and accommodation advice but are rarely the best source of reliable trekking advice.

Tourist offices in Delhi include:

Government of India Tourist Office (☎ 332000; 88 Janpath) is near Connaught Place. It is helpful at answering most questions, has some free literature (including a good map of Delhi) and offers ITDC bus tours of both Old and New Delhi. However, there is a dearth of information regarding trekking.

Jammu and Kashmir Tourist Office (☎ 3345373; Kanishka Shopping Plaza, 19 Ashoka Rd) has reliable information about trekking in Ladakh and nowadays makes more realistic comments about travelling to Kashmir.

Himachal Pradesh Tourist Development Corporation (HPTDC; ☎ 3325320; Chandralok Bldg, 36 Janpath) is the place to book seats on HPTDC buses and any HPTDC accommodation. There is, however, a shortage of literature on trekking.

Uttaranchal Tourist Office (☎ 3327713; Suite 102, Indraprakash Bldg, 21 Barakhamba Rd) has facilities to book seats on their buses and accommodation through the Garhwal Mandal Vikas Nigam (GMVN) and the Kumaon Mandal Vikas Nigam (KMVN; both are state-owned organisations with trekking divisions), who also have offices here. They also have comprehensive brochures on trekking, although some of the information and maps need reviewing.

Bangla (West Bengal) Office (☎ 3732840; A2 State Emporium Complex, Baba Kharak Singh Marg) has basic maps on treks out of Darjeeling.

Sikkim Tourist Office (☎ 6115346; New Sikkim House Bldg, 14 Panchsheel Marg, Chanakyapuri) provides general information and basic trekking maps.

Tourist Offices in Kolkata include:

Government of India Tourist Office (☎ 282 5813; 4 Shakespeare Sarani) is on Chowringhee. Both the state and national tourist offices have counters at the airport.

Bangla Tourist Office (☎ 2825813; 3/2 BBD Bagh) is opposite the post office. Don't expect to find much useful information. There's also an office at Howrah Station (☎ 6602518).

Tourist Offices Abroad

The GITO maintains a number of overseas branches where you can obtain brochures, leaflets and general information about India. The leaflets contain plenty of detail and are worthwhile. Also visit the useful Department of Tourism website **W** www.tourindia.com.

Australia (☎ 02-9264 4855; fax 9264 4860; **e** indtour@ozemail.com.au; Level 2, Piccadilly, 210 Pitt St, Sydney, NSW 2000)
Canada (☎ 416-962 3787; fax 962 6279; **e** India@istar.ca; 60 Bloor St West, Suite 1003, Toronto, Ontario M4N 3N6)
France (☎ 01 45 23 30 45; fax 23 65 33 45; **e** goitotar@aol.com; 1113 blvd Haussmann, F-76009, Paris)
Germany (☎ 069-242 9490; fax 242 9497; **e** info@india-tourism.com; Baseler Strasse 48, D-60329, Frankfurt-am-Main 1)
Italy (☎ 02-805 3506; fax 7202 1681; **e** info.it@India-Tourism.com; Via Albricci 9, Milan 21022)
UK (☎ 020-743 7677; fax 494 1048; **e** info@ind iatouristoffice.org; 7 Cork St, London W1X 2AB)
USA
New York (☎ 212-586 4901; fax 582 3274; 30 Rockefeller Plaza, Suite 15, North Mezzanine, New York 10112)
Los Angeles (☎ 213-390 8855; fax 380 6111; 3550 Wiltshire Blvd, Suite 204, Los Angeles, CA 90010)

Smaller promotional offices are in Osaka (Japan), and Dallas, Miami, San Francisco and Washington, DC (USA).

VISAS & DOCUMENTS

See Land (p266) for the documents required to drive a car in India.

Passports

When obtaining a visa for India, your passport should have at least six months validity. If you lose your passport, report the loss to the local police and return to Delhi as it is practically impossible to travel anywhere in India without it. Most embassies will issue a temporary passport, valid for one year. A photocopy of your lost passport should help speed up the process. Upon receiving your new passport, contact the Foreigners Registration Office in Delhi (see Visa Extensions). Some proof of when and where you entered the country will help matters.

Visas

People of all nationalities, including British Commonwealth citizens, require a valid passport and visa to enter India. Visas are issued at Indian embassies. They are valid for 120 days and must be obtained no more than six months before your arrival in India. If you are planning to visit a neighbouring country such as Nepal, and return to India, a double/multi-entry visa is necessary.

Note that if you apply to visit Arunachal Pradesh or other politically sensitive regions, your application can take up to three months, and sometimes longer, to process. If you are travelling independently, and have any doubts at all about whether this will hinder your plans, don't apply. Once you have applied to visit one of these regions you cannot reapply for an ordinary tourist visa until your original application has been cleared.

Visa Extensions

In India, visas can be extended at the **Foreigners Registration Office** (☎ *3319489; Hans Bhavan, Tilak Bridge, Delhi)* or Darjeeling, or at any office of the Superintendent of Police – eg, in Leh, Manali or Mussoorie. The application is usually straightforward.

If you stay in India for more than 120 days, keep your bank exchange certificates as you will need a tax clearance before leaving the country. The clearance certificate is issued by the **Foreigners' Section, Income Tax Office** (☎ *3317826; Indraprastha Estate, Delhi).* Allow a day to complete formalities.

Travel Insurance

Buy a policy that generously covers you for medical expenses, theft or loss of luggage and tickets, and for cancellations and delays in your travel arrangements. It may be worth

Copies

All important documents (passport, credit cards, travel insurance policy, driving licence, etc) should be photocopied before you leave home. Leave one copy at home and keep another with you, separate from the originals.

Another option for storing copies of your travel documents is Lonely Planet's free on-line Travel Vault. Create your personal vault at Ⓦ www.ekno.lonelyplanet.com.

taking out cover for mountaineering activities and the cost of evacuation. Check your policy doesn't exclude trekking as a dangerous activity.

Without evacuation cover, rescue by helicopter can be very expensive – US$3000 or more – and a helicopter will not be sent unless the Indian Air Force has some guarantee of payment. Most reputable agencies that run treks to the Himalaya can organise policies to cover emergency evacuation; indeed, many insist that this be taken out as a condition of booking. Do not rely on your consulate or embassy to help in an emergency.

Buy travel insurance as early as possible to ensure you'll be compensated for any unforseen accidents or delays. If items are lost or stolen get a police report immediately – otherwise your insurer might not pay up.

EMBASSIES & CONSULATES
Indian Embassies Abroad

The following list includes many of India's diplomatic missions around the world. Inquire locally for consulates or if your country's embassy is not listed here.

Australia *(*☎ *02-6273 3999; fax 6273 3328;* ⓔ *hicanb@ozemail.com.au; 3/5 Moonah Place, Yarralumla, ACT 2600)*
Canada *(*☎ *613-744 3751; fax 744 0913;* ⓔ *hicomind@ottawa.net; 10 Springfield Rd, Ottawa, Ontario K1M 1C9)*
France *(*☎ *01 40 50 70 70; fax 40 50 09 96;* ⓔ *culture@indembparis.zee.net; 15 rue Alfred Dehodencq, 75016 Paris)*
Germany *(*☎ *030-257 950; fax 257 951;* ⓔ *info-indembassy@csm.de; Tiergartenstrasse 17, 10785 Berlin)*

Israel (☎ 03-510 1431; fax 510 1434;
e indembtel@netvision.net.il; 4 Kaufman St,
Sharbat House, Tel Aviv 68012)

Japan (☎ 03-3262 2391; fax 3234 4866;
e indembjp@gol.com; 2-2-11 Kudan Minami,
Chiyoda-ku, Tokyo 102)

Nepal (☎ 071-414940; fax 413132;
e indemb@mos.com.np; Lain Chaur,
PO Box 292, Kathmandu)

The Netherlands (☎ 070-346 9771; fax 361
7072; e fscom@indemb.nl; Buitenrustweg 2,
2517 KD, The Hague)

New Zealand (☎ 04-473 6390; fax 499 0665;
e hicomind@globe.co.nz; 180 Molesworth St,
Wellington)

Pakistan (☎ 051-814371; fax 820742;
e hicomind@isb.compol.com; G5 Diplomatic
Enclave, Islamabad)

UK (☎ 020-7836 8484; fax 7836 4331; India
House, Aldwych, London WC2B 4NA)

USA (☎ 202-939 7000; fax 265 4351; w www
.indianembassy.org; 2107 Massachusetts Ave
NW, Washington, DC 20008)

Embassies & Consulates in India

Most foreign diplomatic missions are in
Delhi (☎ 011; most concentrated around
Chanakyapuri), but there are also con-
sulates in the other major cities, including
Kolkata (☎ 033).

If you require emergency evacuation, the
embassy will generally contact your next of
kin, who will have to guarantee payment.
Some embassies may waive this regulation
in a life-or-death situation, but not otherwise.

Australia (☎ 6888223; fax 6874126;
1/50-G Shantipath, Chanakyapuri, Delhi)

Canada (☎ 6876500; fax 6876579;
7/8 Shantipath, Chanakyapuri, Delhi)

France (☎ 6118790; fax 6872305;
2/50-E Shantipath, Chanakyapuri, Delhi)

Germany (☎ 6871831; fax 6873117;
6/50-G Shantipath, Chanakyapuri, Delhi)

Israel (☎ 3013238; fax 3014298;
3 Aurangzeb Rd, Delhi)

Italy (☎ 6114355; fax 6873889; 50E Chandra-
gupta Marg, Chanakyapuri, Delhi)

Japan (☎ 6876581; fax 6885587;
4-5/50-G Shantipath, Chanakyapuri, Delhi)

Nepal (☎ 3328191; fax 3326857;
Barakhamba Rd, Delhi)

The Netherlands (☎ 6884951; fax 6884956;
6/50F Shantipath, Chanakyapuri, Delhi)

New Zealand (☎ 6883170; fax 6872317;
50N Nyaya Marg, Chanakyapuri, Delhi)

Pakistan (☎ 4676004; fax 6372339;
2/50-G Shantipath, Chanakyapuri, Delhi)

South Africa (☎ 6149411; fax 6143605;
B18 Vasant Marg, Vasant Vihar, Delhi)

UK (☎ 6872161; fax 6872882; 50 Shantipath,
Chanakyapuri, Delhi)

USA (☎ 4198000; Shantipath, Chanakyapuri,
Delhi)

CUSTOMS

The usual duty-free regulations apply for
India. High-value items such as video cameras are likely to be entered on a Tourist
Baggage Re-Export (TBRE) form to ensure
that you take the goods with you when you
leave India. Depending on the customs officer, you may also be required to enter your
camera on the TBRE form. Similarly, some
officers may want to record sporting goods,
including ice axes, crampons and even sleeping bags. However, no duty is levied provided they are re-exported.

Upon departure, your passport will be
checked for any TBRE entries. Customs
officials do not take kindly to police reports
stating that the goods have been stolen and
are just as likely to charge you duty, which
can be prohibitive.

MONEY
Currency

The Indian rupee (Rs) is divided into 100
paise. There are coins of 5, 10, 20, 25 and 50
paise, and Rs 1, 2, and 5. Notes cover Rs 1,
2, 5, 10, 20, 50, 100 and 500. The rupee was
once divided into 16 annas, and you may
hear prices quoted in annas, especially in
markets: 4 annas equalled 25 paise.

Exchange Rates

A good currency converter is w www.oanda
.com. This table shows the exchange rate at
the time of printing:

country	unit	Rs
Australia	A$1	Rs 25.38
Canada	C$1	Rs 30.46
Europe	€1	Rs 42.42
Japan	¥100	Rs 36.35
New Zealand	NZ$1	Rs 20.77
UK	£1	Rs 69.19
USA	US$1	Rs 48.78

Exchanging Money

Time is the big consideration when organising your money for India. ATMs in the major cities make transactions very easy. Going into a bank and waiting in two or three queues – first to sign a travellers cheque, then to cash the money token and finally to wait for an encashment certificate – is not worth the time. Hotels are a good alternative, as are authorised moneychangers.

There are vast areas of the Indian Himalaya where it is not possible to change money or get cash advances. Use the following information for planning:

Ladakh You can change money and get cash advances in Leh, and change money at Kargil. There are no facilities in Padum.

Himachal Pradesh Authorised moneychangers and banks allowing cash advances are in Manali and McLeod Ganj. There are no facilities in Brahmaur, Kaza, Keylong or Rekong Peo. Change money at Manali or Shimla before heading off.

Uttaranchal You change money in Mussoorie, Dehra Dun or Naini Tal but you may have difficulty in towns such as Uttarkashi or Joshimath, or elsewhere in the mountain regions.

Darjeeling & Gangtok There is no problem changing money here.

Cash This is the simplest option; preferably carry US dollars, which can easily be changed at a bank or hotel before starting your trek.

Travellers Cheques These have the advantage of replacement if stolen or lost. Again, carry cheques in US dollars for easy exchange in more remote areas.

ATMs There are now a handful of ATMs in Delhi and Kolkata that accept most major credit cards.

Credit Cards Most cards are generally accepted. Banks can also provide a cash advance in US-dollar travellers cheques or Indian rupees.

International Transfers Having money transferred to India can take time and a lot of chasing around. It is probably faster to have the funds deposited in your account at home, where they can be drawn out as a cash advance.

Black Market There is no longer a significant black market for US dollars in India. Besides being illegal, there is also the risk of receiving counterfeit notes or being short-changed in the street.

On the Trek

If organising an inclusive trek through a local agent, check before you arrive in India that the agent accepts payment by credit card. The trek may also be payable in instalments (ie, 10% deposit, 60% on arrival and the balance after completing the trek). If trekking independently, you have little option but to carry cash with you.

Don't be too concerned with carrying low-denomination notes. Hundred-rupee notes can normally be changed at *dhabas* (tea stalls) along the trail, and the total bill for porters and horsemen is likely to run into many hundreds of rupees. Ensure that the notes are in good condition. Torn or dirty notes are often not accepted in India, especially in remote regions.

Costs

When compiling a budget, try to break down your expenses into a number of categories. The total is still a conservative estimate and there will always be extras, whether it be tipping the porters or discovering that the local bus is out of action and you have to hire a 4WD.

If you are backpacking, your basic food and fuel costs should amount to no more than Rs 200 per day, plus Rs 50/200 per night for camping/lodge accommodation. If hiring horses or porters, budget for an additional Rs 300 per porter or horse per day (this should include relocation, food and clothing allowance). If applicable, add accommodation fees and transportation costs for each porter. If making inclusive arrangements through an agent, budget for $US30 to US$50 per day per person.

Finally, account for the cost of travelling from Delhi or Kolkata to the trekking region, and travelling to the trailhead. See the Getting

Around section (pp268–71) and the Getting to/from the Trek information for each trek.

Tipping & Bargaining

Tipping is the custom in India, so you should budget for tips to room boys and helpers who take you around the market, not to mention the host of other people forever coming out of the woodwork to help. See Guides & Porters (pp49–51) for advice on tipping after a trek.

Bargaining is also an integral part of Indian culture. Where there are no fixed prices, the only way to determine the price is to come to a negotiated agreement, which can involve hours of haggling. This may include bargaining over the cost of a trek, porters, transport and other matters such as the number of trek stages. Don't give up or get upset – remember that you will often lose respect if you don't bargain hard. Before bargaining try to get a good idea of the fair price, as once you agree on a price you must stick to it.

POST & COMMUNICATIONS
Post

Aerograms and postcards cost Rs 8.50 and airmail letters Rs 15 to send from India. Airmail letters to Australia, Europe and the USA will take between a week and 10 days to arrive. Sending letters from India can be a time-consuming process. You first need to queue to buy stamps, before joining another queue to have them are franked. Despite this, the system works and the vast majority of letters reach their destination safely.

Posting packages is also complicated but reliable. First, take the parcel to a tailor and get it stitched up for sending overseas. At the post office, fill out the customs declaration (to avoid duty, state the goods are a gift and the value is less than Rs 1000). Then it's on to the weighing and franking queues. Air parcels take approximately two weeks, while surface mail can take up to three months. Most airlines offer discount airfreight rates provided that you hold a ticket with the carrier and send the goods before travelling home.

Receiving Mail When asking your contacts to send mail, instruct them to underline your surname, Poste Restante and the destination city on the envelope. The poste restante counter is usually in some obscure room in the main post office. Most post offices ask to see your passport before letting you check through the mail. Many lost letters are filed under given names, so always check under both your names. Mail is normally held for three months then returned to sender by surface mail.

Alternatively, companies such as American Express will hold mail for their cardholders (American Express will hold mail if you are using their travellers cheques). Hotels may also hold mail, although many will automatically return mail if the guest is not at the hotel when the mail arrives.

Telephone & Fax

The telephone system in India has improved to the point where you can be reasonably assured of making an international or interstate phone call without undue delay. Most towns have private STD/ISD call booths with fax facilities and direct dialling for both interstate and overseas. They are quick and efficient, and are connected with a digital meter showing the cost. Direct international calls cost around Rs 70 per minute depending on the country you are calling. An interstate call would cost around Rs 30 per minute.

If calling from your hotel, check the rates first. Reverse-charge (collect) calls also attract a service charge from most hotels. The best alternative is to book a call for the minimum three minutes and get your friends or family to call you back.

Phonecards In the Indian Himalaya there is limited availability of phonecards, which will only be useful in cities. Lonely Planet's eKno Communication Card, specifically aimed at travellers, provides competitive international calls (avoid using it for local calls), messaging services and free email. Visit W www .ekno.lonelyplanet.com for information on joining and accessing the service.

Mobile (Cell) Phones There is limited reception in hills and no reception in the mountains.

Email

There are Internet cafes in all the main towns in the Indian hill states. Most are well maintained with reliable servers. Email messages cost around Rs 50 per page to send and Rs 10 to receive. An hour of Internet time costs around Rs 100.

PHOTOGRAPHY

For technical tips, see the boxed text 'Taking Photos Outdoors' (p43).

Film & Equipment

Your camera gear will almost certainly be the heaviest item in your day-pack, so don't weigh yourself down with too much gear.

If your SLR camera breaks, the photographic shops in Leh, Srinagar, Manali or Darjeeling do not repair these cameras. Companies in Delhi, including **Kinsey Bros** (☎ 3324446; A-2 Connaught Place) and **Mahatma & Co** (☎ 3329769; 59 M-Block, Connaught Place) are able to handle mechanical repairs but don't always have the parts to fix electrical faults.

Batteries can be purchased in Delhi and most of the trekking-off points, including Leh, Mussoorie, Darjeeling and Manali. The range of temperatures in summer does not necessitate the camera being winterised (protected against very low temperatures), unless you plan to trek in Ladakh in winter. Waterproof containers are essential to protect your gear in prolonged rainy conditions.

The price of film in India has become very competitive, with good stocks available in Delhi. A roll of slide film with 36 exposures costs around Rs 300. Be aware that film may have been stored beyond the use-by date or subjected to hot conditions. Slide film is cheaper than the print variety, and you can have your best slides printed.

Don't send film back from India by post – it may be damaged by heat or if opened for customs inspection. Keep it cool and secure until your return home. Colour film can be processed in Delhi.

Restrictions

Photographing airports before and after you board the plane is strictly prohibited in India, as is photographing military sites and bridges along the main highways. Photographing dams, TV towers, radio towers and other important communication installations is illegal.

Photographing People

Try to initiate some form of communication before even getting your camera out of its pack. Consider the feelings of the people. In most villages, particularly in Islamic areas, photographing women is normally not acceptable. Ask them if you may take their photograph. If the answer is affirmative get on with it. Do not spend the next five minutes adjusting light settings and checking technicalities, this will only lead to the subject putting on a 'camera face'. Indeed, if the subject is posing, take a second shot when they are less wary of your camera. This is especially true when photographing children.

Airport Security

In some airports, such as at Leh in Ladakh, security authorities may not permit hand baggage on the plane, and that includes cameras. It is advisable to pack them securely in your check-in baggage before departure. Most airports in India also ban all batteries from being carried on the plane.

In India, the X-ray machines are film safe, claiming they will not damage unprocessed film under 1000 ASA. However, given the number of X-rays that your film is subject to during travel, it is imperative that you carry your film in a lead-lined bag. Be aware, however, that the X-ray may be strengthened so that security staff can see the bags. While trekking carry film in a clear plastic container, rather than in individual canisters, for easy inspection.

TIME

India is 5½ hours ahead of GMT/UTC, 4½ hours behind Australian Eastern Standard Time and 10½ hours ahead of American Eastern Standard Time.

ELECTRICITY

The electric current is 230V to 240V AC, 50 Hz. Electricity is widely available in India, but breakdowns, blackouts, time sharing and load shedding are common in most Himalayan regions. Sockets are of the two round-pin variety – it's worth getting a local electrician to make an adaptor that will fit your plugs to the hotel sockets. Batteries are available everywhere in India.

WEIGHTS & MEASURES

The metric system was introduced to India in 1966 and is now generally accepted throughout the country. A conversion chart is on the inside back cover of this guide.

LAUNDRY

One of the great luxuries of returning from a trek is giving all your gear to the local *dhobi* (washerman/woman), who will return the clothing the following day in spotless condition. Payment is small in comparison to the sheer delight of not having to do the washing. Expect to pay a maximum of Rs 100 after a three-week trek.

During the trek, how often you wash your own clothes is for you to decide. Once, while trekking in Zanskar for a month during rather cold weather, I did not wash or change most of my clothes and ended up with a splendid case of body lice! However, the regular washing of socks and underwear can help prevent blisters (see pp71–2) and chafing (p72). Take biodegradable soap and wash your clothes in a bucket away from the river or stream. A washing line and a few pegs is also useful, although be cautious about leaving washing out overnight.

BUSINESS HOURS

In India, Sunday is the weekly holiday. The working week is from Monday to Friday from 10am to 5pm and Saturday morning. These working hours apply to government offices, banks, tourist offices and post offices. Most public holidays and festivals are normally regarded as holidays.

PUBLIC HOLIDAYS & SPECIAL EVENTS

While there are many public holidays in India, which often coincide with main festivals throughout the year, most will have little or no effect on your trekking plans. Those that will include:

Holi (Feb–Mar) One of the most colourful (literally) of the Hindu festivals, with people marking the end of winter by throwing coloured water and red powder over each other.

Id-ul-Zuhara (Feb) A Muslim festival commemorating Abraham's attempt to sacrifice his son. It will be held around 12 February in 2003 and 11 days earlier in 2004 (events on the Muslim calendar fall about 11 days earlier each year).

Buddha Jayanti (May–June) The Buddha's birth, enlightenment and attainment of Nirvana (earthly release) are all celebrated. On the Hindu calendar it is referred to as Wesak, while Tibetans and Ladakhi refer to the date as the Saka Dawa. The festivals are celebrated during full moon, but since the Ladakhi people keep different calendars, the festivals do not necessarily coincide with the same full moon.

Independence Day (15 Aug) The anniversary of India's independence from Britain in 1947. Avoid places such as Delhi and Kolkata as the large crowds can be the target of terrorist attacks.

Dussehra (Oct) The most important Hindu festival, this 10-day event celebrates the Ramayana, starting on the first day of the Hindu month of Asvina. Shops close and it is hard to find a trek crew.

Diwali (Oct–Nov) Celebrated on the 15th day of the month of Kartika. At night many oil lamps are lit as a symbol of their original purpose of showing Rama (an incarnation of Vishnu) the way home from his period of exile. In Kolkata, the festival is also dedicated to Kali (goddess of destruction), lasting five days.

Ramadan (Nov) The most significant event in the Muslim year, this is a 30-day dawn-to-dusk fast. It was on this month that the prophet Mohammed had the Koran revealed to him in Mecca.

Local Festivals These festivals may also interrupt, and enhance, your plans:

Ladakh (mid-June–early July) A famous Buddhist gompa festival, the Hemis festival commemorates Padmasambhava's birthday. It's on the 10th day of the 6th month of the Tibetan calendar.

Himachal Pradesh (Oct) The Dussehra festival in the Kullu Valley celebrates Rama's victory over the demon king Ravana. The festival continues for a week and commences on the 10th day of the rising moon, known as Vijay Dashmi.

Uttaranchal (late April–early May) Temples at Yamunotri and Gangotri are opened on the religious day of Akshaya-Tritya, and remain open till the Diwali festival in October. Temples at Kedarnath and Badrinath open about the same time.

Getting There & Away

There are no flights directly to the Indian Himalaya. This chapter deals with travel from international destinations to India. The Gateway Cities chapter has specific information about getting to the hills from Delhi (pp87–91) and Kolkata (Calcutta; p94). For more general information about travel within India, see Getting Around (pp268–71).

AIR
Airports & Airlines
Delhi is the gateway to India. You will fly into the **Delhi Indira Gandhi International Airport** (☎ 5652011) or, on domestic flights, the **Palam Airport** (☎ 5675121 for Indian Airlines, ☎ 5675126 for other carriers).

For treks out of Sikkim and Darjeeling, the nearest international airport is Kolkata. Its international and domestic airport is **Netaji Subhas Chandra Bose** (☎ 5118787). If travelling via Nepal to Sikkim and Darjeeling, there are convenient transfers from Kathmandu. Many flights between Europe and South-East Asia/Australia or to/from East Africa pass through Mumbai (Bombay).

Air India (ⓦ www.airindia.com) is India's international carrier. The domestic carrier is **Indian Airlines** (ⓦ www.indian-airlines .nic.in), which also operates regional international flights.

You will have no problem booking domestic flights before you depart for India. However, getting those flights confirmed is another matter – you will probably need a day or two in Delhi or Kolkata before heading to the hills.

Departure Tax
The airport departure tax is included in most international tickets. If you purchase your ticket in India, the tax is paid at the airport. For flights to neighbouring SAARC (South Asian Association for Regional Cooperation) countries (Pakistan, Sri Lanka, Bangladesh, Nepal) the tax is Rs 150. To other countries it is Rs 500.

International Fares from Delhi
Delhi is the best place in India for cheap international tickets. There are a number of bucket shops around Connaught Place, but inquire with other travellers about their reliability. Fares will always depend on the carrier, season of travel and travel agent.

The UK
Various excursion fares are available from London to India, but better prices are available through the many bucket shops. The cheapest fares are usually with Middle Eastern airlines such as Gulf Air or Emirates. Uzbekistan Airlines and Aeroflot also offer competitive fares to Delhi. Although more expensive, British Airways and Virgin Atlantic fly direct from London to Delhi, Mumbai and Kolkata. British Airways also flies from Belfast to Delhi or Mumbai.

Most British travel agents are registered with Air Travel Organisers Licensing (ATOL). If your flight is booked through an ATOL-registered agent that goes out of business, ATOL will guarantee a refund or an alternative. Unregistered bucket shops are riskier but sometimes cheaper.

Continental Europe
Fares from continental Europe are generally more expensive than from London. Direct

Warning
The information in this chapter is particularly vulnerable to change: prices for international travel are volatile, routes are introduced and cancelled, special deals come and go, and rules and visa requirements are amended. You should check directly with the airline or a travel agent to make sure you understand how a fare works and be aware of the security requirements for international travel.

The upshot of this is that you should get opinions, quotes and advice from as many airlines and travel agents as possible before you part with your hard-earned cash. The details given in this chapter should be regarded as pointers and are not a substitute for your own careful, up-to-date research.

Baggage Restrictions

The 2001 terrorist attacks on the USA mean airlines worldwide now impose tight restrictions on carry-on baggage. No sharp implements of any kind are allowed onto the plane – this means you need to pack items such as pocket knives, camping cutlery and first-aid kits into your checked luggage.

If you're carrying a camping stove you should remember that airlines also ban fuels (unleaded gasoline, white spirits or any flammable liquid) and gas cartridges from all baggage, both check-through and carry-on. Empty all fuel bottles and buy what you need at your destination.

flights leave from Frankfurt, Amsterdam and Paris to Delhi. Lufthansa, KLM and Air India are popular carriers.

The USA & Canada

Most flights to Delhi and Mumbai are via Europe or South-East Asia. High season for flights to India runs from June to August and December to January. Low season runs from March to around mid-May and September to November.

From the east coast, airlines travelling to Mumbai or Delhi include Air India, American Airlines and Singapore Airlines. From the west coast, Aeroflot has a reputation for discounts, while Cathay Pacific, Korean Air and Asiana Airlines also fly to both cities.

From Canada, most flights go via Europe but there are other options. From Vancouver, Northwest Airlines flies to Delhi or Mumbai via Hong Kong or Singapore, while Air France travels via Paris. From Toronto or Montreal to Mumbai or Delhi, fly via Paris with Air France or Frankfurt with Lufthansa.

Australia & New Zealand

The high season extends from the third week of November till the end of January. Fares from the east coast are slightly more expensive than from Darwin or Perth. Air India and Qantas fly to Delhi via Singapore. Malaysia Airlines, SriLankan Airlines and Gulf Air fly to Delhi and Mumbai. Flights to Kolkata are the most expensive.

There are no direct flights between India and New Zealand; most airlines offer stopovers in Asia. Malaysia Airlines flies from Auckland to Delhi via Kuala Lumpur, while Air New Zealand flies via Singapore.

Asia

Bangladesh Biman Bangladesh Airlines and Indian Airlines fly from Dhaka and Chittagong to Kolkata.

Nepal Royal Nepal Airlines Corporation (RNAC) and Indian Airlines share routes between India and Kathmandu. Both airlines give a 25% discount to those under 30 years of age. Delhi is the main departure point for flights between India and Kathmandu; other cities with direct connections are Mumbai, Kolkata and Varanasi. From Kathmandu, there are daily flights to Biratnagar (Nepal) with convenient land connections to Darjeeling and Sikkim.

Pakistan Pakistan International Airlines (PIA) operates flights from Karachi and Lahore to Delhi.

LAND

Car and motorcycle drivers will need their vehicle's registration papers, liability insurance and an international driver's permit, along with their license from home. You will also need a *Carnet de Passage en Douane*, which is a passport for the vehicle and acts as a temporary waiver of import duty.

Cycling is a cheap, convenient, healthy and environmentally sound way of travelling. Bicycles can travel by air. Ask the airline in advance about check-in requirements, although most airlines treat bicycles as just another piece of baggage.

Bangladesh

A regular bus service between Kolkata and Dhaka (24 hours) is by far the most convenient way of crossing the border.

If you're travelling from Bangladesh to India, you don't need an exit permit unless you entered Bangladesh by air, in which case you need a road permit. Contact the **Immigration & Passport Office** (☎ 02-9556020; *127 New Eskaton Rd, Mogh Bazar, Dhaka*).

If you're travelling from Kolkata, you will need a visa for Bangladesh (see Embassies & Consulates in India, p260). Bus tickets can be purchased from **Shyamoli Paribahan** (☎ 033-2290345; fax 2293715; *51 Mirza Ghalib St*), near Hotel VIP International.

Europe

The classic way of getting to India is overland, although a number of countries may not be safe for travel right now; investigate with your embassy. A number of London-based overland companies operate bus or truck trips across Asia on a regular basis. Check with these operators for more information:

Encounter Overland (☎ 020-7370 6845; W *www.encounter.co.uk; 267 Old Brompton Rd, London SW5 9LA*)
Exodus (☎ 020-8673 0859; W *www .exodus.co.uk; 9 Weir Rd, London SW12 OLT*)
Top Deck Travel (☎ 020-7370 4555; W *www .topdecktravel.co.uk; 125 Earls Court Rd, London SW5 9RH*)

Nepal

To/From Delhi There are direct buses between Delhi and Kathmandu (36 hours). However, it's cheaper and more satisfactory to organise this trip yourself. The route via Gorakhpur and Sunauli (in Uttar Pradesh) is the most convenient. Gorakhpur is an important railway junction: it's a 783km, 14½-hour train trip to/from Delhi. Sunauli is on the border.

To/From Bangla (West Bengal) From Siliguri, the major transport hub en route to Darjeeling and Sikkim, it is only one hour to the Indian border town of Paniktanki. Sharing a 4WD is the best option, followed by a cycle-rickshaw across the border to Kakarbhitta.

Daily buses run between Kakarbhitta and Kathmandu (18 hours). An alternative option from Darjeeling is to hire a taxi that is licensed to travel across the border to the airport at Biratnagar, Nepal. The fare should be about Rs 1650. If you depart Darjeeling

Buying the Best-Value Air Ticket

For short-term travel, it's usually cheaper to travel mid-week and to take advantage of short-lived promotional offers. Return tickets usually work out cheaper than two one-ways.

Booking through a travel agent or via airlines' websites is generally the cheapest way to get tickets. However, while on-line ticket sales are fine for a simple one-way or return trip on specified dates, they're no substitute for a travel agent who is familiar with special deals and can offer all kinds of advice.

Buying tickets with a credit card should mean you get a refund if you don't get what you paid for. Go through a licensed travel agent, who should be covered by an industry guarantee scheme.

Whatever your choice, make sure you take out travel insurance (see p259).

mid-morning, this will connect you with the early-afternoon flights to Kathmandu. These flights can be booked through several travel agents in Darjeeling.

To/From Bihar It is also possible to cross the border at the town of Raxaul (India) and Birganj (Nepal). Buses between Patna and Raxaul take around seven hours.

Pakistan

Due to the continuing unstable political situation between India and Pakistan, there is only one open border crossing. At present, there are no direct bus or rail links operating between Lahore in Pakistan and Amritsar in India.

To/From Amritsar (Punjab) Connecting Lahore and Amritsar, the road crossing at Wagah is open daily from 9am to 3.30/4pm winter/summer. Most people walk across. Regular buses and minibuses (Rs 70) go from Amritsar to the border.

Pakistan is 30 minutes behind Indian Standard Time. Travellers have reported that the exchange rate between Indian and Pakistan rupees is better on the Pakistan side of the border. However, be aware that it is illegal to take Indian rupees into or out of India.

Getting Around

AIR
While there are many flights every day between Delhi and Kolkata (Calcutta), only a handful of services link these gateway cities to the hill states. Contact details for relevant airlines are in the Gateway Cities chapter.

Domestic Air Services
There are only a small number of airports in the Indian Himalaya. These include Srinagar and Jammu in Jammu and Kashmir state, and Leh in Ladakh. The airport at Leh is the most important for trekkers during summer, while during winter it is the lifeline to the outside world. In Himachal, there is the airport at Bhuntar, about 50km south of Manali and Gaggal, and 15km south of Dharamsala. In Bangla, the services include flights to Bagdogra, 90km south of Darjeeling and 114km south of Gangtok.

Following the civil aviation deregulation in the past decade, Indian Airlines no longer has a monopoly on domestic air services. Airlines such as Jagson, JetAir, Archana and Sahara also service the Indian Himalaya, together with Alliance Air, a fully owned subsidiary of Indian Airlines.

Booking Flights
Indian Airlines has computerised bookings at all but its smallest offices, so getting flight information and reservations is quite straightforward. However, most flights are heavily booked so you need to book as far in advance as possible. The private operators are all reasonably efficient and most have computerised bookings or authorised agents in major tourist centres. In theory, you should be able to make your flight bookings before leaving home, but in practise it can be problematic. If your flight has not been confirmed before you leave home,

go to the airline office and get a chance number – that is, be put on the waiting list and hope that it clears. Even if you have an *impossible* waiting-list number, it is still worthwhile going to the airport. Chances are the seats will become available and you will get away on time.

Tickets & Conditions
The following conditions apply to Indian Airlines; regulations, student discounts and restrictions applying to smaller operators should be checked when booking your ticket.

- The ticket must be paid for in foreign currency. To pay in rupees, you will need a cash certificate. Change is given in rupees.
- Refunds on adult tickets attract a charge of Rs 100 and can be made at any office within an hour before departure (this does not include flights out of Leh in Ladakh!) If you fail to show up 30 minutes before the flight. This is regarded as a 'no show' and you forfeit the value of your ticket.
- Unlike almost every airline in the world, Indian Airlines accepts no responsibility if you lose your ticket. They will not refund it although they may issue a replacement at their discretion. It is imperative therefore to treat their tickets like cash, rather than travellers cheques.
- Prices for tickets are higher than the locals' Indian rupee rate. Indian Airlines offer a special youth fare, which is 75% of the standard US dollar fare for travellers under 30 years of age.
- The check-in time is one hour in advance. On some internal routes, as a security measure, you are required to identify your checked-in baggage on the tarmac immediately prior to boarding. Don't forget to do this or your luggage will not be loaded onto the plane. Also for security reasons at some airports, eg, Leh, you may not be allowed any hand baggage. This includes camera gear and valuables, which may have to be stored in the hold.

BUS
Government-run bus companies operate in each state in the Indian Himalaya, and their services are supplemented by private buses.

Between Delhi and the more popular regions such as the hill stations, there is often a choice between luxury buses, some with reclining seats and air conditioning. The more rudimentary, bone-shaking buses are not usually recommended for getting to the hills, although they are often the only alternative when travelling from the hill stations to the trekking-off point.

Most buses to the hill stations depart Delhi or Kolkata in the evening and drive overnight, ensuring that you feel like a dried-up spider by the time you reach your destination. Any notion of sleeping at night or serenity in the day is interrupted by the blaring of the bus horn or a cassette with the latest Hindi movie hits cranked up to full volume. However, videos have been phased out, depriving you of the delight of sitting through three or four movies before you reach your destination.

For the other, more dangerous challenges you'll face travelling in India, see Road Conditions and Road Rules (p270).

Baggage

Trekking gear is generally carried for free on buses but take a few precautions. If the baggage is to be loaded on the roof, make sure that no-one loads a leaking jerry can full of cooking oil or kerosene near your gear, or dumps a heavy tin trunk on your baggage. Ensure that all your gear is packed into heavy kit bags, which provide further insurance from theft and protect your backpack. Although most buses will cover luggage with a tarpaulin, you may also cover your gear with a plastic bag or sheet to further protect it from the elements.

Carry valuables on board with you and make a habit of watching your bags when you stop at a bus station or *chai* (brewed tea) stop. If someone loads your bags onto the roof (with or without asking first), expect to pay a few rupees for the service.

TRAIN

Travelling by Indian trains is always an experience. Rather than travelling all the way to Himachal or Uttaranchal by road, consider these special high-speed trains (see the Gateway Cities chapter for full details):

The *Shatabdi* from Delhi to Chandigarh (for onward travel to the Kullu valley or Dharamsala); Rishikesh (for Uttarkashi and Joshimath); Dehra Dun (for Mussoorie); and Kathgodam (for Naini Tal and Almora).

The *Rajdhani* from Delhi to New Jalpaiguri, which is the railhead for Bangla (West Bengal) and Sikkim.

There are, however, very few railway lines in the Himalayan regions. Most are generally narrow-gauge and of novelty value rather than a means of long-distance travel. They include the trains servicing Shimla and Darjeeling.

Get a timetable before travelling. Indian Railways publishes its timetable at W www .indianrail.gov.in. On arrival in India, refer to the daily newspapers such as the *Indian Express* and *The Times of India*. They publish the details and seat availability of all the main trains departing from Delhi.

Classes & Reservations

There are generally two classes – 1st and 2nd – but there are a number of variations. There are air-con (AC) options, eg, the AC chair car, which is the normal seating arrangement for the high-speed *Shatabdi* trains. Other trains offer a remarkable choice (AC 1st class, 1st class, AC two-tier sleeper, AC three-tier sleeper, 2nd-class sleeper, 2nd-class reserved seat and 2nd class). Not all classes are available on all trains. The AC classes are normally reserved for major trains and routes, but it is these that you normally take when travelling to the foothills or from Delhi/Kolkata to New Jalpaiguri.

Prices vary accordingly. For example, the fare for the AC 1st class is double the standard 1st-class fare; the AC two-tier sleeper fare is 20% higher than 1st class; and the AC chair fare is about 55% of the 1st-class fare. The 2nd-class fares are around 25% of the 1st-class fare.

In Delhi and Kolkata, there are special booking facilities for foreign tourists at the main booking offices – these make life much easier. Reservations can normally be made up to a few days in advance for a fee of Rs 20 to Rs 50, depending on the class of your ticket.

You must have a seat reservation for the *Shatabdi* and *Rajdhani* trains. If you do not have a reservation for the other trains, it's worthwhile arriving at the station early and getting on the train in the reserved carriage department. If there are spare berths/seats, the ticket examiner will allot you one, charging you the normal fare plus the reservation fee. If you want to get a sleeper, ask the stationmaster if there is a tourist quota or a VIP quota. Normally a degree of patience and politeness will ensure something is arranged.

CAR
While it is possible to rent cars in major centres such as Delhi and Kolkata, this is not normally an option. Firstly, driving on Indian roads requires skills that take a lifetime to perfect. Secondly, if you have an accident, chances are your insurance will not cover you for the damage or third-party liabilities.

The best alternative is to hire a car and a driver. This is becoming an increasingly popular way of getting to the hills. With the costs shared between four people it's not overly expensive, particularly when you consider the days you could spend hanging around Delhi or Kolkata trying to get a reservation. It's easy to hire a car and driver, either from the local state tourist authority, at a private taxi stand or through your hotel.

Hiring a car and driver in Delhi will cost around Rs 2000 per day for up to 200km; add Rs 10 for each additional kilometre (or Rs 20 if one way). Overnight charges also need to be factored in, although most drivers tend to sleep in their vehicles while they are away.

Road Conditions
Probably the one factor that puts the fear of God into the intrepid trekker is the precarious nature of India's roads. While most are remarkable feats of engineering, they are frequently unsealed, always narrow, invariably winding and sometimes precariously perched on mountains with precipitous drops that plunge hundreds of metres to the valley floor.

During the monsoon season (mid-June–mid-Sept), the roads can be washed away or rendered impassable by landslides. Flexibility is the key to travelling at this time and a few days should be reserved while you wait for the landslide to be cleared. 'Transhipping' is the normal means to get around a roadblock – you carry your gear over or around the landslide where vehicles on the far side

will ferry you onto the next town or bus station. Chai stalls often spring up on each side of the roadblock to provide refreshments to drenched and mud-caked passengers. Porters will also be on hand, diverting from their task of clearing the blockage to assist with the more lucrative job of carrying passengers' excess baggage.

Road Rules
To further complicate the precarious nature of India's roads, most drivers observe few road rules. Perhaps the most perplexing habit is the use of the horn, which is blasted at regular intervals throughout the journey. You will also be very busy, be it keeping the driver awake in times of boredom or warning oncoming traffic that he has no brakes (or if he has, he's not going to use them!).

Overtaking provides another dimension to your journey. The rule in the hills seems to be 'overtake all and sundry, in particular any vehicle that has just overtaken you'. Any quest to overtake on a blind corner, a steep hill or any other dangerous section of the highway is treated as a divine right. Giving way to oncoming traffic comes second to the more acceptable rule of giving way to uphill traffic – this is faithfully observed, unless your bus happens to be larger or faster than the one coming in the opposite direction.

HITCHING
Hitching is never safe in any country and we normally don't recommend it. However, in India, hitching a ride to get from a remote location, after completing a trek for instance, is a legitimate form of travel – and the driver will expect to be paid. This form of transport is particularly popular where there is a shortage of buses or other public transport, eg, after completing a trek in Ladakh or the Zanskar; when travelling along the road between Leh and Manali; and between Manali and Spiti. The normal method is to flag down the driver with your hand. If the vehicle stops, the driver will want to know where you are going and how much you are willing to pay. The fare will be approximately the same as the bus. Once this has been agreed on, the driver's assistant will help load your baggage

and ensure you have time to clamber onto the roof or get seated in the cabin.

Concerns about safety are usually unfounded, bar the usual concerns about the driver's road skills and the state of the roads. As a precaution, women should not travel without a male companion. It may also be wise to note the number of the truck just in case your baggage goes missing.

LOCAL TRANSPORT

Once you reach the hill station or main town in the hills, the next step is travelling to the road head to commence your trek. There are a variety of options; see the Planning section of each trek for details.

Bus

This is the least expensive option. On ordinary buses the number of people seated generally exceeds the number of seats. Expect the usual mounds of luggage and livestock to be stored under the seat, and at least some of the passengers (the ones next to you) to suffer from travel sickness. The timetables are rarely adhered to, while the journey is frustratingly slow with numerous stops. This is, however, all part of the experience.

It is important that you arrive early to catch the bus. Not because it will ever arrive or depart early but simply to secure a seat. At some stations, tickets are issued in advance, but this does not guarantee your seat. The only way to secure your seat is to get on the bus first. When the bus arrives, it is recommended some of your party load all the trekking baggage onto the roof while the others get on the bus and reserve the seats.

4WD & Taxi

If you have a lot of baggage and want to save time, consider hiring a taxi to get to the trekking-off point. If you share the cost between three or four people, this is a viable option. Even for one or two people, the cost is still reasonable considering the convenience.

A journey that may take a complete day by bus can often take only a few hours by taxi.

There are taxi stands in most towns. Most drivers belong to a cooperative or union so that fares are standardised and displayed at the taxi booth. In Ladakh and the Kullu Valley, the rates are fixed and it is hard to negotiate. Nevertheless, there's no harm in trying before you start your journey. In Uttaranchal, the fare is calculated at around Rs 20 per kilometre. If you just want a drop (one way), you will have to pay around 50% for the return journey. This method is open to negotiation and will depend on the number of passengers and the amount of baggage.

Alternatively, there are shared taxi arrangements in some of the major towns of Uttaranchal, including Haridwar, Rishikesh and Dehra Dun. Shared 4WDs are available in Siliguri; some of the major towns in the Bangla hills, including Darjeeling; and in the main towns in Sikkim. 4WDs depart when they have 11 passengers on board. Rates are two to three times higher than the bus fare.

Auto-Rickshaw & Tempo

An auto-rickshaw (also known as a scooter or auto) is a noisy three-wheeled device without doors, with a driver up front and room for two passengers in the back. They are generally about half the price of a taxi, and are usually metered, with the same ground rules as taxis. If the meter is broken, set a firm rate before you start. This is is a convenient means of transport for exploring hill stations or towns. The driver will often know where you can get spare parts for your stove or batteries for your camera and will normally wait for you (without charge) while you make a purchase.

Tempos are a bit like a large auto rickshaw and, like shared 4WDs or taxis, operate along fixed routes. In particular, they are found in Dehra Dun, Rishikesh and Haridwar.

Cycle rickshaws also operate in the old parts of Delhi, and in Kolkata and Siliguri. Again, fares must be settled in advance.

Language

In Darjeeling, Sikkim and most parts of Uttaranchal and Himachal Pradesh, Hindi is widely understood. The people in the outlying villages of the Kashmir Valley speak only Kashmiri; similarly Ladakhi, a Tibetan-based language, is the only language understood in the more remote valleys of Ladakh and Zanskar (see the section on Ladakhi, pp276–7). In Himachal and Uttaranchal, Pahari and Garwhali respectively are widely used in the village areas.

Hindi

Hindi is written from left to right in Devanagari script. While the script may be unfamiliar, many of the grammatical features will be familiar to English speakers.

All nouns in Hindi have a gender, either masculine or feminine. Different forms of verbs or adjectives are used depending on the gender of the noun. Where necessary, these forms are indicated by (m) or (f).

For a far more comprehensive guide to Hindi get a copy of Lonely Planet's *Hindi & Urdu phrasebook*.

Pronunciation

Most of the sounds in Hindi correspond to the Roman letters used to represent them in the transliteration.

Vowels & Diphthongs

It's very important to pay attention to the pronunciation of vowels and especially to their length. A line over a vowel (eg, ā, ī, ū) indicates a longer vowel sound.

The symbol ~ over a vowel (eg, ã, ĩ, ĩ, ũ, ũ,) indicates that it should be spoken through the nose.

a	as the 'u' in 'sun'
ā	as in 'father'
e	as in 'bet'
i	as in 'sit'
ī	as the 'ee' in 'feet'
u	as in 'put'
ū	as the 'oo' in 'fool'

ai	as the 'a' in 'bad'
o	as in 'both'
au	as the 'aw' in 'saw'
o	as in 'both'

Note that **ai** is pronounced as a diphthong when followed by **ya**, and **au** is pronounced as a diphthong when followed by **va**.

ai	as the 'i' in 'high'
au	as the 'ou' in 'ouch'

Consonants

Most consonants in the transliterations are pronounced as in English, with the following exceptions:

c	as the 'ch' in 'cheese'
g	always as in 'gun', never as in 'age'
ṭ	pronounced with the tongue further back than in English. Curl the tongue back towards the roof of the mouth.
ḍ	pronounced with the tongue curled back towards the roof of the mouth.
r	slightly trilled
ṛ	an 'r' with the tongue placed near the roof of the mouth and flapped quickly down, touching the roof as it moves.
q	as the 'k' in 'king', but pronounced further back
y	as in 'yak'
kh	similar to the 'ch' in Scottish loch
gh	like the 'g' in 'go' but pronounced further back in the throat

Aspirated consonants are pronounced with a breath of air, represented by an h after the consonant (except for **sh**, pronounced as in 'ship', and **kh** and **gh**).

Greetings & Civilities

The traditional greeting when meeting a Hindu is to hold your palms together and say *namaste*. The reply is the same. Muslims, on the other hand, give the greeting *salām alaikum* – literally, 'Peace be on you'. The reply is either the same or *valekum as salām*, meaning 'And also on you'.

Dealing With Requests

Unfortunately, the first greeting from many children in well-trekked areas is of the 'give me' variety, while older villagers will ask for medicine. It is useful to know the following words.

I have ...	*mere pās ... hai*
I don't have ...	*mere pās ... nahī̃ hai*
chocolate	*cāklet*
money	*paisa*
medicine	*davā*

With goodbyes, Hindus again say *namaste*, while the Muslims say *khudā hāfiz*, which means, literally, 'May God bless you'.

When addressing a stranger, particularly if the person is of some standing, then the suffix *ji* is a very polite expression, almost like 'sir'. This term may also be used as 'yes' in reply to a question.

Excuse me/Sorry.	*kshamā kījiye*
Please.	*mehrbānī kar ke*
Thank you.	*shukriyā/dhanyavād*
You're welcome.	*koī bāt nahī̃*
How are you?	*āp kaise/ī haī?* (m/f)
Fine, and you?	*bas āp sunāiye*

Essentials

Yes.	*jī hā̃*
No.	*jī nahī̃*
Maybe.	*shāyad*
Do you speak English?	*kyā āp ko angrezī ātī hai?*
Does anyone here speak English?	*kyā kisī ko angrezī ātī hai?*
I don't speak Hindi.	*mujhe hindī nahī̃ ātī*
A little.	*thorā thorā*
I understand.	*maī samjhā/ī* (m/f)
I don't understand.	*maī nahī̃ samjhā/ī* (m/f)
How do you say ... in Hindi?	*hindī mē ... kaise kehte haī*
I know.	*mujhe patā hai*
I don't know.	*mujhe patā nahī̃*
Where is ...?	*... kahā̃ hai?*
How much is ...?	*... kā dām kyā hai?*
Could you speak more slowly?	*dhīre dhīre boliye*
Please write it down.	*zarā likh dījiye*

Please show me.	*dikhāiye*
I have a visa/permit.	*mer pās visā parmet hai.*
Sir/Madam	*jī*
male	*ādmī*
female	*aurat*

Small Talk

What's your name?	*āp kā shubh nām kyā hai?*
My name is ...	*merā nām ... hai*
Where are you from?	*āp kahā̃ [ke rehnevāle/ kī rehnevālī] haī?* (m/f)
I'm from ...	*maī ... [kā rehnevāl ā/ kī rehnevālī] hū̃* (m/f)
I'm a tourist/student.	*main paryatak/chātra hū̃*
Are you married?	*kyā āp shādīshudā haī?*
I'm ... years old.	*main ... sāl kākī hū̃*
Do you like ...?	*kyā āp ko ... pasand hai?*
I like ... very much.	*mujhe ... bahut pasand hai*
I don't like ...	*mujhe ... pasand nahī̃ hai*
Just a minute.	*ek minat rukiye*
It's all right/ No problem.	*koī bāt nahī̃*

Getting Around

How do we get to ...?	*... kaise jāte haī?*
When is the ... bus?	*... bas kab jāegī?*
first	*pehlā/pehlī* (m/f)
next	*aglā/aglī* (m/f)
last	*ākhirī*
What time does the ... leave/arrive?	*... kitne baje jāyegā/ pahūcegā?* (m) *... kitne baje jāyegī/ pahūcegī?* (f)
plane	*havāī jahāz* (m)
boat	*nāv* (f)
bus	*bas* (f)
train	*relgārī* (f)
I'd like a ... ticket.	*mujhe ek ... tikat cāhiye*
one-way	*ek-tarafā*
return	*do-tarafā*

1st class	*pratham shrēni*
2nd class	*dvitīy shrēni*

Useful Words

big	*baṛā*
cheap	*sastā*
clean	*sāf*
dirty	*gandā*
expensive	*mahēgā*
far	*dūr*
fast	*tez*
go	*jānā*
good	*acchā*
happy	*khush*
heavy	*bhārī*
here	*yahā̃*
his	*uskā/uskī* (m/f)
hers	*uskā/uskī* (m/f)
light (weight)	*halkā*
load	*bojh*
mine	*merā*
small	*choṭā*
that	*vo*
there	*vahā̃*
tired	*thakān*
this/these	*ye*
yours (pl, inf)	*tumhārā*

Around Town

Where's a/the ...	*... kahā̃ hai?*
bank	*baink*
bus stop	*bas stāp*
chemist/ pharmacy	*davāī kī dukān*
post office	*ḍākkhānā*
shop	*dukān*
ticket office	*ṭikaṭghar*

How much is ...?	*... kā dām kyā hai?*
Can I change money here?	*kyā yahā̃ ḍālar badal jaa saktā/ī hū̃?* (m/f)
How do we get to ...?	*... kaise jāte haĩ?*

Accommodation

hotel	*hoṭal*
lodgings	*kamrā*
caretaker	*caukidār*

Do you have any rooms available?	*kyā koī kamrā khālī hai?*

How much for ...?	*... kā kirāyā kitnā hai?*
one night	*ek din*
one week	*ek hafte*

I'd like a ...	*mujhe ... cāhiye*
single room	*singal kamrā*
double room	*ḍabal kamrā*
room with a bathroom	*ghusalkhānevālā kamrā*

I'd like to share a dorm.	*maĩ ḍorm mē ṭheharnā cāhtā/ī hū̃* (m/f)
May I see it?	*kyā maĩ kamrā dekh saktā/ī hū̃* (m/f)
Is there any other room?	*koī aur kamrā hai?*
Where's the bathroom?	*ghusalkhānā kahā̃ hai?*

How much is ...?	*... kā kyā dām hai?*
Do you have a ...?	*kyā āp ka pās ... hai?*
bed	*bistar*
room	*kamrā*
blanket	*kambāl*

Is there (breakfast/ hot water)?	*(naashta/ garam paani) hai?*

Food & Drink

Do you have ...?	*kyā āp ke pās ... hai?*
I am hungry.	*mujhe bhūkh lagī hai*
I am thirsty.	*mujhe pyās lagī hai*
I like hot and spicy food.	*muje ṭīkhā khānā acchā lagtā hai*
I don't like hot and spicy food.	*mujhe ṭīkhā khānā acchā nahī̃ lagtā hai*

restaurant	*ḍhābā*
food	*khānā*
tea	*cāy*
water	*pānī*
boiled water	*ūblā pānī*
cold water	*ṭhaṇḍā pānī*
bread	*roṭī*
chicken	*murgh*
curd (yogurt)	*dahī*
lentils	*dāl*
eggs	*anḍe*
fruit	*phal*
potato	*ālū*
rice	*cāval*
sugar	*cīnī*
vegetable	*sabzī/sāg*

Times, Days & Numbers

What time is it?	*kitne baje haĩ?/* *ṭāim kyā hai?*
It's (ten) o'clock	*(das) baje haĩ*
day	*din*
night	*rāt*
morning	*saverā/subah*
evening	*shām*
today	*āj*
tomorrow/yesterday	*kal*
(meaning is made clear by context)	
day after tomorrow	*parsõ*
now	*ab*
week	*hafte*
month	*mahīnā*
year	*sāl/baras*

1	*ek*
2	*do*
3	*tīn*
4	*cār*
5	*pãc*
6	*chai*
7	*sāt*
8	*āṭh*
9	*nau*
10	*das*
11	*gyārah*
12	*bara*
13	*terah*
14	*caudah*
15	*pandrah*
16	*solah*
17	*satrah*
18	*aṭṭhārah*
19	*unnīs*
20	*bīs*
21	*ikkīs*
22	*bāīs*
30	*tīs*
40	*cālīs*
50	*pacās*
60	*sāṭh*
70	*sattar*
80	*assī*
90	*nabbe/navve*
100	*sau*
1000	*hazār*

100,000	*ek lākh*
(written 1,00,000)	

Emergencies – Hindi

Help!	*mada kījiye!*
Stop!	*ruko!*
Thief!	*cor!*
I'm lost.	*maĩ rāstā bhūl gayā/* *gayī hũ (f/m)*

Health

I need a doctor.	*mujhe ḍakṭar cāhiye*
It hurts here.	*yahãn dard hai*
I have sore knees.	*ghuṭnõmẽ dard hai*
I have blisters.	*chāle haĩ*
I'm allergic to penicillin.	*mujhe penisilan se elargī hai*
Help!	*bacāo!*

Family

Being invited into a family house is one of the most delightful aspects of trekking in the Indian Himalaya.

Is this your ...?	*kyā yeh āp kā/kī/ke ... hai?*
sister	*behn*
mother	*mātājī*
father	*pitājī*
son	*beṭā*
daughter	*beṭī*
elder brother	*bhaiyā*
elder sister	*dīdī*
friend	*dost*

married	*shādīshudā*
unmarried	*avivāhit*

TREKKING

Hiring Porters & Horsemen

You will have little need to negotiate for porters or horsemen using their own language; at the trailhead or town there is bound to be someone who can assist with the arrangements. However, the following terms may be useful.

Will you come with me?	*āp mere sāth calẽge?*
How many horses do you have?	*āp ke pās kitne ghoṛe haĩ?*

I have to go to ...	*mujhe ... jānā hai*
What do you charge per day?	*ek din ke paise lete haĩ?*
Do I provide your food?	*kyā āp kā khānā mujhe denā hogā?*
What food do you need?	*āp ko kyā khānā cāhiye?*
What weight do you carry?	*āp kitnā vajan uṭhāte haĩ?*
What weight does your horse carry?	*āp ghoṛe par kitnā yajan rakhte haĩ?*

Clothing & Equipment

It is imperative to check with porters at the outset of the trek whether they have the right clothing and equipment.

Do you have ... ?	*kyā āp kea pās ... hai?*
boots	*jūte*
gloves	*dastāne*
jacket	*jaikaṭ*
kerosene	*kerosin*
knife	*chūrī*
sunglasses	*dhūp kā cashmā*
stove	*isṭov*
tent	*tambū*

On the Trek

When asking for directions and times in remote villages it is a mistake to ask a closed question, such as 'Does it take four hours to reach...?'. The answer will invariably be in the affirmative as the villager does not want to disappoint you with a negative reply! Likewise, the villager will often shorten the time it takes to reach a particular camp.

Also be aware that most villagers or shepherds will have little conception of time. They often walk for a very long time each day, so an hour or two is not really important to them.

How far is...?	*... kitnī dūr hai?*
Which trail goes to ...?	*kon sā rāstā ... ko jātā hai?*

far	*dūr*
near	*nazdīk*
right	*dāhinā*

left	*bāyã*
north	*uttar*
south	*dakshin*
east	*pūrv*
west	*pashcim*
level	*samtal*
uphill	*caṛhāī*
downhill	*ḍhalān*

Weather

It's ...	*āj ...*
cloudy	*bādal chāye hue haĩ*
cold	*bahut ṭhanḍ hai*
hot	*bahut garmī hai*
stormy	*tūfān*
windy	*tez havā cal rahī hai*

rain	*bārish*
sunshine	*dhūp*

Features

bear	*bhālū*
big river	*baṛā nadī*
Buddhist monastery	*gompā*
goat	*bakrī*
Hindu temple	*mandir*
lake	*jhīl*
leopard	*bāgh*
monkey	*bandar*
mountain	*pahāṛ*
Muslim mosque	*masjid*
pass	*darrā*
peak	*coṭī*
river	*nadī*
road	*saṛak*
rock	*patthar*
sheep	*bheṛ*
spring	*cashmā*
village	*gãv*

Ladakhi

Ladakhi is the language used by most people indigenous to Ladakh and Zanskar. Once similar to Tibetan, Ladakhi is now considerably different, and there are disparate dialects throughout the region. Learning a little Ladakhi will add to your enjoyment and will earn you the respect of the local people. If travelling out of Leh or trekking where little English is understood, it is quite necessary. If you only remember one word, make it the all-purpose *jule* (**joo**-lay), which means 'hello', 'goodbye', 'please' and 'thank you'.

Spelling

Every guidebook, map and tourist brochure can offer up to six or so different ways of spelling a name. For example, there is a famous *gompa* (or *gonpa* or *gomba*) at Tikse (or Thikse, Thiksey or Tiksey). The basic rule is: if it sounds the same, it's the same place.

Basics

Yes.	*kasa*
No.	*man*
How much/many?	*tsam?*
I don't understand.	*hamago*

good	*demo*
rupee	*kirmo*
meat	*sha*
milk	*oma*
rice	*dras*
sugar	*khara*
water	*chhu*

Geography & Climate

In Ladakh, life is completely dominated by the weather and geography. Here are a few words that you may hear:

bridge	*zampa*
cold	*tangmo*
ice	*kang*
lake	*tso*
mountain pass	*la*
mountain	*ri*
river	*tsangpo*
snow	*ka*
stream	*tokpo*
summer	*yar*
wind	*lungspo*
winter	*guhn*

Numbers

1	*chig*
2	*nyis*
3	*sum*
4	*zhi*
5	*nga*
6	*truk*
7	*dun*
8	*gyet*
9	*gu*
10	*chu*

Glossary

alpine – all areas above the *tree line*
Aryans – a people who migrated from Persia and Asia Minor to northern India between 2500 and 1500 BC

Bakraval – goat herders from Jammu and Kashmir
basalt – hard, dense, volcanic rock; solidified lava
beggar – system of forced labour
Brahma – member of the Hindu trinity; referred to as the creator or the source of all existence
Buddha Jayanti – celebration of the Buddha's birth, death and enlightenment
bugyal – a high alpine meadow in the Garhwal region of Uttaranchal

cairn – pile or stack of rocks used to indicate the route or a trail junction
chai – brewed tea (a mixture of tea, milk and sugar boiled together)
chang – barley beer brewed in Ladakh
chapatti – local bread baked on a dry griddle
Char Dham – the popular pilgrimage to the four sources of the Ganges River
chola – woollen cloak worn by Gaddi shepherds in Himachal Pradesh
chorten – reliquary or shrine to the memory of a Buddhist saint; a conical stone monument, often containing relics and symbolising the natural elements
chowkidar – caretaker
chu – Ladakhi word for stream
cirque – rounded, high ridge or bowl formed by glacial action in mountainous regions

Dak bungalows – comfortable rest houses established by the British and still maintained in remote districts
Dalai Lama – spiritual leader of Tibetan Buddhists
Dalit – preferred name for India's Untouchable caste
dandy – a wooden platform or palanquin used to carry pilgrims, supported by a team of porters

darshan – prayers
Devanagiri – script of Sanskrit-based language
dhaba – local tea stall or restaurant
dhal – a lentil-based soup or main dish
dhal bhat – *dhal* with rice
dhobi – washerman/woman
dhura – term for a pass in some regions of Uttaranchal
Diwali – one of the most important Hindu festivals, including the worship of *Lakshmi*
Dogras – rulers from the hill stations of Jammu and Kashmir who established the Jammu & Kashmir state
Drukpa – 17th-century Buddhist order supported by the royal families of Ladakh and Bhutan; the Red Hat sect
Dussehra – Hindu festival commemorating the *Ramayana*

foot – base of a mountain; lower end of a valley or lake
ford – to cross a river by wading
Forest Rest House – built to accommodate forest officers; trekkers may also stay here if there is a vacancy
fork – branch or tributary of a stream or river
4WD – Four-wheel-drive vehicle; jeep

gad – term for river in some regions of Uttaranchal
Gaddi – shepherds from Himachal Pradesh
Ganesh – elephant-headed god of wisdom and prosperity
Ganga – Ganges River; often used to name its tributaries, eg Gauri Ganga
garh – a fort in Uttaranchal
Garuda – the divine eagle, Vishnu's vehicle of transport throughout the universe
Gelukpa – followers of Tsongkhapa, often referred to as the Yellow Hat sect (now also referred to as the sect of the Dalai Lama)
Gita – sacred texts that set out the philosophical basis of reincarnation
glacier – extended mass of ice, formed from accumulating snow, that moves slowly down a mountain or valley

GMVN – Garhwal Mandal Vikas Niwas; in Uttaranchal, a state-owned organisation with a trekking division

gompa – Tibetan Buddhist monastery

GPS – Global Positioning System; a device that calculates position and elevation by reading signals from satellites

granite – coarse-grained, often gray, rock formed by the slow cooling of molten rock (magma) deep below the earth's surface

Gujar – shepherds who frequent many of the less remote valleys in Kashmir, Himachal Pradesh and Uttaranchal

gurdwara – Sikh temple

Gurkhas – military rulers from the Gorkha region of Nepal, who invaded the West Himalaya in the late 18th century

head – uppermost part of a valley

herbaceous – relating to plants or plant parts that are fleshy as opposed to woody

Holi – colourful Hindu festival to mark the end of winter

HPTDC – Himachal Pradesh Tourist Development Corporation

Id-ul-Zuhara – an important event in the Muslim calendar commemorating Abraham's attempt to sacrifice his son

Indra – the Aryan god of the sky

Inner Line areas – areas close to India's borders (with China and Pakistan) that you need an Inner Line permit to enter

ITBP – Indo-Tibetan Border Police; a civilian police force charged with monitoring the border; requires trekkers to show their passports on treks near India's borders

J&K – Jammu & Kashmir State

Jumla – pre-Aryan god worshipped by the people from Malana village in Himachal Pradesh

Kali – goddess of destruction, one of the forms of the consort of *Shiva*

Kargyupa – one of the earlier Tibetan Buddhist schools, with its main centre at Rumtek gompa in Sikkim

karma – the path through the cycle of rebirths determined by cause and effect

khal – term for a pass in Uttaranchal

Khampa – seminomadic Tibetan shepherds

kiang – wild horse

KMVN – Kumaon Mandal Vikas Niwas; in Uttaranchal, a state-owned organisation with a trekking division

kora – ritual walk around a sacred peak

kund – term for lake in Uttaranchal; also *tal*

la – Ladakhi or Tibetan term for a mountain pass or the God of the pass

Lakshmi – consort of *Vishnu* and goddess of wealth

Lepchas – the original inhabitants of Sikkim

lingam – phallic symbol associated with *Shiva*

maharajah – king or ruler

mandir – Hindu temple

mani wall – dry stone wall with many of the upper stones carved with Buddhist prayers

Marpa – noted Buddhist sage who wandered the Himalaya in the 11th century

masjid – mosque

Moghul – Muslim dynasty of Indian emperors

momo – Tibetan steamed 'spring roll'

Mons – early Buddhist missionaries from India who travelled to Ladakh

Naga – benevolent half-snake, half-human being

Naropa – Buddhist sage who wandered the Himalaya in the 10th century

nirvana – the ultimate aim of Buddhist practice, the release from the cycle of existence

nullah – riverbed

Padmasambhava – Buddhist teacher who travelled the Himalaya in the 8th century

Pahari – hill people of Himachal Pradesh

paise – smallest unit of Indian currency; 100 paise make a rupee

Pandava – one of the key families in the Mahabharata

parao – local term for a trekking stage in the Kumaon region of Uttaranchal

paratha – local bread cooked on an oiled griddle

puja – Hindu prayer session

pulao – savoury rice

puri – local bread, deep-fried
PWD – Public Works department

rajah – king
Rajput – Hindu warrior class; the royal rulers of Rajasthan
rakshi – rice wine
Rama – seventh incarnation of *Vishnu*
Ramadan – Muslim period of fasting, acknowledging the time when Mohammed had the Koran revealed to him in Mecca
Ramayana – the story of *Rama* and Sita (one of India's best-known legends)
rani – queen
Ringchen Brangpo – 11th-century Buddhist scholar said to have founded 108 gompas in the West Himalaya
rupee (Rs) – Indian unit of currency

sadhu – wandering Hindu holy man/woman
Saka Dawa – Buddha's birth and enlightenment, celebrated in the Tibetan calendar
sar – Kashmiri term for lake
scree – weathered rock fragments at the foot of a cliff or on a hillside
Shia – Muslim followers of the son-in-law of the Prophet
Shiva – the Hindu destroyer and also the creator, worshipped in the form of the *lingam*
Sikhs – members of the religious body founded in the Punjab in the 16th century, which drew on both Hindu and Muslim traditions
snowmelt – accumulation of slow-melting packed snow
spring line – a place where the water comes straight out of the ground
subalpine – upper forest zone
sumdo – Ladakhi term for village

switchback – a zigzag on a trail that follows a steep grade

tal – term for lake in Uttaranchal; also *kund*
terminal moraine – boulders and scree at the snout of a glacier
thangka – Buddhist religious painting
thach – alpine meadow in Himachal Pradesh
Thakur – titled rulers from Lahaul in Himachal Pradesh
tokpo – Ladakhi term for river
tongba – fermented millet mixed with boiling water, drunk in eastern Nepal and Sikkim
traverse – to cross a slope or ridge
tree line – uppermost (natural) level to which tree cover extends on a mountainside
true left – the left bank of a river or *glacier* when facing downstream or downvalley
true right – the right bank of a river or *glacier* when facing downstream or downvalley
tsampa – roasted ground barley, often mixed with butter tea and drunk by Ladakhi and Tibetan people
Tsongkhapa – Buddhist teacher who established a major reformist school of Buddhism that was adopted by the Dalai Lama

Vedas – ancient set of hymns devoted to the *Aryan* gods
Vishnu – the preserver and sustainer; member of the Hindu trinity, along with *Shiva* and *Brahma*

wallah – worker or doer, eg, *dhobi wallah* (washerman)
walli – the female equivalent of a *wallah*
Wesak – Buddha's birth and enlightenment, celebrated in the Hindu calendar

LONELY PLANET

You already know that Lonely Planet produces more than this one guidebook, but you might not be aware of the other products we have on this region. Here is a selection of titles that you may want to check out as well:

Trekking in the Nepal Himalaya
ISBN 1 86450 231 2
US$19.99 • UK£12.99

Nepal
ISBN 1 86450 247 9
US$19.99 • UK£12.99

Nepali phrasebook
ISBN 1 74059 192 5
US$7.99 • UK£4.50

North India
ISBN 1 86450 330 0
US$21.99 • UK£13.99

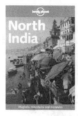

Pakistan
ISBN 0 86442 535 X
US$17.95 • UK£11.99

Healthy Travel Asia & India
ISBN 1 86450 051 4
US$5.95 • UK£3.99

Bhutan
ISBN 1 86450 145 6
US$21.99 • UK£13.99

Tibet
ISBN 1 86450 162 6
US$19.99 • UK£12.99

Hindi & Urdu phrasebook
ISBN 0 86442 425 6
US$6.95 • UK£4.50

India
ISBN 1 86450 246 0
US$24.99 • UK£14.99

Read This First: Asia & India
ISBN 1 86450 049 2
US$14.95 • UK£8.99

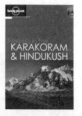

Trekking in the Karakoram & Hindukush
ISBN 1 74059 086 4
US$19.99 • UK£12.99

Available wherever books are sold

Index

Text

For a list of treks, see the Table of Treks (pp4–5).
For individual mountains, ranges and peaks, see under the heading 'mountains, ranges & peaks'.

Bold indicates maps.
For a list of treks, see the
Table of Treks (pp4–5).

Bold indicates maps.
For a list of treks, see the
Table of Treks (pp4–5).

Bold indicates maps.
For a list of treks, see the
Table of Treks (pp4–5).

---

oxed Text

This Book

From the Publisher

This 4th edition of *Trekking in the Indian Himalaya* was produced in Lonely Planet's Melbourne office by editor Angie Phelan and cartographer Karen Fry, with assistance from Marg Toohey and Janet Brunckhorst. Glenn van der Knijff checked the maps and Andrew Smith and Sally Dillon checked the layout. Jamieson Gross designed the cover and Matt King helped out with the illustrations. Emma Koch compiled the language section and David Andrew advised on the wildlife sections. Technical support came from Mark Germanchis, David Burnett and Chris Klep.

Thanks

Thanks to all the readers who wrote in with useful comments about the previous edition of *Trekking in the Indian Himalaya*:

Sharon Abraham, Sumit Adak, Professor Dan Adler, Bill Aitkin, Hum Bahadur Gurung, Mara Benedict, Ami Berger, Karin Blokziel, Antoinette Bouwens, John Bower, Audrey & Roy Bradford, Tom Brichau, Helen Brown, Alice Buchtova, Maggie Carter, Andrew Caulkett, Paul Cleaves, Lisa Dobbie, Laszlo Dora, Mark Duncan, Eric Fabry, Adrian Fawcett, Alexander & Sandy Forrest, Paul Glendenning, Christian Hadorn, Feico Halbertsma, Ryan Hardoon, Stacie Hartung, Olly Harvey, Ahti Heinla, Neville Hesketh, Sandra Hesse, Marco Heusdens, David Holdorf, Berhard Huber, Nicky Hungerford, Tony Hurley, Dirk Huyge, Trevor Ingham, Raghu Iyer, Jean Jacques, Brent Johnson, Tonny Jonckbloedt, David Keitz, Kahe Kell, Alex Koh Wei Hiong, Chintamani Joshi, George Langenberg, Tim Langmaid, Jennifer Lewis, John Liagerwerf, Claudia Loetscher, David A May, J McSweeney & Family, Heather Michaud, David Migdal, John Morrison, Raewyn Moss, Christof Muller, Sue Napier, Don NovoGradac, Lisa Patterson, Jon Petrie, Barbara Pfyffer, Madeline Pikaar, Sue Pickering, Mandy Pocock, Arun S Rana, Sarah Richardson, Ben Ridder, Evan Rieder, Laura Robinson, David Rodriguez, Anna Rogers, Alida & David Romano, Meriel Rule, Shlomo Shapira, Dana Shields, Sainath Shinde, Kim Sinclair, Aisling Sithigh, Ramaswamy Sreenivasan, Niclas Svenningsen, Beth Sywulsky, Mrs & Mr Tawfik, Devraj Thakur, Jennifer Tradewell, Louise Trethewey, Jean-Phillipe Umber, John Urquhart, Dieter van Campe, Frantisek Vitek, Birgit Walter, Dale Wang, Martina Weber, Frank Werning, Felicity Westcott, Karen Whitlow, Chris Willmott, David de Wit.

LONELY PLANET OFFICES

Australia
Locked Bag 1, Footscray, Victoria 3011
☎ 03-8379 8000 fax 03-8379 8111
e talk2us@lonelyplanet.com.au

USA
150 Linden St, Oakland, CA 94607
☎ 510-893-8555 or ☎ 800-275-8555 (toll free)
fax 510-893-8572
e info@lonelyplanet.com

UK
10a Spring Place, London NW5 3BH
☎ 020-7428 4800 fax 020-7428 4828
e go@lonelyplanet.co.uk

France
1 rue du Dahomey, 75011 Paris
☎ 01 55 25 33 00 fax 01 55 25 33 01
e bip@lonelyplanet.fr
w www.lonelyplanet.fr

World Wide Web: w www.lonelyplanet.com *or* AOL keyword: lp
Lonely Planet Images: e lpi@lonelyplanet.com.au